George Lisle

A Faith That Couldn't Be Denied

George Lisle
A Faith That Couldn't Be Denied

Jamaica, 1783–1865

DOREEN MORRISON

WIPF & STOCK · Eugene, Oregon

GEORGE LISLE: A FAITH THAT COULDN'T BE DENIED
Jamaica, 1783–1865

Copyright © 2022 Doreen Morrison. All rights reserved. Except for brief quotations in critical publications or reviews, no part of this book may be reproduced in any manner without prior written permission from the publisher. Write: Permissions, Wipf and Stock Publishers, 199 W. 8th Ave., Suite 3, Eugene, OR 97401.

Wipf & Stock
An Imprint of Wipf and Stock Publishers
199 W. 8th Ave., Suite 3
Eugene, OR 97401

www.wipfandstock.com

PAPERBACK ISBN: 978-1-6667-4036-3
HARDCOVER ISBN: 978-1-6667-4037-0
EBOOK ISBN: 978-1-6667-4038-7

11/23/22

Scriptures marked KJV are taken from the KING JAMES VERSION (KJV): KING JAMES VERSION, public domain.

Scriptures marked NKJV are taken from the NEW KING JAMES VERSION (NKJV); Scripture taken from the NEW KING JAMES VERSION®. Copyright© 1982 by Thomas Nelson, Inc; Used by permission. All rights reserved.

Scriptures marked SFLB are taken from THE SPIRIT-FILLED LIFE BIBLE (SFLB): Scripture taken from THE SPIRIT-FILLED LIFE BIBLE© 2002 by Thomas Nelson Publishers.

In memory of Lynette Maud Morrison (1923–81), Lesma Stewart (1930–2008), and African Jamaicans who were willing to lay down their lives for a people, and a nation, which they knew that they would never see. All remain a constant source of inspiration!

When I walked out of prison, that was my mission, to liberate the oppressed and the oppressor both. Some say that has now been achieved. But I know that that is not the case. The truth is that we are not yet free; we have merely achieved the freedom to be free, the right not to be oppressed. We have not taken the final step of our journey, but the first step on a longer and even more difficult road. For to be free is not merely to cast off one's chains, but to live in a way that respects and enhances the freedom of others. The true test of our devotion to freedom is just beginning.

—Nelson Mandela, *Long Walk to Freedom* (1994)

Contents

Acknowledgments | ix
Abbreviations | xi
Introduction | xiii
Chapter 1: Society and Religion in Jamaica before the Arrival of George Lisle | 3
Chapter 2: George Lisle—American Roots | 33
Chapter 3: Such Promising Beginnings | 47
Chapter 4: The War Begins against the Ethiopian Baptist Society | 60
Chapter 5: The Response of the Ethiopian Baptist Leadership | 71
Chapter 6: The Transference of Power to the Baptist Missionary Society | 100
Chapter 7: A Season of Violent Persecution and Resistance (1826–32) | 120
Chapter 8: Church versus Church (1832) | 150
Chapter 9: The Slow Journey to Full Freedom (1834–45) | 181
Chapter 10: A Season of Joys and Disappointments | 219
Chapter 11: The Final Roar of the EBS: Saint Thomas in the East (1865) | 244
Chapter 12: Legacy | 272
Chapter 13: Epitaph | 285
Appendix 1: Punishments | 293
Appendix 2: Rebellions | 298
Appendix 3: Story of an African Taken into Slavery | 300
Appendix 4: The Covenant of the Anabaptist Society | 302
Appendix 5: Roll of Honor African Baptist Assistants | 305

Appendix 6: Roll Call of the First African Jamaican Ministers Who Attended Calabar College | 306

Appendix 7: Working toward Emancipation, 1837 | 307

Appendix 8: Emancipation Day—August 1, 1838, Song Sheet | 311

Appendix 9: Christian Rituals—Prayer Meetings and Facing Death | 315

Appendix 10: Chapels, Monuments, and Grave Stones | 319

Bibliography | 325

Index | 335

Acknowledgments

THE BASIS FOR THIS study germinated when as a child of immigrants, growing up in England, I was confronted on the one hand by a less than accepting Baptist church, and on the other faced a hostile British society, many of whose feelings were encapsulated in the words of Enoch Powell, Conservative MP. In 1968 he stated that, should British citizens migrating from the Caribbean continue in large numbers, then there would surely be "rivers of blood" on the streets of England. As a family we tended to split our existence between church, school, work, and family, and therefore it seemed to me a somewhat peculiar and hostile statement to make, and this set me on a journey of discovery to understand what it meant to be black.

However, it was when sitting through numerous contextual theology classes, led by Douglas Sharp, that I began to understand that I was asking the wrong question. I needed, rather, to understand who I was as an African Jamaican, and what was my history, that it seemingly placed such fear in British society. I determined that the best way to discover the history of African Jamaicans was to complete a PhD. However, opportunities to take my research outside of England were limited, and so it was not until I had finished my studies that, on being given the opportunity to spend a full six months in Jamaica, researching and curating an exhibition with the encouragement of Horace Russell, Neville Callam, and Robert Johnson, I began to see the possibilities of the book you hold in your hands today.

Yet, given the trials and upheavals of recent years, this book could never have happened without the assistance of many, archivists in libraries, churches, missionary agencies, and the community. So, my thanks go to Emily Burgoyne and Rebecca Shuttleworth at the Angus Library, Oxford, which has not only been my go-to center, but at times felt like my second home. Thanks also to the staff and fellow researchers at the Registrar General's Department in Spanish Town, Jamaica, and community historian Juliet

Gordon, each of whom enabled me to recover documents which allowed this story to be told so fully.

Then finally, this book would never have been completed without the community of friends and family, whose patience, prayer, constant encouragement, and support enabled me to stay focused on the task, and to complete it to the glory of God. So, thank you to Margaret Stewart Richards and Keith B. Richards, Mike Davis (Christ for all Nations), Karen Randle, Laurie Payne, Joan McClymont, Trevor McClymont, Dawn Merrick, Betty Sheen, Corine Stewart, Charles Stewart, Nardia Foster, Barbara Dunne, Godfrey Stewart, Mark Innis, and last, but by no means least, Bevan and Mina Stewart.

Abbreviations

ABCUSA	American Baptist Churches USA
ABMU	American Baptist Missionary Union
BAR	Baptist Annual Register
BMS	Baptist Missionary Society
BUGB	Baptist Union of Great Britain
BQ	Baptist Quarterly
CCU	Colonial Church Union
CSA	Consolidated Slave Act
CSL	Consolidated Slave Laws
CofE	Church of England
CoG	Church of God
EBS	Ethiopian Baptist Society
FMBNBC	Foreign Missions Board National Baptist Convention
HC Deb	House of Commons Debate
HCSC	House of Commons Select Committee
JBU	Jamaica Baptist Union
JNBC	Journal of the National Baptist Convention
JNH	Journal of Negro History
LMS	London Missionary Society
NLJ	National Library of Jamaica
SOAS	School of Oriental and African Studies

Introduction

ASKED TO DETERMINE THE foundations of Jamaican Christianity and Baptist mission in particular, most Jamaican Baptists and those of the Diaspora would talk of the work of European missionaries. In fact, the spread of Christianity amongst African Jamaicans has been well documented by such historians as Philip D. Curtin, Shirley Gordon, and Robert Stewart as having been established and come to fruition under the ministry of European missionaries, primarily through the Baptist Missionary Society and more particularly the work of William Knibb and Thomas Burchell. Subsequent investigations by Diane Austin-Broos, into later developing belief systems of Jamaican Pentecostalism and Rastafari, situate their existence in the work of the American Pentecostal Church, the Church of God, and the "radical" ministries of Marcus Garvey and Alexander Bedward. Lacking has been any significant acknowledgement of the role Africans played in the founding and expanding of Christianity in Jamaica, and so this book seeks to redress that imbalance.

This book is written to tell the story of George Lisle and the Ethiopian Baptist Society (EBS), and their work as the first Baptist mission in Jamaica from 1783 to 1865, and their ongoing legacy, thereby challenging those histories which have previously been written which credit the emancipation of a nation primarily to the 1831–32 resistance movement and the BMS missionaries who survived to tell the tale. For the reality of the evolution of Jamaican Christianity and subsequent religious perspectives, rather than being located in Eurocentric Christianity, is to be located in one of the most successful Baptist missionary movements ever, the EBS, led by a once-enslaved African American, George Lisle, and his cadre of leaders. They preceded William Carey of the Baptist Missionary Society (BMS) by ten years and Adoniram Judson of the American Baptist Missionary Union (now ABCUSA) by some thirty-two years.

This book details how bold Baptists, black and white, in America and Britain, played their part in giving credibility and support to this most unusual of all ministries, often going against the popular wisdom of the day. Individuals and organizations took a stand against the majority who believed that Africans transported into enslavement were no more than animals, a people without culture, identity and faith, and who were therefore undeserving of being treated as human beings, much less ministers and missionaries of equal status and position under God.

Documented here is the rise of the movement. It tells the story of how George Lisle and his fellow Ethiopian Baptists traveled to Jamaica, having been evacuated by the British from America, to not only begin a new life, but to impart their Christian faith amongst an African people who had been enslaved and oppressed for over 100 years by the British. It conveys how their arrival was initially welcomed by the State, as they together with 3,000 British loyalists and their 8,000 slaves swelled the numbers of a people who were under imminent threat of invasion from the French, who were after their triumphs in America seeking to conquer British possessions in the Caribbean, Jamaica being the jewel in the crown.

This book details how the EBS, being the first Baptist missionary movement, was accepted and encouraged by the wider global Baptist family. It documents the work of Lisle and some of the leading characters within the movement, before passing the baton on to the wider church, who by their actions kept alive their belief that God had not forgotten the enslaved of Jamaica, as stated in the Ps 68:31 Bible verse, it being foundational to their understanding.

This book also demonstrates how the Haitian Revolution served as the catalyst for slave owners to declare war on the EBS in 1892, making it clear to Lisle that they considered the EBS to have been cut from the same cloth as their Haitian cousins, and so in seeking to enable the enslaved to rise above their station, would be met by the full force of the law, and if necessary violent repression.

This book tells of the bravery and courage of men and women who in response negotiated not only their enslavement, but the draconian slave laws designed to outlaw their movement, while at the same time overcoming the daily obstacles of racism, intimidation, violence, poverty, imprisonment, and the murder and martyrdom of members, by holding on to the faith which they inherited, and would not deny.

This book shows how for over eighty years the slave owners, supported by the state, undertook a sustained campaign to lessen the role of these illegitimate "Christians," and to blame them, and the first wave of BMS missionary leaders, for being "the sinister force behind society's ill—that must be utterly destroyed."[1] It tells of the EBS's not-too-insignificant role as leaders in the resistance movement and battle for emancipation in Jamaica, and of its members, whose bodies may have been bruised, broken, and destroyed, but refused to bow down to slave masters, and resisted in any nonviolent way they could, reliant solely upon their faith in God.

This book concludes by documenting the culmination of the war in Morant Bay (1865) and with it the public demise of the movement. It tells how after over eighty years of advocacy for the Jamaican nation, persecuted and then deserted by the very same European-led Baptist organization, the BMS (whom they had not only encouraged, but supported some seventy years earlier), they were left to "sleep in the dust"[2] of history, unheralded and alone, but not forgotten by African Jamaicans.

This book uses missionary letters, biographies, government records and eyewitness accounts to resurrect and rewrite Jamaican history from the perspective of the African Jamaican members of the EBS, whose place in history has in the main, been edited out of most historical records. It is written as a continuation of the work undertaken by such eminent historians as Clement Gayle and Horace Russell, who, having laid the foundations, have also created a path on which we who follow are able to tread with pride.

It is also written out of a desire of one who has but a little knowledge, seeking to share Jamaica's faith story from the perspective of the enslaved and free Africans, in order to redress the belief held by many of their descendants who have been made to "feel that [they] never amounted to anything in the creation,"[3] and more particularly that they had no hand in the Christian formation and development of Jamaica. This book instead shows how a people whose only means of hope was a belief in God, faced all manner of persecution (and even death), but never renounced their faith, so that all those who were to follow them might believe that they too could still indeed stretch out their hands unto God, and be made free.

1. Sinalo, *Rwanda after Genocide*, 65.
2. Clarke, *Memorials of Baptist Missionaries*, 76.
3. Fein, "Marcus Garvey," 447.

WHEN TWO WORLDS COLLIDE

1
When two worlds collide,
And one becomes servant and the other master.
Dare to tell the servant that his life is a better one.
And masters have no need of correction.

2
Whether explorer, missionary, pioneer or militia,
history repeats itself. We live and we fail to learn.
Jamaica, Australia, America, South Africa, Myanmar, Tibet,
All are the same.

3
When two worlds collide,
And one becomes master and the other made a slave.
In the agony of years might they not have asked God for freedom,
but the speedy deliverance of a holocaust instead!

4
When wisdom comes at the barrel of a gun,
And God's laws are left to the mere interpretation of men,
Oppressor or oppressed, all humanity becomes the poorer.
Strive to be rich!

Map of Jamaica in the West Indies, c.1700s

"Exterior of a Distillery, on Weatheralls' Estate, Antigua. Slavery Images: A Visual Record of the African Slave Trade and Slave Life in the early African Diaspora, accessed June 16, 2022. http://slaveryimages.org/s/slaveryimages/item/3005

Chapter 1

Society and Religion in Jamaica before the Arrival of George Lisle

THIS IS THE STORY of African American ex-slave, George Lisle, the first Baptist missionary to the world, and his cadre of leaders who planted the first ever Baptist mission, on the island of Jamaica. Full of faith after the liberty which they believed that God had given them, Lisle and his team of Ethiopian Baptists set out on a mission to free all their fellow African brothers and sisters from enslavement, by establishing themselves in Jamaica.

Having been enslaved to British planters in America, one might assume that Lisle would have had only minor adjustments to make in the exchanging the cotton and tobacco fields of America for the cane fields of Jamaica. The climate was very similar, the language was seemingly almost the same, as were the merchants and traders, many of whose families were known in America. Yet for all the apparent similarities, Jamaica was a totally alien situation in many aspects pertaining to life and liberty. This chapter will therefore introduce you to Jamaican plantation society, so that you may understand the momentous task which lay ahead of them.

THE CROWN

Jamaica became a British slave colony in 1665. Though it was not their first slave colony, Barbados, Saint Nevis, and Saint Kitts being established in

1640, by the 1760s it contained almost half of the total number of enslaved people in the then West Indies.¹

As with all their colonies, slavery in Jamaica was a transactional relationship, undertaken by the Crown, with those interested in the trade whereby

> The monarch would assign rights of trade in one specific area to an organization or individual who would pay fees to the Crown and use their own resources to build up the trade.²

"The Arabs among the Benecki." Slavery Images: A Visual Record of the African Slave Trade and Slave Life in the Early African Diaspora, accessed June 16, 2022. http://slaveryimages.org/s/slaveryimages/item/417

So, traders, merchants, ship's captains, plantation owners, and all others involved in the trade received monopoly licenses at the purview of the king, queen, or other members of the royal family. Such was the profits to be made that it is known that individuals would mortgage their property, and even the enslaved themselves, for up to 6 percent interest in order to raise the funds necessary to enter this most lucrative of all trades. One such patronage of the Crown, as represented by then Duke of York was granted to the Royal Adventurers of England Trading to Africa, promising that it would

1. Jones, *Satan's Kingdom*, 13.
2. Jones, *Satan's Kingdom*, 19.

By God's permission furnish the said plantations with at least 3,000 negroes, and will proceed from time to time to provide them a constant and sufficient succession of them so as the Planter shall have no just cause of complain of any Want.[3]

The Crown believed themselves to be the legal owners of the enslaved, with their will being enforced by the British Parliament, who then made sure that it was understood by all to be

A trade of the most advantage to this kingdom . . . for which we have in return gold [elephant's] teeth, wax and Negroes, the last whereof is much better than the first, being indeed the best traffic the kingdom hath, as it doth occasionally give so vast employment to our people both by sea and land.[4]

"A Slave-Shed." Slavery Images: A Visual Record of the African Slave Trade and Slave Life in the Early African Diaspora, accessed June 16, 2022. http://slaveryimages.org/s/slaveryimages/item/1980

There was therefore a determination by all, to make each slave colony as efficient and effective as possible. To this end, they ceded the day-to-day control of each colony to those on the ground, the governor, and colonial legislatures.

---

3. Jones, *Satan's Kingdom*, 20.
4. Jones, *Satan's Kingdom*, 21.

LEGAL PARAMETERS

Those who traveled to Jamaica soon found themselves in a somewhat schizophrenic society. Like most of the British colonies, Jamaica was allowed to establish its own laws through its own legislature, separate from that which was handed down by the British Parliament. There was therefore no consistency as to how the enslaved were treated, and edicts from Westminster were often ignored, refused, or overridden by laws which the Jamaican Assembly put in place in order to circumvent what they considered to be objectionable laws handed down by Westminster.

The enslaved in Jamaica were therefore subject to two "masters," the British government and the Jamaican assembly, which was dominated by the plantocracy. Each legislature made laws governing the practice of slavery, and whereas it would seem rational to assume that that which was passed by the British government had precedence, this was not always the case. For instance, while British law did not recognize marriage, family structures, education or the religious practice of the enslaved, in Jamaica, exceptions were made, with many "Christian" slaveholders being allowed to carry out all these practices on their estates, with the assent of the legislature.

Below is a detailed account of how Jamaican society was structured in the lives of the planters, those who ran the plantations, churches, missionaries and Africans; enslaved and free.

"Spring Garden Estate, St Georges." James Hakewill, London 1825. *Slavery Images: A Visual Record of the African Slave Trade and Slave Life in the Early African Diaspora*, accessed June 16, 2022. http://slaveryimages.org/s/slaveryimages/item/1394.

THE CLASS SYSTEM

Jamaica was a society wherein

> The ruling Jamaicans were European in culture and education: therefore, they might be expected to turn to England for a solution to their problems. At the same time, Jamaican society was very different from British society, and British ideas could hardly be applicable to Jamaican conditions. . . . [They] differed in respect to climate, geography, social structure, and the cultural background of the majority of the people.[5]

The story of the communities within it was therefore a story of status and social class amongst three groups of peoples, the church and plantocracy, colored and white creoles, and enslaved and a minority of free Africans. Though occupying the same island, each community progressed somewhat independently of the others, maintaining and developing their own religious practices in an evolving society, which was new to them all. However, they were all united by one structure: the social class system which determined their place in Jamaica society and defined every aspect of their lives. Theologians Lincoln and Mamiya contend that, while "religion governs the parameters of culture, it is in fact culture which governs how that religion is expressed."[6] This was especially true of Jamaica, as we shall now see, beginning with those at the top, the plantocracy.

Plantocracy

Britain, having found the Caribbean islands to be the ideal place for the much-needed sugar production, first recruited a ruling elite, the ruling classes who saw themselves only as temporary exiles, working to make their fortunes and then returning home to England with increased power, status, and economic capabilities. However, the one difficulty which confronted them all was the fact that they were a minority in a foreign land, with harsh conditions, both climatically and geographically, and in charge of a large enslaved group of people who initially spoke little or no English. This was not England, and so, in addition to creating economic success in this most lucrative of trades, they had to create a new society, a Jamaican society within which they could all live.

---

5. Curtin, *Two Jamaicas*, ix.
6. Lincoln and Mamiya, *Black Church*, 7.

Absentee landowners, having established their plantations, created a tight system of control based on the English class system, which allowed for the functioning of each plantation in their absence. Three grades or classes of people ran the plantation for the owner; the planter-attorney, the overseer, and the bookkeeper. The highest status belonged to the attorney and particularly the planter-attorney, in charge of all the legal affairs of the plantation, and who was in many instances in the employ of established law firms in England. Many had no training to speak of, just a willingness to be there, and a desire to achieve a share of the wealth that was to be found on the island.

Next in the pecking order came the overseer, the manager of the slaves and production. He was the man in charge. However, it is believed that such was the desire of some overseers to maintain their social status that they "insisted on dining alone on the estate, banishing the bookkeepers to their own quarters,"[7] rather than be seen to be consorting with a person of inferior standing. They tended therefore to be an isolated minority, few in number with no other overseer living within miles of their own plantation, and likely to be unmarried. The bookkeeper, the lowest member of the group, was simply the clerk, keeping all the records of the plantation.

This clearly defined class system, once established, translated itself into every area of white society, both in war and in peace. For example, it is said that when war arose, they remained faithful to their class, the attorneys becoming the officers, the overseers the cavalrymen, with horses of requisite value, in keeping with their status, and the bookkeepers were merely foot soldiers, the infantrymen. It was not, however, a static class system; individuals could move up and down, but this then automatically alienated them from those whom they had left behind.

Outside of this class system stood the merchants, and the doctors. Merchants were resented, and considered by the permanent residents to be leeches living in the pleasant circumstances of England or Scotland, while benefiting from the work done by those within the colony. They were solely interested in profit, and so would rather have dealt with free laborers rather than slaves, as it would have been a more profitable arrangement for them.

Doctors, on the other hand, were accepted as providing an invaluable service—keeping enslaved Africans productive until they could no longer be so, at which time they were responsible for having them taken out and thrown down a gulley where they were left to die. The doctors were therefore clearly a valuable addition to the island and while some were trained, many were not. They were assisted by enslaved African nurses who were considered in many instances to have more knowledge than the doctors themselves.

---

7. Curtin, *Two Jamaicas*, 47.

Inside a plantation Great House. Photograph courtesy of D. Morrison.

Clearly in such a guarded society there were tensions. There was the constant fear of a people who were always in the minority and miles from home, having to deal with a much larger hostile and rebellious enslaved African population. They were also often times fearful of their own people, caused by extra marital relationships with enslaved women. So, while they as a group expressed a low opinion of the enslaved, who they determined had no value systems, purely chattel, to be bought and sold at will, it was nevertheless not uncommon for them to have a preference for sleeping with the enslaved women, or at best have them as permanent "housekeepers" (mistresses), to tend to all their needs. This caused great conflict between wives and husbands, and great resentment of wives towards women who had no choice in the matter.

Over time, such was the interaction between members of the plantocracy and enslaved women that a grading system was created by the plantocracy as to who was allowed to have what type of "housekeeper." Planters, and colonial officials, though having wives from England, or having married a creole white, had automatic right to brown or colored girls and women, while overseers were entitled to one from the free colored class, and bookkeepers were expected to seek one from amongst the enslaved women. Many grades of peoples of color therefore developed on the island, and these were gradations which also brought with them status. The grades were as follows:

> Sambo: the child of a mulatto and a black man, Mulatto; the child of a black woman and white man, Quadroon: the child of a mulatto and a white man, Mustee; the child of a quadroon and a white man, Mustaphini: the child of a mustee and a white man, Quintroon: the child of a mustaphini and a white man, and Octoroon: the child of a quintroon and a white man.[8]

Increased financial success also brought with it increased fear on the part of the absentee landlord, who feared that his or her profits were being pilfered by those who managed his plantation, and so over time enslaved Africans were often preferred to run the estate (being so obviously locatable by the nature of his color should he stray), rather than any attorney. Despite these internal squabbles, the economic success which was Jamaica soon meant that the planters became the most powerful of all British businessmen, both at "home" and abroad. Such was their power, and the transformative power of the sugar which they produced on British society, that policies which originated within Jamaica were not only incorporated into all other Caribbean colonies, but grew to affect British domestic policy. They became the sole purveyors of what was acceptable, in terms of social roles and culture for all inhabitants of Jamaica, and that included the church.

Church

The Church of England (CofE) was formally commissioned by Charles II in 1661, and instructed

> To discourage vice and debauchery and to encourage ministers that Christianity and the Protestant religion, according to the CofE, might have due reverence and exercise.[9]

They may have been commissioned by the king of England, but in Jamaica, they were subject to the rule of the plantocracy, who led the assembly government.

Plantation owners initially saw the clergy as possibly their most valuable ally; however, because they had little if any interest in religion, they sought initially to keep the clergy "in their place," fearing that the enslaved Africans would become Christians or be baptized, and then their next natural step would be freedom. Priests were therefore encouraged to "bow down" to the planting class, fearful that to abuse the patronage which they grudgingly received from them would have at best resulted in censorship and at worst, deportation back to England.

8. Erskine, *Decolonizing Theology*, 35.
9. Ellis, *Diocese of Jamaica*, 5.

In truth the plantocracy had nothing to fear, for the evangelization of enslaved Africans was not seen by the CofE ministers as a part of their remit in the colonies. The prevailing view within Christendom, from the time of the Reformation, prior to the missionary endeavors of the nineteenth century, was that the church had no mandate to either preach the gospel to, or establish churches for, unbelievers in foreign lands. The common wisdom at that time held that it was the duty of apostles, not pastors, to preach the good news, and since the death of Christ's own apostles, this role and expectation had died with them.

So according to historian Bisnauth "the 'national' character of the CofE led the church to continue its activities only to those who were considered nationals, and not only were the blacks in British colonies not nationals, they were also chattels."[10] The CofE therefore firmly believed that they had no commission to evangelize, rather their duty was to maintain, and to tend the congregations which God had given them, in fulfilment of their scriptural mandate taken from Rom 1:16–17.[11] They could therefore without conscience ignore aspects of the 1696 Slave Code which demanded that:

> All masters and mistresses who owned or employed slaves were to endeavour as much as possible to instruct their slaves in the principles of the Christian religion, to facilitate their conversion and to do their utmost to fit them for baptism.[12]

So, the Anglican priest who was outside of the class system sought to maintain it in order to receive the favor of the plantocracy. He saw his role as being chaplain to the "Christians," and to the plantocracy, looking beyond their faults and failings, giving them instead the outer trappings of a "respectable" Christian life, baptizing them, marrying them, and presiding over their funerals. However, as industrious as the CofE minister proved in undertaking his duties to the plantocracy, they proved themselves to be deficient in many other areas. The clergy were believed to be the cause of much of the vice and debauchery on the island and churches were more often shut than open, by a clergy often described as "Of character so vile, that I do not care to mention it; for except for a few, they are generally the most finished of our debauchers," and "much better qualified to be retailers of saltfish or boatswains to privateers than ministers of the Gospel."[13]

---

10. Bisnauth, *History of Religion*, 199.

11. "For therein is the righteousness of God revealed from faith to faith: as it is written, the just shall live by faith" (SFLB).

12. Bisnauth, *History of Religion*, 102.

13. Ellis, *Diocese*, 12, 13.

It is believed that there were many amongst them who though sent out by the bishop of London, and approved by the governor of the island, had fled to the Caribbean under self-imposed exile from Britain, in order to escape crimes and misdemeanors which they had committed. It is to be noted for example that John Wesley's brother-in-law, "Westley Hall, a fervent preacher . . . fled to the West Indies with one of his many mistresses."[14]

So, it is no surprise then that when approached by enslaved Africans seeking to attend their churches, they sought ways of excluding them. Ellis argues that though they never clearly stated their indifference to the enslaved African, their actions soon made known their views, and exclusion was easy to do, particularly when acceptance was dependent upon money. For example, if an enslaved African sought the "freedom" gained by baptism, he needed to pay £1 3s 9d, a fee which was impossible for any ordinary slave to raise, particularly given that it was not until the early twentieth century that farm worker's salaries reached 1s 6d per week.

Abolitionist John Wesley, renowned evangelist and well-respected clergyman, went as far as to describe enslaved Africans and their race as "The servile progeny of Ham."[15] Despite the fact that Augustine, born in Tagaste, Algeria, North Africa, had since the first century been referred to as "The greatest [Christian] theologian among the Latin fathers, and one of the greatest of all time,"[16] the prevailing belief amongst many clergy at this time went even further than Wesley, believing that enslaved Africans were there to serve the white man as they were considered to be a people without a soul, without humanity, and therefore suitable candidates for enslavement.

Anglican clergy therefore behaved no differently than the plantocracy towards enslaved Africans, and it was therefore not uncommon that they too were owners of slaves. One notorious Anglican priest was indicted for murdering a female African slave named Elija.[17]

---

14. Edwards, *Christian England*, 49.
15. Wesley, *Thoughts upon Slavery*, 28.
16. Ferguson and Wright, *New Dictionary of Theology*, 58.
17. Walvin, *Black Ivory*, 190.

Society and Religion in Jamaica before the Arrival of George Lisle

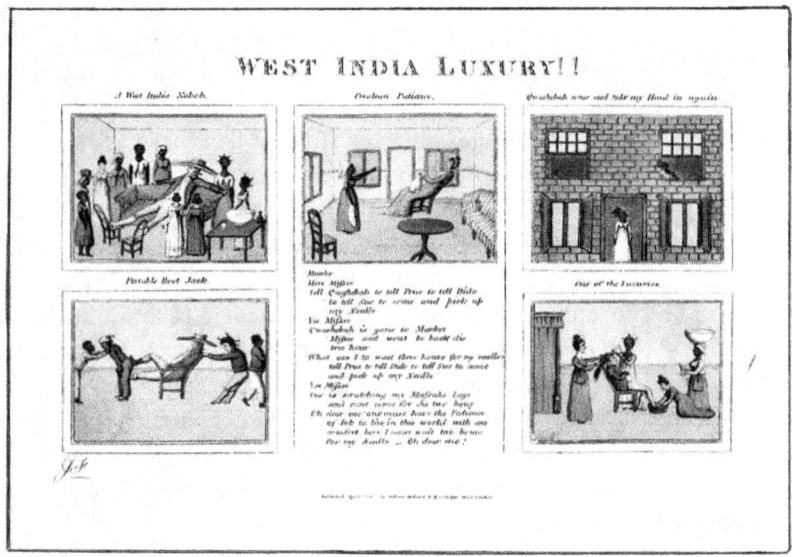

West Indian Luxury!! Anonymous. Published April 1803. *Yale University Library*, accessed https://collections.library.yale.edu.

Coloreds and White Creoles

Next on the status ladder were a class of people who are best described as the first true white Jamaicans. They were not migrants, but Creoles, white people born on the island, and Coloreds, who quickly became a distinct separate group, being the product of sexual liaisons primarily between white men and enslaved African women.

Coloreds

The coloreds created their own controversy on the island, being the cause of much contention between the groups; white males and females, white and mulatto, white and Black, mulatto and Black, and church and society. This was because they were the obvious result of the "superior" white male, "tainting" himself with inferior Black genes. Faced with so much opposition, the colored population grew to define their own cultural identity within Jamaican society, creating a class of their own, but never wavering from their desire to be considered white.[18] Such was their zeal that Curtin argues that they "worked hard to suppress anything that might imply African origin," and even "discriminated socially against the darker members of their own class."[19]

Being the "children" of the plantocracy meant that they were raised as though they were free citizens with minimal limitations. They were given limited rights, education, and economic power, and kept as domestic servants rather than having to work in the fields alongside enslaved Africans. They were accepted for baptism within the CofE, even though the same rule did not apply to their mothers. They learned how to have authority and power, firstly over their African playmates, and as they got older, over all enslaved Africans. They developed a positive self-image, a white self-image—though they were never officially accepted as such. In time the issue of color would become a very contentious one, as the lighter one's complexion, the greater one's social acceptance, and therefore one's job prospects within Jamaican society increased.

White Creoles

These creoles were considered to have less status than the coloreds. Yet they sought to carve out a life for themselves between the superior white British, and those who they nevertheless considered to be their inferiors, the coloreds. White creoles developed their own culture and customs, but as a consequence of their not being allowed to marry their European counterparts, they were forced to make unions with colored women, which then caused them to be labeled as "loose" in the eyes of Victorian society. Creole society, and therefore Jamaican society, developed believing that unions such as these, and the permanent partnerships made with African "housekeepers," were acceptable. So acceptable in fact that there existed legal contracts which made compensation payable to women when and if the man in question legally married abroad or left the island.

Punishments

All of the above classes were allowed to punish, or, as was the case of Jamaica, to use violence against the enslaved. Such was the savagery of the punishments meted out to Africans in Jamaica, that they were considered

---

18. Curtin, *Two Jamaicas*, 43.
19. Curtin, *Two Jamaicas*, 46.

to be the harshest of all punishments ever seen in plantation society in the Americas. Historian James Walvin describes how

> Beneath the veneer of plantocratic sophistication (to be measured in their homes, their wealth, their glittering social world and their metropolitan connections) there lay savage and scarcely controlled violence. Scratch a planter, and a ferocious and vengeful man stepped forth to inflict death and bloodshed on the encircling blacks.[20]

Punishments began soon after their arrival from Africa, with each person being branded with a hot iron, as if they were cattle. Then in order to assist them in "settling" into a life of servitude, they were subjected to a method known as "seasoning." Seasoning was designed to

> Break the slaves' spirits and to loosen their links with Africa by judicious separation of tribes, by teaching them to speak only the master's language and by the most stringent discipline.[21]

So harsh in fact was this method that it is believed that up to one third of those transported to the plantations, died in the process.

Then once enslaved they were subjected daily to brutality and violence in various forms. The everyday punishments were varied and could include any of the following: rape, amputation of limbs, fingers cracked or smashed, beating out of eyes, beatings, torture, castration, babies being dug out of a mothers' womb, starvation, iron masks, the whip, and shackles.[22] The harshness of this system was such that it divested them of all self-esteem with most of their identity and culture destroyed. This was the intent, according to Baptist missionary William Knibb who relayed the following conversation he had with a fellow traveler to Jamaica:

> [A] passenger he has slaves but never favours any but females as they cannot be bought into subjection without it. He is an odious picture of the brutalizing and immoral tendency of this execrable system which calls loudly. I was going to say for the curse of every friend of conscience and decency. He informed me when he could not deny the—-which were addicted that he personally knows overseers who employ an old woman to bring them all young females when they arrive at maturity for the purpose of debauchery and crime and in order to divest them of every feeling of modesty. Usually compels them to wash him in a state of complete nudity,

20. Walvin, *Black Ivory*, 249.
21. Ransford, *Slave Trade*, 104.
22. See Appendix 1 for pictures of different types of punishments.

and it is no uncommon practice for them to cohabit with female slaves for the purpose of increasing their stock.[23]

To emphasize their authority and achieve their goals, the planters created various punishments which were to be meted out to anyone found to be slowing down the means of production. For example, in order to deal with routine disobedience, slaves were allowed to receive thirty-nine strikes[24] of the cat o' nine tales or regular whip, and afterwards, in accordance with protocol, they were commanded to curtsy and thank their master for the punishment which they had received.

It is to be noted that as women made up the majority of the field labor, they were most vulnerable to receive indiscriminate punishments. Typically, the women were flogged after:

> The posterior is made bare and the offender is extended prone on the ground, the hands and feet being firmly [held] by other slaves . . . the driver, with his long and heavy whip, inflicts under the eye of the overseer, the number of lashes, which he may order. Pregnancy did not deter such punishments. Two pregnant Jamaican slaves, who left the field in the rain, were put in the stocks and then flogged.[25]

No indignity was too great, as was seen in the case recalled by plantation owner Thomas Thistlewood, as he celebrated when one of his slaves

> Derby catched by Port Royal eating canes. Had him well flogged and pickled, then made Hector shit in his mouth.[26]

There was definitely no grace shown, even when causing the most innocent of offense, as was once observed by Rev Henry Coor who

> Recalled his Jamaican host having nailed a female domestic to a tree by her ear for having broken a plate.[27]

---

23. Knibb, "Journal Entry."

24. 2 Cor 11:24 sees the apostle Paul speaking of receiving "From the Jews five times I received forty stripes minus one." It would seem that the British government when deciding on the rules for the enslaved, believed that, if, thirty-nine lashes were tolerable for Paul, then it would be appropriate and tolerable for the enslaved to receive (SFLB).

25. Walvin, *Black Ivory*, 122.

26. Walvin, *Black Ivory*, 239.

27. Walvin, *Black Ivory*, 251.

Society and Religion in Jamaica before the Arrival of George Lisle 17

Perhaps the most notorious and violent of all punishments meted out to this point were those concerning three Coromantee men sentenced to death following Tacky's Rebellion,[28] in Saint Mary's, in 1760:

> An eye witness of the execution, and one who is the great apologist of slavery, in his history of the West Indies, details the scene. One was condemned to be burned, and the other two to be hung up alive in irons, and left to perish in that dreadful situation. The wretch that was burnt was made to sit on the ground, and his body being chained to an iron stake, the fire was applied to his feet. He uttered not a groan, and saw his legs reduced to ashes with the utmost firmness and composure; after which, one of his arms, by some means getting loose, he snatched a brand from the fire, that was consuming him, and flung it at the face of the executioner.
>
> The two that were hung up alive were indulged (at their own request) with a hearty meal, immediately before they were suspended on the gibbet, which was erected on the parade of the town of Kingston. From that time till they expired, they never uttered the least complaint, except only of cold in the night, but diverted themselves all day long in discourse with their countrymen, who were permitted, very improperly to surround the gibbet. On the seventh day the commanding officer sent for me, as a notion prevailed that one of them had some important secret to communicate to his master, my near relative. I endeavoured, in his absence, to try an interpreter, to let him know I was present, but I could not understand what he said in return. I remember that both he and his fellow sufferers laughed immediately at something that occurred—I know not what; the next morning one of them silently expired, as did the other, on the morning of the ninth day.[29]

Such were the punishments imposed on the enslaved, who soon learned that their enslavement was to be a neverending ship of misery and violence.

Missionaries

While Europeans, Creole whites, colored populations, and Anglican ministers were concerned about maintaining their social status, newly arrived missionaries were not. Their concern was purely for the salvation of the

---

28. See Appendix 2 for a list of the major rebellions on the island.
29. Madden, *Twelvemonth's Residence*, 1:133–34.

African soul, and their deliverance from heathen ways, through their acceptance of a Christianity which was clothed in Western culture and its attending value systems.

Mulatto and Black females of the upper classes.[30]

There were two waves of missionary activity prior to and shortly after the arrival of the Ethiopian Baptists of George Lisle. The first was led by nonconformist churches (including Moravians, Wesleyan Methodists, Church of Scotland), each working independently of each other, in the latter years of the eighteenth century. It is unlikely that nonconformist missionaries considered that they would be an obstacle to the advancement of African people in the Caribbean, as, in addition to their evangelical zeal, they were committed to bringing about the abolition of slavery, and the establishing of their denomination as the denomination "of the people." However:

> The missionaries often did further damage to their spiritual mission by clumsy failures to understand the inner significance and importance of "native" customs which seemed to them merely "savage" or "barbaric"—customs which for many centuries had regulated sexual relationships and had socialized families, villages and tribes.[31]

They knew that their natural enemies would be the planters, and the CofE, the latter seeing them as a threat because of their emancipatory intent.

30. Phillippo, *Jamaica*, 151.
31. Edwards, *Christian England*, 317.

However, enslaved Africans were also naturally suspicious of them for they were members of the white "ruling" classes and accepted and encouraged the maintaining of the established class system, whereby they excluded Africans as co-laborers when setting up churches and mission stations. It was difficult then for these missionary groups to progress amongst a constituency which would have traditionally been their prime constituents in Britain—the working classes. They were nevertheless determined to succeed and the following are examples of how they fared.

The Moravians

Being the first missionaries to arrive in 1754, the Moravians established themselves on land given to them within the Bogue Estate plantation, in the Western interior of Saint Elizabeth. In order to build the mission station which they needed, they used the labor made available to them, enslaved Africans, and so perhaps not surprisingly, their influence amongst the Africans were initially limited. Also, as was typical of missionaries of the day, they did not assist their cause by failing to seek to incorporate other ways of being church in this new context, and so often sabotaged the little progress they managed to achieve. For example, after one Christmas Eve celebration service they chastised the Africans for carrying out what they considered to be heathen practices—beating drums, dancing, and singing. Such was their single-minded understanding of how faith was to be expressed, and their lack of respect for African customs and cultural practices that they could not identify it as a contextual continuation of the Christmas celebrations, choosing instead to see it as a failure by the people to adopt "civilized" worship practices. One "offended" minister remarked:

> Scarcely was our worship closed, before the heathen negroes on the estate began to beat their drums, to dance, and to sing, in the most outrageous manner.... After breakfast... (I)... expressed my surprise that, having heard the word of God for so many years, they still continued their heathenish customs.[32]

Wesleyan Methodists

This group arrived in 1789, under the leadership of Dr. Thomas Coke. They were a people with worship practices more akin to that of the enslaved

---

32. Brathwaite, *Folk Culture*, 13–14.

Africans, in that they had an expectation and acceptance of the reality of the Holy Spirit. In fact, such was their enthusiasm that they were soon seen by the CofE as fanatical, and a threat to the status quo. Yet, though they had managed to achieve twelve curates in nineteen parishes by 1822, unlike the Moravians, they were not supported by the establishment or given land on which to build chapels or churches. Also, even though they had taken an interest in the plight of Africans, few Africans were inclined to join them, seeing them as being not too dissimilar in their worship practices to that of the CofE.

This resulted in a Methodist church which gained a constituency of Myal men, who saw the church as a haven which could protect them from persecution, and colored people, who saw it as their opportunity to be linked with an acceptable European church, thus fulfilling their desire to be considered white. Methodists in Jamaica ultimately came to be known as the colored sect.

Other Minor Denominations

There were many other minor denominations which also presented themselves on the island, the foremost being the French Catholic Creoles from Saint Dominguez, and the Jews. Both groups were known to have owned slaves and in fact many Jews eventually became planters and merchants in their own right. The Plymouth Brethren, another group, were quite unique in that they came with their conservative attitudes which were in the main, "anti-music, anti-woman, anti-amusement . . . with no doctrinal basis, no organized ministry and no social outreach."[33] Suffice to say their presence was mostly overlooked.

The second wave was spearheaded by the CofE, following the passing of the Abolition of the Transatlantic Slave Trade Act in 1807. Called upon to prepare the African for freedom through conformity to expected social, cultural, and political norms, and notably to assist them in this endeavor, the CofE brought with them their own version of the Bible. Not for them the tried and trusted King James Bible with its sixty-six books, but a unique "Slave Bible," designed purely for the enslaved across the plantations of the British Caribbean. In fact, so unique was it that 957 chapters of the original Bible were redacted, a startling total of some 19.5 percent of the original text! Unsurprisingly, stories of liberation such as that of the children of Israel fleeing from Egypt, and most of the books of the Old Testament prophets, were withheld. However, interestingly they did not redact the book of Acts, which if accessed by the enslaved would have so resonated with their

---

33. Barrett, *Sun and the Drum*, 24.

own worldview that they may have reacquainted themselves with the God of their homeland, as well as a means by which they could trust God to gain access to the freedom and liberty which they so badly desired.

Free Africans

There were actually three groups of "free" Africans present in Jamaica. Firstly, those few, who had received their manumission from "owners" who had either died or chosen to reward an act of faithfulness, and those who had managed to save money and bought their own freedom.

Secondly, there was a small group of people, who though enslaved were able to pay their owners a certain sum of money in exchange for a passport, which gave them the "freedom" to travel about doing business or preaching, for a certain number of days, up to one month.

Then finally, there were the Maroons. The Maroons were Africans who had escaped enslavement, during the time of the British conquest of the Caribbean islands from Spain in 1655. They became a law unto themselves, creating their own settlements and enclaves in the Blue Mountains in the east and in areas in the west of the island. Determined never to be enslaved again, they often came into conflict with the British, who they repeatedly defeated under the leadership of one of the most outstanding military leaders in guerilla warfare at that time, Nanny or "Granny" Nanny, as she was lovingly known. Nanny hailed from Ghana. History tells of how having repeatedly defeated the British, she was then disappointed to hear that in 1839, Cudjoe, the leader of the Leeward Maroons, had signed a peace treaty with the British, promising to no longer harbor runaway slaves and other "criminals" in return for keeping their independence within an area of land, totaling some 1,500 acres.

However, to their detriment and the glorious history, which Nanny had wrought for them, Cudjoe also agreed that his Maroons would take on the role of assisting in the quelling of slave rebellions, as well as acting as bounty hunters, hunting down runaway slaves, and anyone else whom the British government and Jamaican assembly determined were a danger to the peace and tranquility of the island. Their most famous work in this period was assisting in the putting down of Tacky's Revolt in 1760, made easier by the fact that they were African like those whom they chased down. Their ability to camouflage themselves while hunting was legendary in that they were

> Decorated with their well-known "war paint," covered with bushes and twigs of the lignum vitas. . . . Where they lay down nothing was discernible of their bodies-nothing but the living

> bush that covered them. In this way they march without observation, and in this way they spring like tigers upon their prey, who, seeing nothing but a forest of bush, imagine themselves secure.[34]

However, when their population outgrew the acreage which they had been given, 300 maroons, and 200 runaways, demanded more land. This was met with a strong no, and as a consequence the conflict with the British was reignited. However, in 1795 the Maroons chose to negotiate a surrender, for the most surprising of reasons. It is said that

> In December 1795 with the arrival of one hundred Cuban hunting dogs. Maroons (and slaves) were terrified by the animals, which were drawn to their prey by a strong sense of blood. The animals, fabled savagery went before them, the myth of their bloodlust more potent than the reality.[35]

As a consequence of their defeat, Maroons whom the empire deemed the most troublesome were relocated to other British enclaves. Some were transferred to Nova Scotia, after which serendipity came into play, when four years later they were repatriated back to Sierra Leone in Africa, where they actually became the local elite, a status which remains to the present day.

Negro Servants.[36]

---

34. O'Connor, "Black Rebellion," 3.
35. Walvin, *Black Ivory*, 258.
36. Underhill, *West Indies*, 2.

Enslaved Africans

Initially the British had transported working-class people to the Caribbean: the conquered of Ireland, conscripts, thieves, and migrants from other trading posts. However, due to the harsh conditions of the Caribbean, they looked for another people, a working elite more suited to the equatorial climate, and Africans were found to be ideal. Britain concentrated its operations in the southwest coast of Africa, a distance of about 1300 miles. Those snatched into slavery were either captured in war, stolen by the slave merchants, sold by their rulers for crimes committed, or bought and kidnapped by British traders. Approximately fourteen million Africans were taken as slaves to the islands of Caribbean during the entire period of enslavement. They were taken from many different cultures and languages, and the largest group of enslaved Africans came from various regions across West Africa and of them it was said:

> The "Kramanti" (rebellious but strong) or "Coramantyn"—the Ashanti Fanti people of the Gold Coast . . . the Ibo (industrious) of the Niger Delta . . . Mandingo, (peaceable) from the region between the Niger and the Gambia, and to a lesser extent, the Pawpaw's from Dahomey, Congo and Angola.[37]

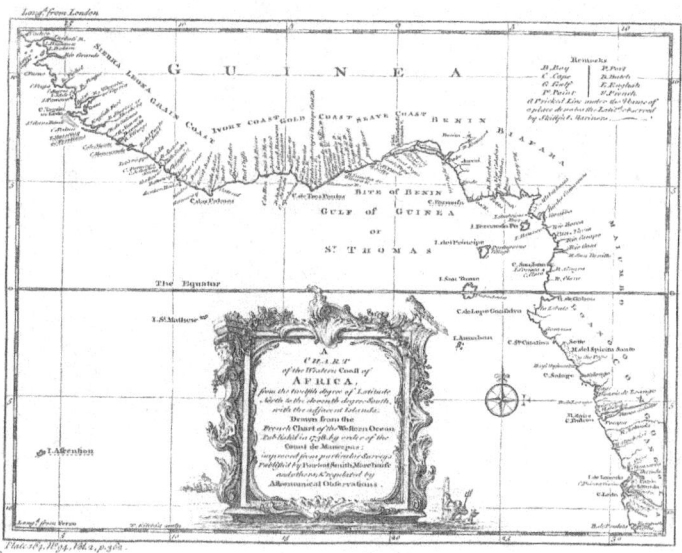

Map of the West Coast of Africa, 1738, courtesy of Nardia Foster, educator.

37. Curtin, *Two Jamaicas*, 24–25.

They were a people of all religions and none, educated and uneducated, and included, men, woman and children, taken to foreign soil, thousands of miles away, to a race of people whose language, culture, mannerisms, customs and expectations, they had no understanding of, but clearly feared.[38] Having experienced the torment of the Atlantic crossing many of them believed that enslavement would lead to them being eaten in cannibal feasts, or other such torments. So, on arrival many threw themselves into the sea rather than take those final steps from the ship into bondage. Dr. Cullen, a noted historian of his day, described how on their arrival most slaves were "skin and bone, too weak to support their languid forms,"[39] and how those who were too weak to be paraded for sale were simply left on the docks to die.

Then, once on the island, all individuality was lost as they were re-defined as "slaves," thereby enabling slave holders to deny them their very humanity. In order to keep profit margins high and competition low, while keeping control of the enslaved, plantations were small and therefore easily policed. They were just like cattle, to be used and abused, and such was the design of slave accommodation that their every move could be observed, thereby making it virtually impossible for them to escape.

Yet, this was but the beginning, as they learned that not only were their lives no longer their own, but that of their children, born and unborn, and the decision as to when, how, and by whom such children should be born. They were not allowed to marry or develop stable unions. They were not able to keep their names and name their children, each was benevolently given by their owners.[40] Plantation owners became as 'God' to enslaved Africans, and expected to be respected and obeyed as such. The only expectation of the plantocracy was that a profit would be made as quickly as possible, and so the enslaved were made to work as effectively as possible, and within as short a time as possible, and given the easy accessibility of Africans, the mortality rates amongst them were therefore unnaturally high.[41]

---

38. See Appendix 2, for the story of one such African taken into slavery.

39. Ransford, *Slave Trade*, 101.

40. It is a common practice in Jamaica that family members have an official documented name, but are also given "pet names," which I believe originated in this time. When the master gave a slave name, the enslaved in resistance chose their own names, which they would then use amongst each other.

41. Waddell, *Twenty-Nine*, 19. The slave trade had been prosecuted by the Jamaica colonists with the utmost recklessness from an early period. In 1698, when the white population was only about 7,000, the Black population had increased to 40,000, and that number was but the half of what had been imported. In 1776 they were introduced at the rate of 18,000 yearly. Up to that date, about 600,000 negroes had been landed, of whom 130,000 had been sold away again, and 270,000 had perished, leaving about 200,000 in the island.

Hoeing a cane-piece, ca. 1830.[42]

Culture

No aspect of their life was their own, not their identity, family, customs, or culture, which was deemed inferior and heathen. European society failed to seek to understand African cultures, society and worldviews, choosing instead to make value judgments simply based on what they had observed in frightened, ignorant people forced from their homes, communities and culture and separated by the barrier of language. An exception to this view, even though it came late into the proceedings, was that of one government official, R. Madden, who makes a measured response to the plight of these enslaved Africans, having heard tales about them in their own country, and then having interacted them in enslavement. He stated:

> If the negro in his own country is not the degraded being he is represented in the colonies, the condition that debased him deserves the blame: that in his own land he is not that lazy worthless being, the testimony of all recent travellers clearly proves.[43]

Then going on to give an example of the experience of one such traveler to Africa, he recalled the following story:

42. Parry et al., *Short History*, between pp. 162–63.
43. Madden, *Twelvemonth's Residence*, 1:141–42.

> Speaking of an affecting interview between a poor blind negro widow and her son, he says, "From this interview I was fully convinced that whatever difference there is between the European and the negro in the conformation of the nose and colour of the skin, there is none in the genuine sympathies and characteristic feelings of our common nature." Of the truth of this observation, he gives a striking example in the conduct of a negro woman, who found him, without food or shelter, sitting under a tree in the country of Bambarra. She conducted him to her hut, carried his saddle and bridle, spread a mat for him, and provided him with food. The women of the neighbouring huts came to see him; and while they were spinning cotton, "they lighted their labour with songs;" and one of the young women sang a ditty which was composed at that very moment . . .
> The winds roared and the rains fell,
> The poor white man, faint and weary,
> Came and sat under a tree.
> He has no mother to bring him milk,
> No wife to grind him corn.
> Let us pity the white man,
> No mother has he to bring him milk,
> No wife to grind him corn.[44]

Sadly, this attitude was not typical of those who visited Jamaica. What they observed instead was an enslaved population who often responded by acting out those identities given to them by their masters, becoming the "fools" and pranksters, "Quashie" figures, "playing the fool to catch wise," and the tellers of folktales in order to survive the oppression of enslavement. As a consequence, much of the primary culture of enslaved Africans was lost to them, and what remained were those things which their "owners" had little or no interest in, but were universal to most African cultures: their belief in God and the supernatural, music, dance, community, folktales, and a respect for their elders.

Worshiping God

Slavers kidnapped Africans of many faiths, including Islam. The enslaved Africans' worship of God remained hidden, it being an unexpected practice in a world in which God was rarely or privately worshiped. Yet no matter their faith, for them worship was a holistic experience; there was no separation of

---

44. Madden, *Twelvemonth's Residence*, 1:141–42.

persons, or life in general, into body and soul, the spiritual and the physical, the secular, as is common in the West. God to them was "almighty, omnipotent, omnipresent, transcendent, a good creator, a God of order, gracious, the source of all life and having all power."[45] The worship of God therefore became the one area of life which they were unknowingly being allowed to remain African, and within which they too could acquire status and power, not simply among their own people, but their masters also.

Occasionally their practices did come into contact with the church, but were soon dismissed by Anglican clergy who, having filtered their rituals through their own worship practices and context, declared them to be irreligious.[46] Such was the view of their most notable practices, John Canoe (Jonkonnu), Myalism, and Obeah. To the British, John Canoe was simply a riotous Christmas display of frivolous and unruly behavior, however, Curtin states that

> Although the planters considered this harmless fun, and the missionaries objected mainly because of the rum-drinking involve, the John Canoe dance was, in fact, very closely associated with the survivals of African religion and magic.[47]

Myalism and Obeah on the other hand were considered by Europeans to be one and the same religion, often referring to them in totality as Obeah. The CofE dismissed its practitioners as "the agent(s) incarnate of Satan,"[48] practicing a form of idol worship and superstition lacking real power. Despite this Obeah was known to drive fear into the hearts of many because of its potential to galvanize the masses into resistance and possible rebellion. They and their followers were therefore considered to be the "enemy" of the Jamaican Assembly, who on the December 21, 1781 passed a law against both the religious practices, and practitioners, who once caught were either tortured if they agreed to reveal their secrets, or faced death by burning, if they would not.[49]

---

45. Erskine, *Decolonizing Theology*, 34.

46. Davis, *Emancipation Still Comin'*, 60. "The Indians and Negroes have no manner of Religion by what I could observe them. 'Tis true they have several Ceremonies, as Dances, Playing, etc, but these for the most part are so far from being Acts of Adoration of a God, that they are for the most part mixt with a great deal of Bawdry and Lewdness." Erskine, *Decolonizing Theology*, 38. He makes the point that "To interpret a people apart from their world is to misinterpret them."

47. Curtin, *Two Jamaicas*, 27.

48. Banbury, "Jamaican Superstition," 7.

49. Erskine, *Decolonizing Theology*, 32; Walvin, *Black Ivory*, 180; Banbury, "Jamaican Superstition," 6. It is stated that the African obeahman carried his obeah magic with him under the hair of his head when imported. For that reason, the heads of Africans were shaved before being landed, or if that was not done, he swallowed the things by

Obeah

Caribbean historians believe that there was a marked difference between the practice of Obeah and Myalism in Jamaica. Many believed Obeah to be either a continuation, not of African religion, but of the African practices of witchcraft and sorcery, or a part of African religion which was too remote from white religion to be called religious and as Africans sought to resist enslavement, Obeah developed into a distinct sect. Its followers professed to be able to not only free people from the shackles and rule of slavery, but to kill or cure in the name of "obi." Such was its rise to fame that most African men, who saw themselves as powerless, often sought the power of Obeah as the means to counter the stealing away of the affection of their African women by their fellow Africans and members of the plantocracy. To physically fight for their affections would have resulted in punishments, and so they would request the appropriate love potion, as their means of fighting back.[50] Obeah as a consequence gained a reputation for evil and was believed by many to be one way in which they could successfully resist the oppressiveness of slavery.

Myalism

Myalism on the other hand, was considered to be the antithesis of Obeah, anti-witchcraft and anti-sorcery. Historians consider it to have been the only form of African religion brought to Jamaica,[51] and therefore the best and truest representation of African religion, culture, and customs as could be seen at that time. Initially it developed without restraint, being "hidden" by the more prominent voice of Obeah. It was primarily concerned with the worship of God, practitioners believing in a spiritual world, as well as spirit possession, with followers being instrumental in carrying out exorcisms and thwarting the spells cast by the Obeah man or woman.[52] Central

---

which he worked in Africa, before leaving.'

50. Erskine, *Decolonizing Theology*, 29. "Most deaths are attributed to the magic of obeah-men, whose services have been purchased by some enemy of the deceased. In addition to causing death, magic may have an effect on the course of a love affair, the well-being of one's crops, one's animals, etc." Horowitz, *Peoples and Cultures*, 136.

51. Beckles and Shepherd, *Caribbean Slave Society*, 295–96. "Myalism . . . is the first documented Jamaican religion cast in the 'classical' African mold. . . . [It] is a collective groups' acceptance of a new religious form consisting of rearranged existing rituals, symbols, and beliefs combined occasionally with new beliefs. Second, the originator is a charismatic leader inspired by dreams and visions. Third, the aim, is a culture which believes that good can and should prevail, is to prevent misfortune and maximize good fortune for the community."

52. Beckwith, "Chapters on Religion," 142. Leaflet available from the Turner

to their worship practices, and particularly to the ecstatic trances, and spirit possession which was necessary for receiving the revelation necessary to heal and to exorcise, was music in the form of drumming, singing, and dancing.[53] However, given that the majority of the white population neither believed that Africans had the capacity to undertake any form of religious practice, or that spiritual activities such as exorcism or healing were possible, they simply dismissed it as mere noise, superstition and sexually immoral.

"Slaves Working on a Plantation." *Slavery Images: A Visual Record of the African Slave Trade and Slave Life in the Early African Diaspora*, accessed June 9, 2022, http://www.slaveryimages.org/s/slaveryimages/item/1037.

Collection, University of Birmingham. "In 1774 . . . a stupor was produced by means of a cold infusion of callalu (an amaranthus cooked commonly as greens but poisonous in infusion), which could be dissipated by applying lime juice and vinegar as restoratives." Cundall, "On Myalism," 587–88. The Obeah man must not be confounded with the Myal-man, who is to the former what the antidote is to the poison.'

53. Barrett, "African Roots," 16. Myals performed a dance known as Kumina. It was a dance done whenever there was a birth, at puberty, marriage, death, sickness, calamity or injury. Folks danced until they were possessed by the spirit, and it was in that spirit possession that the cause of illness was revealed directly, or through the spirits of dead ancestors.

One religious practice which evolved in enslavement was that of the funeral ritual known as "Nine Nights," which

> Believed that the spirits of the dead took nine nights to return home to Africa, and join their ancestors thereby making life's circle complete. There is an expectation that in so doing the Spirit (Duppy) of the deceased will enter the grave and be at rest.[54]

The only way the enslaved saw themselves being free from their confinement was through death. Funerals were therefore a time of celebration for the freedom which it achieved, and also because they then expected God to enable, or allow, them to return home to Africa as a reward for their faithfulness in the midst of their suffering, and more significantly, to make the communities which they had left behind, complete once again. Once again, this too was scoffed at and mocked by those who observed it. With little understanding of their own religious practices, it is understandable that such faith and beliefs were beyond their understanding, as can be seen in the following comments:

> Have you ever heard African Negroes speak of their own country? I have heard them speak very much in favour of their own country, and express much grief at leaving it. I never knew one but wished to go back again. . . . The slaves also believed that after death, they shall first return to their native country, and enjoy again the society of kindred and friends, from whom they have been torn away in an evil hour.[55]

So, this was Jamaica in all its fullness, and into this volatile atmosphere was to come George Lisle, and his cadre of leaders, who were free, bold women and men, the likes of which the island had never ever seen. Yet, what made them believe that they could now make a difference in this jewel in the crown of the British slave trade and the most oppressive of slave colonies? Well, to understand that one must first examine the climate from which he and they came, and how it and God inspired them to take their message of full freedom in God from America, to their brothers and sisters in Jamaica, and the wider world.

---

54. Morrison, "Reaching for the Promised Land," 203.
55. Brathwaite, *Folk Culture*, 3, 9.

George Lisle (1750–1828) Photograph courtesy of D. Morrison

Chapter 2

George Lisle—American Roots

BAPTIST FAITH ORIGINATED DURING the Reformation in England in the sixteenth century. It then emerged in the American colonies in the early seventeenth century, with the first church being established in Providence, Rhode Island (1636–37). While each Baptist church was autonomous, Baptists, like their counterparts in Britain, organized themselves into associations for mutual support and growth. Churches were established along the east coast of America, both within wider society and on the plantations, where Black and white Christians were often encouraged to worship together.

As a result of this "mixing," Baptists were from their earliest beginnings a persecuted people, not only because of their zeal but also because they accepted enslaved Africans into the church. It was in fact not uncommon in Virginia Lisle's birthplace, where James Ireland, a preacher from Scotland, was reported to the authorities for having preached to Black people and allowing them to attend church. He witnessed and reported the punishments meted out to them as a consequence:

> The poor negroes have been stripped and subjected to strips, and myself threatened with being shut up in total darkness if ever I presumed to preach to the people again. It wasn't the first time he had witnessed the whipping of blacks in attendance of a Baptist service.[1]

It was on one such plantation in Virginia, owned by Henry Sharpe, a British subject and Baptist deacon, that George Lisle (formerly named

---

1. Whitt, *Free Indeed*, 2794.

Sharpe), was born and raised a slave. His birth happened at about the time of the rise of the Baptist faith in Virginia which seems to have been as a result of the revival movement known as "The Great Awakening" which started in the New England colonies in the 1740s.

George Lisle's father, Lisle, was believed to have been the first African Christian on Sharpe's plantation, and Lisle in describing his upbringing recalled how members of the both the Black and white community described his father as "the only black person who knew the Lord in a spiritual way in that country."[2] Lisle therefore being raised within a Christian context always had an awareness of the Christian faith and this developed in him, "a natural fear of God . . . which barred [him] from many sins and bad company."[3] It was not, however, until he was an adult that he too chose to become a follower of Christ.

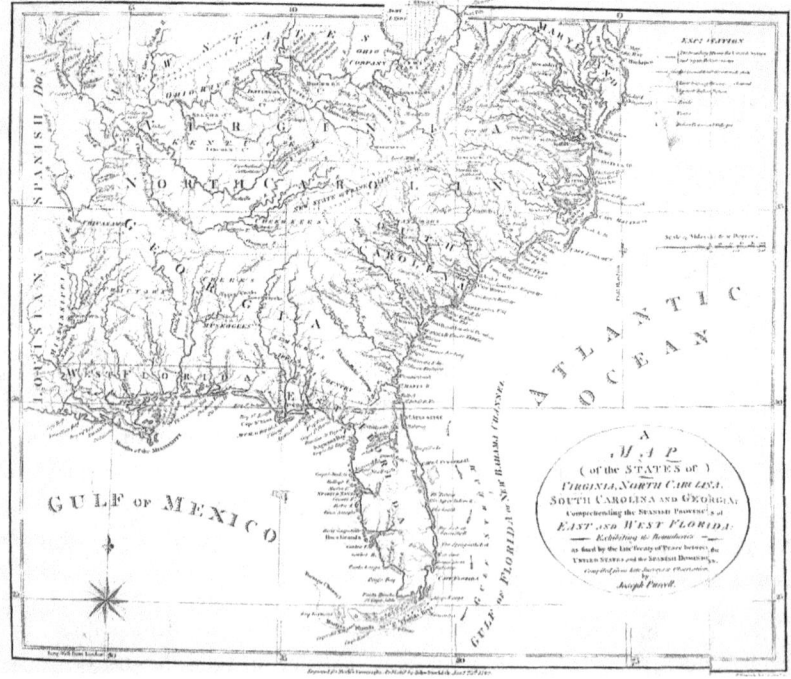

Map of the States of Virginia, North Carolina, South Carolina and Georgia. Joseph Purchell. National Library of Scotland, accessed https://www.flickr.com/photos/nlscotland/7024153737

2. Liele, "Letter Dec 1791," 332–33.
3. Liele, "Letter Dec 1791," 333.

CONVERSION AND EARLY MINISTRY

The year 1770 saw Henry Sharpe relocate to Burke County, Georgia, taking his slaves with him, and it was there, under the pastoral leadership of a Rev. Matthew Moore of Buckhead Creek Baptist Church, that Lisle accepted Jesus Christ for himself in 1773. Of his conversion Lisle stated:

> I saw my condemnation in my own heart, and I found no way wherein I could escape the damnation of hell, only through the merits of my dying Lord and Saviour Jesus Christ; which caused me to make intercession with Christ, for the salvation of my poor immortal soul; and I full well recollect, I requested of my Lord and Master to give me a work, I did not care how mean it was, only to try and see how good I would do it.[4]

Lisle's conviction was sure for all to see, and Moore recognizing his potential for ministry gave him a "call at a quarterly meeting to preach before the congregation,"[5] for approval for ministry. The members voted and the vote was unanimously won, and then having gained the permission of the colonial officials of Georgia, Lisle was allowed to become the first licensed minister of African descent in America. This allowed him to preach four times a year to both Black and white Christians, thereby taking his place as a part of the global Baptist family.

"Church Service at Plantation, South Carolina, 1863." *Slavery Images: A Visual Record of the African Slave Trade and Slave Life in the Early African Diaspora*, accessed June 16, 2022, http://slaveryimages.org/s/slaveryimages/item/1853.

4. Holmes, "George Liele," 340.
5. Holmes, "George Liele," 341.

Lisle was at the same time encouraged to preach on many of the plantations in the area, as well as to the predominantly white congregations around them. He went on to become the first African Baptist pastor of the first Black church in America, Silver Bluff, on the Gaulphin Plantation in South Carolina. In 1775 he was ordained, once again leading the way by becoming not only the first African Baptist minister, but the first ordained African American minister in America. Lisle stated that it was while serving as the pastor of Silver Bluff Church that he came to understand the work which he was to do. He developed a concern for his African brothers and sisters, determining that he would seek to enhance their lives by introducing a relevant contextual church able to speak holistically to their needs, whether they were enslaved or free.

"Silver Bluff Baptist Church, South Carolina."[6]

ETHIOPIANISM AND THE BIRTH OF THE ETHIOPIAN BAPTIST MOVEMENT

It was during this period of awakening that Lisle and his followers co-opted the notion which was sweeping across the African diaspora, that of "Ethiopianism." Ethiopianism was a movement which traveled across America,

6. Accessed at Lowe, "Silver Bluff Baptist Church, South Carolina."

providing enslaved Africans with an independent spiritual, social, and political identity, as people created in the image of God. It was a means whereby they could assert their African identities as they worshiped God, in the midst of oppressive environments. Their foundation stone was the Bible, and particularly texts which referred to Ethiopia, the most significant one being Ps 68:31 (KJV), "Ethiopia shall soon stretch out her hands unto God." Lisle and his followers therefore began referring to themselves as "Ethiopian Baptists," seeing in the Bible a

> Vision of a homeland [which] was the biblical Ethiopia. It was the vision of a golden past—and the promise that Ethiopia should once more stretch forth its hands to God—that revitalized the hope of an oppressed people. Ethiopia to the blacks in America was like Zion or Jerusalem to the Jews.[7]

This notion soon became a part of the wider African worldview, as they understood the term "Ethiopian" to be the Hebrew translation of the Greek word which meant "Black" or "African." This only served to affirm them as Africans, and their increased understanding that they were a part of God's creation, for "civilization came down the River Nile from Ethiopia to Egypt and then to Greece and then to Rome."[8] Many Africans, including Bishop Richard Allen, founder of the Free African Society in Philadelphia (1894; later renamed the African Methodist Episcopal Church in 1916), was one of those early leaders who

> First identified the cause of African freedom with this prophecy in Psalms . . . [and] it is reputed that one black regiment proudly wore the appellation of "Allen's Ethiopian" during the Revolutionary War . . . Prince Hall, a black Revolutionary War veteran and founder of the African Masonic Lodge [when] commenting upon the successful slave insurrection in Haiti (1792–1800) . . . observed: "Thus doth Ethiopia begin to stretch forth her hand, from the sink slavery, to freedom and equality."[9]

Sylvia Frey in seeking to explain the phenomenon suggests that

> The paucity of black church records makes it virtually impossible to determine precisely when early separate churches began to take racially specific names, but the tendency to differentiate themselves racially is clearly there: in the tendency of black evangelicals to . . . define (d) themselves by their place of birth

7. Charet, *Root of David*, 69.
8. Asante and Fazama, *Encyclopedia of Black Studies*, 408.
9. Homiak, "Dread History," para. 6.

as "Ethiopian Baptists," and later to designate their separate churches as "African," designations that connote both a claim to independent social personality and a sense of themselves as a select group of Christians. The emergence of a race-centered focus for community ultimately affected patterns of black resistance.[10]

The development of the use of this term is further attested to by Jamaican sociologist Barry Chevannes who similarly identified Lisle and his followers, as Ethiopians stating that

> With the introduction of Christianity from the 1780s on, the name Ethiopia began to be used. Lisle called his church Ethiopian. Later on, in the early nineteenth century the passage from Psalm 68:31 was used quite liberally by the Baptist Minister William Knibb, in his sermons and prayers, making clear identification of the slaves with Ethiopia, and in the publication of his weekly paper, Baptist Herald and the Friends of Africa.[11]

Lisle and his colleagues were therefore able to use it as a means by which they could embrace their full identity, both politically and spiritually without having to visibly challenge their enslaved condition, while never failing to remind themselves of their neverending historical link to Africa. Roswith Gerloff goes as far as to state that Lisle and his contemporaries in embracing this philosophy "introduce a black theology of liberation and interculturation,"[12] which they were not afraid to declare in their correspondence with the wider Baptist family. The wider Baptist family in turn acknowledged them as Ethiopian Baptists, as can be seen in the following correspondence sent over the years.

Referring to Andrew Bryan, a "disciple" of Lisle, his regional Baptist association wrote in affirmation:

> This is to certify, that the Ethiopian church of Jesus Christ at Savannah, have called their beloved *Andrew* to the work of the ministry. We have examined into his qualifications, and believing it to be the will of the great Head of the church, we have appointed him to preach the Gospel, and to administer the ordinances, as God in his providence may call.[13]

10. Fabre and Benesch, *African Diasporas*, 94.
11. Chevannes, *Rastafari*, 37.
12. Gerloff, "African Diaspora," 10.
13. Marshall, "Journal of Negro History," esp. "Sketches of the Black Baptist Church at Savannah, in Georgia; and of Their Minister Andrew Bryan, Extracted from Several Letters," para. 2. Andrew Bryan, also a disciple of Lisle, was given the following recommendation on January 19, 1788 by an American Baptist Church official, identified as

Lisle too also made the following statement in a letter to Dr John Rippon:

> The gospel is taking great effect in this town. My Brethren and sisters in general, most affectionately give their Christian love to you and all the dear lovers of Jesus Christ in your church at London, *and beg that they and all the other churches will remember the poor Ethiopian Baptists of Jamaica in their prayers.*[14]

Thomas Swigle also a disciple of Lisle, after a disagreement with Lisle, nevertheless continued to demonstrate his alignment with the movement in 1802 when he corresponded with Rippon, stating:

> All my beloved brethren beg their Christian love to you and all your dear brethren in the best bonds; and *they also beg yourself and them will be pleased to remember the poor Ethiopian Baptists in their prayers,* and be pleased also to accept the same from, Reverend and dear Sir, your poor unworthy brother in the Lord Jesus Christ, Thomas Nicholas Swigle.[15]

Clear then is the fact that Lisle and the movement he spawned, self-identified themselves as African through the use of the name Ethiopian Baptists, and by so doing they kept alive the idea in all the minds of the enslaved, that they could one day return to Africa. They also facilitated the acceptance of a link between the people of Africa and the Christian faith and the importance of this cannot be overstated in a context of enslavement wherein the purveyors of Christianity at that time, the Anglicans (CofE) and Moravians, were identified as a part of the inhumane and oppressive systems and structures of slavery. Of this we shall speak more in the next chapter, but let us examine briefly how Lisle and his followers came to the point where they would take their message of "Ethiopianism" around the world.

THE AMERICAN REVOLUTIONARY WAR: CATALYST FOR A GLOBAL MISSIONARY MOVEMENT

The American Revolutionary War began in 1775, and though fought primarily between Britain and America, the Americans were assisted by the French, the Spanish, and some Native American tribes. Henry Sharpe, a loyalist, joined up with the British forces in Savannah, moving his slaves with

---

V. D. M. Marshall.

14. Benedict, *General History*, 202.
15. Benedict, *General History*, 205.

him. However, appreciating the ministry of Lisle, he gave him his freedom so that he could preach freely in Georgia and South Carolina, without restriction. Lisle chose instead to remain in the service of Sharpe for a further four years when Sharpe was killed in battle.

Why he did this has been the source of much speculation over the years. Some have suggested that it may have been that Lisle, forever grateful, committed himself to remain in the "free" service of Sharpe as long as he was needed by him. Others have said that it may have simply been a strategic decision in that:

> Given the volatile socio-political context surrounding his ministry, it is likely that Lisle thought that he might be more effective with planters as a slave, rather than a freeman. As a free man, Lisle would represent an untamed and un-chaperoned threat to whites, while simultaneously acting as a transfigured embodiment of physical freedom to his slave congregations. As a licensed slave preacher, Lisle could comfort whites with his social confinement, showing them that his autonomy had limitations. Lisle might have also felt that he could identify with slaves on a more personal level, if he did not extend himself outside of their social standing.[16]

While I agree with the "truth" contained in these statements, I think that his reasons involved a far more practical concern. The slave laws of the American South were pretty draconian, with some states refusing manumission, while others, in doing so, added caveats, which determined not only how freed slaves should behave, but where they could travel. So, for instance, while Virginia declared that "no slave could ever be freed under any circumstances whatsoever,"[17] and that "hereditary slavery was made an aspect of Christianity,"[18] South Carolina and Georgia on the other hand were more draconian:

> Blacks who were manumitted were often required to leave the county within, for example, six months, in order to discourage an increase in the number of free blacks who might tempt the enslaved black to revolt. . . . Free papers were often required to be in the possession of manumitted blacks, at all times. In addition, a black wanting or needing to be out after dark or leave the

---

16. Futrell, "They Came Up Out," 68.
17. Livingston, "Bond," para. 2.
18. Whitt, *Free Indeed*, 2785.

city/county limits might also have to carry a passport, proving that he or she was allowed to do so.[19]

I therefore believe that while Lisle's manumission gave him a level of "freedom," records do not state that his wife and the children he had then had been given the same freedoms. So, it would likely have been the reality that while he was "free," his family were still enslaved, and so Lisle declaring his freedom would naturally have not only caused the breakup of his family, but it would also have severely hampered his ministry in both Georgia and South Carolina. I therefore suggest that he chose to remain a "slave" of Sharpe, primarily in order to keep his family together.

Lisle nevertheless took advantage of this newfound freedom, using it as an opportunity to travel and widen his appeal. So, despite the war and its restrictions, he founded the first African Baptist Church in North America, now known as the First African Baptist Church of Savannah (previously called the Ethiopian Baptist Church of Jesus Christ). It was the first church within the developing African American Ethiopian Baptist Church movement, and such were Lisle's skills and abilities that the church grew quickly, as did his reputation as a preacher and evangelist. Hughes Oliphant, himself a noted scholar of preaching, said of Lisle:

> His preaching was received by black and white alike. . . . George Lisle was a gifted evangelistic preacher who knew how to present the gospel in the language of his people.[20]

In 1782, the British surrendered to the Americans, bringing the Revolutionary War to an end, and this meant that the British were also expected to surrender all their interests in America at the same time, and this included the "slaves" who had fought with them. Negotiations began, with the Americans insisting that the treaty include the proviso that "the British would not carry away any Negroes, or other Property."[21] However, Guy Carleton, the commander in chief of the British forces in North America, was insistent that

> Slaves promised their freedom should have it . . . He could not abide by anything in the treaty "inconsistent with prior Engagements binding the National Honor, which must be kept with all Colours."[22]

---

19. "African American & Black Canadian," paras. 11, 13.
20. Akin, "Cross and Faithful Ministry," 11.
21. Jasanoff, *Liberty's Exiles*, 88.
22. Jasanoff, *Liberty's Exiles*, 88, 89.

The British, therefore claiming the moral high ground, released many of their slaves to freedom. However, in retaliation many Americans in the South, believing, as General Washington did, that the British removal of human property from New York was against the spirit of the surrender agreement, tried to re-enslave the Africans before their freedom papers could be granted, only relenting, in many instances, if compensated for the loss of their "property."

Lisle himself was considered to be such "property" by the children of Henry Sharpe, and so they had him imprisoned in the hope of re-enslaving him. However, Lisle, fearing a life of slavery once again, produced his manumission papers, and so had to be set free. This then put in motion an urgent need to gain the freedom of his wife and children, to enable them to stay together as a family. He providentially received support from one Colonel Moses Kirkland, a planter and member of the British armed forces. Kirkland lent Lisle $700 and agreed to protect him in Savannah.

First African Baptist Church, Savannah, Georgia.[23]

23. Nielsen, "First African Baptist Church."

Kirkland was based on Tybee Island, at Port Tybee, at the mouth of the Savannah River. Lisle therefore waited along with other freed "slaves," loyalist British citizens, and other sympathizers, for their evacuation to enclaves of their choosing within the British Empire. It is believed that one in forty members of the then American population, about 95,000 loyalists and their slaves became evacuees from America. Some had fled beforehand to New York, to avoid a witch hunt, while others hunkered down in South Carolina and Savannah, Georgia, until ships could be organized. While the British government felt no responsibility for making reparation to these loyalists, it did however agree to compensate them for their losses, if they could submit an acceptable claim. Of the 5,072 accepted claims which were made from both Black and white people, only 2,291 were awarded compensation, with an additional 588 receiving a pension as compensation, literacy being a problem for many.

The evacuation began in December 1782 and with it the beginning of the Ethiopian Baptist missionary movement. Over 30,000 Loyalists left New York and were taken to Nova Scotia and Quebec. Significant amongst those passengers was a man who was once the slave of George Washington, and David George, a friend of Lisle. George had previously been a member and then pastor of the Silver Bluff Church after Lisle had departed. He remained in Nova Scotia for ten years, developing a worshiping community, and planting a church, which despite racial tensions had sixty members, both Black and white. However, facing continual opposition and never having got used to the very cold weather, he relocated with a group of fellow African "Americans" to Sierra Leone, East Africa, in 1792. Once there he again pioneered a ministry which not only made links with the Baptists in Britain, but saw him traveling to the UK and interacting with Baptist colleagues of the BMS, in order to engender sympathy for the Baptist cause in Sierra Leone. Of his standing as a missionary Rippon wrote:

> Governor Clarkson, in the most unreserved manner assured me that he esteemed David George as his brother, and that he believes him to be the best man, without exception, in the colony of Sierra Leone.[24]

A further 8,000 loyalists were taken to Britain, and included in that party was Hannah Williams, a female member of the movement, who was also once a member of Lisle's church in Savannah. Her work has thus far been undocumented, but it is known that on her arrival in England, she

---

24. Brooks, *Silver Bluff Church*, 24.

made links with the BMS and the Baptist Union of Great Britain (BUGB), having received a letter of introduction from Lisle.

Many thousands of slaves were evacuated from South Carolina and Savannah and it is understood that at least 12,000 of them, covertly chose to "re-settle" in America. Such was the case for both Andrew Bryan and Jesse Peters. Bryan and his wife, Hannah, together with Kate Hogue, Hagar Simpson, and Samson Brown and his wife, were converted in Savannah by Lisle, and chose to remain there. Bryan then became the first "official" pastor of the Ethiopian Baptist Church of America, which in a very short time developed a membership of about 300. Such was the effectiveness of his ministry that by the time he died not only was he known to Dr. Rippon and Baptists in England, but the Savannah Baptist Association, a "white" organization situated in the heart of the pro-slavery South, which passed the following resolution on hearing of his death:

> The Association is sensibly affected by the death of the Rev. Andrew Bryan, a man of colour, and pastor of the First Coloured Church in Savannah. This son of Africa, after suffering inexpressible persecutions in the cause of his divine Master, was at length permitted to discharge the duties of the ministry among his coloured friends in peace and quiet, hundreds of whom, through his instrumentality, were brought to a knowledge of the truth as "it is in Jesus." He closed his extensively useful and amazingly luminous course in the lively exercise of faith and in the joyful hope of a happy immortality.[25]

Jesse Peters also once a member of the church in Savannah, chose to return to South Carolina, from where he also planted a work in nearby Augusta, Georgia. Those who chose to leave America from South Carolina traveled to the southern regions of the Empire, primarily the British Caribbean islands. Brother Amos, also of the church in Savannah, pioneered a work in New Providence, in the Bahamas, where he was reported to have had a membership of some 300 people in 1791, growing to 850 by 1812. Records show that Lisle stayed in contact with all of these missionaries throughout his life time, and he never failed to be respected by them as their "pastor." Each one in their own way consolidated the credibility of this movement, not only as a denomination, but as the first Baptist witness to the world, occurring ten years before William Carey, and thirty years before Adoniram Judson.

---

25. Woodson, *History*, 53.

But what of Lisle himself? Well, he together with his wife, Hannah Hunt Lisle, and their four children (Paul, John, George Jr., and Hannah),[26] traveled to Jamaica along with 3,000 Loyalists and their 8,000 slaves. Lisle traveled as the indentured servant of Colonel Kirkland and of that decision and his relationship with Kirkland, Lisle commented that:

> I was partly obliged to come to Jamaica as an indented servant for money I owed him, he promising to be my friend in this country.[27]

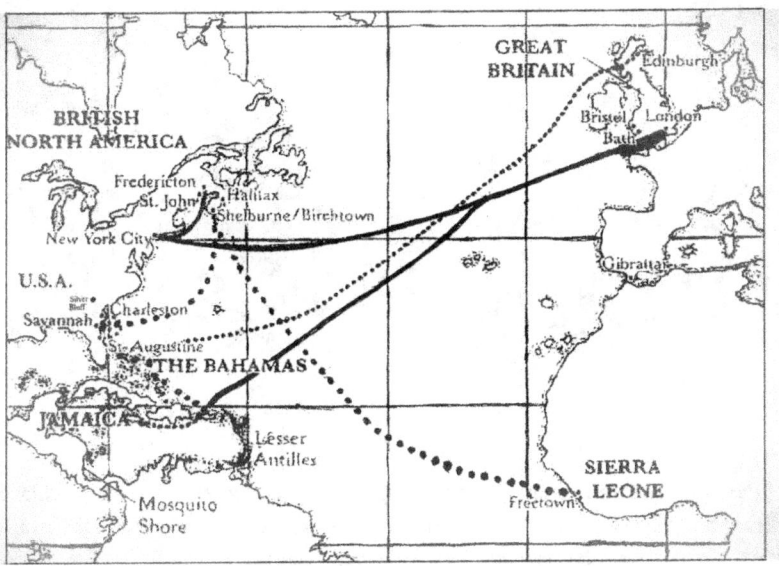

Ethiopian Baptist Society Missionary Journeys, from 1782. Designed by D. Morrison.

26. It is understood from records that George and Hannah had a fifth child, Lucy, who was born in Jamaica. Of her family, we shall learn more later.

27. Payne, "Baptist Work," 21.

"Harbour Street, Kingston." Slavery Images: A Visual Record of the African Slave Trade and Slave Life in the early African Diaspora, accessed June 16, 2022. http://slaveryimages.org/s/slaveryimages/item/729

Chapter 3

Such Promising Beginnings

THE JAMAICA TO WHICH Lisle and his colleagues arrived in January 1783 considered itself to be under "siege." Having been defeated in America, Britain continued to be under threat from the French, who saw this as an opportunity to not only take significant territory from them, but the most significant of all their islands in the British Caribbean, Jamaica, the "jewel in the crown." The governnor of Jamaica therefore had no hesitation in extending a warm welcome to not just the 3,000 loyalists, and the 8,000 slaves who came with them, but also to Lisle and his family, their experiences of battle being seen as a very valuable asset.

LISLE BEGINS MINISTRY IN KINGSTON (1784)

As a consequence of the fear which the war had created, Lisle and his colleagues were able to begin their ministry in Jamaica as a people with favor. Lisle chose to begin the work in Kingston, and over the next ten years it extended to a second station under the leadership of Moses Baker, at Flamstead, in the West. Together they enjoyed a honeymoon period of some ten years, in which they were able to establish their credibility within the wider global Baptist family, being the first and only Baptist witness on the island.

Lisle's ministry on the island was in fact delayed until September 1784, hampered initially by the $700 debt which he had incurred borrowing the money which he used to buy the freedom for his family. However, on arriving in Jamaica with a personal recommendation, he took up employment in the service of General Campbell, the then-governnor of Jamaica. Campbell often called upon him when the island was "under arms" to, as Lisle stated,

> Be on duty . . . being a trumpeter to the troop of horse in Kingston . . . and also by order of government I was employed in carrying all cannon that could be found lying about this part of the country.[1]

Lisle admitted that this was a distraction to his ministry for it took him two years to repay the debt in full, but it was necessary in order to receive his papers which declared that he was indeed a free man. Yet this period of employment nevertheless gave him the foundation on which he built a self-supporting ministry which would enable him to work with an enslaved population who had not the income to pay him as their pastor. Records show that he and his family negotiated over one hundred contracts between 1788 and 1823, which involved such diverse trades as hauling freight, carrying produce, farming, and trading in the local market.

In his own words, he began preaching in September 1784:

> In a small private house, to a good smart congregation, and I formed the church with four brethren from America besides myself.[2]

We know that the four African assistants who traveled with him from America were George Gibb, George Vineyard, John Gilbert, and George Lewis. Later additions were Moses Baker, a mulatto colored barber from New York, Thomas Swigle a colored creole born in Jamaica, Parson Killick, an African creole, and lesser-known persons including Moses Hall, James Pascall and Cupid Wilkin, many of whom I shall speak of later. Given the emotional and spiritual support which was given to him by his team, Lisle was able to concentrate on building up the church in Jamaica. He brought with him from America a significant strategy for mission, known as hub-and-spoke evangelism. This according to Samantha Futrell was a system which Lisle had used with much success in America, whereby

> After securing a stable footing in Reverend Moore's church in Burke County, Lisle spread out to various localities within a couple hundred miles of the church. Using the church as the epicentre of his evangelism, Lisle travelled to plantations all around Burke County. . . . [Also] between Georgia and South Carolina

---

1. Holmes, "George Liele," 345.
2. Holmes, "George Liele," 334.

frequently, establishing amicable relationships with planters and evangelizing like Whitefield among slave communities.³

Applying this system in Jamaica, allowed the Ethiopian Baptists in a short time to take the gospel to the many plantations, and wherever else they were allowed to minister across the island.

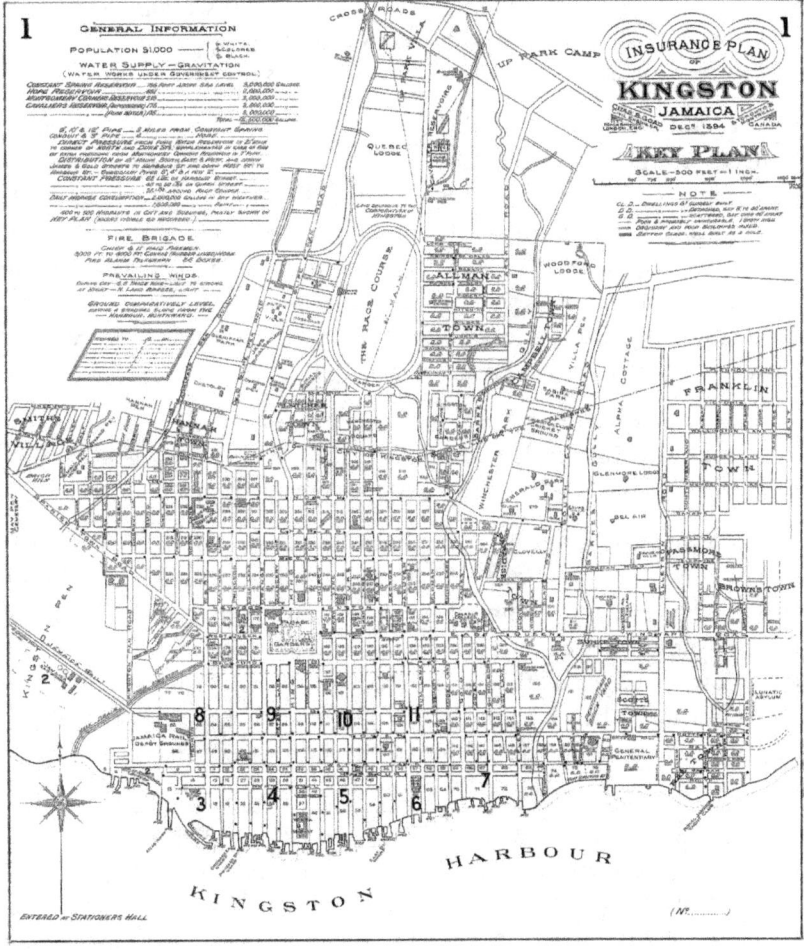

Map of Kingston (1894), accessed http://www.jamaicanfamilysearch.com/Samples2/kgnmaps1894.htm. ⁴

3. Futrell, "They Came Up Out," 59–60.
4. Chas. E. Goad, "Insurance Plan of Kingston, 1894," esp. "Kingston Map 1."

All the leading members of the movement were literate and so they were not only pioneers in establishing churches but schools. They were also able to share their experiences directly with their supporters in the wider Baptist family around the world. Lisle himself was a prolific writer which means that we have a significant number of letters regarding his ministry in Jamaica. Of his own abilities and those of his members, he stated,

> I have a few books, some good old authors and sermons, and one large Bible that was given me by a gentleman. A good many of our members can read and all are desirous to learn.[5]

Together, this team took their self-empowering Christian message on to the streets, preaching regularly at the Kingston Race Course, often to the surprise of many white people who had never before seen such a sight as an articulate African pastor, able to share the gospel in ways which they had not previously heard or seen. Lisle and his team also preached across the plantations and in the interiors of Jamaica, hoping to achieve both a spiritual and physical freedom for their enslaved brothers and sisters. Their message was well received, Lisle reporting that

> Preaching took very good effect with the poorer sort, especially the slaves. The people at first persecuted us, both at meetings and baptisms, but God be praised, they seldom interrupt us now.[6]

Lisle and his leaders being not only Black, but African, therefore had the advantage of being able to communicate in a manner relevant and similar, if not the same, to the culture of the people to whom they were ministering. Also, although the term "Ethiopian," used in referring to Africans, had been known in England,[7] the "silent" message of "Ethiopianism" raised little or no suspicion in Jamaica among the English, while it likely resonated with the people, being a reminder of the Africa which was for many:

> Remembered as a place of freedom and plenitude, especially in comparison to the conditions experienced on the plantations, where work was hard and physical necessities in short supply. Through both of these processes, Jamaican slave culture was successful in the process of idealizing Africa as a garden of Eden,

---

5. Lisle, "Letter Dec 1791," 336.

6. Akin, "Cross and Faithful Ministry," 8.

7. Jones, *Satan's Kingdom*, 18–19. "In 1640 there was a record of a woman called Frances, described as a 'blackamoor amid', 'which thing is somewhat rare in our days and nation, to have an Ethiopian or Blackamoor to be . . . truly converted to the Lord Jesus Christ, as she was . . . this poor Ethiopian's soul sorrowed much for God, and she walked very humble and blameless in her conversation to the end."

which was to prove a potent source for the liberatory hopes of the masses. Ethiopia thus became the African Zion, a source of hope for the slaves in their exile, and provided the location from which the forces of liberation would come.[8]

We know something of Lisle's ministry style from his work in America:

> Lisle connected with his congregation by leading them in musical worship and then explicating "the most stirring parts." This exegesis related the important parts of the hymn to the slave congregations, indicating the significance of these verses as spiritual texts among slave populations.... After spending some time singing and explaining the Christian hymns, Lisle would often discuss how the Lord transformed his heart in a personal testimony to his hearers.[9]

It is noted that one of the earliest sermons Lisle preached was taken from Rom 10:1–3, wherein he compared the fate of the enslaved with Israel's enslavement in Egypt, and their need to be set free. Lisle then described the God of the Bible as being equally

> The God of the African cosmos, who would turn oppression and suffering into victory—a first synthesis of African traditions and historical experience with the biblical message ... the foundation for overt African expressions of the Christian faith and the 'freedom of the African soul.[10]

Lisle's preaching was well received by both Black and white converts, just as it had been in America. In fact, such were his abilities that he could boast of an increased congregation of 350 members, 450 converts and 400 baptisms in just seven years. He carried out Baptisms in the sea at Kingston, and the river in Spanish Town. He gained an additional 1500 members in the country where his converts were primarily the enslaved, whom he described as mostly:

> Poor illiterate slaves, some living on sugar estates, some on mountains, pens and other settlements, that have no learning, not to know so much as a letter in the book.[11]

However, such were Lisle's abilities that he also had white supporters and members, who included "gentlemen" of the highest standing on the

---

8. Charet, *Root of David*, 110.
9. Futrell, "They Came Up Out," 56.
10. Gerloff, "African Diaspora," 11.
11. Liele, "Letter Dec 1791," 343–44.

island, including Stephen Cooke, a member of the Jamaican Assembly, and "One white brother of the first battalion of Royals from England, baptized by Rev. Thomas Davis."[12]

The church which they established included a free school, for the instruction of all children, both enslaved and free. The work grew quickly, and in explaining his methods in 1791 to Rippon, he said:

> I have deacons and elders a few; and teachers of small congregations in the town and country, where convenience suits them to come together; and I am pastor. I preach twice on the Lord's Day (morning and afternoon), and twice in the week; and have not been absent six Sabbath days since I formed the church in this country.[13]

However, this is not to say that the Ethiopian Baptist movement had an easy time as they sought to establish themselves in Jamaica. While it is clear that for strategic reasons, Lisle and his fellow evacuees had been made welcome in Jamaica by the governnor, the plantocracy were not so impressed, choosing many ways to show their disdain of him. Just like many of their peers in America they presented a great deal of opposition to Lisle when they realized that through the sheer strength of numbers this ministry could become a threat to not only their way of life, but their very existence on the island. Antagonism, intimidation and violence were commonplace, as was exemplified in an incident which Lisle's supporters documented at the time:

> As the church prepared to celebrate Holy Communion, an old drunken planter rode a horse into the building and stopped in front of the pulpit, calling out, "Come, old Lisle, give my horse the sacrament!" Lisle with characteristic composure and firmness is said to have replied, "No, sir, you are not fit yourself to receive it."[14]

Despite such incidents Lisle and his colleagues persisted and soon

> Found friends in the magistrates, who appear, by a number of accounts, to have treated George and his religious associates with much humanity and kindness. *(So that when)* they . . . presented a petition to the Honourable House of Assembly, in which they "set forth their distresses, and desired liberty to worship Almighty God, according to the tenets of the Bible." The

---

12. Liele, "Letter Dec 1791," 334–35.
13. Liele, "Letter Dec 1791," 335.
14. Shannon, *George Liele's Life*, 120.

Assembly sanctioned their proceeding, by granting them the liberty they desired; upon which, opposition ceased.[15]

We know that one such supporter of Lisle was Stephen Cooke, a merchant whose testimony to John Rippon resulted in Lisle receiving funds from the wider Baptist family, to pay for the establishing of the church building in Kingston. This, however, did not stop other religious groups who came from a more pietistic background, from perhaps seeing the charismatic tendencies of many Ethiopian Baptists, as too flamboyant in comparison to their own. Yet if such practices were looked at more closely today, the similarities to that practiced within Pentecostal and charismatic traditions might make them seem quite tame. However, at that time those who observed members of the movement, often expressed concerns, similar to this, made some years later, complaining how

> They met at night, sang doggerel songs in place of hymns, and worked themselves up into religious hysteria and convulsions, which were regarded as a sign of being filled with the Holy Spirit. Such old-time practices as sending a candidate into the Bush to "have a dream" before he could be regarded as a fit subject for baptism, may have come over with these misguided teachers; and much of the so-called worship of the wilder Revivalists of to-day is likely to have had the same origin. It cannot be too clearly stated that our Baptist Mission in Jamaica gives no recognition to such practices. Animal excitement is no evidence of conversion, and cannot possibly be the work of that Holy Spirit whose blessed indwelling manifests itself in righteousness, peace, and calm and hallowed joy.[16]

Lisle nevertheless received a great deal of support from Britain, perhaps because of his previous contact and faithfulness to the British cause in America, or the Baptist sympathizers within the Jamaican Assembly, who encouraged his ministry by allowing him to preach in various homes. So impressed were many of them that they also sought support from their Baptist colleagues in Britain, who in turn responded with funds to support the buying of land on which Lisle began to build the first Baptist church on the island, the Windward Road Chapel, located on the south side at the corner of Windward Road and Elletson Road, in 1791. Of it, Lisle stated:

> There is no Baptist church in this country but ours. We have purchased a piece of land at the east end of Kingston, containing

---

15. Benedict, *General History*, 5.
16. Tucker, *Glorious Liberty*, 89.

three acres, for the sum of 155L. currency, and on it have begun a meeting-house, eighty-seven feet in length by thirty-seven in breadth. We have raised the brick wall eight feet high from the foundation, and intend to have a gallery. Several gentlemen, members of the House of Assembly, and other gentlemen, have subscribed towards the building, about 40L.[17]

Windward Road Baptist Chapel, Kingston, 37 x 87, with vestry and galleries around two sides. *Journal of the National Baptist Convention*, September 8–13, 1915, accessed http://media2.sbhla.org.s3.amazonaws.com/aaa/nbc/NBC_1915.pdf.

The church was completed in 1794,[18] and shortly afterwards George Gibb Bailey was sent by the BMS to confirm the person and work of Lisle and the Ethiopian Baptists of Jamaica. Bailey on meeting Lisle and seeing the work which he had planted, including a now-thriving congregation of over 500 people, reported back that

> I have inquired of those, who, I thought, could give me an account of Mr Lisle's conduct, and I can say, with pleasure, what Pilate said, "I can find no fault in this man." The Baptist church thrives abundantly among the Negroes, more than any denomination in Jamaica; but I am sorry to say, the Methodist church is declining rapidly.[19]

17. Liele, "Letter Dec 1791," 336.

18. Liele, "Trust Deeds Windward Road." The signatories to the Trust deeds for the church were George Liele, John Lisle, Windsor Cole, John Gilbert, William Beckford, Thomas Nicholas Swigle, John Harris, Thomas London, George Gibb, Cupid Wilkins, William Kitt, and John Cahill. Trust Deeds for the land for a Baptist church bought from James Whitfield Smith by George Lisle, February 1791.

19. Akin, "Cross and Faithful Ministry," 15.

Such was Lisle's success that many on the island further believed that he and his Ethiopian Baptists would bring about the transformation which Jamaica needed. Rippon is reported to have received the following letter from an anonymous Methodist in Jamaica:

> Another sensible Gentleman, of Kingston, in Jamaica, much attached to Mr Wesley's interest, also says, "I will be very candid with you, and tell you, that I think the Baptist church is the church that will spread the Gospel among the poor negroes, and I hope and trust, as there is reason to believe that your church will be preferred before all others by the Negroes, that those of you who are in affluence will contribute and send out a minister, and support him.[20]

MOSES BAKER PIONEERS WORK IN THE WEST

Moses Baker was the most unlikely of candidates for Baptist ministry, being a mulatto from New York, married in the Church of England, and who on arriving in Jamaica worked as a barber for three years, in Liguanea, then fifteen miles outside of Kingston.

Baker was fortunate in that he gained himself a benefactor in the person of Mr. Isaac Lascelles Winn, a Quaker who owned the Stretch and Sett sugar estate (later named Adelphi) in Falmouth, within the parish of Saint James. Winn had initially employed Baker's wife, Susanna Ashton, to wash his clothes, but then found out that her mother had done the same for him when he was a sailor in New York. Believing he could trust her, Winn then asked her for some assistance with the education of his slaves, and she recommended her husband Moses Baker. Winn therefore sought Baker's assistance, "to instruct my negroes in religious and moral principles."[21]

However, before Baker could take on this role, he began to lose his sight. Desperate, he was advised to go to Kingston and visit George Lisle and his congregation. Baker was impressed by Lisle, stating that:

> Though but little acquainted with him, I thought he was a good man: and was baptized by him at this time.[22]

Soon after that meeting Baker found his sight miraculously restored, having been blind for almost a year. Of his conversion and healing he wrote:

20. Bailey, "Letter to Dr John," 542–43.
21. Baker, "Account of Moses Baker," 368.
22. Baker, "Account of Moses Baker," 369.

> In the midst of my prayer, I felt a great change upon my heart, and seemed to have a sure trust and confidence in God through the metis of Jesus Christ, that my sins were forgiven, and that I was reconciled to the favour of God. I and the brother that was with me were both much affected and we fell to the ground. I could go on no longer in regular prayer, but only called on the Lord for mercy in broken sentences.[23]

Baker became a member of Lisle's church soon after, and once well, accepted Winn's invitation to teach his slaves on the north coast of the island. He traveled to Winn's estate near Montego Bay, arriving on the estate in Flamstead in 1788, and soon

> Commenced his labours, sometime in the year. . . . He faithfully spoke to them of their sins, and warned them of their danger. . . . He soon had access to about twenty other sugar estates. Multitudes of poor down-trodden slaves joyfully listened to the sound of the gospel and not a few abandoned their evil habits, consecrated themselves to God by baptism and were formed into a church at Crooked Spring.[24]

Crooked Spring was to be his home for the entire forty years of his ministry until his death in 1824, receiving favor from Winn who had initially consented to:

> Give thee a list of names of my leading people. I do not mean that thou shalt reside among them any longer than the time thou takest to reprove them: I will give thee a place about a mile off where those who wish to follow thee can come and hear thee, and I will make out a salary for thee, that thy wife and child may live comfortably; and I will protect thee from being molested by anyone, in the discharge of thy duties.[25]

Baker was in a much better position than many of his colleagues within the Ethiopian Baptist movement in that he not only had freedom, but his own home. He went on to pioneer work from Hanover to Saint Mary, using the hub-and-spoke system to establish congregations across the whole of the West and North coasts. In fact, such was the confidence that Baker engendered that another plantation owner, a Mr. Hilton, asked him to visit the slaves on his two sugar estates based in Westmoreland. However, because

---

23. Clarke, *Memorials of Baptist Missionaries*, 23–24.
24. Clark et al., *Voice*, 34.
25. Baker, "Account of Moses Baker, of Jamaica," 469–70.

of his "workload" Baker visited Swigle and asked him for assistance, and Swigle in response sent his assistant George Vineyard to Westmoreland.

DR. JOHN RIPPON AND THE GLOBAL CREDENTIALING OF THE ETHIOPIAN BAPTISTS

While Lisle was the head of the Ethiopian Baptist movement, his own integrity was given global credibility and acceptability by one Dr. John Rippon, Baptist minister and historian based in London, England. Rippon was the first editor of the Baptist Annual Register (1790–1802), a periodical established to chronicle the activities of the Particular Baptists in England and America. He had gained a reputation as the preeminent Baptist historian of his day, even though he was based in England, and such was his enthusiasm to document Baptist history that he was known to have communicated with Baptists as they established themselves all over the world. He pioneered communication with Baptists in Philadelphia, Savannah, South Carolina, Virginia, Dublin in Ireland, and India, and it was through this communication network that he learned of the ministry of George Lisle and the Ethiopian Baptist movement. A mutual acquaintance of theirs, Rev. Joseph Cook of South Carolina who had previously ministered in Bath, England wrote to Rippon in September 1790, just days before his own death, to tell him of

> A poor negro, commonly called among his friends, Brother George, [who] has been so highly favoured of God, as to plant the first Baptist Church in Savannah and another in Jamaica.[26]

Stephen Cooke, merchant and member of the Jamaican Assembly in Kingston, Jamaica, also contacted Rippon in 1791, saying of Lisle that

> He has been for a considerable time past, very zealous in the ministry; but his congregation being chiefly of slaves, they had it not in their power to support him; therefore, he has been obliged to do it from his own industry . . . however, I am led to believe that it has been of essential service to the ministry; however, I am led to believe that it has been of essential service to the cause of God, for his industry has set a good example to his flock, and has put it out of the power of enemies to religion to say, that he has been eating the bread of idleness or lived upon the poor slaves.[27]

---

26. Baker, "Account of Moses Baker, of Jamaica," 469.
27. Akin, "Cross and Faithful Ministry," 14.

Rippon as a consequence sought to find out about Lisle, his supporters, and the Ethiopian Baptists for himself, and so communicated directly with Lisle from 1791. Seeking to establish Lisle's credibility Rippon, sent him more than fifty questions about himself and his ministry to which Lisle appears to have responded openly in the same year. He shared his history, faith perspective, and pastoral ambition, along with information as to the ministers, ministries, and individuals who had supported his ministry. His now-famous letter stated:

> My occupation is a farmer, but as the seasons in the part of the country are uncertain, I also keep a team of horses and wagons for the carrying of goods from one place to another, which I attend myself, with the assistance of my sons, and by this way of life I have gained the good will of the public, who recommend me to business and to some very principal work of the Government. . . . The chief part of our congregation are slaves, and their owners allow them, in common, but three or four bits per week (equivalent to 5–7 pennies then, and 3pence or 3 cents today) for allowance to feed themselves, and out of so small a sum we cannot expect anything that can be of service from them; if we did, it would soon bring a scandal upon religion: and the free people in our society are poor, but they are willing. . . . And Rev. Sir, we think the Lord has put it in the power of the Baptist societies in England to help and assist us in completing this building . . . we place all our confidence in you to make our circumstances known to the several Baptist churches in England, and we look upon you as our father, friend, and brother. . . . Your letter was read to the church two or three times and did create a great deal of love and warmness. . . . I remain with the utmost love, Rev. Sir, your unworthy fellow labourer, servant and brother in Christ. George Lisle.[28]

So began Rippon's relationship with Lisle and this letter was followed up by a visit from a Mr. Green on behalf of Rippon, in 1792. Green returned to England with Lisle's Church Covenant in hand, a document which was approved and witnessed by twenty-four elders, twelve male and twelve female.[29] The covenant was the foundational document of the Ethiopian Baptist movement in Jamaica and was read monthly in each of their congregations. For Rippon it was a testimony of their intent, and being impressed, he passed it on to the Baptist leadership in Britain. They in turn were able to relate to Lisle, he having described his movement as being of the Anabaptist

---

28. Early, *Readings in Baptist History*, 56–57.
29. See Appendix 3 for the full covenant.

persuasion. This was a position which they also held, as was later seen in the sending of John Rowe, their first missionary to Jamaica, who was described in his home parish register, in Saint James, "as an Anabaptist Missionary."[30]

Rippon then chose as a consequence to embark on direct correspondence with the various Ethiopian Baptist missionaries around the world, confirming and documenting the extent of their missionary movement. By the turn of the nineteenth century Lisle and his followers had so convinced Rippon of their intentions that Rippon was able to declare in his writings to the world that Lisle and the Ethiopian Baptists were a credible Baptist witness which was impacting the world in a very significant way. Then, having connected the dots, as it were, he passed on this information and his understanding of the movement to his colleagues across the Baptist world, including two significant persons, David Benedict, an American Baptist historian who was at the same time, also compiling information about this pioneering movement, and John Ryland who became the founder and leader of the Baptist Missionary Society (BMS), which in time became the primary supporter of the work of the EBS in Jamaica.

Yet this good news was not to last, as the growth expected of the EBS failed to come to full fruition because of circumstances far beyond their control, the Haitian Revolution of 1791. This event led to a backlash against the movement not only in Jamaica but throughout the whole of the British Caribbean as the colonial government introduced laws which were designed to permanently stifle and ultimately kill their movement.

---

30. Payne, "Baptist Work," 24.

Chapter 4

The War Begins against the Ethiopian Baptist Society

With the threat of an impending war and invasion by the French having receded by 1784, the Jamaican Assembly turned its attention to concerns on the home front, and they had many. The white loyalists had arrived in Jamaica believing that of all the evacuees, they were to be the most prosperous, having arrived in the most prosperous island of the British slave empire. They hoped to claim a share of the many millions of pounds generated by slavery, which according to the inventories held in regards to the monies generated in loans between 1776 and 1783, amounted to some £1,148,559 sterling (approximately £124,652,069.48 today).[1] Many loyalists had therefore hoped to simply blend into the plantocracy, purchase land, and continue their business with the "assistance" of the 8,000 slaves which they had brought with them. However, on arrival they soon found that their presence was in fact resented by the majority of the 18,000 white creoles, who themselves possessed 210,000 slaves, and owned all the available land, none of which they were willing to share.

At the same time the war had also created trade blockades with America which:

> Left Jamaica reeling and resentful [as] provision shortages, combined with severe drought, led to a famine that reputedly killed at least fifteen thousand slaves.[2]

---

1. This figure was reached by using an inflation calculator.
2. Jasanoff, *Liberty's Exiles*, 251.

These new arrivals therefore simply added to the frustration on the island, and so the government who had "welcomed" them so warmly, seemed to have underestimated the tensions which would occur as a result. The situation was further compounded by the fact that these new arrivals were found to be culturally more American than British, to the increasing annoyance of a plantocracy who then identified them as simply being an extension of the threat which they had faced from America. Tensions developed and continued to increase as the years went by, forcing many loyalists to leave the island, for other enclaves which might prove themselves more welcoming. Their slaves were sold before they left; however, this brought increased complications as these "slaves" were similarly disposed. They naturally found a home within the EBS, and soon shared their experiences of the war, multiracial worship, activism, and the independence to be gained through the developing of a Black church. Gaining strength as a group, the danger for the plantocracy was soon heightened as they looked across the Caribbean Sea and saw seeds of change springing up through the revolution in Haiti.

THE HAITIAN REVOLUTION (1791)

The Caribbean of the 1780s was already a very volatile and therefore fragile place, as ideas of an impending attack by the French and Spanish had loomed on the horizon. However, it was in Haiti that the greatest concern arose, when the revolution broke out in Saint Domingue. Haiti was well known to all peoples in Jamaica, it being about 100 miles from the island, and therefore often used as the final resting place before docking in Jamaica, after traveling across the Atlantic. The revolution therefore left many whites filled with fear, while Africans saw it as a sign of hope.

In September 1791, this seemingly stable enclave was overrun by the enslaved who went on to defeat their French overlords, becoming the first Black republic in the Western world. The colonial world shook with fear as a consequence, and with Jamaica being its closest neighbor, there was a fear that this revolutionary "fever" would soon arrive on their door step, and result in the displacing of the white minority population. The Assembly therefore agreed to take steps to make sure that such behaviors could not happen in Jamaica. Bryan Edwards, a prestigious planter, suggested in the first instance that he and his fellow planters assist the French island of Saint-Domingue in order to prevent the revolution spreading to their island. The government responded by sending

Four vessels of war to provide ammunition and supplies to the planters of Saint-Domingue for stopping the revolution . . . most planters of Jamaica realized that the security of their plantation was linked to the security of societies in the Saint-Domingue, for the Haitian Revolution would inspire the slaves of Jamaica to run to Haiti, or even take up armed rebellion against their masters.[3]

Then as the revolution progressed planters made plans to squash all potential internal threats, and this included the calling out of the militia and the imposition of martial law in Jamaica in December 1791. The enslaved Africans in Jamaica were soon inspired by African runaways who sang songs about their lives, and helped to plan revolts in Kingston, Spanish Town, and Port Royal. However, rather than simply attack the perpetrators of the revolt, the Jamaican government decided to go to war against the only identifiable group of organized Africans, whereby revolution could be fermented, the EBS.

The EBS therefore in a short space of time moved swiftly from being merely a potential danger, to being seen as having the potential to develop into a very substantial "army" which could overthrow the white minority. Their position therefore became critical when the laws of the Consolidated Slave Act of 1792 were enacted against them, thereby beginning what can only be described as a sustained campaign of hostility. The laws were contentious in their content, being designed specifically to remove all vestiges of a believing, faithful Baptist Christianity, from the island. In so doing the planters hoped to put Africans back in their place, as the servants which the "god" of the planters had intended them to be. Their rationale for declaring war on the EBS was a simple one, believing if

> Their minds are considerably enlightened by religion or otherwise, that it would be attended with the most dangerous consequences.[4]

THE CONSOLIDATED SLAVE ACT (1792)

The CSA, having been passed on March 2, 1792, was enacted in 1795, with subsequent significant amendments introduced in 1802 and 1826. Slaves were not a cheap commodity, infants costing as much as £50 (equivalent to approximately £66,400 today), children £40 to £45, and adults £60 to £70,

---

3. Jiang, "Impacts of Haitian Revolution," ll. 10–11.
4. Holmes, "George Liele," 345.

and so the laws contained within the CSA were designed to reassure the plantocracy of their continued prosperity, while pacifying the enslaved by supposedly improving their conditions, thereby, hopefully, preventing the insurrection which they had assumed would naturally follow.

Over fifty laws were introduced which determined how the enslaved African should live. Every aspect of his or her life was prescribed, from what they should be provided in terms of annual clothing, to daily rations, as well as when they could break for breakfast, dinner and supper. Determined also were the hours they worked, and where they could travel to, and for how long, as well as how many children a woman should be encouraged to have so as to maintain the prosperity of the planter. Significant amongst the laws which impacted the church were those which determined when the enslaved could worship, how often and under what kind of leadership. Of these laws, perhaps the most impactful were the following:

> XII And, in order that further encouragement may be given to the increase and protection of negro infants, be it further enacted by the authority aforesaid, That every female slave, who shall have six children living, or who having raised from infancy, and during the period of nurture, a child or children of deceased mothers, and which shall continue to live with her as adopted child or children, shall have of her own, and of such so raised and adopted child or children, six children living, shall be exempted from all hard labour, in the field or otherwise, and the owner or possessor of every such female slave shall be exempted from all manner of taxes for such female slave, anything in the act, commonly called the poll tax law, or any other of the tax laws of this island, passed or annually to be passed, to the contrary notwithstanding, and a deduction shall be made for all such female slaves from the taxes of such owner or possessor by certificate of the justice and vestry; Provided nevertheless, That proof be given on oath, to the satisfaction of the said justices and vestry, not only that the requisite number of children, together with the mother, or adopted mother, are living, but also that the mother is exempted from all manner of field or hard labour, and is provided with the means of an easy and comfortable maintenance.[5]

Set in such glowing terms the law simply meant that any enslaved woman, who produced at least six working children for her owner, entitled him to tax relief. Equally draconian acts were enforced which curbed freedom of movement and therefore attending worship:

5. Assembly of Jamaica, *Slave Law of Jamaica*, 5.

XXX No slave, such only excepted as are going with fire wood, grass, fruit, provisions, or small stock, and other goods, which they may lawfully sell, to market, and returning therefrom, shall, from and after the commencement of this act, be suffered or permitted to go out of his or her master's or owner's plantation or settlement, or to travel from one town or place to another, unless such slave shall have a ticket from his master, owner, employer, or overseer expressing particularly the time of such slave's setting out, and where he or she is going, and the time limited for his or her return, under a penalty not exceeding forty shillings for every slave so offending, to be recovered from the master, owner, employer, or overseer, in a summary manner, before any one justice of the peace, by warrant of distress, complaint being made to him upon oath, unless the master, owner, employer, or overseer of such slave shall prove upon oath before any justice of the peace of the parish or precinct where such master, owner, employer, or overseer may or shall live, or happens to be, that he did give the said slave such ticket as aforesaid, or that such slave went away without his consent, in which case the justice to order punishment; and if such justice shall neglect or refuse his duty . . . shall forfeit the sum of five pounds.

XXXI And be it further enacted by the authority aforesaid, That no ticket *(of leave)* shall be granted to any slave or slaves for any time exceeding one calendar month.

XXXVI And whereas it has been found by experience that rebellions have often been concerted at negro dances and nightly meetings of slaves, and as it has been found also that those meetings tend much to injure the health of negroes . . . but nothing herein contained shall be construed to prevent any master, owner, or proprietor of any plantation or settlement, or the overseer thereof from granting liberty to the slaves of such plantation or settlement only . . . playing and diverting themselves in any innocent amusements, so as they do not make use of military drums, horns, or shells. . . . That such amusements are put an end to by ten of the clock at night.

XXXVII And, in order to prevent riots and nightly meetings among negro and other slaves. . . . Be it further enacted by the authority aforesaid, That all negro burials shall in future take place in the day-time, so that the same may be ended before sunset.[6]

---

6. Assembly of Jamaica, *Slave Law of Jamaica*, 17, 18, 20, 21.

Both of the above two laws were significant in that they challenged the enslaved African belief in the ritual of "Nine Nights" and their hope that they would in death achieve what many of them never could in life, a return to their homeland, which would restore the unity of the community.

> XXXVIII Be it further enacted ... that if any Indian, free negro, or mulatto, or white person shall hereafter suffer any unlawful assembly of slaves at his or her house or settlement, every such Indian, free negro, mulatto, or white person shall, upon due conviction thereof before any court of quarter-sessions, suffer punishment by fine not exceeding one hundred pounds, or imprisonment not exceeding six months.
>
> L And whereas it has been found that the practice of ignorant, superstitious, or designing slaves, of attempting to instruct others, has been attended with the most pernicious consequences, and even with the loss of life: Be it enacted, That any slave or slaves, found guilty of preaching and teaching as Anabaptists, or otherwise, without a permission from their owner and the quarter-sessions for the parish, in which such preaching or teaching takes place, shall be punished in such manner as any three magistrates may deem proper, by flagellation, or imprisonment, in the workhouse to hard labour.
>
> LI And whereas a practice of nightly and other private meetings has frequently taken place amongst the slaves in several parts of the island, and which have been unknown to the owner, attorney, or other person having charge of the slaves of the property, and as such meetings are injurious to the health of the slaves, and of dangerous tendency: Be it further enacted, by the authority aforesaid, That in future all such meetings shall be deemed unlawful, and the person who shall or may attend them, shall be liable to be apprehended and taken before any magistrate of the parish wherein the offence shall be committed ... guilty, he or she shall be committed to gaol, to be tried at the next quarter-session of the parish for the said offence ... sentenced to imprisonment in the county gaol for such period ... not exceeding three months ... if the offender be a slave ... he or she shall be sentenced ... as the court shall think proper or ... flogging, not exceeding thirty-nine lashes.[7]

Additional laws designed to thwart the work of Ethiopian Baptists and all other African preachers were instigated in December 1802, determining that:

---

7. Assembly of Jamaica, *Slave Law of Jamaica*, 22, 28, 29.

> Any person (not duly qualified by law) who should presume to preach or teach in any assembly of negroes or people of colour within the island, should be deemed a rogue and a vagabond; and any magistrate might apprehend and commit him to goal, and on conviction, not before a jury, but before three magistrates, the offender, if free, might be sentenced to hard labour in the workhouse for one month for the first offence, and for six months for every subsequent offence; and if a slave, to a month's hard labour for the first offence, and for every subsequent offence, to "a public flogging, not exceeding "thirty nine lashes." That whenever the offence committed by a white person shall appear of extraordinary heinousness, the justices are required to secure the appearance of every such offender at the next subsequent Supreme or Assize Court, by sufficient bail or commitment . . . and on conviction to such punishment as such Court shall see fit to inflict, not extending to life.[8]

This law was, however, repealed two years later having had an unintended effect also on Methodists and other European missionaries. However, the Kingston Council concerned about the "free" missionaries from the EBS introduced their own laws two years later which excluded African missionaries from preaching until 1814, accusing them of

> The pretended preaching, teaching and expounding of the Word of God expressing a belief that they were influencing an "uneducated, illiterate and ignorant persons and false enthusiasts, who became deranged because of the 'fanaticism' of their preachers."[9]

Additional laws, in the form of the Consolidated Bill, were also passed in December 1816 and enacted by the Jamaican Legislature. Significantly for Baptists, it stated:

> And whereas the assembling of slaves and other persons, after dark, at places of meeting belonging to dissenters from the established religion, and other persons professing to be teachers of religion, has been found extremely dangerous, and great facilities are thereby given to the formation of plots and conspiracies, and the health of the slaves and other persons has been injured in travelling to and from such places of meeting at late hours in the night: Be it further enacted by the authority aforesaid, That from and after the commencement of this act, all such meetings

---

8. Teall, "Jubilee," 910.
9. Gordon, *God Almighty*, 48.

between sunset and sunrise shall be held and deemed unlawful, and any sectarian, dissenting minister, or other person professing to be a teacher of religion, who shall, contrary to this act, keep open any such places of meeting between sunset and sunrise for the purpose aforesaid, or permit or suffer any such nightly assembly of slaves therein, or be present thereat, shall forfeit and pay a sum not less than twenty pounds, or exceeding fifty pounds, for each offence, to be recovered in a summary manner before any three justices, by warrant of distress . . . the said justices are hereby empowered and required to commit such offender or offenders to the common gaol for any space of time, not exceeding one calendar month . . . (law does not apply to) ministers(s) of the Presbyterian kirk, or licensed ministers, from performing divine worship at any time before the hour of eight o'clock in the evening . . . or interfere with rites and ceremonies of the Jewish and Roman Catholic religions.[10]

As the enslaved worked from sunrise to sunset, this law meant that all EBS religious worship and the assembling together for Bible study, or any other church activity, was now unlawful.

THE IMPACT ON ENSLAVED CHRISTIANS

The impact of the 1791 CSA and its subsequent slave laws, on the enslaved population were recorded by the missionaries and leading Baptist citizens of the day. One such story was that of a Mr. Williams. The enactment of the 1802 Act immediately resulted in his arrest. Mr. Williams was a freed man of color and of good character, who was also a local preacher in Morant Bay. The story goes that

> Mr Williams and two others had applied to the magistrates in quarter sessions, to take the required oaths, but were ordered off by the chief magistrate, who said, "They ought to be committed for daring to address the Court." This occurred January 4th 1803. On the following day Mr Williams and about twenty serious persons met for prayer and praise. Information was speedily given and he was brought before five magistrates, and as it was proved, sentenced to one month's hard labour in the workhouse. He was not however, chained to convict slaves, but confined in a small close room with a damp brick flooring. When his month was up, he was required to find bail to appear for trial, at the quarter sessions for having allowed his house to be used for

10. Parliament, *Slave Law of Jamaica*, 108–10.

prayer and preaching. He refused to enter into bail, and after being confined one day beyond his sentence, he was let go.[11]

While the CSL was clear as to how worship should be enacted, the 1802 amendments caused additional laws to be implemented which had dire consequences for the churchgoing population, until the Act expired on December 1811. It may not be a coincidence that just a few months after the passing of the Abolition Bill (1807) which gave the death knell to the Transatlantic Slave Trade, the planters implemented more draconian acts against their slaves, so that while in Britain:

> John Rippon held a special service of thanksgiving at Carter Lane on 27 March to give people of colour an opportunity to spend "a day of prayer and public thanksgiving to God, in prospect of the grant of this astonishing salvation." The assembled congregation included some 4—500 Africans: "such a body of Africans," Rippon recorded, "never before assembled for religious worship in any part of Great Britain."[12]

The Assembly put in place the following clauses:

> No Methodist missionary or other sectarian or preacher shall presume to instruct our slaves or receive them into their houses, chapels or conventicles of any sort or description, under the penalty of twenty pounds for every slave proved to have been there—imprisonment until the fine was paid . . . passed by the Assembly, November 11th 1807.[13]

This resulted in the severest of punishments for those who sought to pursue a life of worship:

> Two persons were cruelly flogged by their masters for persisting in coming to chapel, and for praying to God.
>
> In June (1804) a man was cast into prison for praying too loud, between eight and nine o'clock p.m., in his own house: and (so) an ordinance was passed by the Common Council to prevent meetings from being held before sunrise, or after sunset—thus aiming at the prevention of religious services, excepting on the Sabbath day. Rioting, dancing, billiards, theatrical amusements, might go on as usual; but the service of God, singing, prayer, reading the Word of God, and expounding it could not be tolerated.

11. Clarke, *Memorials of Baptist Missionaries*, 41–42.
12. Briggs, "Baptists and the Campaign," 271.
13. Clarke, *Memorials of Baptist Missionaries*, 43–51.

On the 18th January, 1808 Mr Wiggins applied for a licence, but was refused. Mr Bradnock also presented his licence, with the seal of the Lord Mayor of London; but a decided opposition was now determined upon by the city authorities. The chapel was assaulted with stones in open day; and it was threatened by some that the premises would be set on fire.

April 1808. . . . The chapel doors had to be guarded by day, to admit only free persons into the house of prayer, and the poor slaves were sent back, some of them piteously exclaiming, "Massa, me no fe go to heaven now!" "Heigh! White man keep black man fra serving God!" "Black man got no soul!" "Nobody fe teach black man now!"[14]

In conclusion then the CSL sought to prohibit not just the spread of the Baptist faith, but more particularly the enslaved from coming to an understanding of who they were in God. Their desperate plight was relayed to England, where the British government, and more particularly the BMS, continued to monitor the situation and sought to respond accordingly. However, at this point the EBS had to continue to bear the burden alone. Yet, no matter the persecution they never ceased to try and worship their God, and of their experiences it was said that while:

Prison sentences and fines were designed for free white men. The martyrs of religious persecution in Jamaica were far more the dedicated slaves who had no such redress, nor any such protection.[15]

---

14. Clark et al., *Voice*, 37; Smith, *William Knibb*, 1.
15. Gordon, *God Almighty*, 65.

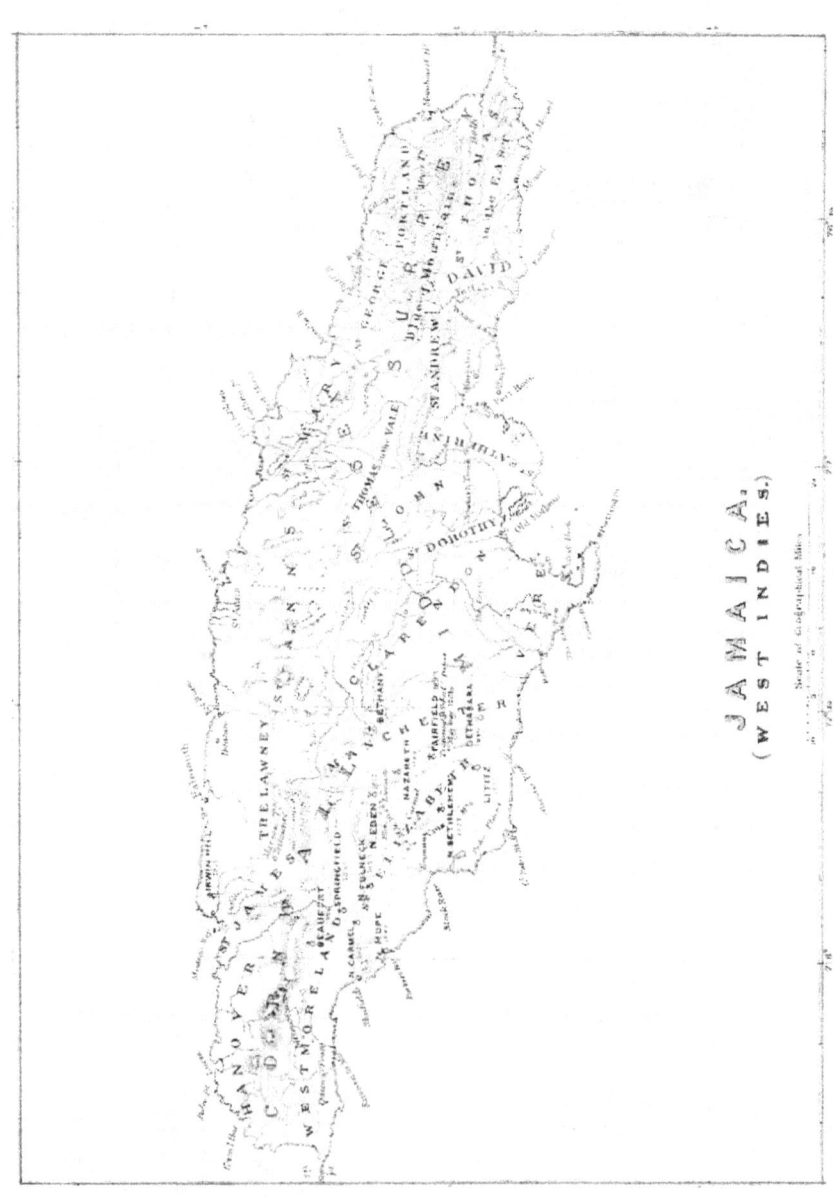

Map of Jamaica, including parishes.[1]

1. Buchner, *Moravians of Jamaica*, 4.

Chapter 5

The Response of the Ethiopian Baptist Leadership

For the weapons of our warfare are not carnal but mighty in God for pulling down strongholds

2 COR 10:4

THE IMPLEMENTATION OF THE CSL made it almost impossible for Baptist church members to attend even social and educational church events. They were required to work from 5:00 am to 7:00 pm, and longer during harvest, and this together with the exclusion of familiar instruments which made their worship so meaningful, their faith was severely challenged. Perhaps the best way to describe the oppression which they faced, is to describe how each leader responded to the persecution, in the parishes and churches across the island.

GEORGE LISLE (1750-1828)

In the face of such opposition, Lisle in the first instance made representation to be allowed to go on preaching, and he was successful, receiving notification directly from James Jones one of the magistrates of Kingston and Secretary of the island. Of this permission Lisle wrote,

> The Hon. William Mitchell Esq. the Custos, had empowered him to grant me license to preach the Gospel, and they have given me liberty to make mention of their names in any congregation where we are interrupted. Mr Jones has given permission for all his negroes to be taught the word of God. The gospel is taking great effect in this town.[1]

So, Lisle expanded the work to Spanish Town, the then-capital of Jamaica, purchasing a piece of land on which he later established the second Baptist church on the island. The funds came from the UK and the USA, at the encouragement once again of Stephen Cooke who had clearly taken on the role of advisor to Lisle. It is perhaps Cooke who should then also be credited with the introduction, though not the content of the 1792 Church Covenant, insofar as he being a politician created a means whereby Lisle was allowed to continue preaching. Cooke himself told of the incident, informing Rippon that:

> I very early saw into the impropriety of admitting slaves into their societies [Methodists], "without permission of their owners" and told them the consequences that would attend it: but they rejected my advice; and it has not only prevented the increase of their church, but has raised them many enemies. Mr Lisle has very wisely acted a different part. He has I believe, admitted no slaves into society but those who had obtained permission from their owners, by which he has made many friends; and I think the Almighty is now opening a way for another church in the capital.[2]

Lisle in fact drafted his Church Covenant in 1792, and defined its purpose and intention as being:

> A collection of some of the principal texts of scripture which we observe both in America and this country, for the direction of our practice. It is read once a month here on sacrament meetings, that our members may examine if they live according to all these laws which they professed, covenanted and agreed to.[3]
>
> The reading of this covenant once-a-month, when all are met together from the different parts of the island, keeps them in mind of the commandments of God.[4]

---

1. Benedict, *General History*, 202.
2. Benedict, *General History*, 199.
3. Benedict, *General History*, 201.
4. Benedict, *General History*, 201.

Lisle, ever the pragmatist, went on to state that it also proved its usefulness in that:

> By shewing the same to the gentlemen of the legislature, the Justices, and Magistrates, when I applied for a sanction, it gave them general satisfaction; and whenever a negro servant is to be admitted, their owners, after the perusal of it, are better satisfied.[5]

Lisle in gratitude boldly declared:

> I have a right to praise God, and glorify him for the manifold blessings I have received, and still do receive from him. I have full liberty from Spanish-Town, the capital of the country, to teach the gospel throughout the island. The Lord is blessing the work everywhere, and believers are added daily to the church. My tongue is not able to express the goodness of the Lord.[6]

So, despite the opposition of the CSL, Lisle's diplomatic skills enabled the Ethiopian Baptists to continue to build a firm foundation in Jamaica. In 1789 he had purchased six acres of land, three acres of which was later set aside for the Windward Road Chapel, and the rest for accommodation of the missionaries, located on what was then known as "the King's Road leading down to Elletson's Wharf."[7] Lisle, however, took nothing for granted and so, in order to avoid any misunderstanding or prohibition of the enslaved attending church, when thanking supporters in Britain for the funds which they sent to support the building of the church, he requested additional funds from Rippon in order to pay for a larger bell, which while calling their members to worship would

> Give notice to our people and more particularly to the owners of slaves that are in our society, that they may know the hour on which we meet, and be satisfied that their servants return in due time for which reason I shall be greatly obliged to you to send me out, as soon as possible, a bell that can be heard about two miles distance, with the price. I have one at present, but it is rather small. The slaves may then be permitted to come and return in due time, for at present we meet very irregular, in respect to hours.[8]

---

5. Benedict, *General History*, 201.
6. Benedict, *General History*, 201.
7. Morton, "Land Sale to George Liele."
8. Holmes, "George Liele," 347.

Lisle's success, however, meant that he was soon negatively "targeted" by the Jamaican Assembly, who, supported by the plantation owners, saw any gathering of groups of Africans as the recipe for a revolution. They therefore utilized every opportunity which presented itself, to prevent him from preaching, and found one in 1794. Lisle, after preaching from the Rom 10:1–3 text, found himself in a court of law where he was compelled to swear that

> He had not the least intention to offer or publish any words that had a Tendency to Stir up Sedition or raise any rebellious notions in the midst of the people of his own Colour or to give offence to the white Inhabitants of the Island nor had [he] any evil intent, whatsoever in delivering such discourse nor was he at the time sensible that the words he made use of were liable to be Construed as injurious to the peace and Quiet of the Inhabitants of this Island.[9]

Nevertheless, it was noted that he was

> Charged with preaching sedition, for which he was thrown in prison, loaded with irons, and his feet fastened in the stocks. Not even his wife or children were permitted to see him. At length he was tried for his life; but no evil could be proved against him, and he was honourably acquitted. [However, he was thereupon] thrown into gaol [jail] for the balance due to the builder of his chapel. He refused to take benefit of the insolvent Debtor's Act, and remained in prison until he had fully paid all that was due.[10]

Despite this, such was his character and commitment to God that he was trusted by his goalers to carry on his ministry while in prison. It is recorded that

> As with Bunyan, his jailor's confidence in his integrity often allowed him to visit the sick of his people and his family by night; he always returned in safety and in time. Thus, amid trials, contumely oppression, and insult, he contrived faithfully to labour and was held in good repute till his death.[11]

On the second occasion of his imprisonment, Lisle and his cohort of leaders were quite creative in securing his release, while at the same time seeking to ensure the continuance of the Windward Road Chapel. In 1798

---

9. Robertson, *Gone Is the Ancient Glory*, 136.
10. Clark et al, *Voice*, 32.
11. Underhill, *West Indies*, 200.

legal documents were drawn up, for Lisle to not only sell the chapel to the trustees and deacons of the church, but also three acres of the six acres of land adjoining it, for four hundred and fifty-three pounds and sixpence halfpenny (£453.0.6).[12] The document lodged with solicitors in Kingston, clearly stated that this would at least pay the outstanding debt to George Whitfield Smith, the original seller of the land.

On his release from prison in 1801, it is believed that Lisle, though he was never prohibited from preaching, was out of favor, facing continual harassment. He was therefore forced once again to take his ministry to the hinterlands of Kingston, and Saint Thomas in the East in order to avoid the vigilantes of the plantocracy, and the government militia. He did, however, remain active, being quite an astute businessman. as can be seen by records which state that he continued to trade and to buy and lease land. For example, in 1800 he leased 100 acres of land at a place called Swallowfield Provision Grounds in Saint Andrew. Then in 1804 he sublet fifteen acres of the same land to John and Catherine Lisle for fifteen years, and a further five acres to a Christopher Mollens and William Bukford. At the same time that he was buying and selling land, he was also involved in the buying of enslaved persons,[13] primarily those who were to be family members, or deacons or members of his church. This shall be discussed in more detail in a while, but it must here be said that the persecution of his followers was such that it would be safer for them to be "owned" by Lisle, rather than a vindictive and cruel plantation owner.

Perhaps the hope of the plantocracy had been that if they were able to remove the leader of the movement, then the work would eventually come to an end. The planter's plan worked in part, in that by the time Lisle had resolved these issues and gained his release from prison, his church had fragmented. However, the main leaders remained committed to the Ethiopian Baptist movement and despite everything, remained committed to the authority of the Anabaptist Covenant and Lisle.

Then, the next time we hear of Lisle is in 1822 when, following an invitation from African Baptists residing in Britain and the BMS, he took a missionary trip to England for four years. Lisle, then aged seventy-two years old, wrote his last will and testament, before traveling to England in 1822, and remaining there until 1826. Records state that Lisle went to England in order to preach to those Africans who were a part of his movement and had

---

12. Liele sells Windward Road Chapel to its trustees and deacons and three acres of land to Whitfield Smith. Liele, "Sale of Windward Road Chapel."

13. Liele, "Indenture Deeds."

relocated to England. We know that he met with the BMS on May 21, 1822. Of that visit BMS records simply state that:

> Mr Burls reported that he & the Secretary had seen & conversed with George Lisle, a black minister from Jamaica, who has come to this country with a view to procure a license for preaching himself, or a minister to accompany him back to Jamaica, under the sanction of the Committee, on which it was Resolved that the Committee cannot sanction the application of Mr Lisle, unless it be concurred in by those brethren in connection with us, who are already in the island.[14]

This seemed a little dismissive and disappointing; however, providence worked its magic, as while Lisle was seeking help in England, a BMS missionary simply happened upon one of his congregations. BMS missionary Joshua Tinson, on finding himself without transport to get to Kingston, was soon invited by Lisle's congregation in Saint Thomas in the East, to pastor in the interim; however, failing to receive a license to preach he relocated to Kingston, standing in for Lisle, at the Windward Road Chapel. With the agreement of the Committee Tinson pastored Windward Road until Lisle's return in 1826. At the same time, the Committee, in agreement with those in Jamaica, consented to find some assistance for the congregation in Marchioneal. The minutes of the annual report of 1823 reveal that they agreed to send Thomas Knibb, a teacher, to provide pastoral oversight. However, upon arriving in Jamaica, Knibb was needed in Port Royal, but the minutes state that the Committee further agreed to the "the adoption of immediate measures for supplying the station at Manchineel, for which help has long been solicited."[15]

So, having traveled to England, Lisle having met with the leadership of the BMS, not only cemented their relationship with the EBS, but he also received the promise of assistance with two of his most significant congregations. It cannot then be overlooked that having had links with Rippon, Ryland, and Wilberforce since the early 1800s, that Lisle might not have played a significant part in the organizing of future missionaries to Jamaica, and just as importantly advised the abolitionists in their developing of the Emancipation Act which was approved by Parliament in 1833. We also know that Lisle being there in 1823 might have been present when the Society for the Mitigation and Gradual Abolition of Slavery (Anti-Slavery Society) was established, and when Buxton stood up in the House of Commons in May of the same year, and introduced a resolution "That the state of slavery is

14. BMS, "Committee," 203–4.
15. BMS, "Annual Report," 25.

repugnant to the principles of the British constitution, and of the Christian religion; and that it ought to be gradually abolished throughout the British colonies, with as much expedition as may be found consistent with a due regard to the well-being of the parties concerned."[16]

Education being important to the movement, it is therefore not beyond belief to expect that Lisle would have tried to inform that aspect of the discussions on the Emancipation Bill which made the Negro Education Grant (1835–45) foundational in the granting of emancipation to the enslaved and their descendants, as it enshrined into law the means by which they could determine their own futures.

Lisle was a visionary leader who throughout his life made space for others to develop their own ministry, whether they were male or female. Having begun the work in Jamaica, he managed despite persecutions, to outlive all of his colleagues. He was pragmatic and forthright as and when needed, but he never compromised his faithfulness to the gospel of Jesus Christ. Of his ministry it was said,

> He was neat in his dress and humble in his manners. He won the highest respect and admiration of the people of the island, white and black. The slaves loved him and their owners honoured him. He was the friend of both. He handled skillfully the sword of truth and drew crowds after him wherever he preached the gospel. When he had established a church in the towns, he made for the interior to unfurl the gospel banner to those who were sitting in darkness and in the region of the shadow of death.[17]

Lisle's Slave Ownership "Controversy"

George Lisle was in life a significant thorn in the flesh of the Jamaica Assembly and the plantocracy because of his preaching and teaching of the gospel to enslaved Africans. It is clear that at his death a smear campaign was undertaken concerning his "ownership" of slaves, which has continued to influence thoughts about him to the present day. Lisle's last will and testament has been seen as a controversial document by many historians today, as it declared him to have been a slaveholder. This they have interpreted through modern lenses, and concluded that it must therefore define him as one who should be disparaged and considered to be less than honorable. However, I would argue that holding such opinions demonstrates little

---

16. Hansard, *Abolition of Slavery*, 275.
17. Love, *History*, para. 2.

knowledge of the contemporary period in which Lisle lived, and especially the pernicious and oppressive nature of the CSL. I will therefore take a brief moment to relate and remind the reader of just two examples of the issues which challenged Lisle and the enslaved populations at that time.

We would probably all agree today that rape is a heinous crime, just as it was back then. The African woman, in Lisle's day, if she were slave or free, could be taken as a housekeeper (mistress), and if enslaved was at the mercy of slavery and subject to "legalized" rape. As stated previously, because of the class system, there were many men who placed many temptations and pressures on women at that time. One such story is told by BMS missionary Cornford concerning one young Christian Martha Magee, who for many years after enslavement was celebrated for having rejected the advances of a rich plantation owner even though it ultimately led to her death:

> Martha was poor. She could only work with her needle for a living, and that was nothing for her, for the payment is so bad. She had her lodging and everything to pay for, it was very hard. That Mr F___, the rich merchant in Linstead, did everything in his power to get Martha to be his housekeeper. He sent two persons to talk to her. They say that Mr F___ was very pleased with her, ___ that she was to have plenty of money and the best of clothes, and that he would build her a fine house, and make it a present to her. And anything in the world she like to ask she was to have. Then, as soon as they [say] all this, Martha get up and say, *"Go back and tell Mr F___ that I want to save my soul!"* So she walk out, and have no more to say. Then two weeks after Mr F___ sent them back to tell her, him can't take no denial: and she shall have her own carriage, and a pair of horses, and servant to take care of them. But she won't stop to hear all, but rise from her seat again, and say, *"Tell Mr F___ I want to save my soul!"* They then leave her alone. . . . She so poor, and so young, and her mother so poor, and no one is there to guide her at the time. But poor Martha, she go through it all like *old* Christian![18]

For the enslaved woman, the CSL therefore presented its own legal obstacles, declaring as already discussed, that should a plantation owner have a female slave who was able to produce six children working on the plantation, then he would receive tax exemptions in regards to her. It was therefore to his benefit to keep all his women "serviced" until they produced the required number of offspring, and there was no room for objections. Lisle, in response, I believe sought to do something about this. One could argue that

---

18. Cornford, *Missionary Reminiscences*, 72.

The Response of the Ethiopian Baptist Leadership 79

the preferred option would have been to free such a slave, rather than own them, but in order to do so, one had to not only pay the cost of freeing the slave, between £60 and £100 for an adult,[19] but then be able to prove that this freed person could be self-supporting for at least ten years, thereby being no burden to the state. For example, an infant slave costing £5 was equivalent to the sum of £66,400 today and that figure would then have had to be multiplied by ten years in order to give that child his or her freedom.

So, while it may have been possible for Lisle and others to work hard and find the money to buy their enslaved brothers and sister, it was rarely possible that they could at the same time, buy them their freedom. Lisle therefore, like many of his contemporaries, concerned especially about the enslaved female members of his congregation, as well as others, possibly bought as many "slaves" as he could afford in order to not only provide for them but keep them safe from harm. This was not an uncommon occurrence for those Africans who could manage it, as can be seen in his home country, America, where Baptist ministers were known to have "bought" slaves in order to not only rescue them from the harshness of slavery, but in order to enable them to fulfil their ministries within the church. For example, a planter visiting a house in Virginia reported that

> I was at the house of a baptist minister in Virginia, who had many slaves, and among them one, who was a brother in the ministry. He was a sensible man and a very acceptable preacher. He had a wife and family all comfortable and happy. He had a good horse, had money at interest, and was called abroad to preach oftener than his master. And here I would observe that, among the African Baptists in the southern States, there are a multitude of preachers and exhorters, whose names do not appear on the minutes of associations. They preach principally on the plantations to those of their own colour; and their preaching, though broken and illiterate, is in many cases highly useful.[20]

Similarly, so, Lisle's colleague Andrew Bryan in Savannah wrote to Dr. Rippon in 1800 detailing his "slaves" in his last will and testament, joyfully declaring that

> With much pleasure, I inform you, dear Sir, that I enjoyed good health, and am strong in body, tho' 63 years old, and am blessed with a pious wife, whose freedom I have obtained, and an only daughter and child, who is married to a free man, tho' she, and consequently under our laws, her seven children, five sons and

---

19. Madden, *Twelvemonth's Residence*, 2:224–25.
20. Benedict, *General History*, 18.

two daughters, are slaves. By a kind Providence I am well provided for, as to worldly comforts, (tho' I have had very little given me as a minister) having a house and lot in this city, besides the land on which several buildings stand, for which I receive a small rent, and a fifty-acre-tract of land, with all necessary buildings, four miles in the country, and eight slaves; for whose education and happiness, I am enabled, thro' mercy to provide.[21]

To own a slave could therefore be seen as an opportunity to save and protect the vulnerable, especially if they were members of one's own family or church. Historical records confirm that Lisle did just that, documenting that amongst the many "slaves" which he purchased was one named Kitty. He agreed a price for her, and any "issue she may have," in 1793,[22] which was quite fortuitous given that she went onto have two children, both girls, Hannah and Lucy.[23] However, it took him until 1794 to be able to afford her "purchase" price of £90 (some £13,902 today), before then happily selling her on to his son John, her intended husband, in 1795,[24] after which time she became known as Catherine Lisle.

In a similar circumstance, we find that Thomas Burchell, BMS missionary to Jamaica, was also known to have "owned' enslaved Africans. In 1831 he was recorded as having thirteen persons on his property at Shepherd's Hall in Hanover.[25] However, records confirm that they were not just any children, but were in fact the children of members of his congregations who had died. Burchell has taken it upon himself to not only provide for their daily needs, but also to train them in the medical skills which he had acquired, and put to good use during the years following apprenticeship and emancipation. In so doing, Burchell not only saved these children from a life of brutal servitude, but equipped them with a profession and a skill for life.

Yet, within the leadership of the EBS, there were also tragic cases highlighted, concerning one's inability to free a loved one who was enslaved. George Gibb, was one such person. Having done so much for others across plantations from Spanish Town in the South, to Saint Mary's in the north, he spent his final years living on a plantation with his second wife who was enslaved. Clearly he, like Andrew Bryan's son-in-law, could not afford to free her, and so any children which she may have had during their marriage was "owned" by the plantation owner. So, it is perfectly understandable, I

21. Bryan, "Letter," 86–87.
22. Simpson, "Indenture Contract Papers"; Simpson, "Indenture Papers."
23. Smith, "Indenture Papers."
24. Liele, "Sale of Kitty."
25. Senior, *Jamaica as It Was*, 284.

contend, that Lisle was determined to save as many of his people as he possibly could, and can see how positive Lisle's "purchases" were, as they were not confined to his family. Casar[26] was purchased as a slave by Lisle in 1792, and manumized by him in 1794. Casar is a gentleman well documented in the history of the EBS, but we know him now as James Pascall, a signatory to the Covenant, and one of the leaders of the Windward Road Chapel.

Secondly, this narrative has already detailed the bravery of men and women who chose to preach the gospel in the face of legislation which determined that even to pray to God could be punishable by death. I believe that Lisle as a consequence sought to "own" as many of his church members as possible, in order to prevent them from facing the threat of imprisonment, or being placed at the mercy of slave masters who were known to have taken a great deal of pleasure in seeing the enslaved suffer. Records speak of the enslaved being punished for the merest of gestures; a lack of a smile or a thank you could see them receive up to thirty-nine lashes. History, I believe, has therefore done, and continues to do, a disservice to George Lisle who, along with his colleagues, is truly a national hero, not just for what he achieved in Jamaica for the Jamaican nation, but because he pioneered a movement which celebrated Africa and African identity, transformed the faith of the nation, and brought the good news of the gospel to a people who could so easily have rejected it, having seen it clothed in the oppressiveness of a slave-owning church.

Lisle fought for the religious freedom of all Jamaicans and BMS missionary, John Clarke, who not only knew, but worked with many of his contemporaries, wrote a rebuttal to the negative accusations leveled against Lisle by those who did not know him. Clarke said of him that

> He . . . was a light in these days shining in a dark place, and among a dark people. He has been charged, by men who came to Jamaica long after his decease, with teaching false doctrine, and following superstitious practices; but on what ground such charges rest I cannot tell. I was well acquainted with Mr Robert Graham, who had been long with him, and heard of no such thing from this good man.[27]

---

26. Liele, "Purchase of Casar."
27. Clarke, *Memorials of Baptist Missionaries*, 11.

MOSES BAKER (D. 1824)

It was primarily as a consequence of Lisle's imprisonment that Moses Baker came to the fore and became the most well-known of all the Ethiopian Baptists in Jamaica and the wider Baptist world. He worked for Isaac Winn and over time for his successor, Samuel Vaughan, visiting an additional 3,000 to 4,000 slaves, on each of at least twenty other plantations in the region. His influence in his life time therefore spread to approximately 63,000 slaves across the many plantations in the region. Of his initial meeting with Baker, Vaughan himself wrote in 1802 that

> On his first coming he showed me his book which is an exposition of his principles and of the doctrines he teaches, which I approved of, as containing sound morality, and as I have never found bad customs introduced, I have left Mr Baker and the negroes entirely to themselves, without any interference, except in the case of matrimony, to which I now require my assent to be given though, in this respect, I have never refused it but once. The too great disparity of ages and the interference of property are, with me, the only reasons of refusing my assent. These are about one hundred couples married at Falmouth and Crooked Spring. . . . The labours of Mr Baker have been pursued nearly eight years viz from the 15th of October 1794 and with increasing advantages to the property and to the negroes.[28]

The extent of Baker's achievements was quite phenomenal given that the implementation of the CSL resulted in his ministry being significantly curtailed to within agreed upon plantations, especially between 1802 and 1814, when he had eight years of underground ministry. Of these restrictions Baker reported in 1806 that

> From Christmas Day I have been prevented from preaching or saying a word to any part of my congregation. From this we can expect nothing but a great falling away of the weaker Christians. The poor, destitute flock is left to go astray without a shepherd. We humbly beseech you all to pray for us, poor distressed creatures that we are.[29]

Such were the difficulties which he and his fellow Ethiopian Baptists faced during that time that it is understood that he received a great deal of financial support from England. One such contributor was Lady Gray of Portsmouth, of whom Baker wrote:

28. Clarke, *Memorials of Baptist Missionaries*, 28–29.
29. Clark et al., *Voice*, 35.

> I have just received a message from Mr Stephen Cooke in Kingstown, who received a letter from Lady Gray of Portsmouth in England directing him to deliver to me the sum of £5 sterling from the honourable Lady Gray for the help and support of my poor, distressed family.... I have also written to her Ladyship and the whole Society has joined me in prayer, love and thanksgiving for the kind offering from her Ladyship to us poor creatures.[30]

Despite these difficulties Baker did not relent or compromise his beliefs in the face of mounting opposition. We learn something of how those years treated him, and his continued resolve after he having returned to public ministry, sent the following letter to Dr. Ryland in 1813:

> I have received liberty to stand up on the Estate of Mr Samuel Vaughan, called Flamstead. Mr Vaughan applied to the General Assembly for a License for me to preach the Gospel, and it was granted on these terms, that I should enter on no estate except his own, i.e., Flamstead and Crooked Spring. But, as the Lord would have it one Gentleman gave his people liberty to come and hear me. Mr Vaughan said "Now Mr Baker I will give you liberty to preach on Vaughan's field, but now you are not allowed to preach, nor teach, nor marry, nor Baptize, nor suffer any other people to come to your Meetings, except Mr Vernon's and my own.... On the appointed day we went to the Meeting-house, and after waiting some time, I stood up and we raised a hymn, the meeting was crowded with strange brethren, not belonging to the place.... Mr Vaughan and some other gentlemen seeing this congregation he was angry, knowing that they were not all his own and said to me Mr Baker, you must order this people away. I answered him, Sir, I am not to leave the word of God, but if these gentlemen do not chuse that their servants should hear the word of God, let them send their Bookkeepers to order them away. From that there was a complaint from every Estate where I had brethren ... and they told him that they were determined to put an end to my preaching, as they found that I was not abiding by the articles of agreement.[31]

As a consequence, Baker was not unfamiliar with imprisonment and the courts. On one occasion, when he introduced a hymn which was considered seditious, his ministry almost came to an end when he found himself before the magistrates, charged with encouraging revolution. Baptist records state that

30. Whelan, *Baptist Autographs*, 163.
31. Whelan, *Baptist Autographs*, 163–64.

A book-keeper who was present, gave information to the authorities that Moses Baker was teaching sedition and stirring up the slaves to rebellion. On this charge he was arrested, and brought down in irons to Montego Bay. Afterwards he was admitted to bail, and when he appeared at the assize court to take his trial, no charge was preferred against him; he was therefore released, and enabled to resume his labours.[32]

BMS Missionary Clarke documents the offending song stating that Baker in conducting a service at Crooked Spring, led the congregation in the singing of Dr. Watt's hymn, "Shall we go on in Sin" which included the "offending" second verse:

> We shall be slaves no more,
> Since Christ has made us free,
> Has nailed our tyrants to the cross
> And bought our liberty.[33]

On another occasion as his folks gathered to meet in a home for prayer, the building was set on fire, with those inside having to run for their lives. Perhaps as a consequence of these and other issues, Baker and his colleague George Gibb, who worked in the neighboring parishes of Saint Mary and Saint Thomas in the Vale, created the "Class and Leader" system whereby leaders or "Daddies" were appointed to oversee communities of believers. Each "member" was given a ticket which both associated them with the church and assisted the leadership in knowing who their members were. This helped to lessen the many attacks upon them, which was often made possible because of the use of Maroons, who "scouted" for the military, and because they too were Africans, they easily infiltrated the movement. The Maroons hunted down runaway slaves and others who had broken the laws of the land, for a handsome reward, which could be as much as forty shillings per prisoner.

Nevertheless, Baker defiantly continued in his ministry until his death in 1824, and while there is little evidence of many of the practices and rituals established under the EBS, we know that his ministry emphasized the work of the Holy Spirit in the life of the believer, and the necessity of being filled with the presence and the power of the Holy Spirit as a means of daily living and overcoming. He also sought to contextualize the gospel to suite the African palate in Jamaica, by introducing hymns of triumph and revolution which spoke of the African predicament of enslavement. In fact, Sam

---

32. Clark et al., *Voice*, 34.
33. Brathwaite, *Development*, 255.

Sharpe, the most "notorious" leader of the "Baptist War" of 1831–32, spoke of hearing his first sermon preached by none other than Moses Baker.

While Baker appears to have had infrequent contact with Lisle and the other leading members of the society in Kingston, it is clear that he was indeed a "disciple" of Lisle, for when asked by his contacts in Britain to explain how he ordered the communities of faith which he oversaw in the region, he wrote a detailed letter to them which was almost a word for word repetition of Lisle's Covenant. So impressed were they by his words that they thereafter referred to him as "The eminent Black Preacher, Moses Baker."[34] In Jamaica too, he made a good impression with citizens and plantation owners alike, making himself available to all who needed him. Of his character one of his white members wrote:

> He came to visit my father, and bid him fare well, when departing with his family for England in 1813. He appeared a plain, home-spun man, rugged as a honeycomb rock. His eyes were then failing; his head was bound with a handkerchief, for he had suffered torture in America, which had injured both eyes and ears. His appearance was that of no common man. His language was direct, and his deliverance was marked with simplicity.[35]

Plantation owners too were unceasing in their praise of him, recommending him to others thus:

> "You will find that he will soon eradicate all Obeah from your estate," wrote one proprietor recommending Baker to another, continuing, "I know of no inconvenience he has been to our property to counterbalance the substantial benefits we have received." A second reported that Baker had married about a hundred couples in the eight years he has visited his estate, and worked "with increasing advantages to the property and the Negroes." A third had been so pleased with the results of allowing Baker onto his estate that he had given explicit instructions to his white staff to by no means hinder the religious teaching or impede slaves in their attendance at meetings.[36]

Significantly the BMS were also won over by him, reporting how

---

34. Baker, "Account of Moses Baker, of Jamaica," 469.
35. Clark et al., *Voice*, 35.
36. Gordon, *God Almighty*, 47.

> Mr Coultart paid a visit to Montego Bay, and saw the then "venerable" Moses Baker who had become so infirm as to be almost incapable of continuing his labours.[37]

Coultart himself also said of him:

> Baker was neither superstitious nor enthusiastic. . . . He possessed good, plain common-sense; he spoke like a spiritual-minded person, and with much feeling. He was decisive and firm in religious discipline; always consistent and influential.[38]

In the midst of persecutions, Baker clearly never lost faith in the goodness of God, boldly and confidently declaring towards the end of his life that, "The heavy trials and persecutions I now labour under but I glory in them, and trust it is the Lord's will."[39] We get an idea of where he got his strength from when he having gone through a period of disagreement with Kitt, a fellow member of the EBS who was sent to him by Swigle during the Windward Road Chapel controversy, after Lisle's second imprisonment, his wife as a result suggested that he abandon his ministry, but he in order to find direction:

> Felt obliged to retire to "a desert place," where he prayed and fasted for six months. . . . His resolution was stiffened by a dream in which he saw himself "taken up, with my heels upward and Hell as it were gaping for me." Waking in terror he decided to return to the estate and face Kitt's criticisms. In the event it became a matter of internal Baptist judgement. . . . Brother Kitt was found guilty of leading an estate slave woman astray and was returned to Kingston with his family.[40]

In terms of his leadership of the movement, Baker eventually became the face of the EBS in Jamaica, and this was perhaps because of his privileged position in that as a mulatto he was not a plantation slave, but an independent preacher, who was therefore afforded more freedom to preach and communicate with the wider Baptist world than his Black colleagues. However, it may also have been because of the phenomenal missionary endeavors which he undertook across the west and northern coast of the island. Over time he was as much a correspondent as Lisle with Baptist groups in Britain, including the New Connexion General Baptists and more particularly John

---

37. Clark et al., *Voice*, 153.
38. Hill, *Lights and Shadows*, 84.
39. Whelan, *Baptist Autographs*, 164.
40. Gordon, *God Almighty*, 44.

Rippon and John Ryland, leader of the BMS. It was he who, together with Lisle, sought to fight fire with fire, by seeking the assistance of the BMS to come and aid them in their work, and "collect, if possible, the scattered flocks of Swigle, Lisle and Baker."[41]

Baker was a zealous servant of the gospel, even making provision for his congregation shortly before his death, requesting that Coultart, "send one to aid him in his work, and carry it on when he should sleep in the dust."[42] He contextualized the gospel for the African in Jamaican, in such a way that by 1814 the Ethiopian Baptists in that region were believed to have numbered some 8,000 members, and considerably more by the time he died in 1824. Such was his passion for his people that a few words contained in his farewell address to them, summed up his life and his ministry. He, "prayerfully wish[ed] that the poor might be rich in faith, and the rich abound in good works."[43] His body now rests in the grounds of his beloved church at Crooked Spring. Of his work I here recall just one of the many epitaphs written about him:

> Not seeking recompense from human kind
> The credit of the arduous work he wrought
> The world gave him no honour—none he sought;
> To one great aim his heart and hopes were given,
> To serve his God, and gather souls to heaven.[44]

THOMAS NICHOLAS SWIGLE (D. 1811)

Thomas Nicholas Swigle was an equally unusual addition to the ministry of the EBS in that he was a free colored creole, born in Jamaica, and so he was the first homegrown church leader of the movement. Born on the island he was baptized by Lisle and his role is best summed up in his own words:

> I am one of the poor, unworthy, helpless creatures, born in this island, whom our glorious master, Jesus Christ, was graciously pleased to call from a state of darkness to the marvellous light of the gospel; and since our Lord hath bestowed his mercy on my soul, our beloved minister (Lisle), by the consent of the church appointed me deacon, school-master, and his principal helper. We have great reason in this island to praise and glorify

41. Russell, *Foundations and Anticipations*, 19.
42. Clarke, *Memorials of Baptist Missionaries*, 76.
43. Tucker, *Glorious Liberty*, 10.
44. Clark et al., *Voice*, 35.

the Lord, for his goodness and loving-kindness, in sending his blessed gospel amongst us, by our well-beloved minister, brother Lisle. . . . The blessed gospel is spreading wonderfully in this island: believers are daily coming into the church; and we hope in a little time to see Jamaica become a Christian country. I remain respectfully, Rev. and dear Sir, your poor brother in Christ, Thomas Nicholas Swigle.[45]

Swigle having begun his ministry as a Deacon and School Master of the school in Lisle's church, overtime, became Lisle's principal helper in Kingston. It was he who took charge of the congregation in Lisle's absence during his first imprisonment. However, after Lisle's second imprisonment leadership squabbles resulted in contentions in the church which caused the Ethiopian Baptist movement to splinter for a while into many independent churches, thereby challenging the very unity of the organization across the island. The cause of this disagreement was believed to be Lisle's desire to have his son Paul installed as the overall leader of the church in his absence, in preference to Swigle, who many believed should have been his natural replacement. Swigle therefore along with some of the deacons objected to Lisle's sons' leadership and wrestled it away from him causing divisions across the whole of the movement. On Lisle's return in 1801, Swigle was disciplined, and excommunicated from the Windward Road congregation.

Swigle, as a result, in 1802 formed the second Baptist church in Kingston, St John's Chapel, on James Street, variously known as Gully Chapel, and then known as East Queen Street Baptist Church. Of its beginnings Swigle wrote to Rippon in 1802 stating that he had been given permission to operate a church, having received

A sanction from the Rev. Dr Thomas Rees, rector of this town and parish, who is one of the minsters appointed by his Majesty to hold an ecclesiastical jurisdiction over the clergy in the island.[46]

His early congregation was large, reporting that they had baptized one hundred and eleven people and had five hundred in attendance, both Black and white. Of them he said,

Some [were] of free condition, but the greater part of them are slaves and natives from the different countries of Africa. . . . We

---

45. Benedict, *General History*, 203.
46. Benedict, *General History*, 203.

have five trustees to our chapel and burying-ground, eight deacons and six exhorters.[47]

Such was the growth experienced by this church that Swigle soon after wrote:

> Our place of worship is so very much crowded, that numbers are obliged to stand out of doors. We are going to build a larger chapel as soon as possible. Our people being poor, and so many of them slaves, we are not able to go on so quick as we could wish, without we should meet with such friends as love our Lord and Master, Jesus Christ, to enable us in going on with so glorious an undertaking.[48]

Swigle also established a second chapel of approximately two hundred and fifty-four members in the High Mountains, on the Clifton Mount Coffee Plantation, Saint Andrew. Speaking of the influence of his ministry and the good relations which he had developed there, he reported to Rippon that

> When I was at breakfast with the Overseer he said to me. I have no need of a book-keeper, I make no use of a whip for when I am at home my work goes on regular and when I visit the field I have no fault to find, for everything is conducted as it ought to be. I observed myself that the brethren were very industrious, they have a plenty of persons in their ground, and a plenty of livestock, and they one and all together live in unity, brotherly love and in the bonds of peace.[49]

In all his correspondence with Rippon, Swigle continued to confirm his continued relationship with all the leaders of the Ethiopian Baptist movement, including and especially George Lisle. We know for instance that in 1801 he and his wife Francis were involved in a land sale to Lisle in Kingston.[50] Then, in 1802 Swigle stated that despite the falling out in 1801 he remained a member of the movement, recalling how:

> Myself and brethren were at Mr Lisle's Chapel a few weeks ago, at the funeral of one of his elders, he is well and *we were friendly together*.[51]

---

47. Payne, "Baptist Work," 23.
48. Benedict, *General History*, 204–5.
49. Benedict, *General History*, 204.
50. Swigle, "Deeds," 212.
51. Swigle, "Letter from Thomas Nicholas Swigle," 1146.

He also commented on Baker's need for assistance in Westmoreland, stating, "I gave him Brother George Vineyard, one of our Exhorters, an old experienced professor to assist him."[52]

Swigle's ministry however had the misfortune to have begun at the beginning of the amended CSL introduced by the Kingston Council on December 25, 1802. As he was not an ordained minister, he too was refused a license to preach, the law being clear in its determination to prevent the spread of the movement. BMS missionary Clarke reporting this incident stated that:

> The persecuting law was signed by Governor Nugent on 18th December 1802, and under the penalty of hard labour in the workhouse, and flogging to any in a state of slavery, all teaching of negroes or people of colour by Dissenters was prohibited unless by "duly qualified, authorized and permitted clergymen." Roman Catholics and Episcopalian ministers were not disturbed.[53]

Swigle nevertheless continued his ministry, but only at the invitation of others. He, like plantation owner, Samuel Vaughan, turned his church into a hospital for the enslaved, and this allowed him to continue to provide pastoral care to those in need in Kingston, without the daily threat of imprisonment by the state.

Swigle's ministry came to an abrupt end upon his death in 1811. Letters by Moses Baker suggest that there followed a power struggle for control of East Queen Street, until the arrival of the BMS missionaries who initially used it as the control center of BMS work on the island, from which subsequent BMS missionaries were dispatched around the island. However, we are given a glimpse of the work which had been undertaken by Swigle and the ministry which he had established through the correspondence of BMS missionary Lee Compere. Compere was the first BMS missionary to pastor East Queen Street in 1816 and shortly after his arrival he wrote home and reported that this pastorate came about as a result of his being approached by many thousands of Baptists in Kingston who were in need of a pastor, and of his then current numbers, he wrote:

> Lord's—day, July 6, 1816. I preached in the morning at six o'clock, again at half past ten, and at half-past two in the afternoon. . . . I, for the first time in my life, administered the ordinance of the Lord's supper, to about two hundred communicants. There

---

52. Payne, "Baptist Work," 23
53. Clarke, *Memorials of Baptist Missionaries*, 30.

are more than ten times as many, who have been members of the different Baptist churches, into which the negroes about Kingston have been divided; but in consequence of their circumstances as slaves, and the irregularities that have prevailed among them, we had no more at this time, who were admitted to communion.[54]

Little is said of his legacy, but significantly, while Lisle's chapel is no more, Swigle's chapel at East Queen Street continues to thrive and evolve.

GEORGE GIBB (D. 1826)

George Gibb is perhaps the least known of the four leaders who arrived in Jamaica with Lisle, but his contribution is no less significant. An African American, Gibb began his ministry in Jamaica as a member of Lisle's church, where he used his skills as a teacher. Records then place him as the pastor of the church built on the land which Lisle had purchased in 1793 in Spanish Town. There he built up a stable congregation of over 700 members, while having other stations going north of the island to Saint Mary's. Such was his success that he was able to minister on the Goshen Estate at the invitation of a Mr. Lang, its proprietor, who invited him to come and preach there to the many slaves which he had acquired from America. Gibb also traveled on the north coast to the Russell Hall plantation near Ocho Rios, where not only did he hold services but baptized several members of the plantocracy including a Mr. Bainbridge, a Mrs. Paisley, Milbro White, and a Duncan. He also traveled to Spring Valley and its surrounding areas, preaching and baptizing those who would come.

Yet as successful as these endeavors were, there were many great moments of trial and persecution for him. For example, in Spanish Town, he faced much opposition with similar stories being told of how

> Frequently was he seized while on the estates at night, cast into a dungeon, and his feet made fast in the stocks—once in Spanish Town for four days—his sole offence the attempt to minister to the spiritual wants of the slave.[55]
>
> Thrown into . . . jail, and confined there for four days, for having been caught teaching the slaves. He was many times found on estates on night, and cast into the dungeon, and his feet placed

---

54. Ministers, *Baptist Magazine*, 74.
55. Underhill, *West Indies*, 247.

in the bilboes, for having dared to enter into a negro house to teach those by night to whom he could not have access by day.[56]

An old member of his church in Spanish Town, speaking to European missionaries, recalled how Gibb

> In the olden time, when in company with a few like-minded with himself the nights were spent in travelling from one estate to another to collect the slaves for prayer and instruction. Many were their hair-breadth escapes from the wrath of hostile planters, and many the souls save through their heroic devotedness.[57]

There are also many recollections of his ministry in Constant Spring, Saint Mary and Saint Thomas in the Vale, where frequent skirmishes with white planters took place, as was the case in Saint Thomas in the Vale, which:

> Bore an unenviable notoriety for its cruelties in the time of slavery. Near to Jericho stood the infamously celebrated Rodney Hall Court House in native phraseology called the 'Hell of Jamaica.' It stood there once, for it is now a ruin. A female member of the church still living gave birth to a child while on the treadmill of the House of Correction annexed to it. In the vestry book of this parish may be found entries of payments made for ears and legs cut off for the offence of running away, and of noses slit for the same crime; some poor wretches burnt to death, and others hanged for breaches of the atrocious slave law of those days.[58]

Yet Gibb never shied away from ministry there. It is believed that Gibb lived there in constant danger as he sought to minister to his flock, often holding his meetings in the surrounding forests and swamp areas. Here too though his work was successful in that he was reported to have:

> Collected many hundreds of people and formed these who believed into a Christian Church, using triune immersion, and so dipping the subject three times. . . . All the ordinances had to be attended to under the shadow of night, in secret, unfrequented places, where the persecutors were not likely to come upon him, or his helpless flock, in whom light had taken the place of darkness.[59]

---

56. Clarke, *Memorials of Baptist Missionaries*, 15.
57. Underhill, *West Indies*, 209–10.
58. Underhill, *West Indies*, 256.
59. Clarke, *Memorials of Baptist Missionaries*, 15.

In Port Maria, in the parish of Saint Mary, Gibb purchased land and built a chapel but it was pulled down as a consequence of the persecutions which they faced. Yet the tale of this event continued to strike fear in many. BMS missionary Clarke told how:

> After some years a piece of land was privately bought and a sort of chapel, of humble appearance, was erected upon it. This was surrounded by dismal swamps, and rising ground covered with trees and bushes. Here, for a short season, they worshipped God concealed from the view of their foes and hoped their secluded retreat would not become known. Soon however, it was found out by two of the persecutors, probably a Judas for favour, if not for money, had revealed the hiding place; the worshippers fled, and the building was speedily levelled to the ground. The white men left exulting their success, but the Divine displeasure followed them. One was speedily called to his account. The other fell sick, and had soon to leave the island. "Who hath hardened himself against God and prospered?"[60]

Despite all these obstacles Gibb was able to continue ministering until his natural death in 1826 at Pembroke Hall. Prior to his death Gibb transferred many of his members in Spanish Town to the ministry of James Phillippo, and they became the founding members of Phillippo Baptist Church. He is fortunate to have left a widow, who was able to tell of his life and ministry, and such were his abilities as a leader that BMS records confess that:

> Some of our best people came from the churches first formed by Lisle, Gibb, and Moses Baker.[61]

GEORGE LEWIS (D. AFTER 1814)

George Lewis was a native of Guinea, originally transported from Jamaica to Virginia where he became a Christian and a Baptist, before choosing to return to Jamaica to preach to his fellow slaves. He too was unusual in that his ministry was conducted primarily as a Baptist minister, under the auspices of the Moravian church, in Saint Elizabeth and Manchester. Much of our understanding of him therefore comes courtesy of Rev J H Buchner a leading Moravian who told of the many exploits of Lewis in his work, 'The Moravians in Jamaica', published in 1854.

---

60. Clarke, *Memorials of Baptist Missionaries*, 15–16.
61. Underhill, *West Indies*, 24.

Moravian churches at that time were somewhat similar to the Baptists in their theology, but found that because of their ownership of slaves, it was almost impossible for them to minister with any meaningful significance amongst their African brothers and sisters between 1754 and 1823. So, Lewis and other African missionaries, who ministered with him, were credited with much of the early achievements of the Moravians, especially on many of the plantations. Of their ministry Rev Buchner said:

> The labours of all these were not without effect; the attention of the negroes was arrested, and not a few were found among them who secretly visited their fellow-slaves, from plantation to plantation, telling them of a Book in which God's Word was declared of Jesus the Saviour, of a heaven to which they likewise might go; and teaching the people a form of prayer.[62]

Such was Lewis's passion for ministry that though a slave and threatened with death, he initially worked as an itinerant preacher in the shadow of the CSL and paid his "owner," a Miss Valentine of Kingston, a monthly sum in exchange for a ticket of leave which allowed him to leave her employ for up to a month and work as a peddler, while pursuing his ministry. As a result of this

> He travelled frequently in the parishes of Manchester and St Elizabeth; preached first to a few, those invited others to come and hear him, and soon he was so well known among the slaves that they assembled round him at night wherever he went. This produced a general inquiry after the truth among the negroes; and, as the brethren were invited to preach about the same time on an estate called Peru, and likewise on other plantations in the May-Day mountains, they became more generally known; and Old Carmel was soon visited by numbers making the inquiry, "What must I do to be saved."[63]

Over time Lewis's was so successful that one Moravian missionary made plans for his freedom:

> Brother Lang conceived such a good opinion of him, that, at his request, he [Brother Lang] proposed that the congregation would collect one hundred pounds to purchase his freedom. This they accomplished and George Lewis became a free man. From that time, he was much with our missionaries at Old

---

62. Clarke, *Memorials of Baptist Missionaries*, 12.
63. Clarke, *Memorials of Baptist Missionaries*, 12–13.

Carmel, and frequently accompanied them on their visits to the different plantations.[64]

His popularity too was real and of the success of his ministry it was said that:

> People often walked twenty to thirty miles on a Saturday night, in order to be at Old Carmel early on Sunday morning to hear the Gospel, and then return home the following night, so as to be at work on the plantation grounds at six o'clock on Monday morning. . . . An old woman who came eleven miles to attend the meetings, being asked how she could walk so far, answered *"love makes the way short."*[65]

We also have the testimony of Robert Peart, who as a result of the preaching of George Lewis, at the age of fifty-six years old, he converted from Islam to Christianity in 1814. Perth then became an evangelist in his own right, preaching until his death in 1845. Of his conversion Buchner wrote the following:

> Robert Peart, at Spice Grove, was by birth a Mandingo; he was taught to read and write, and early initiated into the Mahometan faith, being designed for an expounder of their law. When about twenty years of age he went on a visit to his uncle, previous to his entering "the great school at Timbuctoo" to finish his studies. While there he was waylaid, and carried down the coast to be sold. His relations endeavoured to ransom him, but in vain; he was brought to Jamaica: this was about the year 1777. For some time, he adhered to the Mahometan religion, in which he had been brought up, at least partially, and confessed that whenever he wished to observe one of the Mahometan fasts, he presented to be sick. When G Lewis visited these parts, Robert's attention was arrested by hearing him asking a blessing and returning thanks at his meals. "I saw him," said Robert, "before him eat, say thankee, and when him done, say thankee again. Me say eh!" (an exclamation of surprise among the negroes). Him say to me, "Why don't you pray?" Me answer him: Me do pray. He say to me, "What do you pray?" Me say me believe in God, but not in his Son; for in me country we pray to God and his prophet Mahomet." George Lewis replied: "Dick (this was Robert's name before baptism) you are altogether wrong, you must pray to Jesus Christ, Him the, only right one to pray to. "These words,"

64. Clarke, *Memorials of Baptist Missionaries*, 13.
65. Clarke, *Memorials of Baptist Missionaries*, 14.

Robert continued, "sunk into my heart; I went there, kneeled down, and began to pray: Lord have mercy upon me! Christ, have mercy upon me! Again and again, for that was all I could say. . . . Religion having begun to spread more and more among the Negroes, Robert and some others were taken before a bench of magistrates, and examined as to the nature of the instruction which they had received. His answers having convinced the judges that the gospel will make a man a more valuable servant and a better member of society; he was quietly dismissed.[66]

Perhaps because of such success, Lewis was frequently arrested and imprisoned by planters who disliked him intensely particularly as:

He kept meetings with the slaves at night: and the familiarity and kindness with which the brethren treated him was much spoken against. He was imprisoned repeatedly for this offence of preaching to the slaves; and once he escaped being taken up and confined only through the intercession of Brother Lang.[67]

Yet Lewis continued despite these obstacles and people spoke favorably of him and his ministry, which had enabled them to grow in faith, and caused many of the plantation owners to look favorably on African Christians. He stayed with the Moravians but a short time, choosing ultimately to work in the far end of the parish, but of his work amongst them the Moravians reminisced as to how his reputation was built. One particular incident stands out above all else, it being told how:

Whenever George Lewis came to the estate, they contributed at the rate of three pence each, had a supper, and sat up all night listening to his instructions. They were in the habit of fasting three times a week, eating and drinking nothing from sunrise to sunset. This naturally irritated the planters, who took every means to put it down. One day the overseer, having had the names of three of the praying men mentioned to him, went into the field early in the morning to observe how they could work the day through. When breakfast time came they took none, and as they told him they had eaten enough before it was day, he ordered them to break stones all day, with sledge-hammers, which they readily continued to do till evening without intermission, and so successfully, that he could not refrain from expressing his surprise![68]

66. Buchner, *Moravians in Jamaica*, 50–53.
67. Clarke, *Memorials of Baptist Missionaries*, 13.
68. Buchner, *Moravians in Jamaica*, 52.

Lewis's final sermon was preached in the Manchester Mountains, date unknown, but the story continues to be told of how

> Many years ago a free black man visited the neighbourhood; he talked to the slaves about Jesus, and afterwards baptized some of them. At length, on one of his preaching excursions, he was seized by the opponents of the gospel and hung. If this is true, Jamaica has had her proto-martyr.[69]

Of his life little more can be said, save the fact that his ministry was rooted in a belief in the supernatural, in the works of the Holy Spirit, which missionaries reported, retelling how under his ministry:

> Many had wonderful dreams to tell, which they considered as prophetic visions; some excited themselves by fanatical notions and fell into wild extravagances, which they called "the convince" in which they had full faith, as much as in a Divine Revelation.[70]

Though he spent much of his time working amongst the Moravians, Lewis remained committed to the Baptist faith, and of his ministry, those who knew him and his many un-named colleagues best stated that

> He practised, as the people sometimes expressed it, *"the negroes' home religion and meeting."*[71]

Yet there were those later critics who sought not only to discredit him and his colleagues, but spoke of a man who seemed to have no visible church home, or allegiance, and therefore could not be affirmed as a preacher of the gospel. Clarke most firmly quelled this accusation, stating that

> If Christ was preached how could it be a spurious Gospel? Many of these persons were sincere and did what they could to lead sinners to the Saviour. . . . Be that as it may, there can be no doubt that he contributed greatly to excite among the people in these parts, a desire to be instructed in the Christian doctrine.[72]

---

69. Clark et al., *Voice*, 37, Smith, *William*, 1.
70. Clarke, *Memorials of Baptist Missionaries*, 15.
71. Clarke, *Memorials of Baptist Missionaries*, 14.
72. Clarke, *Memorials of Baptist Missionaries*, 12, 14.

GEORGE VINEYARD (D. CA. 1800)

George Vineyard's ministry was quite brief but nevertheless very significant. He too was an African American who had traveled with Lisle from America to Jamaica. He spent his early days supporting Lisle; however, such was the success of Moses Baker on the north and west of the island that when a plantation owner, Mr. Hilton of Westmoreland, requested that Baker also come and preach to his slaves on his two sugar estates there, Baker declined but said that he would find him a person to assist him. On a visit to Swigle, Baker requested help from him and Swigle responded by sending him, "Brother George Vineyard, one of our Exhorters, and old experienced professor to assist him."[73] It is believed that Vineyard then used this plantation as the base from which he reached out from Hanover and across the whole of that parish. He and his wife Elizabeth also established a chapel at Delve, not far from Savanna-La-Mar, Westmoreland, in his brief period of service, until his early death around 1800.

Not much has yet been revealed about his ministry, save that reported by Moses Baker via Thomas Swigle who wrote to Rippon that:

> Mr Hilton has provided a house, and maintenance, a salary and land for him to cultivate for his benefit upon his own estate, and brother Baker declared to me that he has in the church there, fourteen hundred justified believers, and about three thousand followers, many under conviction of sin.[74]

CONCLUSION

In conclusion then, what can be said of these brave men and women who planted the word of God in the hearts and minds of an oppressed but faithful people, during the trials and tribulations of enslavement and the CSL. The common wisdom of the day amongst the majority of those who witnessed their ministry, concur with the reflections of BMS missionary Clarke, who said of the movement that they were

> Simple minded men, who took the word of God for their guide; and who, in giving instruction to others, had much to suffer, and nothing to gain, but souls won to Christ and the approval of their own conscience, and of God. They sought to do good in the face of obloquy, scorn, contempt, bitter opposition, persecuted,

---

73. Payne, "Baptist Work," 23.
74. Swigle, "Letter Oct 1802," 1146.

punishment and threatened death. Some of them were indeed martyrs at the time of the insurrection of 1832, and after it.[75]

These are but a handful of the hundreds and thousands who established the foundations for freedom, for those who would come after them, and who mindful that they were not be those who would see the promised land, made provision to pass the baton on to those who they had taught and those whom they soon hoped would secure the freedom which they had so bravely fought for, the Baptist Missionary Society.

---

75. Clarke, *Memorials of Baptist Missionaries*, 10.

Chapter 6

The Transference of Power to the Baptist Missionary Society

THE CRISIS IN LEADERSHIP, and the urgency to meet the needs of the over 20,000 Christians in Jamaica came to a head with the passing of the 1802 amendment to the CSL which signaled the death knell of the Ethiopian Baptists, as a visible and prominent presence on the island. As we have seen already, this law soon became a significant barrier to any ministry being undertaken by members of the EBS movement, with the majority of its ministers having to go "underground." It was then that they reasoned that they needed a partner who could help them to circumvent these laws, or at least enable their churches to continue. In desperation Baker wrote to Baptist friends in England requesting assistance:

> Dear Sir, _ In compliance with the last invitation I went down to Kingston, and got a good man to come up and instruct that gentleman's slaves; but all is stopped. From Christmas-day I have been prevented preaching or saying a word to any part of my congregation. From this we can expect nothing but a great falling away of the weaker Christians. The poor destitute flock is left to go astray without a shepherd; yet as the Lord has promised He will not forsake us nor leave us, we have reason to believe that if God is for us we shall endeavour, though all the world be against us, to hold fast our profession to the end; therefore we cry and crave to God, night and day, for His great mercy and assistance. We trust God will put it in your power to send us assistance for the Lord Jesus Christ's sake, and for the sake of so many poor

souls, that will be totally lost for the want of-your assistance. We humbly beseech you all to pray for us, poor distressed creatures as we are.[1]

Concerns were shared with the BMS who were already familiar with many of the issues being faced in Jamaica, by the one whom they lovingly called "The Venerable Moses Baker." John Ryland, Principal of Bristol Bible College, was prompted to respond, writing back in 1804 on behalf of the BMS, stating that they had been considering such assistance for many years, and would be happy, when able, to send missionaries to assist them in the work there. Such a venture was, however, going to take time, not only in terms of funding and training, but more particularly the opposition which the college would receive, being located in the heart of the "slave industry," Bristol. Bristol was in fact one of the three major slave ports in England, with merchants and plantation owners in residence, all determined to maintain its future for the continued prosperity of not only Bristol, but their families, and ultimately Britain.

Ryland, however, sensed that something could be done when the abolitionist argument that there should be no slavery in Britain was upheld in Parliament in 1788.[2] Fortunes then changed further when a bill to abolish the transatlantic slave trade was presented to the British Parliament in 1805. While it was passed in the House of Commons, it failed to achieve the required votes in the House of Lords by a mere seven votes. Nevertheless, this convinced the abolitionists that it was surely now only a matter of time before things would change, and slavery would finally be abolished. They were proved right when Parliament first passed a law forbidding the trading of "slaves" between Africa and the West Indian colonies, in 1806, and then passed the Abolition of the Transatlantic Save Trade Act in 1807. This act determined that Africans were no longer to be stolen and brought to the Caribbean to work as chattel, but it failed to change the position of the existing enslaved Africans already in the Caribbean. It was nonetheless a tremendous victory and one which Lord Granville, the then Prime Minister, described as, "the most glorious measure that had ever been adopted by any legislative body in the world."[3]

Ryland, therefore, seized this moment to speak with abolitionist and parliamentarian William Wilberforce, for his view as to whether the time was then right for the sending of English missionaries to Jamaica. Wilberforce, aware of the opposition which continued to exist in regards to

1. Clarke, *Memorials of Baptist Missionaries*, 28.
2. Jones, *Satan's Kingdom*, 109.
3. Jones, *Satan's Kingdom*, 136.

Dissenting and Methodist missionaries amongst the planters in Jamaica, responded positive, but cautiously stated that

> I am inclined to believe that preachers in a white skin would be likely to be treated better and respected more than black ones. This is all I can now say. When the meeting of Parliament shall bring me within reach of West Indians again, I will try in private to soften the prejudices of some leading men connected with that country; but I fear that the prejudices of the resident colonists, and their irreligious habits, are such as to render all attempts to soften them unavailing.[4]

However, while these issues were playing out in England, there was an increased sense of urgency in Jamaica as many plantation owners, in preparation for 1807, increased the number of Africans on their plantations. However, such an increase in numbers had the unintended consequence of creating unease in an already fearful minority white population. They saw this as a threat to their very existence once again, should rebellion break out. So the Jamaican Assembly, in response, as stated earlier, introduced their own 1807 act, which prevented Africans preaching and gathering together on every plantation on the island. As a result of this, Baker was all the more determined to find a means by which the EBS could be legitimized, and established for the good of all Africans. He and Lisle concluded that the best way forward was to set out a proposal to a missionary organization, whereby they could somehow be co-opted as the visible presence, while being partners in the work. The BMS being the only established missionary organization at that time fitted the bill perfectly.

Back in England, while the Committee was considering a way forward, some Baptists expressed the opinion that there was an urgent need to go, after having read Lisle's Church Covenant, but perhaps not for the reason one might imagine or have expected. According to well-respected minister and theologian, Dr. Payne, many in the BMS reasoned that it indicated an urgent need to provide a right and acceptable interpretation of the gospel, before the needy, uncivilized, and ignorant Africans in Jamaica imbibed heretical ways taught to them by the EBS. He reasoned that

> In view of the sincerity and simplicity here revealed, the dangers of fanaticism and heresy, the difficulties and the opportunities among people who covenanted in this fashion, and the special responsibility of the Englishmen for the West Indies, it is not

---

4. Catherall, "Bristol College," 296.

surprising that Dr Ryland and his friends did not rest until they were able to send missionaries to Jamaica.[5]

So, an agreement was reached between the EBS and BMS, however, it took another seven years before that person was trained and ready to go. It was in 1813, when Ryland announced with much relief in a letter to Wilberforce that "I cannot but think it of great importance to send someone speedily to Jamaica: I have waited several years with great anxiety for some one to send."[6] They had trained their first missionary for Jamaica. However, the question has to be asked here, especially given the response by some to the Covenant, whether, having accepted the call to provide the leadership for African Jamaican Baptists, the BMS were sufficiently equipped, informed and qualified to do so? Was it really simply a matter of replacing Black missionaries with white ones as Wilberforce had hoped? Would they be able to spread the gospel message by providing academically excellent and "civilized" Christians, in place of what they deemed to have been mostly illiterate though zealous Christians with limited knowledge of the ways of God? What about issues of language, culture, and customs? Had they even been considered?

Well, using the experiences of some of those early BMS missionaries—namely, John Rowe, Lee Compere, Joshua Tinson, Thomas Burchell and William Knibb, we shall spend the remainder of this chapter interrogating how the BMS, with little time on their hands, before taking over the reins of leadership from the EBS, discovered that while a white minister may well placate those who "owned" slaves, more needed to be taken into consideration when "partnering" with Africans whose culture, customs, and rituals they neither knew or understood, as well as the climate and the industry of slavery itself.

CLIMATE AND SLAVERY

John Rowe (1788–1816)

Rowe was born in Somersetshire and became a student of John Ryland, training at the Baptist College in Bristol. There was a clear expectation that on the completion of his studies in 1813, he would be their first BMS missionary to Jamaica. His remit was a simple one to "support Moses Baker and to assist the established Baptist presence, the Ethiopian Baptist Society." He was also given a letter of instruction which included the following comments:

---

5. Catherall, "Bristol College," 296.
6. Clarke, *Memorials of Baptist Missionaries*, 69; Tucker, *Glorious Liberty*, 11.

> But let man, whatever be his situation, be the object of your regard—You carry a gospel which addresses itself alike to civilized and the uncivilized; a Gospel that commends itself alike to everyman's conscience and occupies the heart. . . . We wish to assume no dominion over you, but merely to direct your attention to those parts of the mind of Christ which relate to your immediately, and to your undertaking. . . . You are going amongst a people in a state of slavery, and require to beware lest our feeling for them should lead you to say or do anything inconsistent with Christian duty. Most of the servants whom the Apostle Paul addressed in his epistles to the Churches were slaves, and he exhorts them to be obedient to their own masters in singleness of heart, fearing God; and this, not only to the good and gentle, but also to the froward, &c. These exhortations must be your guide, and while you act upon them no man can justly be offended with you.[7]

Rowe and his wife arrived in Montego Bay, Jamaica on February 23, 1814, and received a warm welcome from Samuel Vaughan, on whose property Rowe had expected to reside. However, all was not well, as on hearing of Rowe's arrival Vaughan received opposition from other plantation owners who objected to having another dissenting minister in their locality. Rowe found alternative accommodation in nearby Falmouth, where he then hoped to establish his own mission station, in addition to supporting the work of Baker. However, he too, like his Black colleagues, was refused a license to preach by the local magistrate. When Rowe reported back within weeks that, as far as the Jamaican legislature were concerned all "Baptists were *personae non gratae*,"[8] Baptists in England soon heard that their worst fears had come true.

Rowe therefore concentrated on assisting in the work of Baker, and preaching in his home, where he also opened a school for poor children, enslaved and free. Events however, appeared to change for the better when shortly afterwards he was able to obtain a license, but before he could reap the benefits of it, it was soon suspended again until August 1816, when the Jamaican Assembly passed an act which brought the enslaved African's needs to the forefront of planning for their future, calling upon the Churches to:

---

7. Catherall, "Thomas Burchell," 351; Clarke, *Memorials of Baptist Missionaries*, 74.
8. Catherall, "Bristol College," 296.

Consider the state of religion among slaves, and to carefully investigate the means of diffusing the light of genuine Christianity among them.[9]

So, finally all seemed well, especially for dissenting missionaries. Great must have rejoicing by the BMS as their first missionary to Jamaica, finally had free reign to preach the gospel. Sadly, their joy was short-lived, as before Rowe was able to utilize the precious license, he died of yellow fever, on June 26, 1816. News of his death was sent back to England via Moses Baker, who it is said became somewhat of a father figure to Rowe's son during his time of grief.

Rowe's time in Jamaica was short, just two years, but the impression he left was long-lasting in that he being the first, gave a favorable impression of the BMS to a population who were naturally somewhat suspicious of those who came in the image of their oppressors. However, his death highlighted the fact that clearly the climatic conditions of the Caribbean were something of an urgent issue which needed to be resolved, it having taken the lives of family members of two of the missionaries who followed Rowe. However, before the Committee had time to catch their breath and deal with this issue, another taxing problem came to the fore which could, in and of itself, place the whole Jamaica project in jeopardy.

Lee Compere

Compere was the second missionary to arrive in Jamaica, but his tenure lasted barely a year. Little is said of his time on the island, due to what seems to have been something of a falling out between him and the Committee over his lived experiences while there. Compere was born in Essex, and like Rowe attended Bristol College, after which time he was set apart for ministry in Jamaica. Compere, his wife, together with two members of Ryland's Church left England on November 21, 1815, sailing into Kingston on January 19, 1815. It is said that such was his enthusiasm for his new venture, that on the voyage over, he preached every Sunday, and was well respected for it. Then on arrival he took up a position at Old Harbour, about twenty-five miles west of Kingston. However, he soon relocated to Kingston itself, having accepted an invitation by African believers to take charge of a congregation at a place which they called Gully Chapel, also known by others as East Queen Street Baptist Chapel. Gully Chapel was an African congregation, of both enslaved and free, but not long into his service events clearly

9. Barrett, *African*, 17.

began to take its toll on Compere as he learned of their plight, and the truly inhumane, torturous, and soul-destroying daily grind which was slavery. Compere, shared these experiences in his correspondence with the Committee, and though we have no record of what he had actually observed, we do have some idea of a typical day in the life of the enslaved which he may have observed, and which was shared with the BMS by the Moravians, prior to the BMS becoming active in Jamaica:

> Every morning, with the first dawn of day, the shell was blown to call the slaves to their work, and everyone was expected to appear immediately and join his party. Each gang walked off to the field under the direction of the driver armed with a long whip. The children, from six to twelve years of age, were under the care of an elderly negress, armed with a rod. This infant gang proceeded to the pastures to clean them, or to do any work suited to their strength. The gangs toiled all day in the sun; their covering at that time being only a clothe tied round their loins. There was no remission of work except in the middle of the day to take their meals. Late in the evening, after the setting of the sun, they returned to their homes; but not infrequently, to resume labour by the light of the moon. The work was examined by the overseer. If he was dissatisfied with it, the labourer, whether man or woman, was laid on the ground and flogged. Before the whip descended the third time, the person was covered with blood. Not an evening passed without hearing the crack of the whip and the shrieks of the victims. The missionary's first message in such scenes was supplications, written to the overseer for mercy to those who, on their knees, with uplifted hands begged for pity and intercession. . . . Day after day . . . they witnessed the same toil and the same scenes until Sunday, when the slaves went to the market to bring home a supply for the week, or to their provision grounds to labour for their own support. . . . When, or at what time . . . could a missionary labour among these people?[10]

Not long into his time at Gully Chapel, fellow BMS missionary John Clarke gave an insight into the response of the committee to one of his letters, highlighting a deteriorating relationship between them. He stated:

> When invited to be the pastor of the Negro Church in Kingston, he encountered the difficulties of weak church discipline, exacerbated by the many restrictions placed upon the leadership of dissenting churches. Success in both church and school at East Queen's Street necessitated an appeal for help to the BMS.

10. Tucker, *Glorious Liberty*, 6.

Significantly, the Committee's reply indicated a growing tension between the missionary and the Society, for it was a sharp reminder to him that he was a "nonpolitical" agent and should concentrate on preaching the Gospel.[11]

Imagine how Compere must have felt upon receiving such a letter, the contents of which in part seem like a gentle rebuke. Such a different position to that expressed by the BMS only a few months earlier when they proudly described him as a "devoted and zealous missionary."[12] It seems that Compere's mental state soon became more and more unsettled due in part to the sensitive issues which surrounded him. He expressed the full extent of his pain and the empathy he felt, in one particular letter to the Committee:

> I felt as I never felt before while speaking of the suffering of Christ. I could willingly have died in the pulpit. I enjoyed and unusual degree of utterance, accompanied with an agonizing desire of plucking souls as brands from the everlasting burning.[13]

History tells us that it was soon after that that the relationship irretrievably broke down, as Compere, fortuitously, either became too ill to continue in his role and therefore resigned, or, he was actually forced to resign by said Committee who succinctly wrote the following comment dated October 1, 1816, in regards to his time in Jamaica as their missionary:

> For some time his conduct has not altogether coincided with the views of the Committee, so that he is no longer under our direction, but has embarked with his family for the United States of America.[14]

Evidently the sickness was not so debilitating that he needed to return home to England, Compere able instead to embark on a new mission field, amongst the Creek Indians, in Georgia.

Clearly the issues faced by both Rowe and Compere forced the BMS to address both the problem of adjusting to the harsh climatic conditions, and how to enable their missionaries to achieve the mental strength necessary to coexist with the horrendous system that was slavery. A change of direction therefore ensued, whereby it was decided that future missionaries were to be given a certain amount of time in order to adjust to both the climatic and social conditions which they would face, before taking up roles

---

11. Catherall, "Bristol College," 297.
12. Clarke, *Memorials of Baptist Missionaries*, 72.
13. Clarke, *Memorials of Baptist Missionaries*, 73–74.
14. Clarke, *Memorials of Baptist Missionaries*, 74.

in their individual stations. This they hoped would lead to greater success and stability.

CULTURE AND CUSTOMS

No sooner had the BMS "resolved" what they consider to be the most significant issues, they were soon faced with additional issues of how to minister within the context of a culture and customs which were so significantly different from their own. Letters written home, personal comments, and the experiences of Knibb, Flood, and Phillippo, who embarked on one such visit, as well as the ministry of BMS missionary Joshua Tinson, shed light on the issues raised.

Mrs Coultart

Missioner James Coultart and his wife arrived in Jamaica on May 9, 1817, but no sooner had Mrs. Coultart put down her trunk when she sent the following letter home:

> The inhabitants of Jamaica consist chiefly of black people, rude and superstitious to a degree. At the death of one of them, the relatives and friends meet together at the house of the deceased, and feast, and sing, and riot, during the night. They prepare and keep by them their funeral dress, which is the most gaudy and costly their circumstances will permit them to obtain. They are generally great thieves, unless they are partakers of the holy religion of Jesus Christ. The wild religious part of them fast on certain days, dream dreams, and see visions; nor are those who are really partakers of divine grace totally free from these inconsistencies. There are a number of brown people also, who are nearly of the same stamp, but they consider themselves very superior to the black, and it is with difficulty they degrade themselves by speaking to them. The white people are generally such as make money their idol; many of them live an awful degenerate state.[15]

---

15. Underhill, *West Indies*, 206.

African Funeral Practices.[16]

Clearly, she had no understanding of the harshness of the conditions, the limited food supplies, and other resources given to the enslaved, and the full meaning of chattel slavery which meant that not only were they to be enslaved for life, but so were their children and their children's children, being the sole property of the plantation owner. Their only "escape" therefore was death, and it, being a welcome release, was to be exuberantly celebrated. Her comments were therefore clearly misguided and erroneous, but they have remained in the history books for all time, whereas those whom she spoke of have been made to seem foolish, and even disrespectful. Unfortunately, Mrs. Coultart never got the opportunity to truly understand the culture and customs of the enslaved Africans, as she too contracted yellow fever and died on October 8, 1817.

Such comments came quick and fast, from Europeans whose understanding of what constituted appropriate cultural practices and customs were in some ways defined by what they as evangelical Christians considered to be the right way to not only worship, but socialize, celebrate, and mourn. Acceptable to them was an appreciation of classical music and such dances as the waltz, which they considered "civilized," and the Jamaican equivalent, known as the quadrille. However, unacceptable to them, and considered inferior or heathen, were the preferred forms of African-inspired expressive folk dances, such as Gerreh and Dinki-Mini, which were usually performed after the death of a person, or Bruckin' Party, a dance which was performed at moments of great celebration.

16. Phillippo, *Jamaica*, 244.

There were, however, a minority of Europeans who, in taking the time to observe their practices, especially when at worship, gave favorable reports, describing the dance as a natural extension of who Africans were as a people, and was rather to be admired for the following reasons:

> Nothing could be more light, and playful, and graceful, than the extempore movements of the dancing girls . . . the precision of their step, and the lofty air of their action, the elasticity of their step, and the lofty air with which they caried their heads[17]

"Negro Figuranti." *Slavery Images: A Visual Record of the African Slave Trade and Slave Life in the Early African Diaspora,* accessed March 9, 2022, http://slaveryimages.org/s/slaveryimages.org/s/slaveryimages/item/2482.

Over one hundred and fifty years may have passed since the first enslaved Africans were brought to their "prison" in the sun, but the issues which were there at the beginning, clearly still remained. Sadly, there were those who even complained about how the enslaved, whose only annual holiday was the two or three days at Christmastime, chose to occupy their leisure time, enthusiastically beating drums, dancing, and singing, during the Christmas masked festival known as John Canoe (Jonkonnu). Clearly, the contrasts of culture and customs was clearly one of the most contentious of issues which had to be

---

17. Brathwaite, *Folk Culture*, 11. As was done in Africa, the enslaved danced and sang at work, at play, at worship; from fear, from sorrow, from joy.

negotiated by these new arrivals, if the BMS were to have any hope of success, if the only acceptable musical instrument was the organ.

"Jaw-Bone, or House John-Canoe." *Slavery Images: A Visual Record of the African Slave Trade and Slave Life in the Early African Diaspora*, accessed March 9, 2022, http://slaveryimages.org/s/slaveryimages/item/2311.

Imagine then the "shock" which a delegation of new missionaries experienced when visiting their fellow missionary, Joshua Tinson, and participated in the opening of his church in Kingston, in 1827. However, before we hear of their brief, yet telling observations, it is worth visiting the ministry of Tinson up to that point, to observe how he seemed to have endeared himself not only to congregations, but George Lisle himself, as well as members of his family, with no serious cultural issues reported.

Joshua Tinson (1794–1850)

Tinson, was born in Watledge, in Gloucestershire. Having initially commenced biblical studies in Norwich, he transferred to Bristol College in 1818, where he too came under the guidance of John Ryland. His initial expectation upon graduating was to be a missionary in Asia. However, under Ryland's guidance, his interests soon changed to Jamaica and upon receiving his commission on March 13, 1822, he sailed to Jamaica just four days later.

Tinson and his family arrived in Jamaica on May 31, 1822. His ministry was to have begun in Kingston; however, due to a lack of transport to carry him there, he sought to make Marchioneal, then in the parish of Saint Thomas in the East, the place of his labors. Events began well as members of one of Lisle's congregations in the area invited him to come and preach, and then to assist them in the absence of their pastor who they said had recently departed for England. Tinson accepted the call with great expectation that it would also assist him in obtaining a license to preach. However, despite his being a friend of the local Anglican rector, his hopes were soon dashed when a license was refused, the authorities being concerned, "Lest the parish should be inundated with Sectarians."[18]

Undaunted, members of another of Lisle's congregations invited him to take charge of the Windward Road Chapel, Kingston. Tinson was being given the privilege of pastoring the first and oldest Baptist congregation in Jamaica, and he accepted it with gratitude and much thankfulness, taking up his duties on August 8, 1822. His ministry in Jamaica had well and truly begun. He pastored Windward Road for four years, only relinquishing his duties upon Lisle's return in 1826. It seems that his time there was a success. In fact, so successful was he, and so thankful were Lisle and his congregation that God had provided them with an able shepherd in his absence, that they promised to assist him in establishing a church of his own in Kingston.

A deacon of the Windward Road Chapel gave him a parcel of land on which to build what became known as Hanover Street Baptist Chapel. Lisle then further "gifted" him members of his own congregations to assist him in establishing himself within the wider community. Then on December 24, 1826 Tinson preached his first sermon at Hanover Street, and in attendance and participating in the event were BMS missionaries Phillippo, Flood, and Knibb. We gain some insight into their concerns in the briefest of all sentences, but which in and of itself, said so much. A report to the Committee stated that "Messrs. Phillippo, Flood, and Knibb took prominent parts in

---

18. Catherall, "Bristol College," 298.

the interesting services."[19] Despite their reference to "the interesting service" it is clear that Tinson had negotiated his relationships so well that the issue of culture and customs seemed not to be a significant issue for him and the congregations he pastored. Yet, it seemed to remain so for the missionaries who had visited with him.

The BMS had no model of their own in regards to how to deal with cultural differences and with customs, both social and religious, which had evolved solely in Jamaica. However, having seen their missionaries also face difficulties in Sierra Leone (1795–96), they knew that they had to proceed with extreme caution, particularly as "the work in Jamaica had been established since 1783, so that an organization already existed which the BMS dare not ignore."[20] They wisely chose the pragmatic approach, choosing in the short term to work within the parameters of the culture and customs of which they were to be a part of. In this way there was no fear of them losing the congregations which had been established, and most importantly the effective and significant Baptist presence which had by then been on the island for over thirty years.

So, taking their lead from the EBS and from those missionary agencies which had gone before them, the BMS agreed to continue with many of the established practices of the EBS. For example, they kept the "ticket and leader" system which had been established by Baker and Gibb in order to protect their members from Maroon infiltrators who were working on behalf of the British militia. They also kept the "Daddy" system which gave leadership to African Jamaicans in communities within the larger Baptist congregations. The BMS also advised it's to recruit African assistants, from amongst those who were literate or perhaps could recite passages of Scripture from memory. They were to be men and women who had shown themselves to be capable leaders of the congregations in which they were a part. These assistants would then travel with the missionaries and provide such services, where necessary, such as the translation of their words, sermons and Bible studies into Patois, the newly created indigenous language of the people, as well as make plain to the missionaries the language of the people, when required.

We now know the names of twenty-one of these assistants,[21] perhaps the most "famous" of them being a Miss Cooper who became known not only for her resistance to the laws which declared that she had no right to preach, but because she was one of the few documented assistants named

---

19. Clarke et al, *Voice*, 174.
20. Russell, "Missionary Outreach," 26.
21. See Appendix 5 for the names of the African assistants.

by BMS missionary John Clarke, who worked alongside her in the parish of Clarendon. Of the rest, their names do not adorn the history books nor are they displayed on church walls or plaques like the BMS missionaries, but it is a truth that without them the European missionaries would not have been able to take their message to the parishes of Jamaica.

POLITICAL INVOLVEMENT

There was one foundational and thorny issue that could not be avoided, and encompassed all that the missionary was or was not able to do, and that was politics. Historical theologian Horace Russell expressed the opinion that the BMS entered the Jamaican situation with extreme caution, having seen their one and only previous attempts at mission in Africa fail, through what they publicly expressed as "the provident ruling of God," but privately acknowledged as being caused by their missionary Jacob Grigg, who they accused of interfering in the politics of the country.[22] Politics was therefore not a new issue, and one they knew that they had to deal with, but how? We can see the dilemma they faced in the contrasting fortunes of two of their most prominent missionaries, Thomas Burchell and William Knibb, both of whom were not invited to "consider their consciences" as earlier missionaries had been privileged to do, but rather to preach the gospel, and have no part in the politics of slavery.

Thomas Burchell (1799–1846)

Burchell was born in Tetbury, Gloucestershire. It is known that amongst his relatives was a paternal grandfather who had been a Baptist minister, and another who was the great English mathematician, physicist, and astronomer Sir Isaac Newton. Practical qualities of reasoning and analysis, if inherited, he would need in his future adventures in Jamaica. He had begun his work life training to be a cloth manufacturer, but once he began to attend Shortwood Baptist Church, his mind was turned in the direction of missions, and so he too attended Bristol College. With some understanding of what lay ahead of him, Burchell prepared and equipped himself as best as he could, taking not just classes in theology, but like so many students, acquired practical skills in anatomy and physiology, as well as some basic knowledge of chemistry, as and when his studies allowed.

---

22. Russell, "Missionary Outreach," 28.

Portrait of Thomas Burchell.[23]

Having received his commission on the October 14, 1823, Burchell set sail for Jamaica some five days later, arriving in Montego Bay on January 15, 1824. Once there he was introduced to a church and a congregation which, in a few short years, would change his life completely. He had inherited the churches of Moses Baker, the firebrand leader, who would not only stand toe to toe with any who questioned his right to freely preach the gospel to all who would listen, but who also advocated on behalf his enslave brothers and sisters for better conditions and ultimately freedom. How then to follow that? It seemed a monumental task for one who hated public speaking, and of whom it was said

> Like Marcus Crassus, he made no scruple of confessing that, when beginning to speak before great and intelligent assemblies, he frequently turned pale—was discomforted in mind and trembled in every limb. To platform engagements, especially, he seems to have an almost instinctive repugnance.[24]

23. Burchell, *Memoir*, i.
24. Burchell, *Memoir*, 405.

However, while Burchell may have believed himself to be rather "shy and retiring" in certain circumstances, but it soon became clear that he was actually "cut from the same cloth" as Moses Baker. How the hearts of the people must have swelled with both happiness and relief, when at his very first meeting at the church at Crooked Spring, January 25, 1824, he announced to them the good news of the coming Christ, taken from Luke 2:10, "Behold, I bring you good tidings of great joy which shall be to all people." They were immediately included in his understanding of his mission. He had welcomed them as a part of God's kingdom people, and they graciously received him as God's minister in return.

Those around Burchell quickly came to understand that not only did he have the same passion for the gospel and for freedom as Baker, but that he, like Baker, was also concerned about the physical conditions under which the enslaved were forced to labor. This caused him to attract the attention of the local authorities on many occasions. In one of his earliest encounters, he was called to answer for a letter which he had written, and which was soon after published by his brother William, in the *Particular Baptist Magazine* of 1827. In it he expressed his concern in regards to the way the enslaved were being treated, and the conditions under which they lived. However, after providing ample evidence for the courts, no action was taken against him. Through this incident Burchell soon understood the opposition he was to face, and that he needed to learn fast how to express his displeasure in such a way as to not lead to his own life being physically threatened.

Burchell nevertheless remained resolute in his belief that slavery was a heinous crime against God and man, and for this he was loved by his church members. His congregation grew to such an extent that they were once again actively split between three churches: Salter's Hill, Bethlephil, and Montego Bay, in the parish of Saint James. In fact, soon after arriving, Burchell had gathered around him the largest Baptist congregation in the whole of Jamaica, and of the respect they had for him, Sam Sharpe (or "Daddy Sharpe" as he was known) reported that it was born out of their pastor always encouraging them to find nonviolent ways to resist, and therefore they came to understand that anything they could do "to fight against slavery was to 'assist their brethren [missionaries] in the work of God.'"[25]

Burchell, it seems, had fallen in love with the people of Jamaica, and yet it must be asked of the man who feared public speaking, but was soon recognized as the thundering voice for justice: "Was he always a firebrand or did the church of Moses Baker change him?" That question we may never know the answer to—suffice it to say that the BMS may have hoped for

---

25. Rodriguez, *Encyclopedia*, 2:460.

better things in the group of missionaries they sent out the following year, one of whom was William Knibb.

William Knibb (1803–45)

Knibb was born in Kettering, Northamptonshire. His desire as a youth was to follow in his brother Thomas's footsteps and enter the printing business. However, when they both became teachers in a Sabbath School in Broadmead, Bristol, they came into contact with John Ryland. As expected, both their hearts were soon turned to mission, with Knibb hoping to travel to India, and Thomas to Jamaica. Thomas was the first to be commissioned, arriving in Kingston on January 19, 1823. He began work at East Queen Street, however, after contracting yellow fever, he died just over a year later on April 22, 1824.

It is said that upon the death of Thomas, Knibb felt compelled to go to Jamaica instead, in order to complete the work which his brother had begun. On approaching the committee, his offer was gladly taken up and he was given additional training in order to familiarize himself with both the British and foreign school systems used on the island. He was commissioned and departed for Jamaica on November 5, 1824, arriving in Kingston on February 12, 1825. Letters sent home by Knibb expressed how well received he had been and that this was due in part to the similarities between him and his brother. In fact, such was the likeness that he shared a somewhat tragic incident which happened shortly after his arrival:

> Since I have been here, I have been much employed in giving tickets to the members and followers, to the number of 3 or 4,000. Their conversation generally turns on my likeness to my brother. . . . Ah, sweet Massa, him just like him broder; him voice, him face estare me Massa. . . . Last week I buried a little boy who was formerly one of my brother's scholars. He was taken ill one day, dead the next, and buried the third day. His poor mother will have it that when he came to fetch her ticket, he thought I was my Brother's Patre (?) or ghost, and that it frightened him to death.[26]

While Knibb began his ministry in Jamaica as a school teacher, it was soon after in August of 1826 that he was given his first pastorate at a church in Port Royal. He never went back to full-time teacher after that, appearing to have adapted himself quite well, especially to the climate. Over time he

---

26. Knibb, "Letter to England."

pastored in the hills of Saint Ann in the hotter season and by the coast during cooler times. He had African assistants and established African deacons to assist him as he traveled across the island preaching the good news of the gospel.

In terms of political activity, his correspondence betrays little if anything of his thoughts on the system of slavery, and the enslavement of one person by another. In fact, it is virtually impossible to find any indication that he was either aware of, or supported, the abolitionist cause for the physical freedom of the enslaved African. However, we now know that Knibb, despite all that has been claimed about him being the great abolitionist, was solely and only interested in the spiritual freedom of his converts. In order to confirm this, we must in fact jump ahead of ourselves to one of the few times when his thoughts on the issue of the physical freedom of the enslaved were openly expressed.

During a visit to England, Knibb was questioned for three days by questioned three days by members of the House of Lords and the Committe on the Extinction of Slavery throughout the British Dominions in July 1832. Below is a very brief but insightful part of that conversation wherein he confirmed that he had always only sought the spiritual freedom of enslaved Africans, and never ever their physical freedom, and this he did by any means necessary. The following extract is to be borne in mind when observing his ministry in the pages that follow:

> Is it possible, in addressing an unlettered audience, in inculcating the doctrine of the freedom of the faith of Christianity, not to expose yourself to misinterpretation as to temporal freedom, as contrasted with spiritual freedom?—*Whenever I have had the occasion to speak on that subject, I have explained, that when freedom is mentioned in the word of God, it referred to the soul and not to the body; that there were slaves in the times of the apostles as well as at present.*[27]

Knibb was a religious zealot who never intentionally or knowingly swayed from his commission to never involve himself in the politics of the island, unless instructed to do so. He was committed to simply preaching the gospel of Jesus Christ and challenging the enslaved to be obedient to their slave masters—a life of hell on earth, with the assurance of a reward of spiritual freedom, and eternal joy in heaven!

---

27. Hinton, *Memoir*, 174.

CONCLUSION

This then was the period of preparation and adjustment, and with each step the BMS soon realized that if they were to be effective in benefiting from the legacy handed down to them by the EBS, they had to learn quickly, and be willing to allow the existing EBS leadership and African assistants to help them before the last of the pioneering African leaders, George Lisle, died. However, Lisle died within two years of returning from England, in 1828, and only time would tell if the BMS had done enough to take the baton and carry with them the African Christians who had not only established the Baptist witness on the island but were now hoping that these new Baptists would lead them into their promised land of freedom and equality.

Chapter 7

A Season of Violent Persecution and Resistance (1826–32)

THE DEATH OF GEORGE Lisle brought to an end the pioneering leadership which had brought a relevant contextual Christian witness to the African majority. The EBS was considered by the BMS to now be defunct as they took over, hoping to encourage their new African members to respectfully pray and worship God. However, 1826 saw the implementation of new slave laws which placed a blanket condemnation on all Baptists. This is the story of that period of time, and how it all came to head, in the repression and the resultant resistance of 1831–32.

THE SLAVE LAWS OF 1826

The season of violent persecution began with the introduction of new slave laws in 1826. In so doing the plantocracy declared their intention to continue their sustained attack not just against the EBS, but their new leaders, the missionaries of the BMS. It was a battle which William Knibb noted and wrote home about as early as 1825, stating that he saw Jamaica as:

> The land of sin, disease and death where Satan reigns with awful power, and carries multitudes captive at his will. Here religion is scoffed at, and those who profess it ridiculed and insulted. The Sabbath is violated, and a desire seems to manifest itself, by many of the inhabitants, to blot the Creator out of the universe he has formed . . . but God sitteth on his throne, and all power

is vested in him above: he can control their rage, or make it subserve his purpose.[1]

The following ten years showed the reality of this insightful statement, in that with the increased talk of emancipation by the government in Britain, the plantocracy chose to set in motion certain actions which culminated in a pledge:

> That the members of the Union do bind themselves to use every possible exertion, to prevent the dissemination of any religious doctrines at variance with those of the English and Scotch Churches.[2]

The campaign began with the Jamaican Assembly being slow to grant BMS missionaries licenses to preach. They then set out their intentions when they added a further amendment to the CSL, on December 22, 1826, which was then enacted on May 1, 1827. Its aim was to not only curtail the spiritual education of EBS members, and also the ministry of all Baptist ministers, including those of the BMS but also the physical expansion of the movement. It seemed to be a revival of past laws, and included most significantly for Baptists, the following laws:

> LXXXIII And whereas it has been found that the practice of ignorant, superstitious, or designing slaves of attempting to instruct others has been attended with the most pernicious consequences, and even with the loss of life, be it enacted, That any slave or slaves found guilty of preaching and teaching as Anabaptists, or otherwise without a permission form their owner and the quarter sessions for the Parish in which such preaching or teaching takes place shall be punished in such a manner as any three magistrates may deem proper, by whipping or imprisonment in the workhouse to hard labour.
>
> LXXXIV And whereas the assembling of slaves and other persons, after dark at places of meeting belonging to dissenters from the established religion, and other person professing to be teachers of religion, has been found extremely dangerous, and great facilities, are thereby given to the formation of plots and conspiracies, and the health of the slaves and other persons has been injured in travelling to and from such places of meeting at late hours in the night: Be it further enacted by the authority aforesaid, that from and after the commencement of this act, all such meeting between sunset and sunrise shall be held and

1. Knibb, "Letter to Samuel."
2. Bleby, *Death Struggles*, 178.

deemed unlawful, and any sectarian dissenting minister, or other person professing to be a teacher of religion, who shall, contrary to the act, keep open any such places of meeting between sunset and sunrise for the purpose aforesaid, or permit or suffer any such nightly assembly of slaves therein, or be present thereat, shall forfeit and pay a sum not less than twenty pounds, or exceeding fifty pounds, for each offence, to be recovered in a summary manner before any three justices, by warrant of distress and sale, one moiety thereof to be paid to the informer, who is hereby declared a competent witness, and the other moiety to the poor of the parish in which such offence shall be committed, and, in default of payment thereof, the said justices are hereby empowered and required to commit such offender or offenders to the common gaol for any space of time, not exceeding one calendar month: Provided always, that nothing herein contained shall be deemed or taken to prevent any minister of the Presbyterian kirk, or licensed minister, from performing divine worship at any time before the hour of eight o'clock in the evening at any licensed place of worship, or to interfere with the celebration of divine worship according to the rites and ceremonies of the Jewish and Roman Catholic religions.

LXXXV And whereas, under pretence of offerings and contributions, large sums of money and other chattels have been extorted by designing men, professing to be teachers of religion, practising on the ignorance and superstition of the negroes in this island, to their great loss and impoverishment. . . . Be it enacted by the authority aforesaid, That from and after the commencement of this act it shall not be lawful for any dissenting minister, religious teacher, or other person whatsoever, to demand or receive any money or other chattel whatsoever from any slave or slaves within this island, for affording such slave or slaves religious instruction, by way of offering contributions, or under any other pretence whatsoever . . . such person or persons shall upon conviction before any three justices, forfeit and pay the sum of twenty pounds for each offence . . . in default . . . commit such offender or offenders to the common gaol for any space of time, not exceeding one calendar month.[3]

So, not only were their practices outlawed but this legislation also sought to cut off any finances which they might receive from members, to enable the church to maintain its position and growth. This last clause was followed by the Jamaican House of Assembly setting up the "Sectarian

3. Parliament, *Slave Law of Jamaica*, 108–10.

Committee" (1828), "To enquire into the establishment and proceedings of sectarians in the island."[4] The Committee reported its findings in the local newspaper, using inflammatory language to declare that

> The principal object of the sectarians was to extort money from their congregations on every possible pretext and by the most indecent expedients; that they inculcated the doctrines of equality and the rights of man, and preached and taught sedition, even from the pulpit; that they occasioned abject poverty, loss of comfort, and discontent, among the slaves frequenting their chapels, and deterioration of property to their masters; and that, with an infamous thirst for gain, they recommended females to prostitute themselves in order to get money for contribution.[5]

Through these laws the state gave their supporters the right to not only sanction law breaking slaves, but to attack all Baptists and the BMS missionaries who they believed were the cause of all their ills. Also, though the putting to death of offenders was never legislated for, the actions of the plantocracy and militia demonstrated that the law was seen as the means whereby they could commit legalized genocide against all Baptists. Their war against Baptists soon took on a most reprehensible character, and it began with a war of words. Such was the anger which spread across Jamaica that even the press used its power to increasingly fight against them. One contributor proposed, after a minor rebellion in Hanover, that the people ought to

> Let the magistrates put down the evils of sectarian cank, and banish from our shores the baneful pest and the country will again become morally healthy. Remove the cause, and the effect will cease. Allow no evangelical preaching and we shall fear no further rebellions.[6]

Another argued that

> The reason why the Baptist place of worship was so thronged by negroes rather than by others, was that the preacher inculcated doctrines flattering to their vices, or of an insurrectionary character.[7]

---

4. Hinton, *Memoir*, 92.
5. Hinton, *Memoir*, 92–93.
6. Burchell, *Memoir*, 70.
7. Burchell, *Memoir*, 70.

The result of this was an increased attack not only on the EBS, but a more pronounced and bold persecution of all Baptists, especially the BMS missionaries. Joshua Tinson was one of those so persecuted, and a colleague reported how he responded to his interrogators:

> "Are you a Baptist?" "Yes, gentlemen, I am, and I glory in the name." Brother Tinson narrowly escaped being sent to jail; but I think they have been taught such a lesson, that they will not send for us again.

Others were far less fortunate than he, for while the enslaved undertook many creative means whereby they could "resist" these new laws, the oppression they suffered seemed to far outweigh their victories. Historian Shirley Gordon recorded how the enslaved sought to circumvent the system as well as some of the dire consequences which beset them.[8] She recorded the following incidents:

> The mobility of the slaves in attending the market, going to their provision ground, and providing hired-out services in their locality enabled them to dovetail estate-approved activities with public worship. Market baskets were stacked in chapel yards while vendors attended services; where the estate staff were hostile Sunday clothes were carried surreptitiously to the provision grounds, which then became the point of departure for the services.
>
> At times when slaves defied their managers' orders not to attend, the constable was then called in to stand in the chapel doorway and identify those present without permission. Slaves were also frequently waylaid and threatened in the roads on the way to services. . . . Many more slaves were flogged on the estates and were sent to the workhouses and chain gangs for long periods for their loyalty to their religious observance.
>
> Phillippo reported at least one flogged to death in Vere for holding a prayer meeting on his estate.[9]

In the Parish of Saint Thomas in the Vale there were similar stories to be heard. BMS Committee member Underhill documented the following stories:

> One man born free, and formally in the militia, told us that he had seen men shot for nothing worse than praying, and he had a cousin, a slave, who cut his throat to escape a flogging that he

---

8. Gordon, *God Almighty*, 64–65.
9. Gordon, *God Almighty*, 64–65.

expected next day. He had often seen in the caves of the mountains the bones of fugitives, who, while hidden, had died there.

Another had seen a pregnant woman laid down and flogged; she gave birth to the child while being scourged, and died.

Another knew an overseer who was in the habit of throwing his dead slaves into a deep pit on the estate. He one day thought a man was dead, and ordered him to be thrown into this Golgotha. The poor fellow, still alive, heard the order. "Massa," he said "Me no dead yet." Nevertheless, the order was repeated, and the hole received a dying man.[10]

Burchell himself stated that he had experienced within his own congregations the state seeking by any means necessary to prevent the enslaved from attending church. He too highlighted many incidents, including the following:

Constables and spies had been employed to parade the streets, and to mark the slightest deviation from legal propriety.

[They] would get Anglicans to preach to stop "dissenters" preaching or the overseer would read the prayers to prevent people going to dissenting chapels.

Sent town slaves to the country on a Sunday to work in the field to stop them attending church.

Overseers [in Flamstead] are instructed to apprehend negroes who attend the service there, and send them to the workhouse, under the pretext of suspecting them to be runaways: and I understand that negroes, found travelling the country without proper permission from their owners, may be legally treated thus.[11]

According to Thomas Burchell, if such actions failed, the authorities simply threatened them thus:

"If you do not leave off going to chapel, I'll work you, or beat you, out of your religion." Some are kept away under threat of thirty-nine lashes; and others are sent to the workhouse, which is considered much worse than flogging.[12]

Burchell perhaps summed up not only his feelings, but the feelings of all those who were persecuted as a result of the slave laws when in 1830, having been informed of a proposed tax to be levied only on dissenting

10. Underhill, *West Indies*, 256.
11. Burchell, *Memoir*, 63–79.
12. Burchell, *Memoir*, 79.

chapels, he refused to pay it. His chapel lamps were taken as payment in kind, after which he wrote home declaring:

> I have some thoughts of coming home next year; and if I do, I'll tell a tale. Accursed slavery! That infernal system! From my inmost soul I detest and abhor it! I am tired of living in its midst; though I sincerely love the work in which I am engaged.[13]

REPRESSION AND RESISTANCE (1831–32)

Perhaps the death of Lisle and the seemingly non-interventionist attitude of the BMS had encouraged the state to believe that it was time to bring to pass their new order. However, it would appear that they misjudged the situation for 1828 saw coming to the fore a new generation of leaders, who had sat at the feet of Lisle, and other leaders. One particular leader who came to prominence and brought together religious desire and political will in a way previously unheard of was Sam Sharpe, a "slave" and a Daddy in the Baptist church in Montego Bay.

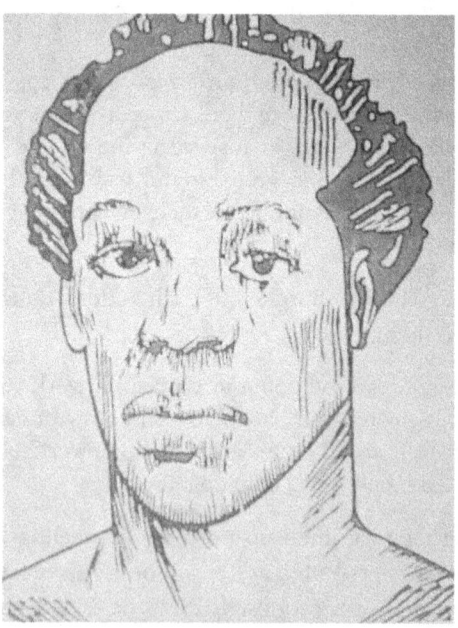

Portrait of Sam Sharpe. Photograph by D. Morrison, Sam Sharpe Monument, Montego Bay, Jamaica.

13. Burchell, *Memoir*, 157.

Sharpe has been credited with being the leader of the resistance movement, which is now more euphemistically called, the "Sam Sharpe Rebellion." However, those planters and clerics of the CofE, which had pursued and persecuted the EBS since 1791, termed it more accurately the "Baptist Wars"—a war against the Baptists which they had hoped would be the culmination of all of their attempts to maintain the status quo, in a world where the British government was coming under increasing pressure from all quarters of society, to put an end to slavery once and for all.

The "Rebellion" is perhaps best understood as, "an 'organised resistance' to an 'organised repression.'"[14] On April 15, 1831, Member of Parliament, and anti-slavery campaigner, Fowell Buxton introduced a motion in the House of Commons concerning slavery in the British colonies. His was a desire to see it ended. This news was swiftly relayed to the planters in Jamaica who in response gathered together, from July to September 1831, holding public meetings, in the various towns and parishes across Jamaica, as well as in the legislature, to agree on how they might best oppose any such bill. Believing themselves to have been betrayed by the British government, the planters sent Lord Belmore to Parliament with their response, which was published in 1832. In it they stated that

> They considered that they were "bound, by every principle, human and divine, to resist;" that "although they might be too weak to prevail, they might prove powerful enough to injure their oppressors;" that, "if they must fall, they would at least perish with honour, as a people not insensible to glory and reputation;" that they "required to be absolved from their allegiance;" and that "the government and people of England" ought to not "endeavour by their acts and treasonable language to excite the slaves to rise up in rebellion, and rob them (the planters) of their property and lives.[15]

These public meetings were often attended by the enslaved, who heard firsthand the news that there was talk of freedom in England, and that it might soon be theirs. Yet, at those very same meetings they also began to hear the intended response of the plantocracy, should such a law be passed. They intimated an increased hostility not only to the British government, but more particularly towards their slaves. The slaves relayed those thoughts to their peers. Tensions soon increased with confrontations becoming the norm throughout the island with many of the following conversations being played out across the land:

14. Gerloff, "African Diaspora," 15.
15. Hinton, *Memoir*, 112.

> The master of one slave told him "That freedom was come from England, but that he would shoot every d-d black rascal before he should get it." Another hears his master say, "the King is going to give us free, but he hoped all his friends will be of his mind, and spill their blood first."[16]

BMS missionary journals confirm this, one entry stating that

> The [plantocracy were in the] habit of taunting the slaves with freedom, clearly establishing that, the slave owners themselves caused the rebellion.[17]

The intensity of the actions of the plantocracy in turn caused the enslaved in response, to begin to seek out the information on emancipation for themselves. Through available newspapers they were able to find the truth, which came directly from England:

> The information thus acquired, although known in the first instance to a few individuals in the towns, was quickly communicated to the slaves on the plantations; and thus the entire slave population of the island became penetrated in a few months with the irritating idea, that their masters resisted the benevolent intentions of the King.[18]

The result was that the repression increased as slave owners sought to find new ways within the CSL to prevent their slaves from receiving the "freedom" which was to come. Once again, they began seeking ways of preventing them from attending church, perhaps assuming that church was the place where the enslaved would hear more news of their impending freedom. However, such actions, according to many who recorded this history, only served to precipitate the crisis, the rebellion. The plantocracy were too late, as events were set in motion on both sides which could not now be reversed, leading observers to declare of them that it was they who "May justly be said to have set their own estates on fire."[19]

One of those who had heard the news was, Sam Sharpe. How he heard about it, and what he decided to do about it, was documented by BMS missionary Cornford, who stated that:

> [He] heard about freedom [when], "A negro boy obtained employment in a printing-office in Montego Bay; and when his

16. Hinton, *Memoir*, 112.
17. Baptist Missionaries, *Narrative*, 161.
18. Hinton, *Memoir*, 113.
19. Hinton, *Memoir*, 113.

naked feet first pressed those boards, the doom of slavery sealed. This lad had an uncle, a deacon in the Baptist church, who, being able to read, watched for opportunities of adding to his little store of information. Some English newspapers were there from time to time carelessly thrown away, some of which were carried by the lad to his uncle. Though a Christian man and a down-trodden slave, the eyes of Sam Sharpe flashed as with lightning when first he read "anti-slavery" intelligence from England. "Hi!" he exclaimed, "we hab friend in England!" Now his thoughts took wing. His spirit panted for a glorious flight, but there were cruelties which bound it down. The precious paper was stored away, to be read again and yet again. . . . The main idea was innocent enough. No conscience was stung. Few hearts quailed. "Look!" said they, "black is more than white. If we say we no work if you no pay, that is right; and white people is not enough to make we." Soon this thought ran like wildfire. . . . But the Christian man, with intensely Christian principles and thoughts, could not limit his plans to Christian minds.[20]

The news once received, soon traveled across the churches and plantations in Saint James, Trelawny, Saint Elizabeth, Westmoreland, and Hanover, and their resolve was perhaps strengthened when in October 1831, and in the absence of Burchell:

Several negroes came to Knibb as their minister, to ask him if what they heard was true, namely, "that free paper was come." When asked how they had heard such a thing, their answer was "when busha and book keeper flog us, they say we are going to be free, and before it comes they will get it out of us. Knibbs' reply was, "No, it is not true. Never let me hear anything of this again. When did busha tell you anything for your good? There is no paper coming. Go home, and mind your master's work."[21]

It was then that Sam Sharpe forcefully responded to Knibb on behalf of all the enslaved present declaring that:

We have worked enough already and will work no more; the life we live is too bad, it is the life of a dog, we won't be slaves no more, we won't lift hoe no more, we won't take flogging anymore.[22]

20. Cornford, *Missionary Reminiscences*, 28–29.
21. Hinton, *Memoir*, 115.
22. Erskine, *Decolonizing Theology*, 49.

In so doing, he repeated the statement which appears to have been the agreed statement of those who had agreed to resist a continued life of slavery. We know this because similar a statement was repeated to the Custos, Mr. Richard Barrett, in the presence of Rev Waddell a member of the Scottish Missionary Society, following a proclamation which Barrett had read demanding that the enslaved, return to work on a plantation in Spot Valley, January 3, 1832. The enslaved responded, seemingly out of fear of the Custos, by repeating the following, almost identical, statement which we know of only Sharpe making to Knibb, in the confines of the church grounds. They said:

> We have worked enough already, and we will work no more. The life we live is too bad; it is the life of a dog. We won't be slaves no more; we won't lift a hoe no more; we won't take flog no more. We free now, We free now; no more slaves again. Then they shouted, and laughed, and clapped their hands. It was really so amusing a scene I could not help laughing with them, and my doing so increased their good humour.[23]

Their following comments reiterating to Barrett, that they would never again work for him or anyone else, declaring, "When your people begin work again me and my children will begin too,"[24] suggests that their laughter was in fact more in fear than mockery. However, more significantly, it serves to confirm Sharpe's status as one of the leaders of the island-wide resistance movement, but just as significantly, it proves that they were in fact a very organized group, with a clear understanding of what they wanted and what they were seeking to achieve strategizing across the plantations of the north coast, after:

> Sam [then] called a council of his friends and committed to them his thoughts. . . . A secret society was formed, with both "the power" and the passion "to add to its number."[25]

---

23. Waddell, *Twenty-Nine*, 59.
24. Waddell, *Twenty-Nine*, 60.
25. Cornford, *Missionary Reminiscences*, 29.

A Season of Violent Persecution and Resistance (1826–32)   131

Area of the 1831 Rebellion with Names and Locations of Estate Properties in the Parish of St. James, and parts of Hanover, Trelawney, St. Elizabeth and Westmoreland. Courtesy of the Jamaica Baptist Union, 2013.

They then met on the Retrieve Plantation in the middle of October, and together made a plan. They agreed that after the Christmas break, they would withhold their labor unless their "masters" agreed to pay them a day's wages for a day's labor. Then two weeks before the Christmas break, the drivers on the different plantations held a meeting to develop their plans for each plantation. At one point there was talk of the use of guns and swords as a possible means of weaponry, one dissenter stating that

> Oonoo, all fool! Buckra no make we go free so! Me say we is to hab sword and gun, and fight for we free![26]

Another argued that

26. Cornford, *Missionary Reminiscences*, 29.

> If the black men did not stand up for themselves and take their freedom, the whites would put them out at the muzzles of their guns and shoot them like pigeons.[27]

While Sharpe agreed with the plan to resist, he refused to take part in any violent actions, stating that he and his fellow Christians had agreed amongst themselves that they would refuse to involve themselves in any violence, affirming that:

> They will not fight nor do any harm unless they are first attacked, and then they must defend themselves.[28]

They were therefore not engineering a rebellion, but forming actions to resist what they believed was their legitimate right to be free. and to strike for it.

Waddell stated that missionaries of all denominations were aware that the Christmas holidays was a time which always led to disturbances, but that this time they knew that this particular holiday would be somewhat different. This he put down to the nature of the enslaved who they had heard were determined to have their freedom, especially knowing for sure the consequences of failure. Waddell stated that they were in the main creoles, who were willing to fight, and if necessary, die for their freedom. He recalled how

> The Creoles—young, strong, and giddy with the new-born hope of liberty, which they said the king had given them and their masters withheld-resolved to stand out for the wages of free labour, and, if needful, to fight for their rights. The old people discouraged the attempt. They had seen worse times, and were sensible of a growing amelioration of their condition. The experience also of former insurrections taught them to dread the consequences of failure. But the counsels of age, attributed to timidity and ignorance, were disregarded. The leaders of the movement,—the captains, colonels, and generals of the insurgents,—fearing that the women first would be persuaded or compelled to resume their hoes, and through them the men, resolved, for their own safety, and the success of their plans, to involve as many as possible, and begin where they knew they must end, by burning down the estates.[29]

It was agreed then by all that fire would be their best weapon as the majority of them were unfamiliar with guns and other kinds of munitions.

27. Parry et al., *Short History*, 161.
28. Cornford, *Missionary Reminiscences*, 33.
29. Waddell, *Twenty-Nine*, 51.

However, before they could fully prepare for the task ahead of them the "rebellion" began on December 27, 1831, when

> A negress at Salt Spring Estate was seized and flogged for some real or fancied fault. Her infuriated husband rushed upon her assailant with a blow, exclaiming that "his wife should never be flogged anymore." In a moment all was uproar,—panic confusion. No one would seize the rebel. Then it was reported that a messenger was sent to Montego Bay for armed resistance. At once the people fled. That night upon the hill aflame arose. Soon it burned more and yet more high. . . . The insurrection was precipitated. Few, if any, were really ready.[30]

Then with the rebellion underway, it was said of Sharpe's role that:

> He simply dwells in their midst to counsel, to restrain, and to bless. . . . So well-known were all his motions amongst the white party, that with them he had the honourable nickname of "The High-priest in the camp."[31]

Thus began the crisis in Jamaica. Plantations burnt throughout the north and west, as the enslaved in their desperation declared their desire for freedom. Such was the case in Saint James where:

> In the yard of one of the estates in the same parish the military were drawn out, probably but for exercise, or because their presence was thought necessary to repress symptoms of revolt; when a woman rushed past them in the direction of the Trash House, [where the remains of the extracted sugar cane was kept] waving frantically above her head a flaming brand, crying as she ran, "I know I shall die for it!—I know I shall die for it! but my children shall be free!" She succeeded in igniting the inflammable mass, but the soldiers were ordered to fire, and she fell lifeless.[32]

On Saturday December 31, 1831, martial law was declared, and concerned about the deteriorating situation, Major General Commanding, Willoughby Cotton, issued a proclamation in the name of the Crown, at their Montego Bay Headquarters, on January 2, 1832, followed by a further proclamation by Somerset Lowry, Governor-in-Chief, which offered a reward of three hundred dollars, for the capture of Sam Sharpe and three of his fellow leaders. It is no surprise then to learn that the plantation owners

---

30. Waddell, *Twenty-Nine*, 29.
31. Waddell, *Twenty-Nine*, 33.
32. Waddell, *Twenty-Nine*, 32.

having "fanned the flames" of rebellion, now dubbed it the "Baptist War," especially as many of the first captives who were accused of being involved, were members of Baptist churches in Montego Bay and Salter's Hill, churches which posed a particular threat by their sheer numbers.[33] Yet the reality of the situation was that Baptists were in fact not the only contributors to the rebellion; members of the Moravian, Wesleyan, and Presbyterian faiths were also involved, as well as those of no faith at all. Nevertheless, the die was cast, the militia and sailors guarded the seaports, while the Maroons were sent up into the mountain regions to catch the insurgents. They also retaliated by burning to the ground the slave villages, before rounding up other Baptists, whose major crime was that of answering to the simple accusation that they were members of the Baptist church.

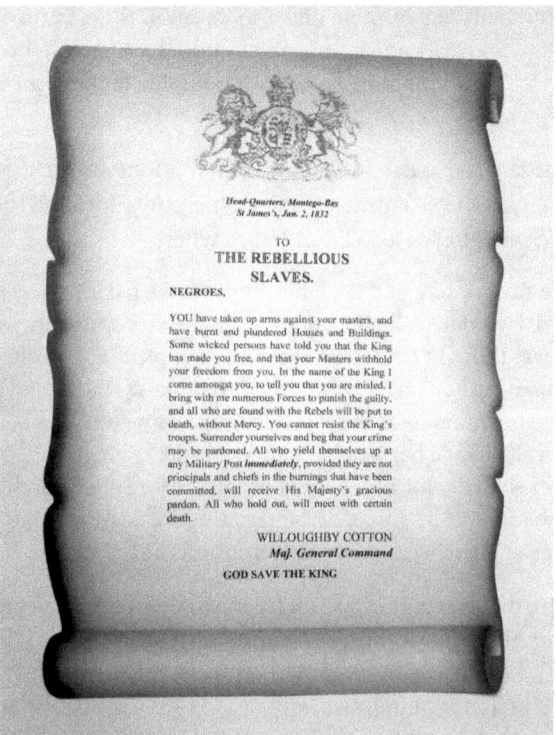

Proclamation: To the Rebellious Slaves, January 2, 1832, accessed *The National Archives, England, CO 137/181*, p. 111. Redesigned by D. Morrison.

33. Baptist Missionaries, *Narrative*, 12, 20. You see at that time, these two congregations had a combined membership of 2,295, with a significant number of "visitors" and "enquirers" in addition, in a region where the total white residential population of Montego Bay was approximately 6,000 to 7,000.

Despite protestations from Knibb, Tinson, and others, and evidence to the contrary,[34] the plantation owners began a persecution primarily of Baptists, seeking to charge as many of them as possible with treason, and executing the guilty. Such was the case at Salter's Hill, Montego Bay, and Windsor Lodge, where

> During the prevalence of martial law *ten* of the members belonging to the Salter's Hill Church were hanged, *seven* were shot, after mock trials, *one* was shot down in his own garden, another in her house, and one was flogged at Montego Bay, who died on the way home, and was buried on the roadside at Spring Mount. A female member was flogged to death by the Maroons. In all *twenty-one* were put to death.
>
> At Windsor Lodge estate seven persons were hanged, two were shot down in their gardens, the heads of five were taken off, and two were fastened on the cooper's shop, and three on the carpenter's. Old Virgil, of Windsor Lodge, a Baptist leader, was led out without trial and put to death. He inquired of Captain Hylton if he was to be hanged for praying to God? The savage man, full of enmity to religion answered "Yes." Then said the old Christian, "Hang me up at once that I may go to my Father." He was one of those put to death because he had taught people to fear God.[35]

Of that time BMS missionary Cornford stated that while it was true that there were many other denominations involved in the rebellion, it was true that resistance also came from Baptists. He wrote:

> It must be confessed that some persons professing godliness from every section of the Christian church took up arms in the cause of liberty. The Baptist churches, as is well known, had throughout the island chiefly attracted the slave population to their fellowship. What wonder then if the planters had evidence that some Baptists, after holding a prayer-meeting on a certain estate, had afterwards spent two or three hours in secret conference with five or six principal men? And what wonder that, having such evidence, it should be widely diffused, and every day

---

34. Baptist Missionaries, *Narrative*, 161. Baptist missionaries at that time actually had evidence that many of their members took it upon themselves to 'protect' as much as they were able, the properties of their 'masters.' This was later proved to be true as the Assembly found that thirty-eight estates were so treated, resulting in 69 enslaved Baptists handing in to the authorities, the 'rebels' as prisoners, twenty-five of them in the parish of Cornwall, but then receiving from the House of Assembly, their manumission (freedom) as a reward.

35. Clarke, *Memorials of Baptist Missionaries*, 161.

more highly coloured with exaggerations, until the white people were unanimous in their resolve to suppress, by all means, and at all costs, every semblance of religion which was not strictly conformed to the Established Church? Hence amongst the slaves the most pious and zealous were often singled out for vengeance at once most bloody, and furious, and blind.[36]

Such were the experiences of many Ethiopian Baptists, who were during this period of martial law subject to much violence: rape, whipping, and the brutal murder of their brothers and sisters. Yet, two very different incidents of that time have survived to the present day, and can now be retold as a testimony to the faith and fortitude of the many who were persecuted. The first is the story of David, a member of a church in Spanish Town, led by one Moses Hall who the authorities had singled out as a means by which they could make an example to others, to prevent the rebellion taking hold in their region. While it is perhaps one of the most tragic stories which has "survived" the passages of history, it is also one which shows the faith and determination of a people wanting to worship the God who they had found to be faithful and true. It is for this reason that the story is perhaps best told directly from the historical records, and a firsthand account:

> At length in other and distant parts of the island the insurrection had commenced. It mattered not that these poor people were far removed from the scenes of strife and wholly ignorant of sedition. . . . What were missionaries but social firebrands? What did these black brutes want with religion? It was denied they had "one soul amongst ten thousand." Should it prove otherwise, it was yet God's will they should be slaves. The Bible plainly said that. Then they were unfit to have religion. . . . Besides, slavery and religion could never exist together. Everybody knew that! What then should they do?" Could they not put an instant stop to this growing rage for religion? Spirits and tobacco lent their mighty aid to this fiery discussion. . . . It was now decided that Moses Hall should be seized at one of the meetings for prayer, and thence brought to trial and execution. The time, the place, the circumstances, were all arranged. Thus satisfied, the party dissolved in comparative contentment, determined meanwhile never to retire to rest without seeing that their arms were duly prepared for every emergency.
>
> The appointed time had soon arrived. The men who have to seize the victim warily advance to the humble cottage where prayer was wont to be made. Above such clusters of negro

---

36. Cornford, *Missionary Reminiscences*, 38.

dwellings one was accustomed to see numerous cocoa-nut trees, whose long feathery leaves would lightly rustle in the evening air whilst they gleamed like silver in the lustre of the moon.... The object of their search is not within.... "This fellow here that is speaking is just the same as the other. I know him. He goes about everywhere holding these meetings. I say, let's take him. As for this other fellow, we shan't catch him in the fact again."

So it came to pass that while David's heart was yet glowing with holy joys, violent hands were laid upon him. Like his divine Master, "he was led as a lamb to the slaughter; and as a sheep before her shearers is dumb, so he opened not his mouth." In the dark damp dungeon, upon cold hard stones, that night he was fain to lay his weary limbs. But call him "rebel" if you will! Load him with ignominy and reproach! Let him stand unfriended whilst things are laid to his charge of which he knoweth not! When the Lord maketh inquisition for blood, the men who dabbled their abominable hands in his may envy him his lot!

David was hurried to the town of Black River, tried, found guilty, and sentenced to death. By special request his head was, after death, severed from his body, and sent back to the men who had been guilty of his blood.... A suitable pole is selected from the woodland. The people of the district are all assembled where various roads meet. The head of the martyr is fixed upon this lofty pole, and the trophy of insane cruelty set up amidst this throng of sorrowing spectators. Around that centre some hundreds of every age are gathered. These with shuddering horror are now made to hear recitals of the rebellion, and its failure,—the wickedness of the impotent slaves.... Such was the strain of threatening invective to which the assembled slaves were compelled to listen. To crown the scene with final and overwhelming effect the name of Moses Hall was now loudly called upon. Answering from the distance, he pressed through the crowd into the ring. Here he is roughly seized and thrust backwards against the pole, upon which, far above him, is the head of his companion and friend. Standing there, he thus addressed:-

"Now, Moses Hall, you have heard what these gentlemen have said; so take warning from this time. Let us see that you understand all about it. Tell us, now, whose head is that above you?" In a firm voice he answers, "Dat's David, massa." "Ha! Yes! Do you know what he is up there for?" "Yes, massa. For praying, sir." "Very well. Listen to me, now. Do you know that it was your head we meant should have been on that pole? And so it would have been, if you had had what you deserve." But David has got what is due to you, that's all. We know all about you, and your doings. Mark you, now. From this time we shall have no more of these goings on. We'll stop your religious nonsense for you. Mind! From this time let us have no more of your 'prayer-meetings' for if we catch you at it we shall serve you as we have served David. You had better take warning. Aye, all of ye! Whoever we catch at such things again,—it matters not who it is,—we'll serve you all alike! Do you hear that, sir?"

Moses did hear it, indeed. His whole soul quivered with excitement at every syllable. What could he do? To bow in calm submission was equal to a sacrifice of his principles and a denial of his Lord. He knew his entire innocence of even the thought of rebellion; but all his protestations would be counted worthless, if not accepted as aggravations of supposed guilt. So suddenly raising and clasping his hands, he kneeled down upon the earth immediately beneath the martyr's head, saying, in solemn voice,—Let us pray! Immediately the whole circle knelt in prayer. What though David had so cruelly and causelessly been put to death! What though the furious persecutors were all present there!! What though their imprecations and threatenings were both loud and deep! The whole throng kneeled down in prayer. And now, before the masters could recover their surprise, the voice of the poor slave in the centre rose clearly over the scene of death-like silence. He prayed that God would "bless al the massa buckra, and make them to know the Lord Jesus Christ,—how he came into the world to save poor sinners,—that they might wash all their sins away in 'him precious blood,'—that so their souls might be saved at last." . . . With such fervour and unction did he pray for them that they were all disarmed. They calmly listened. Defiance and love they had never seen in such firm fellowship before. What could men do who had never prayed for themselves? There was not one who could cast the first stone. The prayer ended, they turned away. . . . The good man, the living martyr, who, though ready to die, they had not the heart to slay, continued his holy enterprise. The sounds of prayer and songs of praise still continued to abound; nor did those masters ever more attempt to stay the progress of that work of God. Moses Hall lived to be old and gray, and never ceased to serve God.[37]

Then there was the story of Miss Cooper who first came to prominence in the 1820s when BMS missionary Phillippo, having slept in the home of a

---

37. Cornford, *Missionary Reminiscences*, 404–5.

Black person, was unable to preach at Harmony Hall plantation. Without a place to preach his mission there was in danger until

> The house of a noble spirited free-black proprietress was offered, and accepted, at Constant Spring, and the Gospel was for some years, amidst much persecution, preached at this place.[38]

The story is told of how she then allowed the missionaries to use her land, and so they

> Preached there beneath the shade of an orange tree and the people sheltered themselves under a booth formed with the branching leaves of a cocoa-nut. A small house was next put up and the people were visited by brethren, Phillips, Taylor and the writer.[39]

However, having been found out, during martial law legal action followed. It was reported in court documents that

> Miss Cooper, a free person of colour, the owner of land on which a little chapel stood, was taken before the magistrate, to answer to the charge of encouraging unlawful meetings, and for attending them. . . . She was bound over to answer the indictment at the Quarter Sessions to be held in Spanish Town. . . . She, undismayed by the threats remained firm to her purpose that on her land a house for the worship of God should stand. What could not be effected by such proceedings, was sought to be reached by readier means, and the destruction of the place of prayer by fire was attempted. That roof being thatched, made it easy to carry this purpose out; but the fire kindled by a discharge from a pistol was speedily subdued, and the place saved.[40]

Miss Cooper nevertheless never ceased to display her faith, wherein at the end of martial law:

> The Gospel was preached there regularly once a month, and in 1834, the Jericho house and land was purchased, and about three hundred of Mr Gibbs's former people, and two hundred of the Spanish Town members formed, in connection with the recently baptized, the Church in this Parish.[41]

---

38. Clarke, *Memorials of Baptist Missionaries*, 18.
39. Clarke, *Memorials of Baptist Missionaries*, 17.
40. Clarke, *Memorials of Baptist Missionaries*, 17.
41. Clarke, *Memorials of Baptist Missionaries*, 17–18.

It was then Miss Cooper who later introduced BMS missionary John Clarke to her community of faith, and together they birthed Jericho Baptist Church in Saint Catherine, which remains to the present day. Of these and other such experiences BMS missionary Cornford who received eyewitness accounts of these activities, set on record his belief that:

> We hold that there is a martyrdom which lives, having fellowship with that which dies.[42]

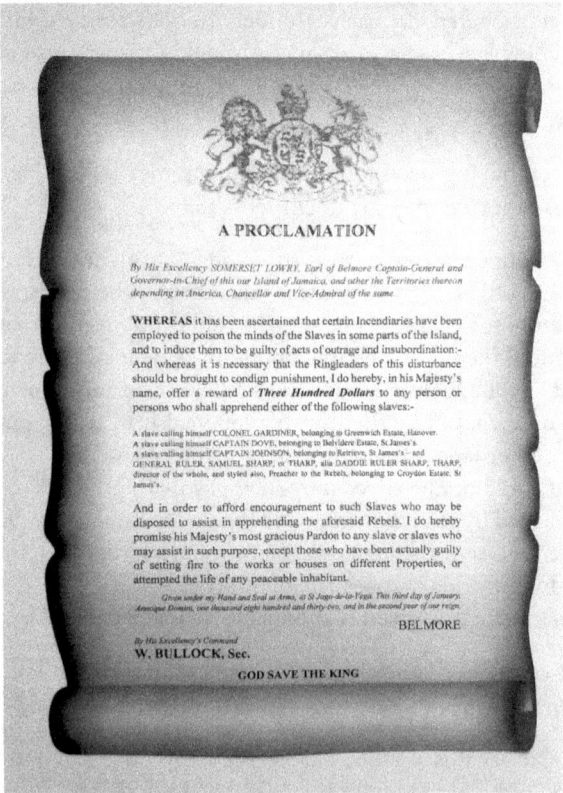

Warrant for the Leaders of the Resistance Movement, 1832, accessed, *The National Archives, England. CO 137/181*, p. 110. Redesigned by D. Morrison.

Back in the heart of the resistance, the rebels were being arrested, and many like Sam Sharpe, fled, going "underground" in the hope of escaping a sure and certain death. However, the assembly whether knowingly or

---

42. Cornford, *Missionary Reminiscences*, 45.

A Season of Violent Persecution and Resistance (1826–32)

unknowingly pulled a master stroke, when having indicated the involvement of Baptist ministers, began arresting BMS missionaries, and charging them with treason and threatening them with execution for instigating the rebellion. Arrests were made, and many missionaries including Thomas Burchell, Francis Gardner, William Knibb, and Joshua Tinson, were imprisoned, put on trial and indicted for beginning the rebellion. Yet, once on trial cases often fell apart as people were often paid to speak against them. This was the case of a man named Samuel Stennet, who on taking to the witness box exposed the falsehood which was going on. During the trial of Burchell and Gardner:

> Mr Manderson then cautioned Stennet against telling a falsehood respecting those whose names had been mentioned, reminding him of the painful effects produced on his mind by his falsely implicating the missionaries. His statement was committed to writing, in the form of an affidavit, which ran thus: "That the affidavit made by him against the Baptist missionaries, Thomas Burchell and Francis Gardner, which led to their confinement in gaol, was false and unjust; that he never heard from them such facts as he had sworn against them; that he was instigated to do so by Messrs. George Delisser, George McF. Lawson, Jun. Joseph Bowen, and W C Morris, the former of whom assured him he would be well looked upon by the Gentlemen of this place; that the country would give him £10 per annum, and that he, George Delisser, would make it £50.[43]

Despite those many falsehoods, the imprisonment of Burchell especially, had the desired effect, for the conspirators had, "*kissed the book not to hurt any parson.*"[44] They had made a pact to lay their lives on the line to protect every minister during the uprising, as was the case of a Mrs. Hudson who had rescued Gardner. The story is told how

> Mr Gardner, set out from Savanna-la-Mar for Montego Bay, to discharge his duties to this church, as acting pastor; and to await there, the arrival from England of Mr Burchell, who was expected daily. He was not aware, of existing conditions in Montego Bay, that the Baptist Chapel had been converted into a barracks for the military; and that the road between Savanna-la-Mar and Montego Bay, was occupied by rebel slaves, who had succeeded in driving the militia, under Colonel Grignon, from Shacklewood Pen: and was in full possession of that part of the country.

---

43. Baptist Missionaries, *Narrative*, 65.
44. Baptist Missionaries, *Narrative*, 40.

> Being mistaken for an escaping slave owner, Mr Gardner was pursued; and might have been killed, had it not been, for the interposition of a Mrs Hudson, a free coloured woman, at Ramble gate. As soon as the rebels were convinced that Mr Gardner was a missionary, he was safely conducted, by slave leaders back [including] one Phillip of Mackfield, whom he had allowed to ride with him in his chaise.[45]

As the leaders of the resistance movement were identified as being members of Salter's Hill, Montego Bay, and Windsor Lodge churches, it suited the authorities to declare that Burchell too must be to blame. Such was their determination to arrest this instigator that as Burchell was arriving back in Montego Bay with his family, on the Garland Grove ship, in January 1832, he was arrested while still aboard. In the months following he was serially imprisoned and kept on trumped up charges, and there was even talk of assassination, before, whether intentionally or otherwise, news was spread abroad that he was to be executed. This then became the pawn which was used to capture Sam Sharpe, who had been indicted as the leader of the "rebellion," even though he had spoken nonviolent resistance and peace throughout the sorry episode. Though a reward was offered for his arrest, and that of his core conspirators, no one had to claim it, for upon hearing this news, Sharpe, speedily with the support of his brother, handed himself in to the authorities. Of his actions it is recorded that

> When Sharpe heard that the ministers and more especially his beloved minister Thomas Burchell were charged as instigators of the slave-riot, he gave up himself to the military, so that he might testify, as to the innocence of his minister.[46]

Burchell was eventually released while Sharpe like so many of his fellow conspirators was convicted and sentenced to die. Those who participated in the resistance, numbered in their "hundreds and thousands."[47] It is believed that of the 221 people who died in the battle that ensued, fourteen of them were white, and 207 of them were enslaved folk. The leaders and their followers, numbering between 310 and 340, were executed for various offenses to do with the insurrection, including the stealing of animals. Such was the enthusiasm of the slave owners to repress further opposition, that it was noted that the "journey" from trial to execution could take but a few hours, as was the case of one George Spence in Lucea:

45. Dillon, *Centennial Review*, 11.
46. Dillon, *Centennial Review*, 9.
47. Waddell, *Twenty-Nine*, 65.

A Season of Violent Persecution and Resistance (1826–32)

> George Spence, belonging to Fat-Quarter, was executed at Lucea early in January, 1832, for rebellion and rebellious conspiracy. He was apprehended on a Friday evening, and the following morning put on his trial, before a Military Tribunal . . . various attempts were made to induce the man to say something that would incriminate Mr Burchell. For instance . . . Burchell told you, you were to be free at Christmas didn't he? Didn't Burchell say you must fight for free? In answer to these and other similar questions, the man stated that he did not know Mr Burchell—he never saw him—he was not a Baptist—he belonged to Mr Watson's (a Presbyterian Missionary) Church. The manifest injustice and partiality of the proceeding . . . induced an Officer present . . . to protest. . . . The man was found guilty, and sentenced to be shot *immediately*. . . . When taken from the Court room, and seeing the soldiers drawn up in readiness to conduct him to the closing scene, he enquired, "What are you going to do with me?" . . . snatching from his back the short jacket he wore, and throwing it over his head, tying the sleeves round his neck, so as for ever to exclude from his sight the things on earth. The Officer, with his own hands, secured the rope by which the man was tied, and then stepped back and gave the command to "fire." In a few seconds the wretched man lay a mangled corpse on the ground. The whole process of the trial and execution did not occupy three hours!![48]

Of their final hours to execution, an eyewitness from Lucea described how:

> They were all, on the day previous to their execution, put into two large carts, drawn by oxen, each prisoner pinioned, with a rope on his neck, and a white cap on his head. In this dress they were seated side by side in the carts, and, on moving off from the jail door, they simultaneously commence a hymn, in which all joined with great composure and fervency. The morning, as usual, was beautiful, the air calm, and the town quiet, and deeply solemnized, as the wagons proceeded slowly along the streets; and the voice of praise was heard at a distance, ascending from the midst of the mournful cavalcade. In this way they were carried up, under a strong guard, into the midst of the burned properties, distances of twelve to thirty miles, and the sentence was carried into effect on the estates, as they successively arrived at them. On each of the melancholy occasions, the unfortunate

---

48. Baptist Missionaries, *Narrative*, 160–61.

men met their death, with a fortitude and cool deliberation that astonished all who beheld them.[49]

Such composure was also seen in Sam Sharpe who was tried on April 19, 1832 and executed on May 23, 1832, and even then, the state could not resist, paying compensation to his owners, after valuing him at a mere £16 10 shillings. Of Sharpe's final thoughts in the days before his death, Bleby who had been requested to visit him in prison, wrote,

> He was persuaded that the British troops would not be allowed to act against the negroes, if they commenced an actual struggle for the liberty which thousands of the British people considered to be most unrighteously withheld from them . . . he learnt from his Bible that the whites had no more right to hold black people in slavery, than the black people had to make the white people slaves. . . . "Minister" he said, while his frame expanded, and his eagle-eye seemed to shoot forth rays of light, "I would rather die upon yonder gallows than live in slavery!"[50]

Of his execution accounts told of a brave and courageous man, full of faith to the end:

> Lewin reported, "I saw him come with his face as bright, and his form as erect, as if he had achieved some glorious victory. His firm foot kept the regular tread of the escort who led him to execution. His calm and peaceful eye singled out his old friends and acquaintances as he passed along, to many of whom he bowed his recognition. In front of the house where many of the family who had called him their 'slave' watched him from the windows, he paused and bowed his last farewell. At the scaffold he ascended with that quick, light step, which was natural to him in the capacity of a butler in which he had served. . . . Seeing the drop, before stepping on it to speak to the assembled throng he tried its firmness with a single foot."[51]

Bleby and Cornford reported how Sharpe confidently declared in the face of death:

> "I depend for salvation upon the Redeemer, who shed his blood upon Calvary for sinners"[52]

---

49. Waddell, *Twenty-Nine*, 65–66.
50. Bleby, *Death Struggles*, 128–29.
51. Cornford, *Missionary Reminiscences*, 35.
52. Bleby, *Death Struggles*, 130.

"I am going to die, because I thought I had a right to be free; I have joined in no outrage against life or property; but have tried to restrain those who did."[53] Finally he said "Ah! My broder . . . you see now de heaben is like brass, and de eart' is like iron. You all know what great trial we hab to pass troo. But God is good. You will see, no sooner is me gone dan God will open heaben, and send down plenty o'rain, and so you will all rejoice."[54]

Reports then tell of a very clandestine reburial some years later, which showed the high regard in which Sharpe, a great Ethiopian Baptist, was held by BMS missionaries and those who continued to watch over his remains. Two independent BMS missionary records tell of how missionaries, in order to give Sharpe, the Christian burial which they believed he deserved, carried out an action which demonstrated the greatest respect for this servant of God:

> His body was buried in the sand, by the side of the harbour; and many years afterwards, his grave was opened. And his bones were gathered, and arranged at midnight, in skeleton form, by Messrs. Lewin, Cornford, J E Henderson, and others; placed in a mahogany coffin; and put in a vault, in the present building [Montego Bay Baptist Church].[55]
> They who had sacrificed him buried him in the sands by the seashore, as one too vile to sleep with the common human race. . . . At last, at midnight, a band of missionaries, and that friend who saw him "die like a man" and like a saint, went to those sands and took away his bones. A beautiful coffin of mahogany was prepared. The skeleton complete was laid therein. A vault was made ready beneath the pulpit in the noble chapel. Sam Sharp was solemnly interred at a midnight hour, in the presence and amidst the loud sobs of those who had admired and loved him. There now those bones are lying. For five years and upwards I stood to preach the word of God immediately above them, whilst to my soul they seemed to whisper a tribute to the glory of my work, and an inspiration to its pursuit even unto death.[56]

---

53. Dillon, *Centennial Review*, 9.

54. Cornford, *Missionary Reminiscences*, 35. This would seem that it could be a reference to Acts 14:17, a text speaking of God's provision through the Holy Spirit. One could therefore interpret it that, while Sharpe himself was going to heaven, they should be encouraged, for God had made provision from them, and would continue to provide for them.

55. Dillon, *Centennial Review*, 9.

56. Cornford, *Missionary Reminiscences*, 36–37.

Of the epitaph he had never publicly received, Cornford wrote:

> Alas, that hitherto "no marble marks his couch of lowly sleep!" No token of any kind records how Sam Sharpe has lived and died. Yet, if ever human being deserved esteem, or admiration, or love,—if ever human deed deserved a bright memorial,—Sam Sharpe should not be forgotten, nor should his bones lie still unhonoured. The mission cause owes him much. His black brethren in Jamaica are exalted and enriched through his voluntary death. But wherever throughout the world "Freedom's battle" is pressed on to victory, the happy issue has unquestionably been aided by the self-sacrifice of this truly Christian hero.[57]

Yet Sharpe though the last to be hung, was only one of the many women and men of that generation of church leaders who were martyred in this season of repression and resistance, but of them all it was said:

> Their ashes flew—No marble tells us whither; with their names. No bard ambalms and sanctifies his song. But they are not overlooked or forgotten by Him to whom "the souls beneath the altar" address their solemn litany, and who will be revealed at the great assize as Judge of quick and dead. Meanwhile, "their witness is in heaven, not a few of their record is on high."[58]

PLANTERS' RETRIBUTION

The insurrection over, yet despite the number of executions, and those murdered for being thought to have involved themselves in the events of the previous four months, many of the planters who having had their crops and property destroyed, believed that a further price needed to be paid to them personally. They wanted, and were determined to provide their own retribution.

So, while those Africans who had not participated in the resistance movement, and had even gone as far as to protect their plantations, were welcomed back, and were allowed to continue in their daily drudgery, for the "guilty" life became increasingly difficult, and ultimately, life threatening. Waddell reported how

---

57. Cornford, *Missionary Reminiscences*, 37.

58. Burchell, *Memoir*, 229. Today we are fortunate that their names and lives are remembered once again, in a memorial near Sam Sharpe's, in Montego Bay, Jamaica.

A Season of Violent Persecution and Resistance (1826–32)

> After the insurrection was suppressed, great confusion and distress prevailed. The people began to suffer more than ever before. The labour was increased, and means of support diminished; over-driving became common, and while many causes combined to coerce them to the utmost of their power, or beyond it, their complaints were nolonger heard. They were under the yoke and the lash, yea, under the wheel, fallen, crushed, abandoned and hopeless. The tale of bricks was increased, and the straw withheld. Defeated, disappointed, and suffering beyond what they had known before, they seemed in most places to give way to despair.[59]

Yet for all that they had been through, and their new added burdens, the planters demonstrated just how tone deaf they were, often being heard to complain to all who would listen, that never before had they seen or owned such a lazy bunch of slaves as they currently had, and it was further stated that they lacked any kind of enthusiasm for the work at hand. Unsurprising, really, given the circumstances, and even Waddell, in response to such grumbling, fearing retribution, responded in his correspondence home, chastising them for expressing what was blindingly obvious to any objective person. He suggested that perhaps the reason for their lethargy was because

> They were half-starved. They had got only fifteen days last year after crop for their provision grounds, and only three or four this year before crop began, and it was now late in the year. How could these poor, hungry people be otherwise than lazy and sulky. Would you or I be any better, working on an empty stomach all day, and little to eat at night.[60]

However, when their lethargy impacted his and the other missionaries church numbers, he too complained, somewhat irrationally, suggesting directly to a people who had seen their prayers seemingly go unanswered, and their labors increased, that

> In that distress we might expect religion would have been their resource for consolation; and, where it really existed, no doubt such was the case. But in themselves, as well as in their condition, appeared a change for the worse, and their improvement for a time was at an end.[61]

Then, compounding his ignorance even further, he surmises that

---

59. Waddell, *Twenty-Nine*, 70.
60. Waddell, *Twenty-Nine*, 74.
61. Waddell, *Twenty-Nine*, 70.

> The wide-spread defection from the profession and piety, over nearly all the disturbed parishes, during the period now under review, shows how empty the profession of it was during the previous period, in the majority of cases, though foolishly dignified, in some quarters, with the name *Pentecostal*.[62]

The enslaved, whose freedom was repeatedly being curtailed, responded forcefully and with one mind, as they expressed their various reasons for not attending church:

> Minister . . . the living we live her is too bad. Our hearts are broken with work and punishment.
> If we don't look for something to eat on Sunday, minister, we must die of hunger. If things ever come better, we will try again.
> It is no use, minister; what can church and prayers do for we again? . . . There is no hope; we will walk after our own devices, and do every one the imagination of his evil heart.[63]

Each of these reasons were simply dismissed by Waddell as excuses, likening them to the children of Israel who "harkened not to Moses, for anguish of spirit and for cruel bondage."[64] In short, he wasn't impressed with their not being able to concentrate on spiritual things, when their bodies were in such pain. His anger also bubbled over towards the planters, who he blamed for their failure to uphold the law of the land, in allowing the enslaved to be able to attend church on a Sunday, thereby preventing him carrying out his spiritual duties to the Crown. Frustrated by both sides' failure to honor the church, missionaries of all persuasions wrote to the House of Assembly, a foolhardy act in fact, given that many of the members of the Assembly were also planter attorneys, and so they got no joy from their many requests. Nevertheless, as the much-sought-after "tranquility" soon returned to the missionaries, they were seen by the enslaved as having had more interest in keeping the law of the land than the laws given by God, which, if adhered to, would have bought them their freedom.

Then suddenly, missionary peace was disturbed when the unlikeliest of saviors, the CofE-led Colonial Church Union (CCU), sought revenge on the missionaries, who they believed had planned and organized the rebellion. By so doing, the CCU inadvertently came to the rescue of the enslaved, who just for a moment could sit on the sidelines, exhale, and watch as

---

62. Waddell, *Twenty-Nine*, 70.
63. Waddell, *Twenty-Nine*, 70, 71, 74.
64. Waddell, *Twenty-Nine*, 71.

nonconformist missionaries of all persuasions scattered everywhere in fear for their lives as the boot was suddenly on the other foot. How the missionaries fared, and how the CCU involuntarily caused the demise of slavery so that its actions became the final nail in its coffin, is a story that in and of itself has to be told, as the enslaved were the last people on either of their minds, as one church confronted another.

Chapter 8

Church versus Church (1832)

The "war" having begun against the EBS, the Jamaican Assembly and the established church, the CofE, looked to consolidate their position by looking for someone or something other than themselves to blame for the acts of insurrection. They soon identified it to be all those who called themselves missionaries, primarily the Baptists, and all who could be identified as being in sympathy with the Baptist cause. However, the Baptist missionaries were not going to take it sitting down.

It now became a matter of church fighting church, the established church of England against the dissenters. What was once a respectable private battle was now being brought into the public domain for all the world to see. Seemingly only one group could win, and while the CofE had the leaders of Jamaican society, judges, magistrates, legislators, and the militia, on their side, what did the Baptists have, especially as they were not political animals, and since they had taken a vow not to involve themselves in the politics of the island? Yet as we shall see, a solution was found which neither side could have predicted.

THE COLONIAL CHURCH UNION

On January 26, 1832, at Saint Ann's Bay, what has since been described as "the most extraordinary Associations ever formed by civilized men in a Christian land"[1] was formed, led by the CofE. The Colonial Church Union (CCU) was established

1. Tucker, *Glorious Liberty*, 26.

> To resist by all constitutional means, the encroachments of their enemies ... to get rid of the rook you must destroy their nests.[2]

The CCU consisted of a group of like-minded white people who came primarily from the leading figures of Jamaican society, the militia, legal profession, the plantocracy, and other significant leaders, but their leadership fell primarily to members of the CofE. Members were required to pay twenty shillings to assist with its establishment, and in order to justify their actions, they undertook the following activities:

> Several companies of the militia, consisting of whites, coloured, and blacks, were called together in the Court-house; when Captain Walker came forward with a paper in his hand, which he read to them, and wished to know if they would all agree to. This paper contained nothing less than a proposal to send off the island every Dissenting Preacher, of every colour; but its meaning was expressed in "such high buckra language," that scarcely one of the blacks, and very few of the coloured men understood it ... one or two coloured men, who understood the matter, declared they never would agree to such a measure; but the majority of the others fell in with it, and consequently the proposal was said to be carried.[3]

Encouraged by this, they then circulated the following statement about an hour later:

> In furtherance of the object of this meeting, the following paper was placarded at several places on the Bay, and printed in some of the island Journals: "Inhabitants of Jamaica! Your danger is great! If you have discovered the source of your disease, lose not a moment in expelling the poison from your veins. Rally round your Church and Kirk, before it is too late, and defend yourselves from all who attack them: the preservation of your wives, your children, your properties, your house, nay, of your very lives, demands it. A Colonial Church Union is all you want to unite the friends of the colony in a defence which must then succeed."[4]

Their aim was threefold:

1. To present a general petition to the Legislature for the expulsion of all sectarian missionaries.

---

2. Parry et al., *Short History*, 159.
3. Parry et al., *Short History*, 95.
4. Parry et al., *Short History*, 95.

2. To prevent the dissemination of any religious doctrines at variance with those of the English and Scottish Churches.
3. To exhibit in their true light the arts which had been used to bring ruin and devastation on Jamaica by publishing an authentic account of the late rebellion.[5]

As the commonly held wisdom of the day was that illiterate Africans could not possibly have planned, organized, and carried out such a daring, though limited, island-wide revolution, it must have needed leadership from some very sound heads, namely their ministers or white and mulatto brethren. Then as the majority of the "rebels" were "proved" to be Baptists, it was agreed that all of the troublesome Baptist ministers must be arrested, tried for treason, and put to death, as well as any other sympathetic missionaries who may also have been involved.

Each denomination was therefore summarily investigated, and challenged to not only prove that they were not a part of the insurrectionist plot, but also most importantly that they were in total agreement with CCU beliefs, and this they could easily prove by joining the movement. Those who refused, and were found guilty, either lost their license to preach, were threatened with being tarred and feathered, or, in the most extreme of cases, had their parsonages and their chapels destroyed, while they themselves were to be executed.[6]

So, for the very first time not only were the African Baptists being subjected to violence and intimidation, but their white counterparts were also, to the point where they were prevented from holding services, and other religious meetings. The CCU therefore took it upon themselves, proclaiming that rebellious Africans had confesses that:

> Certain persons—white persons too, called ministers of religions, [told] them that they were to be free after Christmas, or at the beginning of the year, and that after that period, they were to work nolonger for their masters! Could they be ministers of God, of religion or friends of the human race who would tell them a falsehood?[7]

Baptist missionaries were therefore labelled as agitators, who, "set the negroes to burn and destroy the whole country, and drive all the inhabitants

---

5. Tucker, *Glorious Liberty*, 26.
6. See Appendix 10 for examples of chapels, monuments, and gravestones of the period.
7. Baptist Missionaries, *Narrative*, 63.

into the sea!"[8] They in turn tried to argue that simply because their stations of operation coincided with many of the areas where the resistance had been at its most volatile, did not mean that they were to blame. Now, while it was true that they were able to deny all knowledge of the details of the insurrection, it was nevertheless also true that they were aware that such an event was going to take place. Knibb himself, having had a conversation with Sam Sharpe in October 1831, was also made aware of the events to come by a fellow missionary on December 26, 1831.

Despite their stringent denials, Baptist ministers were rounded up and imprisoned, and charged with being the inspirers and authors of the insurrection. Knibb himself was arrested and kept in prison from January 2, until January 4, 1832. Investigations against him being stopped when, his friend, the Custos, Richard Barrett, having apprehended Thomas Burchell on a ship returning to Jamaica from England, found in his possession, a letter from Knibb which in their eyes, exonerated him:

> There was a letter written by Mr Knibb to Mr B., while in England, clearly stating his views of slavery, and that it was his opinion that persons holding such sentiments could not be permitted to remain in a slave colony.[9]

Being able to return home, it was then on February 14, 1832 that Knibb was finally declared innocent of all charges.

Burchell on the other hand, having departed for England due to ill health, well before the insurrection began on July 9, 1831, was returning well after it had concluded on January 7, 1832, when he was nevertheless arrested as his ship, the Garland Grove, was about to dock in Montego Bay. The captain of the naval frigate, H.M.S. Blanche, transferred him to his vessel; having told him that the island was under martial law, Burchell's property was searched, and he interrogated, and surely his sentiments on the "infernal system" known as slavery would have been easily deduced. He was then transferred back to the Garland Grove, where he was kept as a prisoner until February 10, 1832.

Burchell was then falsely accused by a free colored man, named Samuel Stennet, of instigating talk of freedom within his church. Stennet, however, soon confessed that his testimony had been a lie, but Burchell, the pastor of Baptist leader of the resistance, was kept in prison until March 14, 1832. He was eventually released, as stated previously, when Sam Sharpe gave himself up, choosing to lay down his life for his pastor, rather than have

---

8. Baptist Missionaries, *Narrative*, 102.
9. Hinton, *Memoir*, 123.

Burchell executed for a crime which he had not committed. Burchell was nevertheless advised to take himself and his family off the island, for fear of their lives. So, shortly after he arrived, he was traveling again, this time on a ship to America.

At the same time as missionaries were being persecuted, the CCU's public opposition began with the shouting of abuse, which soon escalated into the destruction of property. They were, it seems, determined to destroy their homes, and so galvanized, by the great support which they had received, mobs came together, and embarked on a period of destruction, following the lead of one Dr. Lawson who:

> From February 5 Dr Lawson, the younger "was going about, endeavouring to form a mob, for the destruction of the Baptist Chapel in Montego Bay" . . . the principal *actors* were eleven magistrates, and numerous officers of the militia.[10]

Between the 7 and 15 February 1832, chapels began to burn. In each instance actions were justified by accusations made against frightened missionaries and their families. In fact, such was the anger of the CCU that many missionaries were forced to flee burning buildings, as well as hordes of angry and violent antagonists with drawn swords. The mob gathered, and the destruction of the Baptist chapels began with the burning down of the three most significant chapels during the war: Montego Bay, Falmouth, and Salter's Hill. The first, "Salter's Hill, eight miles from Montego Bay was attacked by a party of the Saint James's militia."[11] Knibb's chapel in Falmouth, which they called "that pestilential hole, Knibb's preaching shop,"[12] followed, with the days' action completed with the destruction of Burchell's church in Montego Bay. Of the burning of the Montego Bay chapel and the action which followed, it was reported that

> By two o'clock that large building was razed to the ground. . . . The missionaries then received information, from several sources, that an attack was meditated on their persons and lodgings. . . . Mr John Coates, Justice of the Peace, had said "he would not be in one of those missionaries skins tonight, on any account!"[13]

Coincidentally, John Coates was one of the three Justices of the Peace who presided over the trial and sentencing to death of Sam Sharpe. So, led by such a "hero" of the plantocracy, events progressed quickly, so that over

10. Baptist Missionaries, *Narrative*, 59.
11. Tucker, *Glorious Liberty*, 27.
12. Parry et al., *Short History*, 159.
13. Baptist Missionaries, *Narrative*, 59.

the next eight days, ten more chapels were either destroyed or severely damaged. Stewart Town was partially pulled down, Brown's Town was pulled down, as was Lucea, and Savanna-La-Mar. Fuller's field (Ridgeland) was burnt down, as was Saint Ann's Bay, Green Island, Ebony at Hayes, Savanna in Vere, and the chapel in Rio Bueno.

The attack on Baptist and other nonconformist ministers was intense, as exemplified by the experiences of the Rev. and Mrs. Nichols. Nichols was at home with his wife, infant child, female servant, and two other children, when their home which was attached to the chapel at Saint Ann's Bay was attacked. The story is told how

> At ten at night, just when Mr and Mrs Nichols were retiring, there came a violent knocking at the chapel door. After a few blows the door gave way, when a number of people entered, and immediately began to dash to pieces the windows and pews. Every window but one was smashed, and the broken bits of the pews were hurled out into the yard. Mr and Mrs Nichols, with their little children, were in a room only separated from the chapel by a thin partition. Mr Nichols shouted for help, and a resident who was a magistrate fetched out men from the main guard, before whom the rioters dispersed. It is mentioned as a curious circumstance that, though the soldiers who quelled the disturbance had their guns with them not one of these was loaded, nor had they brought any cartridges.[14]

Vigilantes at the same time intimidated and attacked Baptist congregations and their places of worship in the interior. In Saint Thomas in the Vale for example, it was reported that

> During the excitement of the insurrection of 1832, the people met together in peril of life; the huts in which they assembled were destroyed, many were severely flogged for daring to pray, and the chapel which had been erected was set on fire.[15]

Houses too were broken into, and nightly people were under threat of violence which included the threat of being "tarred and feathered." The oppressors were no respecter of persons, as can be seen in the following stories regarding two female Baptist members. The first incident happened to a poor woman in Savanna-la-Mar, where

> On the night of the attack, 8th August, when driven from Mr Kingdon's lodgings, she was obliged to flee to the morass behind

14. Tucker, *Glorious Liberty*, 27.
15. Underhill, *West Indies*, 249.

the back street of Savanna-la-Mar. While running through from the yard shots were fired at her and others, they being pointed out to the rioters—she went from one house to another, secreting herself till the morning. On September 4th, the party who had been that day committed to gaol, for assaulting Mr Case, and had been let out in the evening, hunted about for her and others, to tar them—she was forced to hide at Mr Deleon's for three days . . . [then] on Friday night the 7th . . . she must leave his house, as he was unable to protect her. . . . She then went into an out-house, and the rioters afterwards broke into Mr Deleon's negro houses, and searched for her . . . the next morning, at four o'clock she went barefoot through a morass to a distance of three miles. . . . On the 20th September she saw Mr Medley, one of the rioters, in the back street, who said, "This night every one of the Baptist houses shall be set on fire, for we'll burn them out."[16]

The second incident took place in Stewart Town, and concerned a Mrs. Case:

> Captain Andrew Drummond, Mr Scott and Lieutenant Fearon, of the Clarendon Regiment, lodged at the house of Mrs Case of Stewart Town in the parish of Trelawney, during Martial Law. When they were about to quit, she brought forward her bill. Adjutant Thompson received it, and said, "You need not think that I will pay this bill." Mrs Case asked the reason: and Mr Thompson replied, "Because you are a Baptist. I would rather give £10 to anyone who is not praying, than 10d to one that is." She was therefore not paid, nor are we aware that she has been paid since.[17]

Such were the experiences of all who called themselves Baptists, and when the missionaries sought redress for the actions taken against them, the response led by the planters were several, but all contemptible. A flavor of their contempt can be seen in the following responses:

> When you look around you, and see the devastation that has been occasioned by your pernicious doctrines, if you had the feelings of men, you would not be able to hold up your heads.[18] Joseph Bowen, another Justice of the Peace [had] said, "he would destroy any person's house who dared to give a night's shelter to any of them."[19]

---

16. Baptist Missionaries, *Narrative*, 146.
17. Baptist Missionaries, *Narrative*, 129–30.
18. Baptist Missionaries, *Narrative*, 57.
19. Baptist Missionaries, *Narrative*, 59.

Knibb, Whitehorne, Burchell, Abbot, and Gardner nevertheless petitioned the governnor of Jamaica, Somerset Lowry, Earl of Belmore, for justice, seeking protection as "British subjects, devotedly attached to their gracious Sovereign and his government."[20] Lowry in return issued the following proclamation on 13 February 1832:

A Proclamation

> By His Excellency the Right Honourable Somerset Lowry, Earl of Belmore, Captain General and Governor-in-Chief of this His Majesty's Island of Jamaica, and the Territories thereon depending in America.
>
> Whereas I have received information that several Chapels and Places of Worship, belonging to the Sect called Baptists, situated in the towns of Falmouth, Montego Bay, Lucea, and Savanna-la-Mar, have been wantonly and illegally destroyed by riotous assemblage of People: And whereas such proceedings are disgraceful to the Colony, subversive of order, and of dangerous example: I do hereby call on all Custodes of Parishes and all Magistrates to seek out and discover the authors of these outrages, that they may be punished according to the authors of these outrages, that they may be punished according to Law: And I also require and enjoin the said Custodes and Magistrates, to employ the whole force which the Constitution has entrusted them, in protecting property of every description, whether belonging to private persons, or Religious Societies, in quelling all disorderly Meetings, and in bringing to exemplary punishment every disturber of the Public Peace.
>
> Given under the hand and seal at arms, at Montego Bay, this thirteenth day of February, in the second year of His Majesty's reign, Aunoque Domini, One Thousand Eight Hundred and Thirty-Two.
>
> Belmore.[21]

Despite Belmore emphasizing that this proclamation was sent in the name of the king whose island Jamaica was, the CCU in response simply held a further meeting on February 15, and passed two additional resolutions, "one of which was to bind themselves to support and protect the chapel breakers"[22] and the second was to bind themselves, by agreeing that "Who-

---

20. Baptist Missionaries, *Narrative*, Appendix 1 (2), 2.
21. Baptist Missionaries, *Narrative*, Appendix 1 (3), 3.
22. Clarke, *Memorials of Baptist Missionaries*, 128.

ever gives information respecting the above, shall entitle himself to be tarred and feathered!"[23] They then went on the offensive seeking to find ways

> To prevent hereafter a re-introduction of the Baptist sect into this parish and to recommend our Representatives to use their exertions in the Honourable House of Assembly, to expel them from the island.[24]

At this same meeting, which was held at the Montego Bay Court-house it is reported that

> Mr Gray (Senior Magistrate) said, alluding to the destruction of the Baptist Chapel, "he regretted he was not present at the time as he would have joined heart and hand, with his fellow parishioners, in destroying it." Mr Coates spoke to the following effect. "That they (the meeting) must get rid of the Baptists; that they must petition the Honourable House of Assembly, and if petition would not do, they must use other measures for expelling them; that the voice of the people was for expelling them, *and the voice of the people was above any law*; that they must make laws of their own; and that they (the people) would not be at rest until all the Baptists were sent off the island.[25]

These were clearly dangerous times. The enslaved were used to being persecuted and threatened with death, both night and day, but for the missionaries, this was clearly a new experience. Fortunately, while many Baptists and other missionaries were arrested, charged and threatened with death, none were in fact injured during this period. The nearest any of them had come was Thomas Burchell, who as he prepared to pack and leave Jamaica, was re-arrested on January 11, with the sole intention being, that he would be murdered by members of the CCU. In fact, such was the reality of this, that it was said that:

> Mrs Burchell, who was left on board, with Mr and Mrs Dendy, was sorely broken with grief: fully expecting, from all that she had heard that her husband, would be murdered, immediately on reaching the shore.[26]

---

23. Baptist Missionaries, *Narrative*, 62.
24. Baptist Missionaries, *Narrative*, 63.
25. Baptist Missionaries, *Narrative*, 63.
26. Dillon, *Centennial Review*, 14.

However, what they may have meant for bad turned into triumph as he was rescued by a group of colored people. He described how shocked he was at the level of hatred towards him, when:

> On landing, the most ferocious and savage spirit was manifested, by some of (what are called) the most respectable white inhabitants, that ever could have occurred amongst civilized society. They began to throng around me: hissing, groaning, and gnashing at me with their teeth—some with water in their mouths to spit upon me. Had I never been at Montego Bay before, I must have supposed myself, among cannibals, or in the midst, of the savage hordes of Siberia; or the uncultivated and uncivilized tribes, of Central Africa. Some cried out, "Have his blood"; others "Shoot him," others "Hang him." But as they attempted to approach, several coloured persons surrounded me, and dared them to touch me; and I am fully persuaded, had it not been for the protection afforded me, persuaded, had it not been for the protection afforded me, by the coloured part of the population, natives of Jamaica, I should have been barbarously murdered,—yea, torn limb from limb, by my country men,— yea by *enlightened! respectable! Christian Britons!!!*[27]

Things being so out of control the missionaries petitioned the new governnor of the island, the Earl of Musgrave, requesting that their right to preach the gospel be restored. In response, having anticipated this need, he issued a proclamation which was to be placed across the island. In it he

> Called on all custodes of parishes and justices of the peace to seek out and discover the authors of such outrages, in order to their being punished.[28]

The proclamation was promptly torn down and ignored, the CCU issuing their own proclamation in response stating that "Whosoever gives information respecting the above, shall entitle himself to be tarred and feathered!"[29] This was followed up with a notice of their own being placed directly beneath one of the proclamations. It was a clear and unapologetic threat to all who presumed to think like Thomas Burchell:

---

27. Dillon, *Centennial Review*, 14.
28. Burchell, *Memoir*, 207.
29. Burchell, *Memoir*, 207.

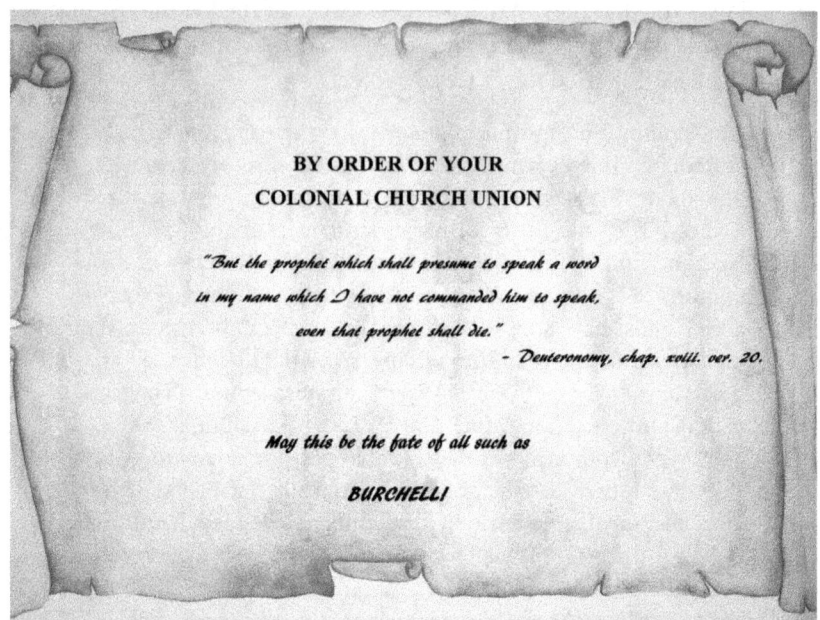

Warning: By order of your Colonial Church Union. Redesigned by D. Morrison.[30]

Ultimately, it was an edict issued by the King of England calling for the disbanding of the CCU which brought the whole sorry episode to a head when suddenly members if the CCU found themselves in a similar position to those whom they had for so long persecuted. They in response threatened to claim their independence from Britain, in the same or a similar fashion to that done over fifty years earlier, by their brethren in America. A statement of intent was published in the *Jamaica Courant* on March 3, 1831 calling upon its members to:

> Let us petition the Assembly . . . to place our own clergy under our own control, and that of our representatives in vestry, even to the expulsion of those missionaries and curates who are still here, paid by, and under the influence of, our enemies, and who have already been detected in their vile vocation. The old church government and discipline was better than the present—*let then the old laws revive.* The episcopal government has here been an experiment, which has failed; for under it sectarianism came with that system; *let them expire together.* We have lately seen the danger of trusting our people to the instruction of those who

30. Burchell, *Memoir*, 208.

are not under our own control; let us, therefore, henceforward, hold the purse and power in our own hands.[31]

In so doing, the CCU by their actions had finally caused the BMS and the enslaved to be united as one in their opposition to the CofE led plantocracy. Now, while the enslaved could not change their circumstances or fight back, the missionaries believed that they still had one more card to play. They would ultimately petition the British Parliament, asking them to pass legislation to end slavery once and for all, thereby bringing the power of the plantocracy to an end, while at the same time saving the Christian witness on the island and removing a very real threat to their own lives, and of course preserving the loss of this most valuable slave colony. The enslaved were not their main consideration. However, this would demand a change in direction on the part of the BMS Committee back in England, agreeing to involve themselves in the politics of the island. Would they be amenable to such a change? What might the Baptist response be? Well, reliant upon the word of God, they soon discovered that "All things are possible, to him who believes,"[32] as we shall now see.

THE BMS RESPONDS

I think it would be fair to say that the early beginnings of the BMS missionary work in Jamaica was in the main uneventful on their part, and seemed at times to be less than sympathetic to the plight of the enslaved African, beyond that of seeking their salvation. The missionaries for the most part never strayed away from the remit given to them by the Committee, "Not to interfere with politics, but simply to preach the Gospel of Christ."[33] However, they petitioned the BMS committee for a way forward, and a way forward was found in private correspondence sent by William Carey to John Ryland. From the letter it is now clear that not only did Carey have a hand in forming the remit under which the missionaries were to operate in Jamaica, but he also indicated a proviso, detailing under what circumstance they could actively engage in politics. He said,

> I hope the failure of the African Mission will teach us more and more, though we have made it a point to avoid every word or action that looks like intermeddling with politics. We have no disposition to do it and if we were at all dissatisfied (which we

---

31. Hinton, *Memoir*, 136.
32. Mark 9:23 (SFLB).
33. Baptist Missionaries, *Narrative*, vii.

are not) yet it is a matter of conscience with me to be submissive to the powers that are for the time being; so that let my opinions about the best mode of government be what they might: yet the Bible teaches me to act as a peaceful subject, under the government which is established where providence has placed me, provided that Government does not interfere in religious matters so as to constrain my conscience.[34]

Carey had clearly stated that non-interference was agreeable, "provided that government does not interfere in religious matters," and now through the actions of the planters, servants of the Crown, they clearly had in the eyes of the BMS. This gave them the "green light" as it were, to believe that they could "fight" fire with fire, for the spiritual freedom of the people of Jamaica, for

> The issue was no longer whether or not religious instruction should be given but whether the system which prevented religious instruction being given should be destroyed.[35]

As the BMS missionaries began to examine themselves, John Clarke commented somewhat regretfully of the years past in which slavery had been ignored by the majority of them, asking

> Was Lee Compere before his time in his hatred of slavery and was this the real reason for his leaving the work of the BMS.[36]

A meeting was then held in Spanish Town, in 1832, at which time they resolved to do something about the repression of nonconformist missionaries on the island. Their rationale according to Hinton was that, having been influenced by the thoughts of Knibb:

> Hitherto they had gone, as their instructions from home prescribed, on the principle of saying nothing about slavery, and of doing all they could consistently do to conciliate the planters; but when they found that the planters could not be reconciled at all to the efficient religious instruction of the slaves, but that, for the sake of maintaining the system of slavery intact, they would violently expel Christianity, they declared hostility against slavery itself, and resolved to identify themselves with those who had long been seeking its abolition. Knibb's resolution was then taken, never to rest till he saw this object achieved . . . the

---

34. Russell, "Missionary Outreach," 28.
35. Parry et al., *Short History*, 159.
36. Catherall, "Bristol College," 297.

missionaries were in deliberation on the propriety and necessity of sending one or two of their number to England, to plead their cause with the British public.[37]

William Knibb. Photograph courtesy of D. Morrison

The Elevation of William Knibb

Decision made; it was then a question of who should they send? Who could both represent the missionaries and the enslaved Africans case? At this time there were actually three main strands of Baptists on the island. There were those who followed Parson Killick, the inheritor of Lisle's mantel, who still had the largest group of Baptist on the island, Thomas Burchell, the most beloved of the missionaries, by Africans residing under the BMS umbrella, and William Knibb, popular amongst his colleagues, other missionaries on the island, the legislature, the BMS Committee and a small but significant number of Africans who had refused, under his command to join the resistance movement.

Parson Killick stands as a reminder of the fact that the work of the EBS did not in fact cease at the death of Lisle, or with the arrival of the BMS. They continued to "draw" converts to Jesus Christ, and away from the BMS whose style of worship was more formal than they had been used to. Killick was baptized by Lisle in 1801, ordained by him in 1811, and then received his mantel, becoming the minister of Windward Road Chapel, whose name

37. Hinton, *Memoir*, 13637.

he changed to the Independent Baptist Chapel in 1828, upon the death of Lisle. BMS missionary testimonies speak of his having had chapels not just in Kingston, but Spanish Town, Saint David's at Bethany and across the whole of the parish of Saint Thomas in the East where he was for a considerable time, the sole minister there. However, Killick was in reality never going to be considered as a messenger for them all, he, having thus far having never received any kind of olive branch from the BMS signaling that they wanted to include the EBS or any of the other independent Baptist groups which had sprung up since the death of Lisle and his other leaders, in events going forward.

Burchell, on the other hand, while the most popular of all the missionaries amongst the enslaved population, and having been the pastor of Sam Sharpe, together with having the second largest BMS congregation,[38] being a poor public speaker with health issues gave him little chance of being seen as the lead missionary, able to adequately represent the BMS to the government in England. Who they were therefore left with was the eloquent William Knibb, who was seemingly popular amongst his colleagues, the plantocracy, and those whom he pastored. Unsurprisingly then, he was chosen to go, the meeting deciding that

> Considering the present distressed state of our mission, the impossibility of occupying several of our stations, the consequent redundancy of missionaries, and the manifest improbability of obtaining redress here, we deem it expedient, for the just representations of our wrongs, and the advancement of the society's funds, that one of our brethren be appointed as a deputation to proceed forthwith to England, to act under the direction of the committee; and that brother Knibb, on account of his intimate acquaintance with the mission in the disturbed part of the island, and his knowledge of circumstances immediately connected with the rebellion, be appointed for that purpose.[39]

While Knibb had supporters across all mission groups, as well as Thomas Burchell, he had little support amongst the wider African population, who may nevertheless because of their love for Burchell have given him a second chance; one which he truly needed, based on his attitude towards them prior to the insurrection. He was known to have repeatedly chastised them and all who would listen, for believing that they could soon be free.

---

38. Baptist Missionaries, *Narrative*, 20. In a report on the state of the churches in April 1831, Burchell's congregation at Montego Bay consisted of 1572 members, while East Queen Street had 2937 members.

39. Hinton, *Memoir*, 138.

Knibb had earnestly encouraged members to desist from any rebellious actions, even going as far as to admonish them when he preached at the opening of Crooked Spring Chapel, (renamed Salter's Hill), on December 27, 1831, just hours before the rebellion began, stating:

> My dear hearers and especially those of you who constantly attend at the chapel, and are members of Crooked Spring, or other Baptist churches, pay great attention to what I am about to say. It is now seven years since I left England to preach the gospel to you; and when I came, I made up my mind to live and die to promote your spiritual welfare. Never did I enter the pulpit with such painful feelings as at present. Till yesterday I had hoped that God had blessed my poor labours, and the labours of your dear minister, now in England for his health, who loves you and prays for you and who tells me that he hopes soon to return to you. But I am pained to the soul to hear that many of you have agreed not to go to your work after Christmas; and I fear it is too true. I learn that some wicked persons have persuaded you that the King has made you free. Hear me, I love your souls—I would not tell you a lie for the world. What you have been told is false—false as hell can make it. I entreat you not to believe it, but to go to your work as usual. If you have any love to Jesus Christ, to religion, to your ministers, to those kind friends in England who have given money to help you to build this chapel, be not led away by wicked men. You are too ready to listen to and believe what they tell you, instead of coming to your minister, who you know will tell you the truth. God commands you to be obedient to your master; if you do as he commands, you may expect his blessing, but if you do not, he will call you to an account for it at the Judgement Day. If you refuse to work, and are punished, you will suffer justly; and every friend you have must and will turn his back upon you.[40]

Then, once the rebellion was underway, Knibb not only undertook a spell in the king's militia, but he also contrived to encourage his members to bring to court the offenders, as the following incident recalls:

> When three slaves from Green Park estate, named Joseph Henry, James Virgo and Lewis Atherton, members of the Falmouth church, brought down from York two rebels, whom they had captured while attempting to burn Green Park—Henry and Virgo went to Mr Knibb, and related this circumstance; stating that the magistrates had rewarded them with a doubloon, and

---

40. Baptist Missionaries, *Narrative*, 29.

given them a pair of handcuffs, with authority to go and do the like again if necessary. They asked him whether they had done right, as they had been taunted for taking up their own colour, by some irreligious negroes, who said they did it for money. Mr Knibb commended their conduct, and strongly urged them to go on defending their master's property, and capture as many rebels as they could.[41]

Knibb then continued to preach obedience from such texts as Col 3:22–25, reminding them of the obedience of servants to their masters.[42] While his words may have succeeded in influencing many to withdraw from the rebellion, he at the same time had irritated the majority of enslaved peoples to such an extent that it is said that after hearing him speak at Salter's Hill on December 31, 1832:

> The hearers generally were displeased with it. Some of them said that the white people had bribed him not to tell the truth, "Minister never said a word about freedom before; why does he come and talk to us about freedom now? The white people must have bribed him to it." The members of his own church, however, gave him credit; but one of them said to him at a later period, that "If minister had not been so urgent, he really should have believed, from the conversation of the planters and the slaves, that freedom was come."[43]

Finally, it was known that Knibb was one of the two ministers who interviewed the imprisoned Sam Sharpe on behalf of the Jamaican legislature. Perhaps knowing that he would not lie to a minister, Knibb was able to confirm that Sharpe had indeed been the leader of the resistance. Of that event, Knibb testifying to the House of Lords Slavery Committee recalled that

> I said, "Sharp, now tell me, that is a good man, just how you did at Retrieve." . . . And Sharp said, "I was the first man who took the oath. We had the Bible brought." . . . I got up before them, and took the bible in my right hand, and I said, "if ever I witness against my

---

41. Baptist Missionaries, *Narrative*, 30.
42. The SFLB states, "Bondservants, obey in all things your masters according to the flesh, not with eye service, as men-pleasers, but in sincerity, of heart, fearing God. And whatever you do, do it heartily, as to the Lord and not to men, knowing that from the Lord you will receive the reward of the inheritance, for you serve the Lord Christ. But he who does wrong will be repaid for what he has done, and there is no partiality."
43. Hinton, *Memoir*, 118.

brothers and sisters anything connected with this matter, may hell be my portion," and the whole of the rest did the same.[44]

While Sharpe never broke his promise and kept silent as to who his fellow "conspirators" were, Knibb on the other hand, was seen to be assisting in condemning to death, of the "champion" of the enslaved and a much loved and respected Baptist leader.

Yet, only months later, having read the caveat from Carey, Knibb agreed to work against the injustices meted out to his church members. Injustices which were in fact typical of the persecutions all of the enslaved had had to endure in simply trying to live, and in many instances, worship God. He recalled how

> An excellent young man of the name Sam Swiney, a deacon of my church in this place, is now in chains for his love to Jesus. During my sickness he and others, both bond and free, met at my house to pray. Information of this was carried to the magistrates; and though I procured three respectable persons, neighbours, including the head constable, to prove on oath that no noise was made, which the informer had sworn to, the poor fellow was convicted. The magistrate would have it that preaching and praying were the same. I tried to convince him of the difference, but it was of no use; so for offering a prayer to God, and nothing more, this poor fellow is sentenced to receive twenty lashes on his bare back, and to be worked in chains on the roads for a fortnight. I did all I could to save him, and so did his owner, a respectable gentleman of colour (Mr Aaron de Leon), who told the magistrates that he had his permission. Next morning I went to see him flogged, determined to support him as well as I could, however painful to my feelings. There he was, a respectable tradesman though a slave, stretched indecently on the ground, held firmly down by four slaves, two at his hands and two at his feet. The driver was merciful, or every lash would have fetched blood. "Oh, what have I done?" was the only exclamation that escaped from his lips, accompanied by a moan extorted by the pain. He was raised from the ground, chained to a convict, and immediately sent to work. I walked by his side down the whole bay (Savanna-la-Mar), to the no small annoyance of his persecutors. Amidst them I took him by the hand, told him to be of good cheer, and said, loud enough for them all to hear, "Sam, whatever you want, send to me and you shall have it." The good people here have behaved nobly to him,

---

44. Miles, *Second Letter*, 112.

encouraging him by every means in their power; I shall see that he wants for nothing, and by my public notice of him show that I consider him a persecuted Christian.[45]

Then when accused of planning the insurrection Knibb was reminded how, even the "respectable God-fearing gentlemen" who had once befriended him, soon showed themselves to be a part of the opposition rallying against him and his colleagues. Mr. Roby was one such "friend" who admonished he and his comrades thus:

> [He] informed them that very great prejudice existed against them, because many of the rebels who had been taken were Baptists. He observed, that many charged the missionaries with having intentionally excited the slaves to rebellion; but he thought they were innocent in intention, though he believed, that by an injudicious selection of texts, (such as fight the good fight of faith. If the son make you free, ye shall be free indeed, &c) and by dealing too much in the abstruse of mischief, and had misled the slaves. He let the missionaries know, that as Sectarians he "most cordially hated them," for that he was "a staunch churchman"—that his love of justice constrained him to interfere on their behalf—that popular clamour ran very high against them.[46]

Knibb was also reminded of how he was the subject of many personal attacks:

> On the Lords' Day, January 8th, public worship being impracticable, the missionaries assembled the family of the house in which they lodged, for a devotional exercise; the whole company, including themselves and their servants, consisting of twelve to fifteen persons. In addition to prayer, a sermon was read, and they ventured to sing a hymn or two. But this quiet and peaceable attempt to keep holy the Sabbath day was not allowed to pass, without an effort to make it a punishable act. For on Tuesday the 10th Mr Roby received a message from Major Coates, by a constable, requiring him to produce the missionaries at the Court-house . . . for what purpose he knew not. . . . Major Coates told them, he had received information that Mr Knibb had been preaching to a large concourse of negroes on Sunday morning in the house at Jackson Town, and it was not licensed![47]

---

45. Miles, *Second Letter*, 95–96.
46. Baptist Missionaries, *Narrative*, 52.
47. Baptist Missionaries, *Narrative*, 54–55.

It therefore made sense to him that he could now be the one to lead the opposition to the planters. He therefore accepted the commission to go to England and together with Thomas Burchell, "Plead the cause of the slaves, and of Christian Missions in the West Indies, more especially in Jamaica."[48] Yet there were many missionary voices at that time, from all denominations who stated that Knibb believed that this could be achieved, not simply by garnering support in England, but by utilizing the dissatisfaction amongst some of the enslaved, who he knew wanted physical freedom and were growing increasingly dissatisfied with the mundanity of their enslavement. Historian J. R. Ward noted that

> The management of Creoles was becoming more difficult, especially when they received menial tasks. Among the field men at Good Hope in 1804 nine of the thirty-eight Creoles, but only one of the sixty-six Africans, were considered to be "lazy," "indolent," or habitual runaways.[49]

The planters it would seem, had been hoped that the enslaved creoles would have been content with being a buffer between the plantation owners, and the Africans. However, they wanted to be no man's "slave" or proxy, and were more than happy to become central players in the resistance movement. The missionaries, including Knibb, therefore understood, especially after the disturbances, that the creoles' desire for physical freedom could be manipulated and utilized for the cause of religious freedom on the island. So, on April 26, 1832 began a journey which in the eyes of many did not only see Knibb become the completer of his brother's task, but also, in part, that of George Lisle and the EBS.

This was the beginning of the elevation of William Knibb. He became a man on a mission, and toured churches in England in order to gain support for the preservation of religion, by speaking out against the religious persecution of his congregants, caused by the evil that was slavery. He frequently preached from Exod 7:16, "Let my people go, that they may serve me" (SFLB). At the same time he wrote letters to the enslaved, expressing how hard he was working for their freedom, while at no time mentioning that he was not pursuing their physical freedom as a human right given by God, and had no interest in changing their status as "slaves." However, their support enabled him to say to his supporters in England that he did in fact represent the enslaved peoples of Jamaica, whose desire was to be set free in order to serve God. By so doing Knibb could realistically garner support for

---

48. Dillon, *Centennial Review*, 21.
49. Ward, *British West Indian Slavery*, 229.

the freedom of the gospel being an established principle on the island, while at the same time believing that it would lead to the planters being driven from the island or at the very least be made powerless.

One of the most significant speeches he gave, was that made to his colleagues. It was perhaps his most defining speech in support of the BMS work in Jamaica and the need to abolish slavery in order to preserve freedom of religion on the island. In it he pleaded,

> I appear as the feeble and unworthy advocate of 20,000 Baptists in Jamaica who have today no places of worship in which to meet, their chapels have been destroyed, and no Sabbaths, and I believe and solemnly avow my belief, that by far the greater part of that twenty thousand will be flogged every time they are found praying. I call upon you all by the sympathies of Jesus, whose mission was, and is, to bind up the broken-hearted, and to proclaim liberty to the captives, and the opening of the prison to them that are bound. O Lord, open the eyes of Christians in England to see the evils of slavery and to banish it forever from the earth.[50]

PARLIAMENT DECIDES

It was fortunate for Knibb and disadvantageous to those of the CofE that long gone were the days when the latter could have simply have looked to their king or queen for support, thereby enabling one or two of their enemies to be locked up in a tower or beheaded. These were the days of the British Parliament being the final arbiters for justice in the British Empire, and fortunately for Knibb the government of Charles Grey as clearly abolitionist.

Such was his impact that he was invited by both the Houses of Parliament to testify. Over a three-day period from July 17 to 19, 1832 he testified before the Committee on the Extinction of Slavery throughout the British Dominions. Two of his recorded conversations highlight his attitude to slavery, and his only desire being the spiritual freedom of the enslaved. Firstly, on his way to the Committee hearing, Knibb entered into a conversation with the Earl of Harewood, wherein the following dialogue ensued, which would seem to many to have been a missed opportunity to speak out against the institution of slavery itself, if that indeed had been his position:

> "Mr Knibb, I have been quite distressed by the account you gave us of what was going on on some of our estates; it has broken my rest. Now, Mr Knibb, you and I differ on some matters; you

50. Holmes, "George Liele," 350.

Church versus Church (1832) 171

are a dissenter and I am a churchman, but I believe you are a Christian, and I trust I am one too. Now be frank with me. Is that the state of things on my estate? If you say it is, I will by the next mail direct the removal of my manager, but he shall never know that it is in consequence of information received from you." Knibb informed his lordship that happily it was not the case on his estate; that his manager was a moral man, and did what he could to promote morality on the estate. "I wish I had known this at the same time with the statement," said the earl, "I should have slept better: but now, Mr Knibb, give me your hand, and make me this promise, that if, when you return, you find anything of the kind going upon my estate you will immediately inform me . . ." Knibb assured his lordship that he should feel it his duty, if he perceived anything of the kind, to inform him.[51]

Knibb then accompanied the earl into the committee room, where he revealed his theological position in regards to slavery. The following is but a short extract of the discussions which took place between Knibb and the Committee:

> What were the doctrines at all bearing on the temporal condition of the black population, which you inculcated?—*I never touched upon the subject in my life.*
>
> In preaching to the slave population, have you not found it very difficult to keep altogether separate spiritual concerns of that black population form their temporal situations?—*It is difficult, but every good man would do it.*
>
> Is it possible, in addressing an unlettered audience, in inculcating the doctrine of the freedom of the faith of Christianity, not to expose yourself to misinterpretation as to temporal freedom, as contrasted with spiritual freedom?—*Whenever I have had the occasion to speak on that subject, I have explained, that when freedom is mentioned in the word of God, it referred to the soul and not to the body; that there were slaves in the times of the apostles as well as at present.*
>
> Did you find it necessary to abstain from quoting particular passages of scripture for the purpose of avoiding the exciting any undue feeling in the mind of the negro on the subject of liberty?—*I thought it my duty so to do.*
>
> As the slaves who can read having access to these scriptures would naturally find passages of that description, did they never come to you to ask you questions on passages of that kind?—*They never did.*

51. Hinton, *Memoir*, 173.

> No inquiries were made with regard to passages of that kind, which occur frequently in the holy scriptures?—*No; whenever we received a member in the church we always enforced the duty of obedience to masters, which would lead them to suppose that we considered slavery quite compatible with Christianity.*
>
> You were understood to say that when you preached the doctrine of spiritual freedom, you always endeavoured by explanation to make the slaves understand that what you said did not apply to freedom as distinguished from slavery?—*I used every effort in my power.*
>
> According to your conscientious belief of the doctrines of Christianity, is it possible that you could preach at all without preaching spiritual freedom?—*No; when it is asked whether we could preach at all, I understand to be meant preach the whole counsel of God; I do not mean to say that we could not preach a single sermon.*
>
> Could you possibly administer religious instruction, so as to make the slave comprehend the pure doctrine of Christianity, without preaching spiritual freedom?—*No.*
>
> In your opinion, would not a Baptist minister in undertaking to instruct slaves, omitting to speak of spiritual freedom, take away an essential part of its doctrine?—*Most certainly.*[52]

This clearly confirms his theological position, and the mission he was sent to achieve. Surprisingly, it was a view which was in sharp contrast to that held by then-British foreign secretary George Canning who, as early as 1826, expressed his view that

> The treatment of the West-India negroes is a stain upon a Christian age, and upon a country professing itself Christian. If the slaves be made acquainted with religion, they must learn that slavery is inconsistent with the Christian religion; and will you shut out religion, in order that you may maintain slavery.[53]

An interesting turn of phrase here that "slavery is inconsistent with the Christian religion." Cannings' argument was that it was either religion or slavery, rather than Knibbs's argument, that it could be both religion and slavery, but not religion and the plantocracy. Clearly Knibbs's beliefs were more in keeping with those held by the slave-owning House of Lords, and at this point were somewhat even more reprehensible than those of the Colonial Legislature, whose representative at least confessed to Parliament that

---

52. Hinton, *Memoir*, 174–75.
53. HC Deb, *Ministerial Proposition*, §1217.

It was right that the people of England should know, that the deputies acting on behalf of the West-India interest went to the full extent of admitting the principle of emancipation. It was right that those who contended for the West-India proprietors should know that the time for emancipation had arrived, though, for his own part, he was not one of those who believed slavery and Christianity to be incompatible with each other. He conceived, however, that emancipation must take place.[54]

It seems that of the major players, only the more liberal House of Commons was truly determined to see the end of the enslavement of Africans. This was an unfortunate turn of events for the enslaved, many of whom had believed that they had found a champion in Knibb. However, the House of Commons parliamentary records tell us that Knibb did not need to convince Parliament as to the need in taking power out of the hands of the plantocracy. On May 14, 1833 when Mr. Secretary Stanley rose to his feet in the House of Commons and led the house in an impassioned argument for the need to finally answer the issue of slavery and emancipation, he stated that despite the cost to Britain's economic concerns both on land and at sea and the past opposition of the Colonial Legislatures who, having failed to legislate for abolition, were now at their most amenable, there was a greater and more priceless consideration which demanded that the Commons interfere and act now, and that was because

> The happiness of the descendants of those for whom I now propose to legislate—that generations yet unborn are to be affected for good or for evil by the course which this House may think proper to adopt.[55]

The Committee had in fact been wrestling with the issue of the emancipation of the enslaved, and retaining control of their colonial enclaves, from as early as 1823 when

> Lord Bathurst forwarded to those islands directly governed by this country certain directions, which pointed out several modifications desirable to be adopted as the ground-work for an altered state of society. They were intended, by a gradual alteration in the domestic habits of the slaves, to bring about the total abolition of slavery, and the conversion of the negroes into free labourers. The main principles were the abolition of Sunday labour and Sunday markets, constituting the sacredness of the

---

54. HC Deb, *Ministerial Plan*, §78.
55. HC Deb, *Ministerial Proposition*, §1194.

marriage contract, the placing of restrictions on the punishment of the slaves, the establishing of Saving Banks, and other regulations calculated to prepare the slave for the station and the performance of those duties and obligations which civilized life imposes. . . . But how were these salutary and humane provisions received by the colonial legislatures in 1824? Without one single exception, they were unanimously rejected by every colony having a legislative assembly of its own.[56]

Parliament then having received the threat of Jamaica, ceding itself from Britain, were clearly annoyed, one parliamentarian going as far as to suggest that

There are three possible modes in which Parliament might deal with the people of Jamaica; first, as I have said, it might crush them by the application of direct force; secondly, it might harass them by fiscal regulations and enactments restraining their navigation; and, thirdly, it may pursue the slow and silent course of temperate, but authoritative admonition.[57]

On hearing of the retaliatory threat against them, negotiations were soon the order of the day. Both parties were encouraged to meet, parliament having threatened fire with fire. A second committee meeting was therefore arranged to take place some sixteen days later, on May 30, 1833, and it was agreed that a delegation of the Colonial Legislature would be invited to attend. Present at that meeting in May was Sir Richard Vyvyan, who voiced the opinions of the Colonial Legislature in Jamaica. He stated that since the passing of the 1823 Reform Bill, they were aggrieved in that they had lost the indirect representation which they had previously had. Since that time, they had been sent missives from parliament, discussing their lives and livelihoods, without them actually being able to be involved in the conversations. They then expressed the belief that the discussion on abolition was the final straw, in that they were being presented with a fait accompli, that slavery was to be abolished and they would in return simply receive a loan in order to establish themselves in other businesses. Vyvyan then had a few choice words and home truths to say to his fellow Parliamentarians. He began,

As this House never did recognize the Resolutions of Parliament in 1823, as this House never did admit the right of the House of Commons to legislate on the internal affairs of Jamaica, even

---

56. HC Deb, *Ministerial Proposition*, §1199.
57. HC Deb, *Ministerial Proposition*, §1200.

when the West-Indies was indirectly represented in Parliament, we never can concede that a House of Commons, which is to exist upon the principle that actual Representation should be the foundation of legislation, can justly claim to legislate over us, their election, by whom in consequence, we are not represented; who are strangers to our condition and interest, and whose attempt to dictate to us would, consequently, upon all their own principles—the principles of their own existence as a legislative body—be tyranny and not legislation. . . . No one could deny . . . that the West-India interest had some reason to complain at being deprived of that indirect Representation which it had enjoyed in that House previous to the passing of the Reform Bill. . . . In fact, it was notorious, that persons connected with the West-India interest could not obtain seats at the last election, unless where they happened to be supported by his Majesty's Government.[58]

So, there you have it. There were in fact two battles going on at the same time regarding Jamaica, and neither directly concerned the enslaved. Knibb was unhappy with the planters who had tried to end his ability to preach, while the planters were equally troubled in that, having taken out patents and contracts with the Crown, now the Crown, through his Parliament, had chosen not to include them in any legislative matters concerning the island since 1823. They were absentee "landlords" who were now removing the "tools" of their trade. What use was there, he argued, of land without the "tools," the enslaved, to work on the land? The Crown's intent was to seemingly make them paupers, with no recourse. He argued that they were not having it. The contracts were being broken and Parliament had to admit that it was their fault. The planters of Jamaica wanted a voice in the matter, and would resist every attempt to leave them homeless and penniless. The events of 1831 and 1832 therefore now seem to have been collateral damage from the anger which had been brewing for over eight years, with the decisions being reached on the place of colonial slavery within the British Empire, the final straw as far as they were concerned. The planters expressed their frustration that the Empire, now rich, was ready to neglect what had been the financial engine which had actually built the wealth of the British Empire. This alone was as much the cause, if not the defining cause of the insurrection, as their agitating on the island against the nonconformist missionaries, who in many ways they could see as doing the Crown's bidding.

So, on being present in parliament, they were determined that the government should understand the true costs of what they were proposing,

58. HC Deb, *Ministerial Plan*, §§114–16.

if they chose to immediately emancipate the enslaved. Vyvyan sought to explain that for them it was not simply about emancipation, as they had accepted that it was coming; rather, it was about the consequences of that emancipation upon themselves and others connected to the trade. In order to clarify the position of those in Jamaica, he read the following letter from Richard Barrett, then-Speaker of the House of Assembly of Jamaica:

> If by emancipation is meant the substitution of a system of free labour, in the room of slavery, which shall secure to the planters the cultivation of their lands, the Committee are to require compensation equivalent to the portion of labour, of which they may be deprived, and to the risk of loss and suffering which so complete a change may bring with it. The Committee are bound to insist, that the expense of an adequate police, and all other costs of the arrangement, shall be defrayed by Government. They are also to protest, in the most decided manner, against any interposition or Parliament in their internal affairs. The Assembly of Jamaica are always ready, on the invitation of the Crown, to discuss the measure of emancipation, compensation being first provided by Parliament, but they will not yield their legislative rights, except to violence, which their confidence in the justice of their fellow-subjects will not permit them to apprehend.[59]

The Jamaican Legislature, having finally been given a seat at the table, demanded consideration, or else there would have no hesitation in defending what they saw as rightfully theirs, even if that included a physical war between them. The Committee was forced to take their threat into consideration, fearing that the loss of Jamaica would lead to other slave colonies following their example. This being acknowledged, the Committee was further reminded that they also needed to take into consideration the dramatic loss of income that not only the planters would suffer, but also other vested interests, particularly those in Britain. He highlighted the fact that

> The interests connected with the West-India islands were numerous and important. Vast numbers of manufacturers were kept in employment throughout all the manufacturing districts, by the demands of the West-India markets. Enormous sums of money were spent by West-India proprietors in England. The shipping interest was greatly involved. . . . There were not less than 1,000 ships of 300 tons each employed in this trade. There were 500 vessels employed in the northern coast trade.[60]

---

59. HC Deb, *Ministerial Plan*, §§121–22.
60. HC Deb, *Ministerial Plan*, §§122, 131.

Suffice it to say that a great deal of thought was then put into reviewing the plans for emancipation. This was not mostly due to the persuasiveness of the argument presented on behalf of the plantocracy, who simply reminded Parliament of the contracts and patronages which they had paid for and received from the Crown. Parliament, in its admission of guilt, could do nothing but acquiesce to a great many of their wishes. The churches on the island therefore had little or no influence in the decision made regarding how and when slave colonies were to end, and the people given their freedom. Their church-versus-church fight paled in comparison to the greater issues which were at stake. The BMS were simply the visible presence of the anger which the planters had towards those whom they considered to be abolitionist sympathizers, and the enslaved—well, they were simply collateral damage, caught in the crossfire. Ultimately, an agreement was reached whereby Parliament, in order to appease the plantocracy (who were rightly frustrated, after years of disinterest, which allowed them to be left alone to undertake whatever brutalities they wished against the enslaved), saw the need to provide reparations in order for slavery to end:

> Parliament granted £300,000 as a loan to assist the planters whose plantations had been destroyed by the slaves. The Sectarians obtained £20,000 to indemnify them for the destruction of property occasioned by the whites. The committee of the House of Assembly, on the subject of the late rebellion, in their report estimate the injury done to property at the sum of £1,154,583; to which is to be added, cost of quelling the rebellion, £161,596. The Baptists, on the other hand, estimate the loss occasioned by the demolition of their chapels by the militia and church colonial unions, at £23,250.[61]

So, in reality neither church won a victory against the other, but neither church lost in that they were to be restored to the very conditions which they had been in prior to 1831, receiving adequate financial compensation to rebuild their places of worship. The primary winners were the British government, who not only retained all their possessions in the Caribbean, and the planters, who were assured of a more-than-adequate compensation package, not only for the loss of their properties and livelihoods, caused by the disturbances, but for the loss of their slaves when emancipation finally did come. Once again, the biggest losers were the enslaved, who had not only lost their lives but had been punished harshly for a disagreement which they had little or nothing to do with causing.

---

61. Madden, *Twelvemonth's Residence*, 2:250.

Thoughts of a quick and complete freedom were soon dropped. It was to remain an elusive dream after both the major parties agreed that an apprenticeship system was to be established, designed to prepare the enslaved for their lives as free citizens. Parliament's belief was that the enslaved needed to be taught a trade, as well as how to handle their freedom. In truth this was such a disparaging statement made about a people who had, in all but name, managed the plantations for absentee owners (who in many instances trusted them more than their fellow white citizens). So, on August 28, 1833 Parliament received royal assent to the passing of the Emancipation Act, whose full title was "An Act for the Abolition of Slavery throughout the British Colonies, for promoting the industry of the manumitted Slaves, and for compensating the Persons hitherto entitled to the Services of such Slaves." However, given the legislative freedom in Jamaica,

> In 1834 the British Act for the abolition of slavery was amended by the House of Assembly in this colony, and the amended Act came into operation the 1st of August. By it slavery was said to be abolished in Jamaica: a state of apprenticeship was substituted—four years for negroes employed as house-servants; six years for those employed as field-labourers; all children (not all negroes destitute) declared free at once; entitled to freedom who had been with owner's consent brought to Great Britain; negroes entitled to demand a valuation of the unexpired term of their apprenticeship , and on payment of award to be set free; abolition of field-punishment; exemption of female apprentices from flogging; transfer of judicial authority over negroes from local to special magistrates; power of corporal punishments taken from masters and their agents; labour limited to forty-five hours a week, except in certain emergences; four and a half of the forty-five hours subsequently allotted for the cultivation of the negro's grounds. Master bound to maintain his negroes as heretofore; no apprentice to be taken off the island, or to be separated from his wife or child in removing him from one plantation to another; every Saturday to be allotted to the negro; Sunday markets to be abolished. There are a variety of minor regulations respecting the jurisdiction of the special Justices, the classification of apprentices, and the imposition of fines and punishments for specified infractions of the law. But the grand features of this Act are, that slavery is to be abolished, not nominally, but virtually, in the year 1840; that the power of adjudicating between master and apprentice is confined to persons specially appointed, and supposed to be disinterested Judges; and that the power of inflicting arbitrary punishment is

taken away from the overseers. For duly carrying this law into effect, the sum of £20,000,000, as a compensation for the ultimate loss of slave labour, was awarded by the British Parliament to the planters.⁶²

"Sunday Morning in the Country." *Slavery Images: A Visual Record of the African Slave Trade and Slave Life in the Early African Diaspora*, accessed March 9, 2022, http://slaveryimges.org/s/slaveryimages/item/2507.

The enslaved lost out even further, once again with the abolition of the Sunday market. This action was designed to encourage them to attend European churches once again; however, it had the knock-on effect of limiting the time which they had to socialize and shop. While this pleased the missionaries, in that it preserved the right to have the gospel preached, once again the needs of the enslaved were being not just neglected but ignored. So, while Knibb could technically claim that he had achieved all that he had hoped for, he had yet to explain the Act and its amendments to those who mattered most: the enslaved, many of whom had trusted him, and still others who had given him a second chance because of their love of Thomas Burchell. Yet no letter can be found wherein Knibb explained to the people, before his return to Jamaica, that it was their spiritual freedom which he had

62. Madden, *Twelvemonth's Residence*, 2:252–54.

wrought on their behalf. Instead, as his biography states, he simply kept in touch with them, joyfully reporting how he and Burchell had achieved their much-longed-for freedom. Such then was the ignorance of the people regarding this fact that, on hearing of his impending return, the people prepared a warm welcome for their hero, and so impressed was Knibb that, shortly after his return, in 1834, he wrote home, joyfully letting them know how

> The people saw me as I stood on the deck of the boat. As I neared the shore I waved my hand, when they, being fully assured that it was their minister, ran from every part of the bay to the wharf. Some pushed off in a canoe.... They took me up in their arms, they sang, they laughed, they wept, and I wept too. "Him come, him come, for true." "Who da come for we king, king Knibb. Him fight de battle, him win de crown."[63]

Little did they know that their joy was soon to turn to mourning, once they heard the decisions made in England, on their behalf; that the freedom which they had long sought for was still not come.

---

63. Hinton, *Memoir*, 194.

Chapter 9

The Slow Journey to Full Freedom (1834–45)

Knibb received a hero's welcome on his return, both from his colleagues and the enslaved. The missionaries celebrated the fact that they were no longer in danger of the plantocracy, and that they would once again be free to share the gospel, not just in Jamaica, but across the entire British Caribbean. However, the story was a different one for the enslaved, who were told the finer points of what the British government, planters, merchants, and missionaries had "achieved" on their behalf. That was what they had meant when they said that August 1, 1834 would indeed be the date when "freedom was come." It was to be a freedom only for the mulattos and coloreds, and those taken abroad to England. They were being given priority, while there was to be no freedom for the Black majority, those over six years old, until 1840.

With the non-Black emancipation only weeks away, the Africans soon realized that not only had they been deceived, but that this in fact was the missionaries plan from the beginning. Spiritual freedom was all that had mattered to them and when confronted by the enslaved, the missionaries continued relying upon the Pauline scriptures as a justifiable reason as to why Africans could continue be enslaved. It was a poor answer for what many believed to be what was rightfully theirs in God. There was no consolation to be had from the BMS who continued to tell them to respect Scripture, which demanded of them that they

> Let every man abide in the same calling wherein he was called. Art thou called being a servant? Care not for it: but if thou mayest be made free, use it rather.[1]

Why, they asked, was it perfectly acceptable in the British psyche for Africans to be stolen from their homes and families, against their will, and against the laws of God and to be brutalized, but not then be able to protect their wives and children by resisting their bondage, as that would be against the laws of man? This was an interesting twist of logic, and the reason why Sharpe and so many others were prepared to die for the freedom, which their unredacted Bibles continued to tell them could be theirs, just like the children of Israel, who had also been kept in bondage against their will.

So, once again the enslaved had to pick themselves up, dust themselves off, and then somehow stretch out their hands to God, to find hope and the strength to continue for another day, while having lost so much of their will to fight on, especially when it became clear that full freedom could have been theirs, but for the seemingly paternalistic decisions which were made on their behalf. Conversely, the enslaved population of the islands of Antigua and Saint Kitts was to go free on August 1, 1834, together with a parcel of land on which to build their own lives. At the same time, they also came to understand that while those who "owned" them were to be financially compensated, the enslaved were to have schools built, teachers trained, and the prospect of future success for their children and grandchildren, but under the guidance and tutelage of these very same missionaries.

Nevertheless, with their success shared with the people in England, the BMS spared no time in busying themselves, raising funds for their burnt-down chapels (in addition to that already previously agreed by parliament), through the selling of emancipation hymn sheets. This served to confirm and enforce in the people of England that that emancipation had been wrought for all, with congregations coming together to hold thanksgiving services and singing songs such as this one in celebration and triumph, after the events of 1831:

SATAN HEARD AND TREMBLED

> 1
> Satan, Satan heard and trembled
> And, upstarting from his throne,
> Bands of Belial's sons assembled,

---

1. 1 Cor 7:20–21 (SFLB).

> Fired with rancour all his own,
> Madly swearing,
> "Christ to slaves shall not be known."
> 2
> Tidings, Tidings of salvation!
> Britons rose with one accord,
> Swept the plague-spot from our nation
> Negroes to their rights restor'd;
> Slaves nolonger!
> Free-men, free-men of the Lord.[2]

Folks in England thought that they had contributed to a great deliverance indeed, while Africans simply saw as the exchanging of one slave master for another. Britain was in ignorance as to their real fate, and there was nothing that could be done about it, as the church was now seemingly working hand in hand with the colonial government, having been coopted to

> Mould the thinking of the apprentices, to encourage habits of industry, to build churches, and to establish stable social patterns that would induce freedmen to remain in settled estate villages when the system ended.[3]

Somewhat resigned to, if unhappy with, their fate, once again it was their duty to pretend to be obedient, docile, compliant and grateful Christians to their new "masters," if they were ever to have any hope of receiving their freedom. Unsurprisingly church attendance reduced significantly as this news was absorbed by all.

So, in this chapter we will examine the slow journey to what enslaved Africans hoped would finally be their full freedom, and we begin with the apprenticeship system, and then the establishing of free villages and towns, before concluding with the Negro Education Grant, which for many came to be seen as the ultimate betrayal of all that they had hoped for after having placed their trust in William Knibb and the BMS, who had promised them so much.

THE APPRENTICESHIP YEARS (1834–38)

The decision made as to what the journey to emancipation would look like, the then-governnor, the Marquis of Sligo, had the following proclamation read out to every plantation by a magistrate:

2. Robertson, *Gone Is the Ancient Glory*, 163–64.
3. Heuman, "Legacy of Slavery and Emancipation," 2.

My Friend,

Our good King, who was himself in Jamaica a long time ago, still thinks and talks a great deal of this island. He has sent me out here to take care you, and to protect your rights; but he has also ordered me to see justice done to your owners, and to punish those who do wrong. Take my advice, for I am your friend—be sober, honest, and work well when you become apprentices, for should you behave ill and refuse to work because you are no longer slaves, you will assuredly render yourselves liable to punishment.

The people of England are your friends and fellow subjects—they have shown themselves such by passing a Bill to make you all free. Your masters are also your friends: they have proved their kind feeling towards you all by passing in the House of Assembly the same Bill. The way to prove that you are deserving of all this goodness, is by labouring diligently during your apprenticeship.

You will, on the first of August next, no longer be slaves, but from that day you will be Apprenticed to your former owners for a few years, in order to fit you all for freedom. It will therefore depend entirely upon your own conduct whether your Apprenticeship be short or long; for should you run away, you will be brought back by the Maroons and police, and have to remain in Apprenticeship longer than those who behave well. You will only be required to work four days and a half in each week; the remaining day and a half in each week will be your own time, and you may employ it for your own benefit. Bear in mind that everyone is obliged to work—some work with their hands, others with their heads, but no one can live and be considered respectable without some employment. Your lot is to work with your hands: I pray you therefore, do your part faithfully, for if you neglect your duty, you will be brought before the Magistrates whom the King has sent out to watch you, and they must act fairly and do justice to all by punishing those who are badly disposed. Do not listen to the advice of bad people; for should any of you refuse to do what the law requires of you, you will bitterly repent it; when, at the end of the appointed time all your fellow-labourers are released from Apprenticeship, you will find yourselves condemned to hard labour in the workhouse for a lengthened period, as a punishment for your disobedience.

If you follow my advice, and conduct yourselves well, nothing can prevent your being your own masters, and to labour only for yourselves, and your wives, and your children, at the end of four or six years, according to your respective classes.

I have not time to go about to all the properties in the island and to tell you this myself, I have therefore ordered this letter of advice to be printed, and ordered it to be read to you all, that you may not be deceived and bring yourselves into trouble by bad advice or mistaken notions. "I trust you will all be obedient and diligent subjects to our good King, so that he may never have cause to be sorry for all the good he has done for you."

Your friend and well-wisher,
SLIGO,
Governor of Jamaica.[4]

Having then heard it confirmed, that their freedom was to be set back for up to six years, and could be extended beyond that, it naturally created a great deal of anger across all of the islands, even if in later reports to parliament it was said that the Africans in Jamaica were compliant and grateful slaves who simply adjusted to this traumatic disappointment with a "Thank you, Massa." It truly was to be just slavery by another name, and the enslaved knew it to be so, especially when they were told that they would have to remain under the control of those masters who had treated them so badly previously.

In Trinidad, it is said that every day from August 1, 1834 until the July 31, 1838, the enslaved picketed the governor's home and resisted, and as one, they would chant,

Pas de six ans. Not Six Years. No six years!! Not six years, we will not have six years. We are free, the King has given us liberty.[5]

In Essequibo, British Guiana, they occupied church grounds for three days from August 9, seeking to encourage their compatriots to resist Apprenticeship. In Jamaica too, they were having none of this. In Saint Ann parish the enslaved went on strike once again, refusing to return to work, unless they received a days' pay for a days' work. They even went as far as to question when the proclamation had really been issued by the king, or had simply emanated in Jamaica:

1st. Is it the King's law? 2nd. Would you sear that the King make it? 3rd. Did not the Jamaica House make it? 4. Did not Lord Sligo put him name to it because him have slaves? 5. Could you swear it is Law of Jesus Christ?[6]

4. Madden, *Twelvemonth's Residence*, 2:255–57.
5. Frye, "Enslaved," para. 7.
6. Heuman, "Legacy of Slavery and Emancipation," 4.

Upon receiving no satisfaction, such was the anger of the enslaved that rumors soon abounded with tales of how they had vowed that they would rather be shot, or have their heads cut off before they would work as apprentices. However, realizing once again that nothing was going to provide redress, they transitioned into the apprenticeship system, wherein they had to serve their current "masters" without pay, for a minimum of forty-five hours per week. but used all manner of means to protest. However, they would seek to make those forty-five hours as torturous for the planter as it was for them. Their resistance took many forms, such as arriving late to work, working slowly, or just generally answering back and challenging those who managed them.

Frustrated and angry with the disrespect they believed themselves to be receiving, and with what many of them saw as the slowing down of production, it came as no surprise to many that, as apprenticeship proceeded, they too found other ways in which to extend apprenticeship of many, such as by reclassifying house servants as field laborers. They wasted little time before proving to all that

> As a social institution slavery disappeared under what the preamble calls "a general manumission;" but it came back as a system of industry.[7]

Yet, this was perhaps the aim of many from the outset as

> The general consensus was that Africans were somewhat lacking in mental ability and the therefore would only be capable of being a working class, servant people, therefore they needed to be trained as such. Of them Rev George Wilson Bridges, and Anglican Rector of St Ann's Bay, stated, "The human scale goes downward from the white to the Hottentot, where the gap to the highest of animals, the orangutan, is not great."[8]

The CofE itself went even further in expressing its disquiet that Africans could not be anything but slaves, declaring that

> Any drive towards conversion should be tailored towards the slaves' greatly inferior mental capacities. Suitably converted and fed an appropriate diet of quiescent theology, blacks could, it was determined, become perfect slaves; compliant, accommodating and socially calm.[9]

---

7. Mathieson, *British Slavery*, 243.
8. Curtin, *Two Jamaicas*, 41–42.
9. Walvin, *Black Ivory*, 182.

Professor Douglas Hall explained the thinking of the planters, explaining that

> Many of the slave owners and the slave managers regarded the apprenticeship as a part of the compensation, a short and partial reprieve granted that they might squeeze the last juice out of the compulsory labour before the great ruin of freedom set in.[10]

To assist them in their task draconian laws were put in place should they rebel. Soon reports came in from all over the island of the atrocities being committed in the name of "apprenticeship," assisted by the deference and therefore the freedom given to the Jamaican legislature and legal system, which enabled them to continue to treat Africans as slaves.

Tread-Wheel.[11]

Apprenticeship as a means of "partial" freedom was therefore short-lived, with planters reverted to type, and carrying out acts of brutality on a daily basis. They exacted some very harsh conditions and punishments on the apprentices, including sending many of them to the workhouse, the dungeon, or the whipping post. Governor Sligo himself introduced the treadmill in workhouses across the island, believing that it was a better instrument of punishment than the whip, particularly for women. However, in the hands of the planters, it soon became the most heinous instrument of torture used during this period. The Rev. James Thome and Joseph Kimball,

10. Hall, "Apprenticeship Period," 3.
11. Phillippo. *Jamaica*, 173.

on visiting one such workhouse in Saint Andrews, described observing its violent actions:

> The first sound that greeted us was a piercing outcry from the treadmill. On going to it, we saw a youth of about eighteen hanging in the air by a strap bound to his wrist, and dangling against the wheel in such a manner that every revolution of it scraped the body from the breast to the ankles. He had fallen off from weakness and fatigue, and was struggling and crying in the greatest distress, while the strap, which extended to a pole above and stretched his arm high above his head, held him fast. The superintendent in a harsh voice ordered him to be lifted up, and his feet again placed on the wheel. But before he had taken five steps, he again fell off, and was suspended as before. At the same instant a woman also fell off, and without a sigh or motion of a muscle, for she was too much exhausted for either, but with a shocking wildness of the eye, hung by her half-dislocated arms against the wheel.
>
> As the allotted time fifteen minutes had expired the on the wheel, eight in number were released to rest. The boy could hardly stand on the ground. He had a large ulcer on one of his feet much swollen and inflamed and his legs and greatly bruised and peeled by the revolving of wheel. The gentleman who was with us reproved the superintendent most severely for his conduct and told him to the boy from the treadmill gang and see that proper care was taken of him. The poor woman who fell off seemed completely exhausted, but as soon as she was unbound, she tottered to the wall nearby, and took up a little babe which we had not observed before. It appeared to more than two or three months old and the little thing stretched out its arms and welcomed its mother. On inquiry we ascertained that this woman's offence was an absence from the field an hour after the required time (six o'clock) in the morning.[12]

Many other tales were told of how

> Runaways could be punished with imprisonment; negligent or disobedient apprentices were to have their malfeasances "corrected." The precedents under British Law legitimized the continued "enslavement" of plantation workers in the West Indies after emancipation by providing an alternative form of binding and social control that was traditionally accepted at home,

---

12. Thome and Kimball, *Emancipation in the West Indies*, 286–87. Please see Appendix 1 for instruments of punishment.

whereby apprentices were bound to their masters in Britain by an indenture for a fixed period of time, usually seven years.[13]

The worst tale of Apprenticeship came out of the prisons as the conditions were harsh with some ex-slaves made to work in chains, while others were placed in solitary confinement. Other punishments were flogging, [and] starvation.[14]

> To-day I saw a poor negro from Potosi estate, tied to a cart in the square before the court-house, and severely flogged with a cat; immediately after which he was chained to one of the workhouse gang . . . all is going well for the master. . . . Many are severely lacerated, under order of the special magistrates; others are sent to the treadmill, on the most trivial of complaints . . . others are sentenced to work their own day and a half per week for the benefit of their masters, and that for weeks together; and still they bear it with patience.[15]

As these stories came in, telling of the duplicitous actions of pro-slavers, Fowell Buxton raised the issue in the British Parliament on June 19, 1835, requesting

> That a Select Committee be appointed to inquire whether the condition on which the 20,000,001, were granted for the Abolition of Slavery have been complied with.[16]

In essence, with such a wide range of concerns, he believed that

> It was their duty, under the circumstances he was about to detail, to take some decisive step, or to adopt a positive resolution to prevent the money apportioned by way of compensation to the owners of slaves, or rather as the ransom of the slaves themselves from their state of bondage, from being disbursed until the promises and stipulations should have been fulfilled.[17]

There then ensued a conversation instigated by parliament, with many of the stakeholders and correspondence from others who not only held positions in the British Parliament, but also had roles and responsibilities within the islands of the Caribbean; governors, judges, planter supporters, merchants, and missionaries. The Commons sought from them an update and answers to many of the following issues and concerns which had been

13. Tyson et al., "Accounting," 3.
14. "History Notes," para. 63.
15. Burchell, *Memoir*, 294–95.
16. HC Deb, *Abolition of Slavery*, §918.
17. HC Deb, *Abolition of Slavery*, §919.

raised prior to the passing of the act. Parliament began by asking whether the partial freedom given to the enslaved had been accompanied with "rivers of blood—with scenes of unexampled desolation,"[18] as many had expected in 1833. This was answered with a resounding "No." It was rather stated that

> Not one act of violence was committed-there was no boisterous merriment-no uproar of joy. On the evening of the 31st of July, as the moment of liberation was approaching . . . that moment found every chapel and place of worship thronged with worshippers. It passed over in deep and solemn silence . . . profound tranquility.[19]

It had also been asked:

> Suppose Emancipation was granted this evening, what would be done to-morrow morning?" His answer (then) was,—To-morrow morning is an early day. Perhaps they will enjoy themselves a little. I should say, that on the following Monday they would proceed to work.[20]

However, Lord Sligo, then-governor of Jamaica, while he would have been able to give an actual report of the day itself and the dissatisfaction expressed by the enslaved, he chose instead to lie to parliament, simply stating that

> On Monday the apprentices turned out to their work, with even more than usual readiness, in some cases with alacrity, and all with good humour.[21]

Conversely, reports came back from plantation owners expressing their discontent. It was said of the Africans on one estate that "their laziness is unbearable . . . the people do not work." Yet when he was asked to provide a summary of how unproductive his estate had become, he presented the following information below, which for all intents and purposes actually proved that his estate had been doing better since apprenticeship than it had done prior to the granting of the partial freedom, at a time when he had had more people under his control.

---

18. HC Deb, *Abolition of Slavery*, §920.
19. HC Deb, *Abolition of Slavery*, §§920–21.
20. HC Deb, *Abolition of Slavery*, §921.
21. HC Deb, *Abolition of Slavery*, §921.

Table 1:[22] Hogsheads of sugar potted					
1833		1834		1835	
January	5	January	10	January	10
February	10	February	9	February	14
Hhds.	15	Hhds.	19	Hhds.	24
The industry of the two first months of 1835 then produced five more hogsheads than 1834, and nine more than 1833, OF RUM.					
None was made in January in any of these years.					
1833		1834		1835	
February	0	February	95 galls.	February	128 galls
NUMBER OF PERSONS EMPLOYED					
1833		1834		1835	
Grown person	103	Grown person	99	Grown person	83
Children under 12	51	Children under 12	52	Children under 12	2
	154		151		85

Another planter confirmed that he had also observed two significant changes since 1834, the first being that for the first time there were no disturbances during the Christmas holiday period, and secondly that

> Universal, among the negroes in some parishes—"the negroes have shewn that they are easily to be satisfied with wages." I never knew them so greedy for money, so industriously anxious to earn it, I have been hiring apprentices to dig cane boles, in their own time, at from 40s. to 50s. per acre cheaper than the current price paid to jobbers.[23]

Clearly, by the questions which had been asked in the parliament of 1833 had caused them to spend a considerable amount of time planning for the "failure" of this experiment. Violence and the inefficiency of freed Africans had been the expectation, but it had now been proved a myth. However, what they had not given adequate consideration to was the duplicitous nature of those planters who were pro-slavery, and who, in spite of their financial windfall, would continue to brutalize the African body. The House had presumed that there would be a great many contentious moments between employer and employee, most of which would be caused by

---

22. HC Deb, Abolition of Slavery, §§925–26.
23. HC Deb, *Abolition of Slavery*, §927.

the enslaved. In order to preempt this the Crown ordered that one hundred additional independent stipendiary magistrates be appointed throughout the Caribbean. Their role was to

> Administer equal justice to the rich and the poor, the black and the white, who will watch over and protect the negro in his incipient state of freedom, and will aid and direct his inexperience in forming a contract with his master, which must have so material an effect upon his future life.[24]

However, Parliament had not contended with the fact that

> Out of twenty-one or twenty-two magistrates, seventeen were planters, or attornies, or agents; and in a third, there were thirty special Magistrates connected with the planters.[25]

This was then compounded by the fact that for every law passed, the Jamaican Assembly would undermine it with laws of their own. Such was the case of one James Beord, who sought to challenge the apprenticeship system in the courts. He took his case to the magistrates court where he was told in no uncertain terms that God had indeed made all Africans slaves, and therefore, if they refused to continue in slavery, they would be flogged and imprisoned. To the British Parliament, however, their major concern was not that Beord had appealed the system of apprenticeship, but the fact that he had been threatened, and by extension all the enslaved were being told that a failure to comply would end in floggings and imprisonment. Little had changed, but it appeared that Parliament was determined that issues of violence, though accepted for over two hundred years, were not now acceptable, having declared

> That no taint of the servile condition should be suffered to remain as respected the apprentice. That no corporal punishment should be inflicted; or should he or his connexions be insulted by the use of the lash.[26]

Most of the stipendiary magistrates, loyal to the plantocracy, gladly ignored such instructions, with the exception of a few. One such person was Dr. Richard Madden, a doctor, abolitionist, and employee of the colonial office. He was sent to work in both Jamaica and Cuba from 1833–39, and was appointed as a stipendiary magistrate when apprenticeship came into being. In his report to Parliament, he told how he,

24. HC Deb, *Abolition of Slavery*, §933.
25. HC Deb, *Abolition of Slavery*, §933.
26. HC Deb, *Abolition of Slavery*, §930.

After residing there for more than a year, and endeavouring to do his duty in a truly English spirit, being determined to uphold the integrity of the Abolition Act, and protect the negro from oppression, had met with such persecution from the local magistrates and persons connected with the planters, and the Colonial Union, that he had felt himself obliged to give up his appointment in disgust, and return to England.[27]

However, he filed a report detailing what he had both seen and heard. He reported how

On one occasion, a woman was pointed out to me as a shammer by an overseer. . . . That is no shamming; observe how the woman drags her left leg after her . . . she is dead on one side, and she is not able to work . . . three weeks . . . the same paralytic had been to my house . . . for refusing to work she had been flogged on her paralytic hand. . . . Since August, 1834, various outrages have been committed by white people on negroes. One planter has been indicted for shooting at an old woman, and, after wounding her severely, discharged the second barrel at her, but fortunately without effect. The Grand Jury ignored the bill. Another gentleman was indicted for the murder of his negro, by shooting him, and was sentenced to nine months' imprisonment. Another gentleman, an overseer, was committed to goal a few weeks ago, for the murder of a boy, by shooting at a number of negroes assembled in a hut, in the act of singing hymns. . . . Another gentleman was tried in October last, for causing one of his negroes to be severely torn by dogs, for going without permission to bury his wife, who had been dead three days, and had been refused sufficient time to prepare her coffin.[28]

Madden was sincere in his endeavors, and was to be commended in his efforts, for despite the threats to his own life, he did not simply look at what was happening to enslaved Africans, he got to know them. He visited with the pastor of the oldest and more than likely still the largest Baptist denomination in Jamaica, Parson Killick, staying near to his church in Kingston.

Of Parson Killick Madden said that he contributed significantly to his report, describing him personally as

A pious well-behaved, honest man, who in point of intelligence, and the application of Scriptural knowledge to the ordinary duties of his calling, might stand a comparison with many more

27. HC Deb, *Abolition of Slavery*, §954.
28. HC Deb, *Abolition of Slavery*, §955, §958.

> highly favoured by the advantages of their education and standing in society. . . . I have visited three sectarian chapels in this town and if I were to particularise any sectarian instructor whose constant endeavours were directed to the public advantage, as well as the moral improvement of his flock, I might name a poor negro preacher of the Baptist persuasion "Parson Killick."[29]

In terms of the BMS's own response to the Committee, while Phillippo is said to have called the apprenticeship system "slavery disguised,"[30] Burchell's detailed report remains, and it seems to have summed up the feelings of the majority who responded to the Committee:

> The apprenticeship system is working much better than I anticipated it would. The apprentices have conducted themselves with the most admirable propriety, where they have been treated as human beings and not as brutes. The ships are returning home literally laden with produce, notwithstanding predictions to the contrary. The canes have not rotted upon the ground; the crops are finishing earlier this year than last; in one word, all is going on well for the master. I wish I could say as much for the apprentice; but this I cannot. Many are severely lacerated, under order of the special magistrates; others are sent to the treadmill, on the most trivial complaints; and, on the slightest occasions, others are sentenced to work their own day and a half per week for the benefit of the masters, and that for weeks together; and still they bear it with patience. Most of the specials who have been appointed, have proved themselves to be just so many hard-hearted drivers, doing their best to meet the wishes of the planters, and assimilating the present system as nearly as possible to the old. Every day our streets are paraded by men chained together; yea, and women chained together also! This very day men chained, and women chained together also, in the service of their masters, and in fulfilment of the special's sentences. The complaint alleged against the apprentices, that they are not willing to work in their own time, arises from this one fact, that the masters for the most part will not pay them their hard-earned wages . . . much remains to be done by British Christians. . . . Parliament ought to inquire into their proceedings; otherwise the negro will yet be crushed.[31]

---

29. Clarke, *Memorials of Baptist Missionaries*, 31.
30. Phillippo, *Jamaica*, 171.
31. Burchell, *Memoir*, 295.

Such a sad refrain regarding the enslaved, from one who intimately knew of their plight. Ultimately, the Committee agreed that funds could not be withheld by Parliament from the slaveholders across the British Caribbean just because of the vagaries of those in Jamaica. Buxton, therefore withdrew his charge, but soon after the apprenticeship system was declared to have been a failure, and it was summarily agreed that the enslavement of Africans should finally be brought to a premature end on August 1, 1838. However, it is to be noted that from the day of the decision until July 31, 1838, punishments continued, but with an extra degree of anger, if such a thing were possible. Abolitionists monitoring the situation, reported the following case which occurred in February 1836:

> Five women had been sentenced to two day's imprisonment with hard labour on the treadmill for disobedience of orders, when in consequence of the reported death of one of them on the mill, ordered an inquiry, the result of which is stated in the following words: "The women who refused to work on the treadmill were fastened to it by ligature round the arms for twenty-four successive hours, in such a manner as to endanger the lives of all, and actually to occasion the death of one of them!" In the report of the custos on this case, we find no expression of regret at what had occurred, no promise of amendment for the future, but an attempt at justification, with which he hoped the governor would be satisfied.[32]

Freedom couldn't come soon enough, but the question many of the enslaved must have been asking themselves was, would they be alive to see it, or had the planters finally found a legal means by which they could fulfill their pledge in 1831, to kill every one of them before they would ever experience it?

FREE TOWNS AND VILLAGES

While the apprenticeship system which BMS missionaries had negotiated on behalf of the enslaved was proving itself to be an abject failure, the BMS nevertheless encouraged the enslaved to participate in their next project, which they hoped would at least provide them once free, a basis on which to plan a future, through having their own land on which to build a home.

During negotiations for emancipation, there were discussions in regards to the wages to be paid to the enslaved; once free, however, there

---

32. McCornock, *British and Foreign Anti-Slavery Reporter*, 801–2.

were those abolitionists like lawyer and plantation owner Henry Ross, who argued that it was more important for them to have a piece of land which they could call their own, and work to make money for themselves. Ross suggested that there was a system which could be beneficial both for the land owner and for the freed African who had good husbandry skills. His radical idea was to:

> Pay no more in wages for the cultivation of the land-reform your entire system—reverse the tables—place yourself on the safe sideinstead of paying wages to the negro, let the negro pay you, not money but in kind, a proportion of the staple products, which, be sure, he now knows well, and will hereafter know still better how to cultivate to the best advantage,—throw off the master, and become his landlord,—trust him (by degrees) as your tenant—identify your interest with his in the land and staple products of the estate,—let him clearly see and find his own advancement, credit, and profit in that union . . . let him share with you a due proportion of the anxiety, risk and loss, as well as profit. Make him your partner at once, by making him your tenant.[33]

Ross was suggesting the system known as sharecropping and it seemed as though it would have been beneficial to both landowner and African. However, the landowners had many varied reasons for saying no. Firstly, they were not prepared to consider changing the way in which they farmed, preferring labor which they could command. Secondly, given the class system on the island, they were also not prepared to see the social status of the African improved, never mind thoughts of being equal with them. Thirdly, others were concerned that Africans could not be trusted to have a level of "ownership" which could in the long term leave the landowner with much less profit than he could command if he were in charge. Ultimately, what they had wanted was to continue to exercise a level of paternalism as well as maintain their social status, and so a sharecropping project could not succeed. The exception to this was the legislatures in Antigua and Saint Kitt's who embraced the notion of giving all their emancipated people a parcel of land together with their freedom in 1834. However, it is understood that the planters soon found ways of manipulating the situation on their island, in order to get them to work once again on the plantations.

The BMS and other churches in Jamaica, eventually agreed to adopt and adjust a model which was already present in Jamaica. They agreed to

---

33. Ross, *Thoughts*, 46–48.

create free villages and towns similar to the following model which was explained to a government select committee in 1832:

> How do the free blacks maintain themselves? -Many of them in various ways; there is a district of country called Cavaliers attached to the Pepine Estate, in the parish in which I lived; it had originally been a sugar estate, or coffee work, belonging to the Wildman family, but the negroes had been withdrawn, and when I came into possession of the place the land was parcelled out amongst free people, chiefly persons who had got their freedom some how or other, and not being able to get employment in town, for the trades were overstocked there, those individuals retired to this district, and they were all parcelled out in small pieces of land; they took an acre, two or three acres; they under look to pay 30s. an acre; they had three acres and a house chiefly. When I got possession of the estate, I found this run of land rented to one tenant, a white man; he sublet it to those tenants; Mr. Wildman had made that arrangement; he found it very difficult and troublesome to collect the rents, and so he rented this land to this individual, who cultivated part by means of some free negroes, by giving them wages, also by subletting the land, that was the only instance in which I ever knew of freedom being tried upon a scale beyond individuals, for I suppose there were 2 or 300 men women and children. . . . What articles did they cultivate generally? Provisions, corn, and yams; it was a mountain district, well watered, rich land, and some little coffee bushes and arrow root; there was an abundant supply of water, something similar to the Maroon cultivation.[34]

Knibb's trip to England had proved that his thinking was more aligned to that of the plantocracy, so, while sharecropping would have benefitted the most people, because of the class system, to accept Africans as being equal to them, would have been a mortal sin, a step too far, even for missionaries. At the same time, in purchasing land, the missionaries would have the freedom to then add to any town or village, chapel or mission station, allowing them the freedom with which to train up these enslaved children in the things of God, so that when they grew up, they would not depart from it—or more particularly, they would have a denominational allegiance which would likely remain for generations.

Given that the Africans were to come to the labor market up to seven years after the coloreds and mulattoes, who had been given a head start in 1834, this seemed like a good fit. It became the preferred choice, not just

---

34. HCSC, *Report*, 4: §53.

because the missionaries believed such a project would advance the status of freed Africans, and enable them, regardless of employment status, to be able to feed themselves as well as their families, but because it would be more socially acceptable. So, gaining the agreement of the enslaved, the plan was then that once it was known that emancipation was on the way, then churches would purchase land which they would then resell, at cost price, to freed Africans on the day of their liberty, when able to purchase land. By so doing, the BMS believed that it would enable Africans to begin their new lives as independent citizens, able to determine their own futures.

Yet this was not a one-sided deal, for the enslaved did their part too. They worked covertly for many years as they made preparations for emancipation and their new status as free people and landowners.[35] They were determined, and not even the many hours which they had to work as apprentices put them off, or the quarter of a million lashes sixty thousand of them received, or even the fact that fifty thousand of them were brutalized in the workhouses by the treadmills, floggings, and chain gangs, all during that time.[36] They would till the soil and sell the produce, or hire out the skills which they had acquired in enslavement for money. Their goals were simple ones: to buy a piece of land and build their own homes, and they knew that they could achieve this as they had already built the master's houses, churches, and state buildings on the island. If there was any money left, then their aim was to buy their freedom and that of their families, as soon as possible, or at the very least provide an education, if not for themselves, then for their children. However, educator and historian Shirley Gordon makes it clear that

> The majority of free villages were secured without missionary help. Particularly in parishes where missions had not been strong before emancipation, such as Clarendon, Manchester and St Catherine, many ex-slaves bought land directly with their own savings. This trend continued as more and more sugar estates failed and their proprietors sold or rented land in small lots.[37]

---

35. See Appendix 7 for jobs done as they worked towards emancipation.
36. Griffith-Hughes, "Mighty Experiment," 110.
37. Gordon, *Our Cause*, 28.

The Slow Journey to Full Freedom (1834–45)

Free Village: Sligoville, with Mission Premises.[38]

The future was finally looking bright, with everyone seemingly playing their part in creating a foundation not only for themselves, but generations to come. While this was a positive step and worked for many, clearly it required that freed Africans were of relatively good health in order to be able to undertake such levels of work. From the evidence gleaned from one slave colony, this would not be the case, for "leaving [aside] the children, the aged, and the infirm [amounted] to two-thirds of the whole, to remain a burden upon the estates.[39] It would therefore not be inappropriate to suggest that similar percentages of infirmity would be found in Jamaica on August 1, 1838.

By the time full emancipation finally came, there were free villages in Clarendon, Manchester, and Saint Catherine, and free towns in Sligoville, Saint Catherine, Saint James, Hanover, Trelawney, Saint Ann, Saint Mary, and Saint Thomas in the Vale. Surely now one might ask, "Could anything spoil this atmosphere of joy and seeming future happiness?" Well, the Africans, having overcome so much in this volatile situation, were to be further disappointed by the final project designed to assist them in their development as a people, the Negro Education Grant, which was so atrociously handled that it damaged relationships between African Christians and the BMS, perhaps irreparably.

---

38. Phillippo, *Jamaica*, 222–23.
39. HC Deb, *Ministerial Plan*, §142.

THE NEGRO EDUCATION GRANT 1835-45

The Negro Education Grant (NEG) was the final part of the agreement which the BMS missionaries had made on their behalf, and the enslaved, having been disappointed by apprenticeship, saw this perhaps as their "compensation" for all that had gone before, enabling them to leave a legacy for future generations. It was established in order to assist in the "civilizing" of the African. It was a grant of some £30,000 which had to be shared between Mauritius, the Cape, and all the British Caribbean colonies, except those nations who had refused it, choosing instead to deliver immediate and full freedom to their enslaved population. However, such a seemingly great sum was really quite paltry in reality, being less than 1.2 percent of the £20 million "compensation" paid to the plantation owners, and on a par with the amount to be spent on the education of the working classes in Britain. On August 1, 1838, 750,000 "slaves" were to be freed, and Jamaica, the largest slave-owning island was to receive £2,000, while other islands like British Guiana received £1,950.

The plantation owners and legislature took no interest in the NEG in the early years, still grieving over the loss of their slaves, even though they were handsomely paid, twice over. The government therefore offered it to the one institution that it believed could carry out its plan to provide the religious and moral education which they desired the enslaved to have, thereby transitioning them into a compliant, docile peasantry, "trained" to be happy in servitude. It was a purpose shared by most people in Britain at that time, whether they were for or against abolition. William Wilberforce, believed "champion" of emancipation, went as far as to declare that he himself did not want

> The slaves when they became free, or the working classes for that matter, to aspire "beyond their station in life" after they had received an education.[40]

Churches throughout the islands were offered a commission to undertake "The building of school houses for the instruction of the Emancipated Negro population."[41] The mandate was twofold; to build schools and to train Africans to be the teachers in their own schools. Jamaica's designated annual grant of £2,000 was to be for the first six years of the grant's existence, after which it was to be reduced by one fifth each year until its demise. Of the money provided the government determined that "match funding" would be the best way to take the project forward. Missionary agencies

---

40. Bacchus, *Utilization, Misuse, and Development*, 269.
41. Martin, *Statistics*, 612.

were therefore called upon to pledge one-third of the funds needed and this would be matched by the NEG, providing the other two-thirds.

Most missionary organizations accepted this almost immediately, except for the Baptists and the Methodists, who first demanded reparations for the churches which had been destroyed during the terror carried out by the CCU. For the Baptists there were, however, additional theological and practical concerns which they had to consider; whether the BMS could accept monies on behalf of their independent Baptist missionaries, whether each individual missionary should or could in fact accept the monies being offered by the government; whether they should instead choose compensation for the enslaved or advise them to accept monies for an education which was designed to keep them as free people in subservience, or instead encourage them to raise funds with which to pay their own way in society. Ultimately, the BMS agreed that as a denomination they would not take money from the government, but would leave it to each individual missionary to make up his own mind. Burchell and Knibb, having gone to England to argue the case for emancipation, returned to Jamaica with a Parliamentary grant of £5,510 and £6,195 from christian members of Parliament, as "compensation" for the chapels which had been destroyed and the debts which they had accrued on them. They also received a further £13,000 from members of the church in Britain in order to establish their schools.

Once back in Jamaica BMS and other missionaries discussed the issues amongst themselves and then they informed their congregations. Prominent in their thinking, they argued, was not just education, but the link which they had identified in terms of compensation for slavery, and the evangelizing of the then "unploughed" harvest fields of Africa. Taking a lead in those initial discussions were Buxton, an Anglican; Sturge, a Quaker; and Knibb, who had hoped that this "seed" of educating Africans in Jamaica would ultimately lead to them taking the good news to the "heathen" in Africa, as we shall later see. Sturge and Knibb argued that it would be beneficial for the freed slaves to be "educated" to be hardworking, literate, and self-supporting Christians who could take the lead in the Jamaica of the future. Knibb, therefore, having previously agreed to accept funds from the NEG, changed his mind at a meeting of the north-side missionaries in March 1837, speaking against receiving any further assistance. We get an insight into his reasoning from the impassioned plea (harping back to the words of Governor Sligo), which he convincingly made to his church members:

> A fair scale of wages must be established, and you must be entirely independent! If you continue to receive those allowances,

which have been given during slavery and apprenticeship, it will go abroad that you are not able to take care of yourselves, and that your employers are obliged to provide you with these allowances to keep from starvation. In such a case you will be nothing more than slaves. To be free, you must be independent. Receive your money from your work; come to market with money; purchase from whom you please; and be accountable to no one but the Being above, who I trust will watch over and protect you.[42]

African Baptists, having successfully resisted the plantocracy, gained their own emancipation, developed many varied skills in enslavement, and worked their own pieces of land in preparation for emancipation, embraced this strategy, realizing that it was perhaps their final hope of providing for their futures. Despite everything, they demonstrated a willingness to more than do their part in the education of future generations of African Jamaicans. So, it was decided that the BMS were to provide education without turning to the government for support, but in so doing they had promised to provide a better level of education than that which had been expected. This, they believed, would enable Africans to not simply be prepared for "service" but to one day take the lead in the nation, the church, and most excitedly for the BMS, on the mission fields of Africa.

However, within three years of the grant beginning, the colonial office reported that many missionary organizations were in difficult times, for various reasons; there was an overeagerness to get the money, and then they were unable to purchase the land necessary on which to build the schools; there was poor leadership and planning; little if any coordination between religious bodies; and what Charles Latrobe, the government's inspector of schools, described as a "petty play on sectarian feeling" with missionaries being "small minded and jealous" of one another.[43] Let me explain.

Land Purchase and School Building

Difficulties began in the purchasing of land for schools, with missionaries of all denominations working independently of each other, often building their schools near to those of other denominations. It was clear that each group had an ulterior motive, believing that education would be a gateway for them to greater Christian conversion. Latrobe, who had once been a champion of BMS missionaries, declared that each organization had become a law unto themselves, and though many received funds, they failed to keep

---

42. Hinton, *Memoir*, 284.
43. Rooke, "Evangelical Missionary Rivalry," 343.

accurate records in terms of attendance and conduct, and so the success of their work could not be assessed. He informed the British government that

> The strained relationships between denominations . . . resulted in confusion as to the objectives, evasion of financial accountability, and mismanagement of the Grant could not be depended upon to give the slightest information to be depended upon concerning each other's proceedings or even to acknowledge the existence of rival schools.[44]

It was a "scramble for souls" and the Baptists were by no means innocent in this regard, Phillippo expressing sectarian territorialism as he declared to all how they as Baptists would win this "war":

> The whole land is before us and when once we take possession of it, which we as a denomination are doing in a most unexampled manner, the warfare to a great degree will be over.[45]

This neither endeared the BMS to other missionary organizations or encouraged collegiality amongst them. In fact, such was the animosity demonstrated by the church towards itself at this time that in 1839, BMS and Methodist missionaries were observed openly brawling in the streets, to the bemusement and amazement of all around them. Records state that such behavior was replicated across the entire British Caribbean, to the shame of all who called themselves followers of Jesus Christ. Then, in terms of the building of schools, here too all denominations fell woefully short of what had been expected of them. In their zeal to evangelize and educate the children of the enslaved and those soon to be free, the BMS, like all other denominations, sought ingenious ways of killing two birds with one stone. The monies which should have been set aside for the actual building of the school buildings soon became funds which could aid them in their evangelistic outreach, and so were often diverted to be used for the building of churches.

Missionaries of all denominations initially encouraged their colleagues to accept the NEG or write home to ask for funds to build schools, or what they called Sabbath schools, but with the clear intention of using any received monies to build churches, in which would be placed said school. Colleagues were further encouraged not to state that the funds were to be used for this purpose, but that they were simply to be used for the funding of schools. A clear example of this can be seen in a letter written home to England by BMS missionary Henry Dutton in 1840. On the surface, Dutton

---

44. Rooke, "Evangelical Missionary Rivalry," 342–43.
45. Rooke, "Evangelical Missionary Rivalry," 343.

seems an industrious missionary, doing his best for a people whom he described thus:

> The Negro population are a simple, grateful, pious and warm hearted race—That they are ignorant, I admit:—and how can they who have not enjoyed the advantages of education, whose bodies have been fettered by the cruel bonds of slavery, be anything else but ignorant? . . . But to say to say that they are destitute of common sense; that they are deficient in intellect, that they are the connecting link between man and ape; is a libel upon their characters, as gross as it is malicious and as wicked as it is gross . . . only Education is wanted to make them equal in every respect to their fairer neighbours. . . . The Sabbath School in Browns Town contains from twelve to fourteen hundred scholars—embracing all ages from the infant of four or five years to the venerable African Patriarch of three score years and ten, and of all colours from the jet black negroe to the white creole.[46]

However, the letter continues to ask for funds, making it clear that it was to fund not one, or two, but five churches, with the accompanying mission houses where necessary. Yes, this one missionary was furiously building churches, not just in Browns Town where the capacity was being enlarged to cater for one thousand to two thousand congregants, but also at Bethany, Clarkensville, Mount Lion, Clarendon, and Sturge Town. One missionary building five churches and the adjoining buildings in one year, begs the question, of when he actually had time to undertake any missionary duties at all. Then, if he was typical of the work being undertaken not just by the BMS, but other missionary agencies, having already received funding to rebuild the chapels destroyed by the CCU, and donors in England, then this was truly a cruel and very selfish thing to do.

One can still see the legacy of this in Jamaica today, as in the Baptist church in Gibraltar, Saint Ann, which is a fine example of how schools were placed in the basements of churches. William Knibb was its pastor at that time, and its role as the basic school for Gibraltar remained so until 2010 when the Gibraltar Basic School had its first building, some 150 years after it was originally intended.

Education Provision

In terms of the actual education provided, in order to understand what took place, one has first to understand the racial climate of Jamaica at that time,

46. Dutton, "Letter."

The Slow Journey to Full Freedom (1834–45)

as expressed by Knibb in a letter which he wrote to England in 1839. In it he stated that

> There are infamous laws existing in the island, which we must try to get abolished. One of them has been alluded to in the House of Commons, by the Under Secretary for colonies. It is to this effect:—"All rogues, vagabonds, or other idle persons, found wandering from place to place or otherwise disorderly, may be apprehended by the constable, and taken before a magistrate, who is empowered to order him or her to be whipped on the naked back, not exceeding thirty-nine lashes." . . . This act makes it lawful to send any coloured person who comes within the act to the workhouse, to be set to work for any time, not exceeding six months; but all white persons committed for the same offences are to be fed, lodged, and worked, separate and apart from the free negroes, mulattoes, and slaves. This law makes the distinction of complexion the rule for the measurement of punishment. The white man, or the white female, who is taken up as a vagrant, is to be fed, lodged, and accommodated with comparative comfort; but the black man, or the black female, is to be subjected to the withering influence of cruelty, and to all the agonies that may be inflicted by the cart whip. This law was never made for freemen; it was made for slaves. Send it to Cuba, send it to America, or anywhere else you please; but it won't do for Jamaica! . . . My opinion is that every law which makes any reference to colour at all ought instantly to be repealed.[47]

So the British, having abolished slavery, introduced racism into an already class-driven Jamaican society. How it showed itself in the lives of the missionaries was that though they took on the mandate to educate the indigenous population, they were hesitant to do so, not only because many of them saw that the natural consequence of such an action would be to make themselves redundant, but more significantly, most of them regarded Black people as inferior. Teachers of all denominations were recorded as being most cruel in the treatment of their charges. One case documented by Tucker, and described as "quaint," concerned a Baptist teacher who was called to his headquarters to report on his work:

> "What have you done with the boys of your school to keep them occupied while you are away?" "Please, sir," he replied, "I went round with the cane, and gave them all a good thrashing."[48]

---

47. Hinton, *Memoir*, 315–16.
48. Tucker, *Glorious Liberty*, 120.

Generations of African Caribbean people, educated in Jamaica and living in Britain today, can attest to having been "trained" by the cane, which they were taught to "affectionately" refer to as "Dr Do Me Good." Racist attitudes also prevailed in the establishing of schools, in that it was reported that parents of "colored" (mulatto or mixed race) children and the missionaries themselves often demanded that their children should not be educated with Africans, who according to one teacher were "Little negroes whose truly degraded habits (stealing, lying and swearing) exceed his own expectations."[49] In fact such were their anxieties that parents demanded that other schools or separate classes should be established so that their children would not be educated with Africans. This resulted in funds being stretched beyond measure in the developing of different types of schools; one with "superior" education for the rich white children, and one for those of rich Black children, with a third one providing "inferior" education for the poor African masses who were simply left to fulfill their destiny, and become the agricultural workers they were "destined" to be, with no pretentious expectation that they would ever attend high school.

BMS missionaries taught using the Lancasterian School system whereby, in the morning, the children were taught the three R's, reading, writing and religion, the Bible being the central textbook. Then in the afternoon, the girls were taught needlework, while the boys were taught agricultural skills. An example of the typical sentences which children up to sixteen years of age practiced writing (at least four times each sentence) can be seen below.

Table 2:[50] Lancasterian School Writing Exercises
Remember thy Creator in the days of thy Youth. Child, 14 yrs
Lying Lips are an abomination to the Lord. Lying Lips, Slave, 12 yrs.
My son if sinners entice thee, consent thou not. My son. Child, 11 yrs
Jesus Christ came into the world to save sinners. Child, 12 yrs
Blessed are they that mourn for they shall be comforted. Child, 14 yrs
If a ruler harkens to lies all his servants are wicked. Keep the commandments. Child, 11 yrs

This was "Bantu" education, like that experienced by young people in Soweto in the 1970s, designed to achieve no real-life prospects for its students. Happy then was a government and a church whose initial concerns, as expressed by George Dennis, inspector of schools in Guyana, was being fulfilled:

---

49. Bacchus, *Utilization, Misuse, and Development*, 262.
50. British and Foreign School Society, "Specimen."

If schools taught the black child "to read, write and cipher alone" . . . he [would] be so puffed up with his acquirements as to forsake the occupation of his fathers.[51]

Only those with "potential," the Black middle class, were allowed the "privilege" of attending high school, and being exposed to the sciences, mathematics, classical languages, and grammar. White middle-class children were considered to have natural ability and therefore were expected to study subjects akin to those studied in the public schools of England, such as Latin, Greek, and Algebra. Shockingly, Phillippo, who passionately led the drive for education amongst Baptists, placed both types of schools in one and the same building, making the differences visible for all to see.

At the outset of the grant the prospect of schooling had filled the enslaved with such great enthusiasm that they participated in large numbers, as can be seen in four of the schools established by Knibb: Suffield, Wilberforce, Waldensia, and Camberwell, which recorded a combined student roll of fifteen hundred students. However, as discrimination and injustice raised its ugly head, all schools saw their rolls falling away, as it became obvious that the planned education for equality was never going to be, and central to its failure were the missionaries themselves.

Native Teachers

Disappointed too were the creole African teachers who had expected to be trained as teachers, but instead saw their opportunities falling by the wayside, as their training funds had also been spent on evangelism. Once again racism and classicism conspired to prevent Africans from achieving their ambitions, as the next generation of leaders. They soon learned that without having been educated in a middle-class high school, they could never hope to qualify as a teacher, their only option being to "teach" at the primary level.

Yet in the midst of this native teachers had a "champion" in the colonial office, who oversaw the establishing of the schools and teachers. As the grant neared its end, the government complained that each organization (BMS, LMS, WMMS, CMS, Anglican and Methodists) was failing abysmally in its mandate to fulfil the training of native leaders. The BMS, on being asked why men who had shown great promise were only partially trained, and put in charge of a school to "do the best they could,"[52] responded by arguing that due to the ignorance of the enslaved, the large numbers of children to be

---

51. King, "Education in the British Caribbean," para. 14.
52. Tucker, *Glorious Liberty*, 120.

educated, and in many instances adults too, then the quality of the teaching provided to trainee teachers had to be sacrificed in order to increase their numbers as quickly as possible. Phillippo even went as far as to argue that it was not their academic potential which was of the utmost concern, but rather their moral and spiritual certitude. He argued that

> Most of our converts . . . hav[ing] emerged from a state of semi-heathenism it is scarcely to be expected they should endure a critic's eye or that there should not be found amongst them occasional inconsistencies and sins.[53]

Even more disparagingly he was heard to argue privately that he believed that the training of Africans as teachers was a morally unrealistic expectation, declaring to a colleague that

> Because of the damage done to their personalities and values during slavery, it would take some time before their moral development could reach the "desirably superior order" required for "teachers of religion or of any other subjects for that matter . . . [black teachers] were lacking in moral and intellectual talent . . . were ostentatious, mystical, ambiguous, indirect and verbose.[54]

If this was the view of folk known to be "friends" of the Africans, then one can only wonder what other anxieties and biases contributed to maintaining the ignorance of a people whose only desire was equality of opportunity, so that they could determine their own futures, and that of their families. Tensions therefore naturally erupted on all fronts as African Baptists saw their great expectations received with a great deal of disrespect. This resulted in diminishing respect for missionaries of all persuasions, and especially the BMS, in whom many had placed such faith and confidence.

The BMS missionaries, just like all other missionary societies, had shown themselves to be a people who were more than happy to educate the rich, but not the poor, who should not be encouraged to seek to move above their station in life, ultimately believing that "the time was 'not yet ripe' for the despised children of Ham to take over positions of Christian leadership."[55] However, as dispiriting as this and all the aforementioned contributory factors were in undermining the NEG, it ultimately failed because of Knibb's desire to "evangelize" Africa, and this led to a shift in the

---

53. Rooke, "Evangelical Missionary Rivalry," 347.
54. Bacchus, *Utilization, Misuse, and Development*, 308.
55. Rooke, "Evangelical Missionary Rivalry," 350.

utilization of resources, away from the education of the majority in order to concentrate on an elite Black minority who they could train to be ministers and teachers, in their likeness.

Africa Must Be Saved

As alluded to earlier in this chapter, BMS leaders, and in particular, Knibb had long harbored a desire and belief that emancipation should be the catalyst for the repatriation of a freed educated African back to Africa in order to pioneer a new evangelistic move across what they deemed to be a vast and un-ploughed territory. By the time emancipation came along, Knibb especially, had received the gratitude of the people, just as if he were Moses leading them to the promised land. They therefore trusted him to lead them through the wilderness years as they began to form themselves into a society and a nation. However unbeknownst to them, central to his decision-making were discussions on reparations, compensation, education, and the African mission, which somehow all became entwined into one project.

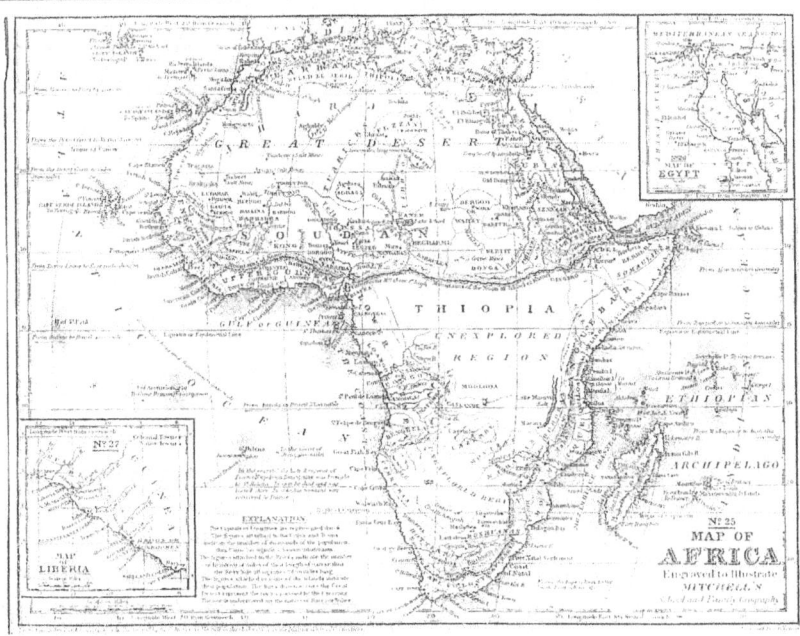

Map of Africa, ca. 1836, courtesy of Nardia Foster, educator.

Knibb was one of the first Baptists to see the possibilities of "free" Africans returning "home" to take the good news of the gospel to Africa. He first raised the subject with the BMS in 1832, agreeing with Buxton who believed in the need to plan ahead, beyond 1845, declaring that

> I am more and more impressed with the importance of normal schools. It is not that there will be a great demand for schoolmasters in the West Indies, but I have a strong confidence that Africa [will] be opened to commerce, civilisation and Christianity: and then there will be need, indeed, of educated and religious black schoolmasters. The idea of compensation to Africa through the means of the West Indies is a great favourite with me and I think we shall see the day when all shall be called to pour a flood of light and truth upon miserable Africa.[56]

However, despite the case which Knibb made for an Africa mission, the BMS Committee rather, encouraged him to concentrate on completing the work with the Africans in Jamaica before seeking to embark on a new mission in Africa. Knibb however was determined, and these thoughts never left him. We have seen overtime how manipulative he could be in his actions, so it might be cynicism on my part, or simply fact that he sought other ways to engender support and get what he ultimately wanted. In 1835, Knibb established *The Baptist Herald and Friend of Africa* newspaper, hoping perhaps just as Lisle had done, when naming his movement the EBS, that it would encourage African support. Knibb possibly had the expectation that the newspaper would once again serve to stir up similar feelings of Africa as their true home. However, this time he could emphasize to them that returning home to Africa was more a reachable goal than ever before, and that they would also be going with the power of the denomination behind them, as well as the blessings of the God of Ps 68:31. Soon after, he then created a missionary journal through the Jamaican Baptist Mission Agency, which was established in 1842.

The coming of emancipation seemed to have turned heads, just as Buxton had expected, especially after the number of school children began to decline, African Baptists having seen the lack of opportunity through the education system. BMS missionaries, rather than examining their own role in this, instead saw it as a lack of interest on the part of the African to receive an education. So began their increased interest in pursuing other fields which were considered to be ripe for harvest, and Africa would be made easier to conquer, if only they had a willing minority of African Jamaicans to help them. The BMS interest therefore increased in an African

---

56. Buxton, *Memoirs*, 458.

mission, and Knibb returned to the subject in 1840 while in England, where a British public was anxious to not only see him, but to hear news of emancipation, the freed Africans, and the state of the mission there. It was at a meeting at Exeter Hall on May 22, 1840, that Knibb spoke of the successes of the Jamaican mission and how in freedom the BMS mission, with the selfless giving of African brethren, had proved itself to be self-sufficient, and therefore ready for another challenge. He enthusiastically stated how

> When the apprenticeship came our chapels were in ruins, and our people were scattered; but such is their attachment to the house of God, and such their delight in his ordinances, that where only eleven small chapels stood, twenty large ones have been erected. . . . I am happy to inform you that I need now only your prayers. You kindly as a society supported me when my brethren were in bondage, but they determined, that the moment they were free, they would take the delightful work on themselves. . . . The fact is, that since my return to Jamaica, we have erected three chapels, two school-houses, and a mission-house, connected with my own church, at a cost of about £18,000 currency, and we have paid it all.[57]

Fortuitously he had brought with him impassioned statements of Africans who were desirous to go to Africa. He therefore implored the people to provide the means whereby they could embark on this great adventure, recalling how earnest the Africans were, relating how

> I asked him when he would be ready to go, "Tomorrow," was his reply. I said to them, "Perhaps you would be made slaves if you were to go." What was their answer? "We have been made slaves for men, we can be made slaves for Christ." These are men that ought to go, and whether you send them or not, go they will. . . . You tell us you have not the money. You have it, and, if you don't bestow it, God may take it away. . . . Will you, my brethren in the ministry, deny me this one request, the introduction of the gospel into Africa?[58]

With such good news Knibb then felt confident enough to write with some frustration to the BMS informing them also of the fact that he had begun to put his proposal of raising up African missionaries for Africa into practice. Given the facts presented concerning declining interests in

---

57. Hinton, *Memoir*, 357.
58. Hinton, *Memoir*, 363.

education, and the prospect of a new mission in Africa, it is no surprise that the BMS Committee had a change of heart. They were encouraged to learn that African Jamaicans were willing to take the gospel to Africa, thereby making it a more feasible proposition than their having to train up, and fund "foreign missionaries" as had been suggested when the subject was first mooted.

So, on June 3, 1840, just halfway through the implementation of the NEG, the Committee agreed that Africa "would be saved" through the missionary endeavors of African Jamaicans, stating confidently that

> In compliance with the representations of our brethren in Jamaica, and following what we apprehend to be the clear indications of Providence, we determine, in reliance on the divine blessing, to commence a mission to Western Africa.[59]

So, led by Knibb, Burchell, and Phillippo, the BMS committed to raising funds for a new work in Africa and as a result the Jamaica Baptist Mission was formed in 1842, separating itself from the financial support of the BMS. This cohort of missionaries, though they often disagreed about many aspects concerning the educating of African Jamaicans, were united when as one they then turned their attention to establishing a college in Kingston for the training of said African Jamaican missionaries and ministers. Calabar College led by Joshua Tinson was established in April 1843[60] with initial funds being provided by the British Baptist Home Committee.

However, Calabar also proved to be the beginning of the development of a truly African Jamaican middle-class education system. Calabar High School for Boys, soon followed, "designed to educate the sons of Jamaica ministers, Church officers and members of good standing who . . . became fitted to be clerks and accountants, or for apprenticeship to one of the learned professions."[61] At the same time Westwood High School for Girls was developed, wherein the best of womanhood in Jamaica were taught "Bible . . . needlework, cooking, [and] house-management."[62]

So, what did this all mean for the NEG and African Jamaicans as the educational emphasis of the church changed? Well, no longer was their priority to provide education and teachers for the majority of Jamaicans. Now they were only concerned with the ploughing of a new harvest in Africa through a small minority of educated, elite, African Jamaican Baptists, and

---

59. Hinton, *Memoir*, 366.
60. See Appendix 6 for a roll call of the first African Jamaican graduate ministers.
61. Tucker, *Glorious Liberty*, 122.
62. Tucker, *Glorious Liberty*, 123.

such was the determination to educate Africans for a great new missionary work in Africa that even the government of the day got involved. Accounts tell of a government who, on capturing renegade Portuguese and other slave ships in Caribbean waters, freeing the enslaved, took them to the nearest Baptist church, where it was expected that they could most easily be integrated into Jamaican society, as well as make themselves available to assist the BMS in the developing of the language skills of their Black Baptists. So successful in fact was this that the name "Baptist" became synonymous with "African," building up the expectation in many that one day soon, they would all be repatriated to their motherland, leaving Jamaica to the vagaries of a now defunct plantocracy.

However, before anything could be achieved, firstly the envy or upset created by BMS churches becoming the dominant church on the island led to other missionary organizations laying charges against Knibb in England, and he did nothing to improve the situation when he involved himself in politics. However, this time, it had nothing to do with "higher" concerns; it was purely political, thereby increasing his unpopularity amongst all parts of society, the enslaved, planters and other denominations. Firstly, he took part in an election campaign in 1837 on behalf of Richard Hill of Falmouth, and then in 1840, he actually stood as a candidate on behalf of small traders on the island.

As a result of this the BMS missionaries were seen as having been compromised on so many levels, with Knibb considered to have betrayed his role as an impartial player, which he had for so long claimed and championed. So compromised was he, in fact, that Burchell, reflecting on events since emancipation, expressed the following concerns in a letter:

> We are at present in this island in difficult circumstances—Our Mission is down in the estimation of all. Public meetings have been too many—they have satiated-they have disgusted—the refusal of Lord Russell to allow Bro. Knibb a personal interview at the Colonial Office will do much to keep us down. My firm conviction has always been and still is that a different course ought to have been pursued after 1st August 1838 than had been pursued and which would have saved us from the present difficulties—however we must recover our ground in the present difficulties—however we must recover our ground in the best way we can. Recovery is perfectly practicable were we all of one mind, but there is at present no union of views and consequently little union of feeling or action—we are not what we once were.[63]

63. Catherall, "Thomas Burchell," 359.

All BMS missionaries, as a consequence, faced increased hostility from the missionaries of other denominations, who also accused Knibb and his colleagues of allowing African leadership to thrive through the continuance of what they considered to be the syncretism begun by Lisle's EBS. Having kept the "ticket" and "leader" and "Daddy" systems, together with allowing charismatic practices, he was left open to the charge of

> Letting congregations grow beyond the personal supervision of the minister, giving too much power to the leaders, and selling tickets for veneration as a charm. The leaders, in turn, had been requiring special dreams and seizure by "the spirit," as a qualification for baptism, and had made baptism by immersion into a superstitious rite. In short, the official Baptists were charged with having taken on the characteristics of the (so-called) Native Baptists.[64]

Knibb's antagonists then took their complaints once again directly to the BMS Committee, who in turn began to express their own doubts in regards to the validity of the work in Jamaica. Knibb was recalled home in 1842 to explain his actions, but he, rather than be overwhelmed by this mounting opposition, forcefully declared in regards to one of his accusers,

> I would much rather receive into my house the vilest slave owner Jamaica ever produced, than some of the agents of the London Missionary Society. I feel no enmity to them, but such mean, snake-like, crawling conduct inspires my unqualified disgust. Under anonymous signatures and through the vilest papers they have attacked us. But do not fear that we shall reply.[65]

On returning to England Knibb pleaded his case, bringing with him one of the much criticized "tickets," which had the name of one of his members, which just so happened to be the same name as one of his leading opponents on the BMS Committee, a Mr. Edward Barrett. Needless to say, despite all the opposition Knibb's skills won the day, and he was victorious on all accounts. However, while in England, he and Burchell also passionately pleaded their cause amongst the British public and the BMS for a Jamaican Baptist church led by Africans. He and Burchell developed doubts as to whether there could ever be acceptance and support for Black-led churches within the BMS.

---

64. Curtin, *Two Jamaicas*, 165.
65. Francis, "Baptist in Jamaica," 7.

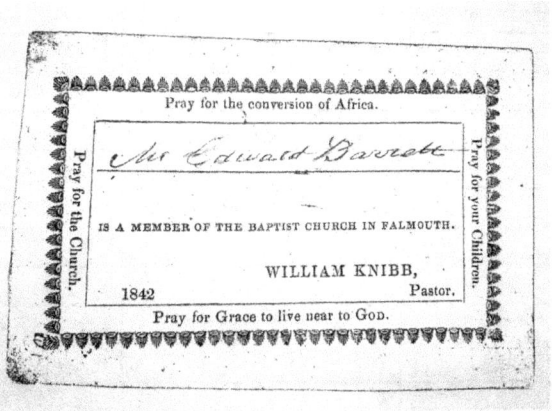

Ticket, Edward Barrett—William Knibb, 1842. Used with the kind permission of the BMS Archives, Angus Library and Archive, WI/3

Burchell and Knibb therefore determined that on their return to Jamaica, rather than consider reuniting with the EBS, and by then many other independent Baptist congregations, they would separate the church from the BMS and establish a "native" church, thereby allowing African Christians to be able to develop in their own culturally appropriate way, and of course assist Knibb in preparing for the new mission to Africa. Africans excited by the prospects of returning home soon returned to using many of the languages which they had spoken prior to their enslavement. Creoles as well as those African-born members, though able to use patois, chose at the same time to renew many of their cultural practices, including the use of words remembered from their mother tongue.

In 1842 Dendy, in a letter to John Clark, stated that his membership at Salter's Hill Chapel included the following African-born members:

Table 3:[66] African Languages spoken in Jamaica, 1842

Ethnic Group	Members	Inquirers
Koromantees	19	7
Eboes	119	15
Popaws	17	2
Mandigoes	5	1
Bandas	3	2
Warnee	1	1
Kongoes	29	25
Guineas	40	11
Clambs	6	1
Nangos	5	1
House	1	4
Moko	5	1

The lexicon of patois expanded as African words were added, and historian Barrett explains a word used then which has remained in use to the present day:

> When one was told that one nyam one's food, this is a mild rebuke for greediness. The word comes from the Twi, meaning "to move quickly" or "to destroy a thing quickly."[67]

They were creating a new culture in a new world and Knibb, undaunted and undeterred, saw himself as simply responding to the needs around him. On returning to Jamaica, he and Burchell gained the support of their colleagues to separate, from all regions, except that which was led by Phillippo in the east. They nevertheless declared the home mission's independence on the fourth anniversary of emancipation, August 1, 1842. However, soon after drought and a hurricane struck Jamaica, and this resulted in an economic decline which led to great unemployment and poverty. Knibb once again had to return to England, but this time he was accompanied by T. F. Abbott, in order to seek assistance once again from the BMS for the home society. The BMS agreed but with the proviso that as the churches in Jamaica were now independent of the BMS they would no longer receive direct funding from England.

It was shortly after this, in 1845, that Knibb contracted yellow fever and died with Burchell who had remained faithful to him, nursing him in

---

66. Francis, "Baptist in Jamaica," 7.
67. Barrett, *Sun and the Drum*, 24.

the full knowledge that he too would more than likely also die of the same. It was in fact a year after himself contracting the fever that Burchell, seeming to be in remission, chose to travel to England for what many had hoped would be a successful recouperation. Prior to leaving, he paid a visit to all the churches which he had pastored during his time in Jamaica; suffice it to say that when the news came in 1846 that their beloved pastor had died in London, England, their hearts were truly broken. The demise of Knibb and Burchell also meant the demise of their ambitious plans for an African Jamaican mission to Africa. While it failed to take root, it had nevertheless begun, and so they were able to leave a second legacy of the NEG, a mission on the Gold Coast, Ghana. Ghana's gain was Jamaica's loss, and more particularly, a loss for all future generations of African children who aspired to be more than "hewers of wood and carriers of water."[68]

Such was the tragedy of the NEG, that by the time of the grant's expiration in 1845, the colonial office was able, justifiably so, to accuse the missionaries, of all persuasions, of misappropriating the funds which they had received. In the ten years of the administration of the NEG, it was proved that they had failed to use the funds set aside for the educational improvement of Africans across the British Caribbean, instead using it either to build church buildings, increase their denominational territories or to form the foundation for a new missionary venture in Africa, all aided by petty denominational rivalries which brought shame to the European missionary movement across all the islands.

African Jamaicans were grieved to see these events unfold. Many of them had expected to enter their promised land of freedom by either returning "home" to Africa, or create a firm foundation for the future of their children and grandchildren. All found their dreams dashed. They were a people who had endured the apprenticeship system and paid in blood, for their own emancipation, while assisting the BMS in the building of new churches, as well as buying land to build their new homes, in the free towns and villages for their children's future, but without equal educational opportunities, they saw it all suddenly drain away. They had been treated horrendously, disrespect, prejudice, contempt, and paternalistic and superior attitudes, had left them at the bottom of the economic and social order, the majority having little or nothing to show for it. Spiritual considerations had once again taken priority over their practical and physical needs. Africans were once again slapped in the face but this was a falling out which was never repaired, with many Africans returning once and for all to the only available religious systems which

68. Josh 9:21 (KJV).

allowed them to be themselves and have equality of opportunities, however meager those opportunities were. In independence they returned to the Black church.

Chapter 10

A Season of Joys and Disappointments

Black, white, and bond, and free,
Castes and proscriptions cease;
The Negro walks in liberty,
The Negro sleeps in peace;
Read the great charter on his brow,
"I am a man, a brother, now."
—Philip Henry Cornford

THE DAY EMANCIPATION CAME must have been a bitter sweet experience for those who had finally achieved it. Bitter in that it had taken so many years for the British government to acknowledge their humanity, and therefore return to them their dignity. Sorrow too for those who had not survived, many of whom had lived their entire lives enslaved. However, though emancipation was finally to come, there were diehards in society, and the church who saw this as a retrograde step. Men such as Presbyterian minister Rev. Gardiner Spring were typical of those around them, who when asked his thoughts on emancipation "announced publicly, that could he emancipate the slaves by a prayer he would not offer it."[1] Despite such protestations,

---

1. Bland, *African American Slave Narratives*, 934.

warnings, hypocritical instructions, and threats, they could do nothing further. The Emancipation Proclamation was read throughout the island, declaring that

> Whereas an Act has been passed by the Legislator of Island of Jamaica for terminating the present System of Apprenticeship on the First Day of August next and thereby granting the blessing and privileges of unrestricted freedom to all classes of its inhabitants and whereas it is incumbent on all the inhabitants of this our Island to testify their grateful sense of this Divine Favour.
>
> We do therefore by and with the advice of our Privy Council of this our said Island direct and appoint that Wednesday the said first day of August next be observed in all churches and chapels as a day of general thanksgiving to almighty God for these His mercies and of humble intercession for his continued blessing and protection on this most important occasion and we do hereby call upon persons of all classes within this our said island to observe this said day of August next with the same reverence and respect which is observed and due to the Sabbath.[2]

As instructed, the marking of the event began the night before, and it lasted the following two days. It was a time of great celebration, thanking God for answered prayer. Tucker, describing the event, stated that

> The evening of July 31, 1838, in Jamaica, was a time like that of the Exodus from Egypt, never to be forgotten. At all the largest centres of our mission—Spanish Town, Savanna-la-Mar, Brownstown, Falmouth, Montego Bay—special evening services were held resembling watch-night services. As the hour of midnight approached the crowded audience bowed in prayer, and after it had struck, rose up to praise and thank God. . . . The scene at Falmouth, where William Knibb presided . . . he declared "The monster is dying," he said as the clock began to strike; and after the last stroke: "The monster is dead; the negro is free." . . . The first day of freedom was spent in religious services, chiefly of praise and thanksgiving; the second, in giving a good time to the young. . . . He (God) let the oppressed go free.[3]

---

2. "History Notes," para. 1.
3. Tucker, *Glorious Liberty*, 37.

A Season of Joys and Disappointments   221

Emancipation of the Negroes.[4]

Full freedom was given to 30,000 men, women, and children. Liberty trees were planted and liberty graves dug, wherein chests were placed in the ground and it is known that in each of them, "lie buried a driver's whip, a neck-chain, handcuffs and like symbols of slavery,"[5] together with any other items each congregation saw as a relevant testimony to a life lived in enslavement.

We can learn a great deal about the EBS by what additional items were put in the chests. The truth of what some of those additional items were was shared with me by a Mr. Nathan Cunningham, now a member of Grace Baptist Church in Clarendon, but who as a child attended the school attached to Gurney's Mount Baptist Church in Trelawny. Mr. Cunningham testified as to how, when a boy, he knew nothing of liberty trees until a hurricane blew down one such tree, in his school yard, and the chest was exposed.

4. Madden, *Twelvemonth's Residence*, 1:1.
5. Tucker, *Glorious Liberty*, 37.

In the chest the school children not only found the items described above, but also Spanish and British gold coins. Being children, he said, they simply took them to the shop and exchanged them for sweets. Imagine, a people who had endured enslavement, with little or no material possessions, but their hatred for their European "masters" was such that they would rather bury the slaver's gold than keep it to start a new life for themselves and their families.

That said, the event itself did not take place without significant recognition being given to the work of those early pioneers, who by their very presence and beliefs began the drive towards, and built the foundations for, emancipation. It is to be noted that on Emancipation Day each church was given a song sheet, containing three original hymns, written for the occasion. We are fortunate to have today, one of these song sheets which was used by the members of all BMS congregations.[6] Significantly if one looks at the cover of the song sheet, there is contained within it a testimony in remembrance of those of the EBS who had gone before. The hymn sheet gives them the ultimate accolade by simply recording the following words, "Ethiopia shall soon stretch out her hands unto God."

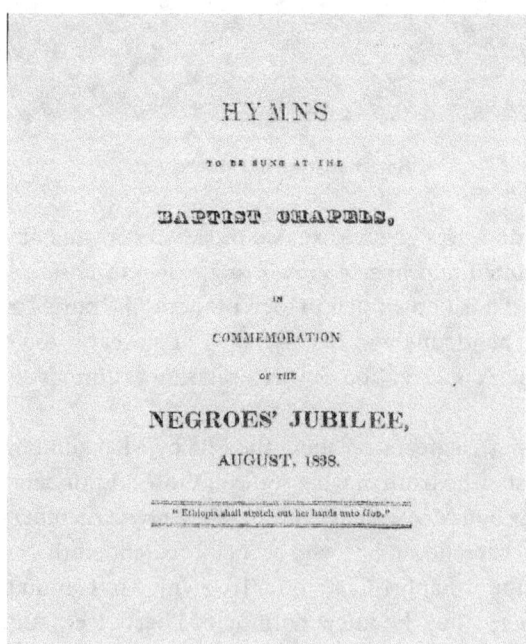

Emancipation Day Hymn Sheet, Cover, courtesy of D. Morrison.

6. See Appendix 8 for hymns sung on the day of emancipation.

THE BMS CELEBRATES

The generation of BMS leaders who took charge of many EBS congregations finally had something to celebrate. The goal had been achieved and so it seemed that the pioneering generation of the BMS could, for once, well and truly pat themselves on the back for staying the course. Yet before we go any further in this chapter in pouring praise on the BMS, one missionary stands out above all others for his contribution in enabling so many children and their families to reach their full emancipation, and that is Thomas Burchell.

Thomas Burchell becomes Doctor Burchell

It is also a little-known fact that Burchell used the medical skills which he had acquired at Bible College to become an integral part of the medical provision provided to African children and others during the period known as apprenticeship, and then after emancipation. This was necessary as many of the estates withdrew their medical provision to the children who had been freed in 1834, the medical doctors presuming that as there would be no more plantations after 1838, then their services were no longer needed.

Burchell therefore took it upon himself to provide such assistance in the form of a dispensary at Mount Carey, in Hanover, where it is said that

> When at length a debilitated constitution compelled him to seek a residence among the hills, Mount Cary assumed the character and the importance of a dispensary in relation to the surrounding districts; as many as from two to three thousand of the coloured peasantry annually receiving gratuitous relief. The obtaining of medicine from England, however, in requisite quantities, became too expensive; hence he further turned his chemistry to account by making his own resins, tincture, etc; yet even then, his outlay was heavy, amounting in the latter period of life to nearly £100 per annum. The reader will probably remember that, at an earlier period of life, Mr Burchell had an opportunity of attending a course of lectures on physiology and anatomy. The knowledge then acquired he now employed in the practice of surgery to some extent; and occasionally he used the knife. To assist him in dressing of wounds, he took into his house, from time to time several orphan children of his members, whom he trained to that beneficent service, in which they showed much expertness.[7]

7. Burchell, *Memoir*, 304.

It was Burchell also who, following the refusal of Knibb to implement a policy whereby the missionaries would "purchase" the enslaved, in order to give them their freedom, found another means whereby they could do so. He was one of the main motivating voices, who directed his fellow missionaries to impress upon their slave-owning members, to forego any further claims on their slaves, and to give them their freedom, one year earlier than expected, on August 1, 1837. More than forty such individuals were given their freedom within his own congregations. However, it is a sad dichotomy that within the same Baptist congregation were both slave holders and the enslaved, one perhaps thanking God for the increase in production, while the other grateful for having escaped the lash, and surviving another day. Nevertheless, once emancipation was achieved, Burchell was praised once again for demonstrating, through the baptism of his daughter in 1843, his belief in the equality of all peoples, in what he hoped would be a new Jamaica. Of that event he rejoiced stating that

> It was my happiness to baptize her in the "Great River," four miles distant from Mount Cary, on Sunday morning the 1st of January, together with about seventy others. Between two and three thousand spectators were present . . . my beloved daughter entered the river, hand in hand, with our servant girl. As soon as she was baptized, the assembled multitudes broke forth in strains of gladsome and thrilling melody, giving utterance to their feelings in the well-known doxology, "Praise ye the lord. Hallelujah!" Eshranna is the first child of the mission family, born and brought up on the island, and publicly baptized, and that too in company with the natives. In this the people take special delight, saying, "Now we see there is no distinction!"[8]

In return for his goodness, the people were more than happy to assist him in any project which he undertook. This was a joy which seemed for a while, at least, to translate across the whole BMS.

---

8. Burchell, *Memoir*, 304.

Male and Female Baptismal Service, Jamaica. Royal Museums Greenwich, accessed https://www.rmg.co.uk/collections/objects/rmgc-object-254872

INCREASING DISSATISFACTION WITH THE BMS

Such was Knibb's contentment that a year after emancipation, he wrote home, responding to the concerns which had been raised in regards to giving Africans full freedom, declaring that

> You ask me how we are getting on, how freedom is working. I speak the feeling of a heart overflowing with joy when I say that my most ardent expectations have been more than realized. If ever the finger of God has been seen it is in Jamaica. We read the blessed effects of freedom in a contented, cheerful and industrious peasantry, in empty jails, in absence of pauperism, in crowded chapels, thriving schools, and in a stimulous to internal trade, unprecedented in the annals of Jamaica. This is not romance nor fiction. In the whole of this parish in which were full 27,000 slaves not one of the emancipated as far as I can learn has sought parish relief. A beggar, except from old age, I have not seen. Argus could not find a vagrant, and the amount of crime was last Quarter, two persons, convicted, or one I forgot which, of petty theft—in the first year of freedom in Jamaica, when 300,000 human beings were in one day set free, the militia was virtually disbanded; the police on the island was discharged, and a few parochial constables enjoy a perfect synacure in pursuing the peace of the Island.[9]

---

9. Knibb, "Letter to Mr Charles."

Tablet. For the Emancipated Sons of Africa, August 1, 1838. Picture by D. Morrison, Webb Memorial Baptist Chapel, Falmouth, Jamaica.

Yet, for all of this good news, an increased dissatisfaction began to come to the surface in regards to his own denomination and mission board. He constantly challenged every attitude which he believed, belittled, or denigrated his African brethren. Together with Burchell he frequently took a stand against the BMS, who they felt had actually failed to make a firm commitment to the abolition question. Relationships with colleagues too had often been strained as a result, and after one particular incident he

> Was accused of being an "officious meddler" when he attacked the idea that missionaries could buy slaves, even if it was argued

that it would thus be easier for the slaves to purchase their freedom.[10]

Knibb, already a "thorn in the flesh" of many, nevertheless pursued a course of action which demonstrated, he believed, would bring about a relevant African Jamaican church, as a witness to the world. While he did not use the term "Ethiopian" to refer to them, he often used the term "Africa" and "African" to identify his African brothers and sisters in the church. There were also tensions in wider areas, concerning church governance, where the people now free and independent wanted to be included, which at the very least meant being a part of the decision-making processes of their churches. One particular incident comes to mind, concerning the leadership of Phillippo Baptist Church. In 1841, Phillippo, due to sickness, traveled "home" to England. Thomas Dowson, a newly appointed missionary, was given the pastorate of the church in his absence. He pastored the church for nearly three years, before Phillippo's return. Dowson then withdrew to England for six months; however, on his return in 1844, the congregation expressed the desire to call Dowson as their minister instead of Phillippo much to the latter's annoyance. The matter was referred in 1845 to the BMS in England, and they replied succinctly that

> The Committee having given up mission work in Jamaica, there is no propriety in their interfering at all in points in dispute between churches and ministers.[11]

However, rather than seek to resolve the issue in house, according to the Covenant which Lisle had left them, or the ecclesiastical principles abided by the Baptist churches, Phillippo instead decided to take the matter to the High Court of Chancery, where he won the case on November 4, 1850. Despite this, he faced two more attempts to unseat him, and the matter was only finally concluded when Thomas Dowson established a new independent Baptist congregation, also in Spanish Town.[12] Understandably, however, members of the congregation became increasingly disillusioned and discouraged, that in simply seeking to replace their minister, as allowed, their opinion did not matter. According to Underhill, such issues of correct church polity were secondary in comparison to the twenty or so years of service which Phillippo had given to the church. Such a display

---

10. Catherall, "Bristol College," 299.

11. Underhill, *Life of James*, 228.

12. Dowson and nine elders from Spanish Town soon established a new congregation and purchased property on the corner of White Church Street and Duke of Wellington Street. Robertson, *Gone Is the Ancient Glory*, 177.

of ingratitude and lack of respect for Phillippo was therefore seen as being quite sinful. Underhill wrote this:

> There can be no doubt that the painful incidents of this conflict greatly affected Mr Phillippo's judgement of the Negro character. The bright side had ever presented itself to him in the early years of his missionary life. He had hitherto known the people as remarkably accessible to kindness, and to the influence of those who had sought their freedom and the advancement of their highest interests. He had seen them as peculiarly impressionable to Divine teaching, docile to those in authority, and grateful for sympathy under their oppressions. But now he had to learn that slavery could not be abolished without leaving behind a legacy of evil, and that its mischievous effects were not to be at once removed by the righteous act of emancipation. . . . "Half our virtue," says Homer, "is torn away when a man becomes a slave, and the other half goes when he becomes a slave let loose."[13]

In enslavement they had to be compliant, therefore such comments signified that even after so many years, members of the BMS mistook forced compliance and obedience for gratitude. Yet, not all BMS missionaries demanded such deference of those who were once enslaved. The ecclesiastical principles were in fact honored in the case of Rev Dendy and his congregants of Salter's Hill Baptist Church. Together they agreed and signed a letter of complaint about the remittances to be paid to the Presbytery of Jamaica.[14] They were included and this made the response by Phillippo, the most senior of the missionaries at that time, seem simply unconscionable. This and other such incidents, particularly by those whom they had respected, resulted in the majority of churchgoing African Jamaicans simply remaining in them, in order to receive the benefits of the now "acceptable" church in terms of such things as baptism, employment opportunities, and the limited educational opportunities available to them. At the same time, they were known to pursue the creating of their own new Black-led churches, or attended where they could communities of the EBS, wherever they could find them.

How the BMS missionaries felt as a result of this upheaval, with the knowledge they were no longer fully in charge, is best summed up in the words of BMS missionary John Clarke, who lamented,

> How different now is the life of a Minister in Jamaica to that of a Missionary a few years ago. Then it was all happiness—almost

13. Underhill, *Life of James*, 230.
14. Dendy, "Letter."

> unmingled joy. Wherever one went multitudes came flocking to hear the good news. Almost every Monday I would have 20 to 100 anxious enquirers—Baptisms large and frequent—scarcely any exclusions—all at peace in the Mission. Now congregations are as good as ever—but comparatively few come forward enquiring what must we do to be saved Baptisms are few and far between—cases of discipline are numerous and painful, and our missionary band is rent asunder.[15]

Yet, it wasn't long before tensions were ratcheted up once again, as onto the stage came a new governnor, John Eyre, who saw his task as righting the wrongs of 1831. He was joined by a new generation of BMS missionaries who, knowing little of Lisle and his cadre of leaders, were not hesitant in expressing their disdain for what they deemed to be a people who were in the main uneducated and uncivilized. A people who could only benefit from professional, educated, trained ministers and teachers such as themselves. This they believed would enable the churches of the newly formed Jamaican Baptist Union (1854) to both mature and grow; however, Burchell was not so impressed with them, leaving this stark warning, which by 1865 many may have wished that they had paid attention to

> Those who have recently come out have acted as tho' they were influenced by any spirit rather than a Christian Missionary spirit. . . . It has appeared to me (I shall be glad if I am in error) that our recent friends have been anxious to procure the most important vacant situations without any regard to the destitute districts—Souls have lost sight too much—I have felt almost disgust at the grasping after the best stations. When we came out we had no stations—we had to work for them and I grieve to see these things.[16]

NEW RESISTANCE

It had begun well, this season of freedom; however, dissatisfaction in the church was matched by a growing dissatisfaction amongst the dispossessed, the planters. I cannot imagine that when the Emancipation Proclamation was delivered to all the peoples of Jamaica in 1838, the African Jamaican majority anticipated in any way that the freedoms which they had so passionately fought for were to be only a fleeting temporary thing. That the

15. Gordon, *Our Cause*, 29.
16. Catherall, "Thomas Burchell," 359–60.

anger which lay in the hearts of the "dispossessed" white minority who now held power within the Legislature would rise up and lead to the genocide of many.

Concerns about the future plight of the free African majority and their place in Jamaica was raised by William Knibb in 1839 when the ink had barely dried on the Emancipation Proclamation. The government, no longer able to divide the society by the terms "slave" and "free," determined that society should be defined by the color of one's skin. Knibb, in response, expressed his opposition, stating that

> There are infamous laws existing in the island, which we must try to get abolished. One of them has been alluded to in the House of Commons, by the Under Secretary for colonies. It is to this effect:—"All rogues, vagabonds, or other idle persons, found wandering from place to place or otherwise disorderly, may be apprehended by the constable, and taken before a magistrate, who is empowered to order him or her to be whipped on the naked back, not exceeding thirty-nine lashes." Suppose a person like one whom I could name, who is so well known for the tender mercies he possesses, were to see my deacon, Mr Brown, or his wife, upon his property, some day just after he had had his dinner, and should order his constable to take hold of them as idle vagabonds, and lay them down, and give them each thirty-nine lashes, would that be right? ("No.") is that the way freemen are to be treated? ("No, no.") No, my friends, it is not; and I will never rest till this law is repealed. This act makes it lawful to send any coloured person who comes within the act to the workhouse, to be set to work for any time, not exceeding six months; but all white persons committed for the same offences are to be fed, lodged, and worked, separate and apart from the free negroes, mulattoes, and slaves. This law makes the distinction of complexion the rule for the measurement of punishment. The white man, or the white female, who is taken up as a vagrant, is to be fed, lodged, and accommodated with comparative comfort; but the black man, or the black female, is to be subjected to the withering influence of cruelty, and to all the agonies that may be inflicted by the cart whip. This law was never made for freemen; it was made for slaves. Send it to Cuba, send it to America, or anywhere else you please; but it won't do for Jamaica! . . . My opinion is that every law which makes any reference to colour at all ought instantly to be repealed.[17]

---

17. Hinton, *Memoir*, 315–16.

However, the following years saw a governing "plantocracy" who increasingly found ways in which they could put their separatist plans into action, plans which culminated in the events which took place in Morant Bay and the wider parish of Saint Thomas in the East, in 1865. The task took on a greater sense of urgency when the Legislature gained a new champion in their camp, the new governnor, Edward John Eyre. Eyre arrived in Jamaica in 1862 with a plan which quickly used the nervousness of a fearful white minority to show them that they were a part of the continuing "battle" begun in 1831. This time, however, he argued that they were facing an empowered "slave" population, who were seeking to not only undermine their positions, but remove the white population completely from the island, by whatever means necessary.

Ever fearful they looked around Jamaica and identified the reality of what Eyre had been talking about. Firstly, their profits from exported goods declined considerably, but this was in large part due to the fact that

> Some proprietors at emancipation drove their labourers from the estates, and one who was living in the north side of the island. He swore that he would not allow a "nigger" to live within three miles of his house: Of course the man was speedily ruined.[18]

At the same time African Jamaicans, able to now work their plot of land, found it to be extremely profitable. Such was their success that it was reported how prosperous many of them had become. Underhill testified that

> They have purchased 354,575 acres of land, at the rate of say 30s. an acre, a sum far below what was paid at the time when the settlements were first formed. They have provided themselves with clothes, to the value say of £4 for each family. They have stocked their freeholds with pigs, goats, horses and carts, say a the rate of £3 each family. Following the calculations of the Hanover Society of Arts, these freeholders would be possessed of upwards of then thousand small sugar mills; but considering that in districts like Westmoreland and Vere, where the sugar estates are large, and the people produce little sugar themselves, and that in other parishes, pimento or coffee cultivation absorbs much attention, I will put the number of sugar mills down at five thousand for the entire island, at £10 each, as valued by the Society of Arts. And finally, the deposits in the Savings' Banks

---

18. Underhill, *West Indies*, 268.

amount to £49,399. The total of these accumulations reaches to more than two million sterling.[19]

At the same time, he also observed that with this newfound wealth and independence came a generosity of spirit which was second to none. Underhill saw many acts of kindness, especially by the free, towards those who had once oppressed them, challenging the narrative of those who cared only for themselves. He wrote how

> Near to Linstead lived a lady who had enjoyed a handsome income from hiring out her numerous slaves. In her last years she became poor, and was sustained by the affection and benevolence of her former bondsmen. One advanced money to bury her, and was repaid by a few acres of land. In another case, a black woman sought out, in Kingston, the daughter of her former owner, who had fallen into sin. She took her home, nursed her, fed and clothed her, and sought to reclaim her. After some months, the girl was again tempted to go astray by a white man; she became a castaway; but the black woman weeps for her still. In another parish, I saw a man who had made a little money since he became free. He and his wife were in a state of contention, because she wishes her husband to leave their little property to her old mistress who is in poverty, and to set aside their son, which the husband is naturally reluctant to do.[20]

A more unlikely group of oppressors one never did see, especially as many them, in freedom, had returned to the EBS. It is believed for example that the membership of all Parson Killick's congregations numbered approximately 3700 members in 1841. They had also begun to prosper as a part of a free Jamaica, Killick himself receiving financial support from the state to actually build a chapel in Bethany, as well as £200 from the House of Assembly to repair his chapel in Saint Thomas in the East. What a turn of events. His church soon attracted friends and members from the House of Assembly, including a George William Gordon, and Charles Price, both of whom we shall speak of later.

There were many other significant characters and events which, while in and of themselves innocent in that they simply showed African advancement and self-empowerment, together they served over time to highlight to the ever-fearful white minority that the threat which Eyre spoke of was

---

19. Underhill, *West Indies*, 420–21. In an inquiry made in the congregation of the Rev. J. Thompson of Mount Charles, Saint Andrew's, it was found that among seventy-three heads of families, there were seventy horses and mules.

20. Underhill, *West Indies*, 257.

real. Therefore, the battle began to exclude them, especially from the upper echelons of society. Such was the case of one Robert Gordon.

Robert Gordon

Gordon had been the ideal candidate to work with his CofE colleagues, having been acculturated into the Jamaican middle classes, and alienated from his own culture. He believed that the 'native' churches lacked education, and the appropriate spiritual authority, and therefore should be considered 'less than' those established by the European Missionaries. He was of the opinion therefore that the development of the Black population could only be achieved through attendance at churches with an 'educated' clergy rather than as he put it:

> Self-ordained native ministers—who were of the same class as the people whom their presumption made them think themselves qualified to teach.[21]

However, Gordon, an ordained, qualified CofE minister, by his experiences soon came to realize that whereas his future was once determined by the term "slave," now he was being identified as a Black man, and as a Black Jamaican, no amount of "seasoning" into Western Christianity would as he had hoped, make him equal in the eyes of his white Anglican counterparts. His life therefore became one of having to challenge the status quo in a Church which refused to accept Black people as equal under God.

His experience typified the difficult position which educated middle class Black Jamaican elites found themselves in, in their continuing fight for the right to be treated equally. Gordon became a symbol of all those calling for justice for the Black majority who were denied leadership positions purely because of the color of their skin. He and others of his "class" were however made to learn that they may have developed the skills required to become a priest, but they would never be given a mandate to preach, and be called priest in a church led by their white peers.

His repeated requests to be a priest in his own land being repeatedly denied caused him, over time, to change his position, as he was forced to challenge the status quo to no avail. Despite the fact that he had been accepted as a minister in both Canada and England, he died never having been allowed to minister in the country of his birth, Jamaica.

Gordon served out his ministry as the headmaster of Wolmer's Grammar School in Kingston, and was an eyewitness to the events which

---

21. Stewart, *Religion and Society*, 104.

happened later in Morant Bay. Towards the conclusion of his ministry, he expressed the hope that the Anglo-Saxon race would see and accept that it was:

> Their moral duty to do everything in their power . . . to assist in elevating them [black people] to whatever stations in life they may have the qualifications for filling . . . [and] . . . to place no superable bar in their way, on the grounds of colour.[22]

The Great Jamaican Revival (1860–62)

It is said that Pentecostal fervor, revivals of faith, often takes root in communities where there have been social and political upheavals with people suffering from oppression and degradation and in need of justice. Jamaica was no different in this regard, and so was ready for a revival, particularly as change and equality for all was proving slow to be realized, the newly arrived missionaries simply seeing African Jamaicans as ignorant heathens who practiced superstition. As a result of this, they often came into conflict with them, continually trying to exclude them from the decision-making processes of the church. This impasse resulted in many contentions and it was in the midst of these tensions that the Great Revival came as a whirlwind.

Never was such a joyous occasion the cause for such disunity, leading to increased religious and social divisions. Many missionaries had hoped that a revival would come to bring the heathen back to Christ, while the Africans hoped that a revival would open up the hearts of the heathen ministers. Well, come it did in September 1860, embracing the whole island. It began amongst Moravian youth in Fairfield and moved to New Carmel, before expanding to the churches in Saint Elizabeth, each one significantly having been the missionary centers evangelized by George Lewis and his team of leaders.

Initially folk thanked God for answered prayer, saved lives, and the turning away from "sin" as church numbers dramatically increased. European church leaders legitimized it, declaring that "Prayer has not been offered in vain, for a Pentecostal shower has come down,"[23] having heard how churches had "collected evidence of witnesses particularly of . . . intelligent men, not credulous or fanatical, or easily imposed upon."[24] Of his own experience of the revival LMS missionary Duncan Fletcher, happily complained:

22. Stewart, *Religion and Society*, 103–4.
23. Erskine, *Decolonizing Theology*, 32.
24. Erskine, *Decolonizing Theology*, 32.

> I had no sooner begun to carry into effect in September last, than the Holy Spirit was manifestly poured out and our prayer meeting were multiplied in number, and greatly increased in attendance . . . 400 solemnly professed they had been converted in our chapel during one month.[25]

Services erupted everywhere, with people undeterred by a lack of ministers to officiate, by simply organizing their own prayer meetings and services—some of which lasted up to five hours at a time—believing that all that was necessary was the presence of the Holy Spirit. No denomination was left untouched, and no church doubted that God was visiting them in the power of the Holy Spirit. People were being "slain in the Spirit," and there were surprising unexpected confessions of sin from a people who had so often been considered to be beyond civilizing. Even the doubting Phillippo reported how during one service:

> The building was filled from top to bottom, and soon after the service commenced the greatest excitement prevailed. In one direction were poor unlettered Africans pouring out their supplications in some such language as this, and in the words of one of them with the utmost earnestness, his voice heard above the tumult; 'Lord, save me—me a sinner—me a drunkard, me a tief, me de Sabbat-broker. . . . O Jesus, save me by dy precious blood.'[26]

Reconciliation was reported to be happening amongst husbands and wives, parents and children, healing that which the missionaries had spent many years trying to force. All was now being accomplished by the Holy Spirit, with LMS missionaries reporting how the following scenes were being repeated at many of their mission stations:

> Some were kneeling, weeping and praying: confessing their sins to God, naming them . . . this they did audibly; sometimes not only specifying and deploring their crimes, but also praying for the companions in guilt, by name. . . . People were weeping and wailing aloud . . . we had a few extraordinary cases of persons "stricken" or prostrated and dumb for days and in one or two instances weeks together.[27]

People in the grip of revival fever flocked to the churches to worship God, and there were unusual happenings being reported everywhere.[28] Rum

---

25. Findlay and Holdsworth, *History*, 374; Fletcher, "Letter to LMS."
26. Austin-Broos, *Jamaica Genesis*, 58.
27. Alloway, "Letter."
28. See Appendix 9 for examples of prayer meetings and attitudes when facing death.

shops voluntarily shut down, gambling ceased, and highways and byways were the scene of marriages, baptisms, and visitations of the Holy Spirit. In fact, such was the enthusiasm for the revival, that it is believed that 37,000 Bibles were sold within the first eighteen months of the revival, the Bible once again receiving elevated status as people sought to read it for themselves. However, after a year many missionaries became increasingly concerned that the African Jamaicans' increasingly "African" response to the revival signaled a return to so-called heathen practices and more particularly syncretism. Therefore, just as they had done in the early days, they began looking for signs of this, and identified it in such things as the use of cologne (a local alcoholic beverage) and water instead of wine during the Communion service, and "dancing in circles . . . showing signs of possession."[29] Also, when the people wept with joy at having experienced the power of the Holy Spirit, it caused fear in missionaries who dismissed such outbursts as "overstep[ping] all bounds of order and propriety."[30]

One can only imagine how African Jamaicans must have felt when as they worshiped using their preferred genre of music and demonstrated an ecstatic worship style, they were shunned by those with whom they had previously celebrated. In fact, so poorly were their cultural practices received that despite the revival continuing for another year, the missionaries took it upon themselves to declare that the revival had come to an end in 1861, thereafter accusing Africans of feigning "conversion," and once again declaring them to be a people who were:

> So emotionally unstable and so steeped in ignorance and sensuality, despite its surface knowledge of Christianity . . . brought discredit upon the work of God.[31]

A minority of missionaries, primarily the Moravians, did however try in vain to defend the essence of the revival, pleading that:

> For some months this memorable revival, which soon affected old and young alike, was disfigured by what the critic may call excesses; and yet, on the other hand, we must remember that those excesses were no worse than those which occurred in England during the Evangelical Revival . . . in reality the main features were the same; and nearly every incident that happened in Jamaica might be paralleled by something similar in England.[32]

29. Gordon, *Our Cause*, 91.
30. Johnson, "Evangelical Christendom," 34.
31. Findlay and Holdsworth, *History*, 374.
32. Hutton, *History*, 226–27.

Baptist Worship, Spanish Town.[33]

33. Phillippo, Jamaica, between pp 288-89.

They were, however, in the minority. The majority simply bemoaned the fact that the African could be much improved, even civilized out of their heathen, paganistic, and heathen ways, if only they could be divested of their degenerate culture. The majority of the white population were soon filled with fear, and took to carrying guns for the remainder of the revival, fearing that it would naturally lead to rebellion once again.

This then brought to an end any kind of enthusiasm the missionaries had for "converting" African Jamaicans to their understanding of Christianity, confirming their belief that they were an ungrateful, unreachable people, who after such benevolence granted to them were after all beyond redemption. Mission agencies therefore reduced their funds before totally withdrawing from the island in 1865, to begin new works in Africa. However, this did not deter the African majority working-class people who, having experienced the presence and the power of the Holy Spirit at work in their midst, were more resolute than ever to continue to worship God in their own way. The revival revitalized many who thereafter, whether in life or in death, celebrated the fact that they had truly found a faith which could not be denied.[34] Many thereafter called themselves Revivalist Christians, men and women who followed the leading of the Holy Spirit which ultimately added to the unease being experienced by the white minority, who believed that African churches were an unnecessary evil.

The Methodist Society "Ticket" Controversy (1863)

Such was the increasing fear within the white community that they constantly looked for incidents in which the African majority could be considered to be stirring up rebellion. They believed that they had found it in white Christians, especially the Methodists, who seemed to have chosen to cleave to the "dark side." One of the most significant incidents which, if taken out of context, would perhaps seem laughable, but was then spread abroad by Governor Eyre, stirred up such anxiety in the people, that it led to the arrest of many African Jamaicans in 1863, charging them with plotting against the government, and planning destruction of white and colored people on the island. It is the sorry tale of a deceased man and a ticket. The story is told of

> A Methodist Society-ticket being found in the box of a deceased slave[35] by the plantation authorities, bearing the printed inscrip-

---

34. See Appendix 8 for stories of faith recorded by European visitors and ministers.

35. Yes, even after fifteen years of freedom, Africans were being referred to as "slaves," thereby signifying that even amongst the most liberal of commentators, their position was being continually undermined.

tion "The Kingdom of heaven suffreth violence, and the violent take it by force." Too ignorant to understand that this was only a verse of the New Testament, which was printed on the ticket and given to the possessor of it as a token of Church membership in the Methodist Society, the intelligent officials on the estate, and the astute magistrates, and other, authorities of the parish, to whom the circumstance had been referred as wearing a most suspicious aspect, at once jumped to the conclusion that some fearful conspiracy was on foot to destroy the lives of the white inhabitants, of which this "seditious paper" furnished the "proof strong as holy writ." When it further came to light that the Methodist Missionary residing in the town had given out some hundreds of similar documents among the slaves in the neighbourhood, nothing could be more certain in the estimation of these wise men, than that this most timely discovery of the dreadful plot had saved the island from all the terrible consequences of a slave rebellion. The militia were called out, and the parochial authorities assembled in all possible haste; scores, if not hundreds, captured. It was gravely proposed that the island should be proclaimed under Martial Law; and the wildest excitement and terror prevailed, until the Methodist preacher, who had been summoned before the civil and military authorities, assembled in solemn conclave, revealed the hitherto unsuspected truth, that "the highly seditious words" on the supposed treasonable documents, were simply a quotation from St Matthew's Gospel; (proof of which was given, after some delay in hunting up the fragment of a Bible used for swearing witnesses in the parochial courts;) and that the paper which had created such a profound sensation had been given in recognition of the fact that the deceased slave was a communicant in the Methodist Church. Thus, fortunately the bubble burst before any serious evil had been done.[36]

No harm done, but then came to the fore a champion of the people, who was both ensconced in the Assembly, and the EBS. Clearly now the threat was more than real in the person of George William Gordon.

George William Gordon (1820–65)

George Gordon was a member of the Jamaican Assembly, and he played an increasingly central role in the African Jamaican demand for justice and

---

36. Bleby, *Reign of Terror*, 56.

equality. He was the son of a white plantation owner and a mulatto slave mother, and was married to a white creole. Raised in the CofE, he spent some time in the Presbyterian Church, before being baptized in the EBS, wherein he established the Kingston Tabernacle. As a Baptist leader he made speeches across the island stating his opposition to the inadequate leadership being provided by Governor Eyre and his fellow assembly members. Suffice it to say that this did not endear him to the Legislature and more particularly Governor Eyre, who saw such "interference" from Gordon, on behalf of the disenfranchised African majority, as contemptuous at the very least and, more significantly, a threat to his political dominance on the island.

George William Gordon, 1865, courtesy of D. Morrison.

Gordon's speeches were also considered by the white population to be inflammatory, both because of his couching his comments in Scripture, and his leadership role within the EBS:

> He gave a religious imperative to his message in begging the people to help themselves, "then heaven will help you." What the established authorities regarded as incitement was far more in the tradition of the native [so-called] preacher. "Remember that he only is free whom the truth makes free," admonished Gordon again, "you are no longer slaves but free men; then as free men act your part."[37]

---

37. Gordon, *Our Cause*, 100.

He being an influential person of independent means who not only owned two properties in Saint Thomas in the East, where he was also a Vestry member, was undaunted by the increasing opposition. He continued to preach in Kingston and then expanded his ministry by building a chapel in a place called Spring which was situated next door to Stony Gut, also in Saint Thomas in the East.

Gordon was a part of the new generation of church leaders and involved himself in the implementation of new church rules, as can be seen in the following prayer format which he introduced:

> Today is a fast day—to call to mind our sins.
> To implore God to grant us mercies and to help us in our necessities.
> To bless our relations and our friends.
> To pardon our enemies.
> To take away the reproach of sin from our land.
> To bless all Lands with the light of Gospel truth.
> To grant prosperity to our Cause for His Glory in this city.[38]

So then, having established both his political and religious credentials, he raised his political profile to such an extent that he became the political voice of opposition, stirring the people to action against the injustices which were being done against them. Three incidents in particular made him an enemy of Eyre and his fellow Legislators. They concerned

> The rector of St Thomas-in-the-East . . . [who] being solicited for alms by a diseased wanderer, took the extraordinary course of sending the poor man to lock-up: an act which he had no authority to perform, as he was not a magistrate. The wretched outcast, thus sent to a place used only for punishment, and having no better shelter assigned to him than the privy of the establishment in a most disgusting state of filthiness, died there, with no hand to aid him in his last moments, and was then buried, contrary to law, without an inquest being held.[39]

Gordon, on hearing of this incident, took his complaint to Governor Eyre, who responded by censuring him and removing his commissions as a magistrate in various parishes, citing as his reason Gordon's daring to call into question "the humanity of the rector."[40] Undeterred, Gordon went on to publicly accuse Eyre of fraud and the misappropriation of public funds in the Legislature, before writing to the Colonial Secretary, challenging the fact

---

38. Gordon, *Our Cause*, 106.
39. Bleby, *Reign of Terror*, 25.
40. Bleby, *Reign of Terror*, 26.

that in Port Maria, "hard labour should include the treadmill, shot drill, and crank."[41] Needless to say Eyre became increasingly annoyed at this public humiliation and sought to remove this agitation. He soon found his opportunity and the excuse he needed, when a small group of residents rioted at the Morant Bay Courthouse in Saint Thomas in the East, the home of his principal opponent.

The joy that had been, the dissatisfaction which remained, soon turned to hatred, as the ministry of the EBS faced its final challenge in Morant Bay.

---

41. Bleby, *Reign of Terror*, 29.

Chapter 11

The Final Roar of the EBS: Saint Thomas in the East (1865)

PREAMBLE

THE YEAR 1865 AND the events which took place in Morant Bay and across Saint Thomas in the East as a whole, were one of, if not the most significant happenings in the religious landscape of Jamaica. It changed the emerging African Jamaican religious and social culture, and therefore the overall culture of the island.

Saint Thomas in the East had the reputation of being the most oppressive of all the parishes in Jamaica. It was closed to missionary activity and so antagonistic, in fact, were the planter attorneys in the region, to the gospel message, that they denied licenses to all ministers who sought to gain the right to preach there, except for those of the CofE. The only other ministry which could be undertaken was that which could be done covertly, by those who could inconspicuously merge with the enslaved population, hence Lisle and then Parson Killick being able to minister there. Such was their success that Edmund Lyon, a special justice in the region at the time of apprenticeship, said of them that

> The apprentices of St Thomas in the East I do not hesitate to say are much superior in manners and morals to those who inhabit the towns.[1]

1. Thome and Kimball, *Emancipation in the West Indies*, 364.

Such "perfect" behavior being able then to undermine the plans of Eyre meant that in order to achieve his destructive ends, the annihilation of Gordon and the EBS, he needed support. This he received from the two of the major factions on the island. Firstly, the planter magistrates' longstanding hostility towards those who were now free was well known, with BMS missionary Tucker commenting that

> In earlier years, through their intense hostility of the planter magistrates, the east end of the island had remained closed to missionary effort, and one may well suspect that this was one of the reasons why the relations between employers and employed was strained to the breaking-point in this particular parish.[2]

Eyre at the same time had also garnered the backing of the majority of the Jamaican Assembly and planter magistrates, utilizing their lawmaking capabilities in order to make sure that

> In the Legislature, the principal object of the ruling party, never lost sight of, was to keep down the emancipated classes, and so shape the laws enacted from time to time that the great burden of taxation should fall upon them, and as lightly as possible upon their employers. The peasantry were even compelled to pay a most unequal share of the enormous expense incurred in several abortive schemes of immigration, intended solely to lower and keep down, as near starvation-point as possible, the wages they were to receive for their labour.[3]

Naturally this inequitable system soon caused tensions, and such was the anger on both sides that by the early 1860s even the most innocuous event took on significant political meaning. This was the case when in 1864 Parson Killick, who was by then at least seventy years old and concentrating on his ministry in Kingston, found himself being visited at his home by a deputation of BMS missionaries, J. E. Henderson and Hewitt. They, perhaps joyfully, informed him that they had preached the Sunday before at his chapel in Morant Bay. Killick, aware of the political climate, was said to be very displeased that this event had taken place, and not only that these "unknown" white missionaries had imposed themselves upon his people, but that his deacons had exercised such poor judgement in allowing them to do so. He declared it to have been a "liberty his deacons had granted without first consulting him."[4]

2. Tucker, *Glorious Liberty*, 84.
3. Tucker, *Glorious Liberty*, 10.
4. Clarke, *Memorials of Baptist Missionaries*, 32.

In the current climate he more than any other EBS member, having lived through major disturbances, including that of 1831–32, was perhaps more aware than they of the effect that such a visit would have on an outraged people who found themselves being "ministered" to by ignorant English Baptist ministers from abroad who were of the same color and heritage as those who were continuing to oppress them. Suffice it to say that tensions in the parish increased as a result, with the whites using it as a means to publicize the "racist" nature of the EBS, claiming that they were distrustful of educated white Baptist colleagues, preferring instead the ignorant "Native" Baptist preacher.

It was clearly an incident which was remembered by all as events became increasingly confrontational and lines were being drawn. The dispossessed plantocracy naturally intensified its hatred, as they continued to bemoan the loss of their "slaves." Then as relationships deteriorated, plantation owners resorted to foul means to exact their revenge. Rev. Henry Clarke told of one of the most heinous plots which the landowners implemented during this period:

> [They] moved the Negro villages periodically, in order to prevent the labourers from profiting by the bread-fruits, cocoa-nuts, and other trees of slow growth, which they plant around their dwellings. Every village of the estates in this district, of five thousand inhabitants, has been moved within the last ten years; and as the people have to pull down and rebuild their cottages at their own expense, they have got into the way of erecting miserable little huts, in which the poor things are compelled to live, like pigs in a sty.[5]

However, despite the intransigence of the ruling white minority, African Jamaicans continued to possess a boldness buoyed up by their religious conviction that there would one day truly be justice and equality for all. Leading the resistance once again were the faithful remnants of the EBS. Inspired by what would today be termed a prophetic word, and what they understood as the Voice of God, was a word shared by one of their members, which they truly believed gave them the "green light" to move forward and demand their human rights. God, he said, had instructed him to

> Tell "the sons and daughters of Africa that a great deliverance will take place for them from the hand of the Opposition." Magistrates, proprietors and merchants were identified as the oppressive opposition. The people were to "sanctify themselves

---

5. Bleby, *Reign of Terror*, 10–11.

for the day of deliverance." Failing this, the Voice would bring a sword into the land "and the sword would come from America."[6]

So, once again they had a cause and direction, and they felt it was a just one. The fact that it was somewhat reminiscent of the word spoken about deliverance coming from America, in the 1830s by Sam Sharpe, soon convinced them of its truth. Their human rights agenda was initially supported and even encouraged, not only by the BMS in England, but members of the JBU. Prominent amongst them was Dr. E. B. Underhill, then-secretary of the BMS, who sent his now famous "Underhill Letter" regarding the prevailing situation in Jamaica to the secretary of state for the colonies, Edward Cardwell. In it, Underhill stated that

> Numbers of persons in various parts of the island are in a starving condition. The greater number have the greatest possible difficulty to support themselves and their families. . . . Among the foregoing causes of poverty and distress, we have referred your Excellency to the want of employment. In some districts, numbers of people are known to walk from six to thirty miles in search of work. Numbers, even in crop time, applying to the estates for employment, are turned back without obtaining it. . . . In all parts of the island a reduction of wages is expected, in most cases to the extent of from twenty-five to fifty per cent. . . . In many districts Creole labour has been displaced wholly or in part by that of Coolies,[7] Chinese, and Africans. . . . The small settler has to pay for his horse or mule eleven shillings, and for his ass three shillings and sixpence; while the working stock on the estates—steers, mules and horned king—are taxed only six pence per head.[8]

Emancipation therefore was simply serving to place the economic burden on those who had once been enslaved, and they were now at the mercy of employers who repeatedly failed to pay a decent wage. The African Jamaicans' position was further compounded by a drought which lasted for two years, causing a depression in Jamaica by 1865, which left many in a desperate situation. So, Underhill, taking this also upon himself, made it known that as a consequence

> There was hardly any employment for labourers on the sugar estates through the failure of the crop. The provision grounds of

---

6. Gordon, *Our Cause*, 99.

7. Another name for people who came from India, over time used to describe Jamaicans with long straight black hair which looked similar to those from India.

8. Bleby, *Reign of Terror*, 12–13.

> the people scarcely produced anything (through the prolonged drought); for corn-meal and flour all classes had chiefly to depend on imported supplies. Even to buy these the poor had to run into debt at the island stores, thus crippling their resources for years. In some districts the mango-plum, growing wild by the wayside, was the only food of the people. . . . Hence the alarming increase of crime, especially larceny and petty theft. The people steal because they are too poor to buy food. Hence also the ragged and even naked condition of so many of them, so contrary to their usual taste for dress. . . . Hardly a boy under ten years of age has a frock to cover him, and adults from the raggedness of their garments go about not decently clad.[9]

As a result of the Underhill Letter, the people, believing that the English led BMS was with them, felt able to express their dissatisfaction across the island. This showed itself most visibly when they came into contact with the court system, where they almost always lost, no matter the circumstances of their case. In fact, such was the "corruptness" of the courts, that the people began to set up their own system of justice, holding public meetings known as the "Underhill Meetings." The government saw them as a direct challenge to its authority, particularly as Gordon was often the main speaker.

The intensity of the hostilities dramatically changed when in April 1865, African Jamaicans sent a petition directly to their queen, Victoria in Britain, expressing their concerns regarding their circumstances. They received a reply, known as the "Queen's Advice," but to date no one is quite sure if it was in fact responded to by the queen herself, or more local representatives, as "Its tone was curt and harsh, and it was felt by the people to be a mere mockery of their distress."[10] Many discerning church leaders, including Rev. J. Garrett, rector in Vere, and Rev. H. Clarke, curate of Westmoreland, were so convinced that it was not directed by the queen's hand that they refused to display it in their communities. Clarke even went as far as to blame Governor Eyre, accusing him and his supporters of being those who

> Mocked the cry of the poor, and showed themselves the mere partisans of the class opposed to the negroes, and engaged in an act of sheer recklessness.[11]

Eyre responded to them in May 1865 by sending a report to the colonial office, in which he blamed the increasing agitation amongst the African majority, just as his predecessors had done in 1832, expressing the view that

---

9. Tucker, *Glorious Liberty*, 77.
10. Tucker, *Glorious Liberty*, 79.
11. Stewart, *Religion and Society*, 164.

Serious mischief done amongst an ignorant and easily led population when the missionaries residing amongst them, and professing to be their friends and teachers, endorse such statements as those contained in Dr Underhill's letter.[12]

Many voices of dissent then arose, as EBS ministers, together with their Black counterparts within the JBU, openly expressed their dissatisfaction with the status quo in Jamaica. Rev. James H. Crole, and EBS pastor at the Kingston Tabernacle, went as far as to release the following resolution on July 29, 1865, at an Underhill meeting in Saint Ann's Bay:

> That this meeting desires to give expressions of gratitude and thankfulness to Almighty God for his unspeakable goodness, and mercy vouchsafed to the lately emancipated people of this Island, and would implore the divine interposition at this juncture in connection with the oppressed, distressed, wretched and deplorable condition in which the larger proportion of the population is placed by drought and other causes, but especially by the unusual indigested and oppressive system of Government which is pursued, and feel that investigation and remedy are now loudly called for.[13]

This was then followed by another petition sent to the Queen, but this time via Governor Eyre, on September 5, 1865. It said,

> We most humbly beg to implore Your Majesty's attention to our humble communications. When we were slaves we never had such heavy work; and after having finished those number of chains with the expectation, at the end of the week to obtain the amount of six shillings, we generally get one shilling and sixpence to two shillings and sixpence for the whole week's pay. The island has been ruined consequently of the advantage that is taken of us by the managers of estates. Whenever we have a case which may be taken before the planter magistrates, they give us no satisfaction whatever but combine with each other and take away our rights. We most humbly beseech Your Majesty that it may please Your Majesty to appoint a stipendiary magistrate to sit at every court day, as may enable us to obtain satisfaction. All we ask is, that Your Majesty may be pleased to consider over the state of this island, and render the poor some assistance; and that Your Majesty's life may be long

---

12. Tucker, *Glorious Liberty*, 79.
13. Stewart, *Religion and Society*, 165.

spared, and that the blessings of those ready to perish may rest upon you.
By Andrew Ross and thirty-nine others.[14]

This by all accounts was a respectful and polite letter, but it was one which so caused the ire of Eyre that what followed in Morant Bay saw the minority white population exacting the most violent revenge on those who presumed to petition "their" queen, Victoria.

Morant Bay Riot (1865)

The quiet war that was simmering between the fearful and disgruntled white minority, and the increasingly independent and successful African Jamaicans, came to a head on Saturday October 7, 1865, at the courthouse in Morant Bay. The day's events have historically been defined as a rebellion; however, primary sources attest to the fact that it was so named by Governor Eyre, who defined the event as being far more serious than it actually was. Most historians and religious organizations attest that it was simply a riot which, because of Eyre's desire to ratchet up tension amongst fearful whites, got completely out of control as they took "revenge" on a mythical plot to bring down the Jamaican government and to chase the whites from the island.

The day began quite innocuously, the same as any other day at the courthouse. The proceedings, a case of trespass, was presided over by "Two planter justices of the peace—Mr. Walton, the owner of a plantation in the vicinity, who was among the slain the following week, and another."[15] On the defendants being found guilty, observers in the gallery "suggested" rather loudly that the accused only pay the fine, and refuse to pay the additional court costs which were given to him. The magistrate called for the observers to be arrested; they resisted, and violence ensued which led to the case being adjourned, to be resumed again on Monday, 9 October. However, a similar situation erupted once again on the Monday, when the court sought to deal with a similar case of trespass against a Mr. Lewis Miller, a farmer and a resident of Stony Gut village. Miller had sought to stop surveyors selling off abandoned estate land which he and many peasants had farmed for many years. He too was found guilty, and ordered to pay a fine and costs, but once again his supporters, just as other supporters had done on the previous

---

14. Bleby, *Reign of Terror*, 14–15.
15. Bleby, *Reign of Terror*, 33.

Saturday, heckled from the gallery, suggesting that he only pay the fine and not the court costs.

Amongst those present was Paul Bogle, an EBS minister, who had been ordained as a deacon at Gordon's Kingston Tabernacle Chapel. As well as being a pastor in Stony Gut, Bogle was also a small farmer, and so before leaving the court, he stated that they would appeal the decision. Three to four police officers were immediately dispatched to Stony Gut to arrest approximately twenty-eigh people. However, as they tried to do so, the villagers came to their aid, imprisoning the officers and demanding that they as Black men should "swear to 'cleave to the black' and to 'join their colour.'"[16] The officers were later released unharmed, Bogle choosing instead to send a letter of protest on behalf of the people, to Governor Eyre, requesting justice due to them:

> [The] Overbearing manner of the police acting on the orders of the justice; they asked as loyal subjects of Her Majesty, for the governor's protection, and added the challenge: "which protection if refused to [we] will be compelled to put our shoulders to the wheel, as we have been imposed upon for a period of 27 years with due obeisance to the laws of our Queen and country, and we can no longer endure the same."[17]

Bogle spoke about being "imposed upon" for twenty-seven years, and therefore not just since the arrival of Eyre, but since emancipation. He and they had clearly had enough. Eyre's response was swift. Firstly, one of the policemen, who was accused of "favouring the escape of Bogle, when he was almost within the grasp of the soldiers [was] hanged."[18] Then, on Tuesday, 10 October, warrants were issued for the arrest of "Parson" Paul Bogle, and his fellow protesters, having been charged with not only leading the disturbances on both the Saturday and the Monday, but also interfering with the police in the execution of their duties.

Bogle and his supporters, which included folk from many EBS congregations, sought to answer the warrant by attending the courthouse on Wednesday, 11 October, while the quarterly meeting of the parish vestry was in session. Gordon was a member, but was absent that day due to sickness. The meeting soon erupted as the two sides confronted each other. The Custos, accompanied by the local militia, sought to address the gathered crowd, who threw stones in response. A dispatch was quickly sent to Governor Eyre, which exaggerated the facts while asking for the protection of

16. Stewart, *Religion and Society*, 154.
17. Stewart, *Religion and Society*, 154.
18. O'Connor, "Black Rebellion," 3.

the military. A riot then ensued whereby the people used stones and the members of the parish vestry used guns. The courthouse was set on fire, and thirty to forty of the protesters killed, as well as a member of the much-hated CofE,[19] the curate of Bath, and the Custos.

Martial law was declared the next day, Thursday, 12 October, Governor Eyre himself then identifying not just Bogle, but his "archenemy," assembly member Gordon, as the ringleaders of the insurrection, perhaps choosing to believe once again that Bogle was not capable of planning such an enterprise on his own. It is, however, more likely that Eyre, seeing Gordon as his nemesis and the most vocal in his hatred of the oppression which the people were experiencing, saw this event as the opportunity to remove him.

As such an opportunity may never have repeated itself, it was an opportunity which could not and would not be missed, Eyre perhaps applying the premise that Gordon was

> One of these men, in short, of whom a prudent and wise Government must rid itself (of trouble makers) when it finds a legitimate occasion to do so.[20]

Eyre had found that "legitimate" occasion, and through the use of much publicity, both in Jamaica and England, he not only got the white minority on side, but also the church (all persuasions) and the British government. It is said that

> Frightful stories were circulated concerning indignities and barbarities which the Negroes were said to have practised upon the dead bodies of their victims. These stories were gathered up and repeated by Mr Eyre, and had currency given to them in his dispatches.[21]

One such fanciful storyteller was the Rev. John Radcliffe, a minister of the church of Scotland, who wrote to the *Times* newspaper in London, England, stating that

---

19. While the people were starving Bleby said of the role of the rector and his family in Saint Thomas that "he and some members of his family were, the head, ran riot in oppression and injustice" and that the rector "was one of the old-time, slave-holding clergymen, two of his sons filling public offices in the same parish; so that this family with its connexions gave whatever direction they please to parochial affairs; and the Vestry, which this family largely controlled, possessing the power to impose parochial taxes, (including the demands made for various ecclesiastical purposes) on the Nonconformist congregations, which included a great majority of the people, were subjected to unjust burdens that were keenly felt." Bleby, *Reign of Terror*, 13, 19–20.

20. Harvey, *Paris*, 286.

21. Bleby, *Reign of Terror*, 41.

In a few minutes the dead bodies of the Custos, of the magistrates, of a clergyman, of the two sons of the rector, of several men of property, and of officials, were lying about in the street—some chopped to pieces, some with their tongues cut out, some with their bowels torn out, some with indignities that cannot be mentioned.[22]

Morant Bay Courthouse and Leading Politicians, 1865[23]

---

22. Gordon, "Robert Gordon," 2.
23. Bleby, *Reign of Terror*, i.

As a result of this well-orchestrated plan, no part of the elite of Jamaican society raised any objection when Gordon, Bogle, and the forty people who had signed the petition were singled out for punishment. Warrants were issued for their arrest. Gordon was in Kingston when he was told of the warrant and he in response simply handed himself in to the authorities. He was then quickly transported by water, on the *Wolverine*, to Morant Bay along with others. This ship then became his courtroom, where he was accused, tried, and found guilty of planning the insurrection on October 21, 1865.

During his trial he was questioned as to whether he gave his followers bad advice, Gordon responded thus:

> No friend, I never gave the people bad advice, I only told them the Lord would send them a day of deliverance.[24]

Justice was swift and without mercy. Gordon was executed along with eighteen others on October 23, 1865. In the hours before his execution, he wrote his final letter to his wife, confirming his faith and further stating his firm belief that

> It is however the will of my heavenly Father that I should thus suffer in obeying his command to relieve the poor and needy, and to protect, as far as I was able, the oppressed; and glory be to his name, and I thank Him that I suffer in such a cause. Glory be to the God and Father of our Lord and Saviour Jesus Christ, and I can say that it is a great honour thus to suffer, for the servant cannot be greater than his Lord. I can now say with Paul the aged, "The hour of my departure is come, and I am ready to be offered up. I have kept the faith, I have fought a good fight, and henceforth there is laid up for me a crown of righteousness, which the Lord, the righteous Judge shall give to me."[25]

Of his execution, author Thomas Huxley was seen to speak on behalf of many of the opponents of Governor Eyre in Britain, including scientist Charles Darwin, and philosophers Herbert Spencer and John Stuart Mill, when he declared that

> The killing of Mr Gordon can only be defended on the grounds that he was a loud and troublesome man; in short, that although he might not be guilty, it served him right![26]

---

24. Stewart, *Religion and Society*, 96.
25. "Case of Mr George William Gordon," 77.
26. Levy and Peart, "Secret History," 8.

In contrast, Bogle, on hearing that a warrant had been issued for his arrest, went on the run, and the government in response offered a $2,000 reward for his capture. The Maroons, who were known to be particularly meticulous and violent in their apprehension of all those associated with the rebellion, "flogging and executing the rebels at a fearful rate and scouring the countryside for others,"[27] captured him in Hayfield. Bogle was then unceremoniously tried, found guilty, and executed, all on the same day, October 24, 1865.

His enemies having been executed, Eyre, in his concluding report of the so-called "rebellion," continued to lie, including the following fabrications, in order to justify his murderous actions:

> The most frightful atrocities were perpetrated. The island curate of Bath, the Rev. Mr Herschell, is said to have had his tongue cut out whilst still alive, and an attempt is said to have been made to skin him. One person (Mr Charles Price a black gentleman, formerly a member of Assembly) was ripped open, and his entrails taken out. One gentleman (Lieut. Hall of the Volunteers) is said to have been pushed into an outbuilding, which was then set on fire, and kept there till he was ultimately roasted alive. Many were said to have had their eyes scooped out; heads were cleft open, and the brains taken out. The Baron's fingers were cut off and carried away as trophies by the murderers. Some bodies were half burnt, others horribly battered. Indeed, the whole outrage could only be paralleled by the atrocities of the Indian mutiny. The women, as usual on such occasions, were even more brutal and barbarous than the men; the only redeeming trait being that, so far as we could learn, no ladies or children had as yet been injured.[28]

Such statements were found to be pure "fantasy," as indicated in a letter to a London newspaper from a Mr Hepburn, a gentleman from Amsterdam, who declared that

> I met in Kingston one of the persons reported to have been killed during the riot on the 11th October, at Morant Bay.... Mr Joseph Williams. This person was cut in two or three places on the head and received a very severe blow on the arm and head ... the reports that went the round of this city-that is that the tongue of Rev Victor Herschel was cut out of his mouth after death, and that the brains of Baron Kettlehodt were mixed with

---

27. Gordon, *Our Cause*, 113.
28. Bleby, *Reign of Terror*, 43.

rum and gun powder, and drunk by the rioters. . . . He assured me that neither assertion was true, and that beyond cutting the Barons fingers, his body was otherwise in no way mutilated, and that Mr Hershel's tongue was never cut out.[29]

There was, however, one incident of the many reported which did actually take place. The Baron's fingers on one hand were indeed cut off, as rioters tried to get the ring which was often used to seal their fates, off his finger. It is said that many taunted him, shouting, "Now, you write no more lies to the Queen against us." In all other respects it was proved that there was no violent action by the rioters and the mutilation of bodies which were spoken of by Eyre. Mutilations were in fact the work of the John Crow, vultures, which simply helped themselves to the bodies which had been left to rot in the sun outside of the courthouse.

So, in reality the violence which was undertaken was, in all but one case, carried out by those in power. The people were armed with only stones, while Governor Eyre's henchmen had swords and guns. It was therefore most probably them who were the ones who had fatally wounded the only Black gentleman present, Charles Price, whose death was recorded in various parts of the English press:

> Black Price, merely on account of his association with white people, was subjected to the most horrible and appalling indignities. After his body had been cut up with cutlasses he was held on his feet while the women cut his bowels and strewed them on the street. . . . Mr Cooke [clerk of the peace] lay concealed under the house . . . and could tell the victims by the exclamations of the mob. He heard the dying groans of Mr Price, who lay with his entrails protruding, having been ripped open by women.[30]

Now while the eyewitness account of the violence with which Charles Price met his end was most probably true, there is no eyewitness account as to who actually killed him. However, he was more than just a gentleman. Price was a member of the EBS, a sitting or ex-member of the Jamaican Assembly, and he may well have also been attending the vestry meeting. He would therefore not have been an "anonymous" person to either side, as he too got caught up in the events of the day. Charles was in fact a very significant person to all African Jamaicans. Recollections of him are written in BMS missionary records, he being known to such missionaries as John Clarke, who described him as a man who "attended the East Queen

---

29. Hepburn, "Negro Riots," para. 9.
30. O'Connor, "Black Rebellion," 3.

Street School in 1830 . . . became a member of the House of Assembly, and frequently showed good ability and love to his country."[31] So why, one may ask, was such a record kept of this Black gentleman who, it was claimed, was killed because of his "association" with white people? Well, it was because Charles Price, the son of Lucy Price, was the grandson of George Lisle.

Mr. Charles Price, *Photograph Album Documenting the Morant Bay Rebellion, Jamaica 1865, and More*, accessed at https://www.slideshare.net/GailannBarry/documentingthemorantbayrebellion-110224230232phpapp01-1?qid=b913327c-ebc6-401b-8168-746e76cd771c&v=&b=&from_search=1.

So, if a BMS missionary who had only arrived on the island in 1829 knew his exact identity, then it is only reasonable to expect that both sides of those involved in the fray would also have known who he was. It is therefore unlikely that fellow members of the EBS, for they were the majority in attendance, who so revered his grandfather and his service to the nation, would then have killed his grandson. It is, however, probable and far more likely that he had unfortunately placed himself in harm's way that day, perhaps as he tried to mediate a peace between the parties. It is further likely that one

---

31. Clarke, *Memorials of Baptist Missionaries*, 11.

of Eyre's sympathizers, taking advantage of the milieu, just as Eyre had done in the case of Gordon, used the opportunity to lay to rest the grandson of George Lisle who, like his grandfather, had lived and died in the service of the peoples of Jamaica.

Genocide: The Slaughter of the Innocents

Eyre's final report to the Legislature was dealt at the same time as the "work" he had commissioned against the general populace of Saint Thomas in the East. Not satisfied with the execution of Bogle, Gordon, and more than likely Price, Eyre had also received support to go ahead and "put down" the "rebellion" at its supposed center, Morant Bay, the bastion of the EBS in Saint Thomas in the East, and Portland, where he believed were

> Persons who, leaving their proper sphere of action as ministers of religion, [have] become political demagogues and dangerous agitators.[32]

Eyre's plan worked, as not just were the ministers of the EBS demonized, but the whole community of believers, to such an extent that even in England the *London Times* declared that those who had participated in, and supported said "rebellion" were "Baptist . . . rebellious panthers [who] wantonly drank rum mixed with gun powder and the brains of their victims."[33] Under the guise of bringing peace and justice, Eyre then proceeded to carry out what can only be described as an act of genocide, the religious cleansing of an unprepared and unsuspecting, vulnerable and starving people of faith, all of whom he had determined were members of the EBS.

History records how Eyre, in order to aid him in his task, "Quickly deployed increased military forces with Maroon assistance in the parish, and parts of Portland."[34] While his forces traveled across chosen areas, killing a nonresistant people who were in the main innocently residing in their homes and places of worship, the Maroons were involved in similar activities, but it is to be noted that in many instances they went one step further in that, having caught the guilty, they were known for "holding their own court martials"[35] before executing them. Of the events which took place across Saint Thomas in the East, Robert Gordon, by then the headmaster of

---

32. Gordon, *Our Cause*, 159–60.
33. Headsman, "1865: Paul Bogle," para. 9.
34. Stewart, *Religion and Society*, 155.
35. Gordon, *Our Cause*, 115.

Wolmer's Grammar School and a priest in the United Church of England, reported in the *Daily News* newspaper in London that

> There was no more than 18 killed [Militia], including the volunteer, whilst at least 3,000 including infants, children and others, who could not possibly have had anything to do with the riot, were sacrificed on the altar of the white man's rigid vengeance.[36]

Such was the outcry by many in Jamaica and England in regards to the injustices which had taken place that Eyre's vengeance, the deeds of his henchmen, and the true facts did not go untold. A Royal Commission was ordered in the months following to look into the matter, and it revealed the following stories (and more) which were typical of the wrongs which had taken place on the darkest of all days in Jamaica. Each event detailed below is self-explanatory and needs no additional explanation, save to say that the genocide took place after martial law was declared on October 13, 1865. The "slaughter of the innocents" began the very next day, until martial law was ended on November 13, 1865, by which time Eyre had achieved his goal of ridding the nation of a those whom he had deemed to have been a troublesome group, all "rioters" having been executed by November 3, 1865.

A story was told in the Royal Commission which concerned a Mr. Cowell, who was once an official at the Stony Gut Chapel. It was reported that by 1865 he was "old and emaciated, powerless to participate actively in any rebellion,"[37] but this did not stop the government choosing to execute him as a rebel. Bleby documented this, as well as the following incidents, which clearly show that at no time was an African hand ever raised in order to oppose the bloodthirsty agents of the Crown, or in turn to gain their freedom:

> Colonel Hobbs said, "I shot nine of the Fonthill rebels in a chapel, where their leader commenced with prayers, and ended with blasphemy and sedition; and I there adopted a plan which struck immense terror into these wicked men, far more than death; which is, I caused them to hang each other. They entreated to be shot, to avoid this, which appears to me to be far more dreadful an ordeal to them than death. . . . Before the victims were hung, they were first shot; and the general body of prisoners, whether tried or not were ordered to take up the bleeding bodies of their former friends and neighbours and hang them to the rafters of the building where together they had engaged in the worship of God.

36. Gordon, "Negro," para. 7.
37. Stewart, *Religion and Society*, 166.

Colonel Hobbs shot thirteen men at Monklands.... He had a trench dug, and made the unfortunate men kneel with their backs towards it. The soldiers drawn up for the purpose fired at the sound of the bugle, or the word of command. Some, not killed, cried out with pain; and the soldiers ordered them with brutal curses to shut their mouths, or they would blow their brains out. They gave two or three who were wounded a close shot to finish them. Even after this one George Rankin remained alive. The soldiers were in the act of throwing the earth on the trench to fill it up, covering both the living and the dead, when Hobbs gave orders that the pick axe should be used to finish Rankin... if not [killed] he was buried alive.

At Stony Gut a boy was wantonly shot by Lieutenant Oxley's party when they visited that locality. The little fellow had unexpectedly come upon the military; and when he saw them, he turned round and attempted to run and escape, when these gallant soldiers fired upon and killed the lad.... The body lay unburied until the vultures gathered about it, when the neighbors summoned courage to hide away the festering remains in the earth.

At a very pleasant and flourishing village, called Somerset there resided an old man named Richard Graham, blind and infirm through old age, so that he could not move about without being led. On Tuesday 17th October, when the soldiers of the *gallant* 6th were displaying their courage in burning the houses of the helpless inhabitants, this blind old man was found sitting quietly at the door of his cottage, in the sunshine, supposing that his age and infirmities would be sufficient protection from the violence. But the gallant 6th respected neither age nor infirmity. It was enough for them that any person that had a black skin; that was sufficient proof in their eyes that he must be a rebel. A nephew of the old man who lived with him, when he saw these heroes approaching, hid himself in the bush until the soldiers should take their departure. From his hiding-place close at hand, the young man heard a gun fired in the yard; and on coming forth after the destroyers were gone, he proceeded to the spot, and found the old man dead.

At Mount Libanus, two soldiers of the same battalion seized a woman, Mrs Rebecca Telfer, and demanded from her, her marriage ring. She said it was lost; but one of the soldiers said he did not believe her statement, and cried out, "Shoot her! Shoot her!" She bent down, and said, "Good massa, don't shoot me, for I don't know anything at all. If you shoot me, who is to take care of my little children?" She begged hard for her life, and gave them two shillings, which was all the money she had, to induce them to let her go. Her house had already been burnt down, and she was sheltering in a small kitchen that had escaped the flames. The soldiers then seized upon her, and endeavored to force her to enter the small building with them. She resisted them with all her might; when, just at that juncture, her father-in-law, John Telfer, who lived near at hand, appeared upon the scene, having heard the noise she made in struggling with them. The soldiers, irritated at his appearance to interfere with their vile purposes, instantly seized their rifles, and shot him down; and she took the opportunity of their releasing her, to snatch up her two children, and escape into the bush.

On the 22nd of October, four white soldiers . . . returned . . . to David Mayne's shop at Long Bay . . . there [were] two prisoners, named James Sparkes and Johnson Speed. They proceeded at once to tie Sparkes to a tree, and gave him a hundred lashes. They then tied up Johnson Speed, and had given him eighty-five lashes, when the cat broke. One of the soldiers ran into the shop, and brought a horse-whip to finish the flogging; but the other interfered, and prevented him, saying it was not the right thing to beat a man with. One of the bystanders who was there asked by the soldiers whether the man Speed had done anything during the disturbances; evidently seeking a pretext for further villainy. He replied that, when Mr Hinchelwood's house was burning, Speed was there. The soldier who was flogging him then said, "Where is my rifle?" The man cried out, "Lord, I don't do nothing and I going to dead." The soldier levelled his rifle, and fired; but either it contained no ball, or he had missed. He loaded again, and fired, hitting the poor victim in the middle of his back, as he was tied to the tree. Another soldier then stepped up, as he dropped writhing upon the ground, as far as the cords would allow him to fall, and, putting his rifle to the man's ear, scattered his brains all around.

Some Maroons went to Mill's River, to the house of a black man named Robert Bailey. His wife was standing at the door of the cottage, and the man who was leader of the party bade her "good evening," and inquired for her son, William Bailey. She said he was in the house, very sick with fever. The Maroons entered the house, and shot the sick youth as he lay upon his bed. They afterwards laid hands upon the father of the young man, and made him turn his face towards them, and then wantonly shot him down in the yard, with another man, named Robert Walker, who happened to be present. After this they set fire to the house, and then took their departure; carrying with them the clothes of the murdered men, and whatever else they chose to bear away.

At Harbour Head (Port Morant) some Maroons entered the house of John Noble, a black man. He was sick, and had been lying bed-ridden for many years. They directed him to get up and go out of the house. He said he could not, for he was not able. They then forced him out, tied him up to a tree, and shot him, leaving him there dead, and giving instructions that the body was to remain there and not to be buried. Briscoe, one of these ruffianly Maroons, who was identified with many acts of wanton cruelty and murder, and called himself *Captain Briscoe*, said, in his examination before the Commissioners, that the man was shot for the crime of having a son who was a rioter.

A black soldier belonging to the 1st West Indian Regiment . . . proceeded to Long Bay, where he found in the custody of a person named Berry six black prisoners suspected of stealing a sow, the property of one Christopher Codrington. The late manager of the Jamaica Cotton Company (then a justice of the peace) was present, with James Codrington, Mr David Mayne, and several constables and assistants. In the presence of them all,—and such was the panic-stricken condition of the whole country, in consequence of the misrepresentations of Governor Eyre, and the atrocious proceedings of the military authorities, that none dared to interpose by a word, this single soldier was permitted to take these untried prisoners out, one by one, and put them to death by shooting them with his rifle, while the persons above named quietly stood by and looked upon the butchery. . . . The next day after this brutal massacre had taken place, the sow the murdered men were supposed to have stolen . . . came out of the bush with a litter of young pigs, which sufficiently accounted for her disappearance.

Mr Kirkland sent to say I [Thomas Beckford, a butcher] must go and assist to flog the people. I said I didn't able to flog and to be killing beef. He said, if I did not flog, I would get a hundred lashes. I was compelled, for the sword and gun of the Maroon were around me. It was about the middle of marital law. On Friday the 13th, the regiment came up from Kingston. On Monday I began to kill beef for the Maroons; and on Wednesday October 18th, I flogged forty-nine people that day. I know that one, Alick Taylor, had one hundred lashes, and was hanged. George Tyrer had one hundred, William Burke had one hundred, Thomas Bolton had one hundred, Daniel Taylor had one hundred, Toby Butler had one hundred, and was hanged. All the rest had fifty, twenty-five, or thirty. Nobody helped me that day. All the females had sixteen lashes. I cannot tell exactly how many were women; about twenty. I think one Fanny Junor, who was heavy with child, had nineteen lashes. She said she was, and she was sent to be examined, and they said she was not. Married women examined her. She was big with child at that time. The female cat was like this, a piece of knotted twine. Some had seventeen and some sixteen lashes strung with it, all with knots the same as this. The men were flogged with this cat (specimen produced). There were about sixteen or seventeen strands like that, all with wire round in that way, and all that length, put into a good piece of stick. I took that piece, and kept it since that time. My hand got tired with flogging, and I cried out, and they mixed a glass of rum and water to give me strength. Mr Kirkland sent it to me. I began about nine in the morning, and never left off till about four in the afternoon.[38]

Portrait of Colonel Fyfe and Maroons, Morant Bay, *Photograph Album Documenting the Morant Bay Rebellion, Jamaica 1865, and More*, accessed at https://www.slideshare.net/GailannBarry/documentingthemorantbayrebellion-110224230232phpapp01-1?qid=b913327c-ebc6-401b-8168-746e76cd771c&v=&b=&from_search=1.

Such was the flavor of the events which took place during the days of Martial Law, when "not a single soldier or sailor had even been wounded."[39] Of his accomplishments Governor Eyre proudly declared that

38. Bleby, *Reign of Terror*, 58–79.
39. Gordon, *Our Cause*, 111.

Under his authority, the retaliatory toll of floggings, executions, and destruction of peasant property exceeded that which had been exacted after the 1831 32 slave rebellion. Governor Eyre wrote on 2 November. The retribution has been so prompt and so terrible that it is never likely to be forgotten.[40]

History has in the main "forgotten" and even erased the violence which was meted out against an innocent population, together with the injustices which they had had to endure. However, the records are many, and we are also afforded the truth, spoken by brave and bold eye witnesses such as Rev William Clarke Murray, who had been on the island since 1863, and who in fearing the possible repercussions, reported covertly to his home mission, the following analysis:

> Escape for a black man was scarcely possible whatever may have been the character of his offence. I feel a thrill of horror as I recall the hasty, and to my mind vindictive, manner in which thousands of souls were hurried into eternity offering no resistance to Her Majesty's troops. As for the atrocities committed by the Maroons the tale would scarcely be credited in enlightened and Christian England.[41]

Of Saint Thomas itself in the aftermath, BMS missionaries Phillippo and Thomas Lea, visited in March 1866, and reported how:

> They saw sad signs of the devastation occasioned by the outbreak, and its suppression, and heard sad tales of ruin and bereavement from the sufferers. Especially melancholy was it to visit hamlets where the houses had been burnt down, women and children wounded by stray bullets, and there were hardly any men left.[42]

Of these events in Saint Thomas in the East, the Royal Commission soberly concluded that:

> It is clearly shown that the outbreak at Morant Bay, in the parish of St Thomas-in-the-East, was simply a local riot, magnified by the craven fears of the civil and military authorities of the island into a dreadful rebellion and made the occasion and pretext for shocking excesses, to which it will be difficult to find a parallel in British Colonial history.[43]

40. Stewart, *Religion and Society*, 155.
41. Gordon, *Our Cause*, 115.
42. Tucker, *Glorious Liberty*, 84–85.
43. Bleby, *Reign of Terror*, 5.

The Final Roar of the EBS: Saint Thomas in the East (1865)

Graves of 80 Dead, Morant Bay, *Photograph Album Documenting the Morant Bay Rebellion, Jamaica 1865, and More*, accessed at https://www.slideshare.net/GailannBarry/documentingthemorantbayrebellion-110224230232phpapp01-1?qid=b913327c-ebc6-401b-8168-746e76cd771c&v=&b=&from_search=1

A "NATIVE" BAPTIST ENDING TO THE EBS

The increased tension which the repression in Morant Bay created on the island led also to clear contentions developing along "color" lines, amongst the clergy. Suspicion was raised against Black ministers, not only those of the EBS but other independent groups also, so that

> Several coloured Ministers of religion were amongst the prisoners arrested by Governor Eyre's orders, and sent on to Morant Bay, to be tried and put to death, because some months before they had, in the exercise of their rights as British subjects, taken part in public meetings at which his own administration was not always spoken of in flattering terms. These men were marched out, under the orders of Ramsay, day after day, and compelled to look on while the Negroes were butchered, eighteen or twenty at a time, and others cruelly flogged. One of these coloured Ministers, who had been selected for the slaughter, and kept a prisoner for several weeks, told me that he always kept his eyes turned away from Ramsay when he was near, not daring to look upon him, lest he should resent it as an offence, and order him out to be flogged. "How dare you look at me?" said he to a poor trembling creature, whose look had been fixed upon him with the sort of fascination with which men sometimes regard

a horrid monster. "Take him out, and give him a dozen!" It was thus that this man suffered and, indeed, authorized by Governor Eyre to treat the free subjects of Queen Victoria in 1865.[44]

Prominent African Jamaican ministers of mainline denominations, including those of the recently established JBU, were similarly treated. The story is told how

> Rev Edwin Palmer, a black Jamaican parson in the Baptist Union, minister of the Hanover Street Baptist Church in Kingston; Rev James Service, another black minister of the Baptist Union; Rev Roach, an independent pastor, originally from Barbados and formerly a Methodist preacher; and Rev Crole, already mentioned, associate of Gordon . . . and pastor of the Kingston Tabernacle. These "dangerous" men, arrested for sedition, imprisoned without trial, maltreated, and later released for lack of evidence implicating them in the rebellion, barely escaped the fate of Gordon and Bogle.[45]

BMS ministers having once again been declared to be the motivators for the "rebellion" were pursued by the state who believed that they had been inspired by Clark, Dendy, and Phillippo's book, *Voice of Jubilee*, which they termed "a Baptist 'book of martyrs' and which allegedly extolled the example of Baptist slave rebels who died during the rebellion of 1831–32."[46] As there were many such books written during the same period, many of the Baptist missionaries questioned whether the influence of that specific book was the cause, or whether it was simply one of the many books which were written at that time, and therefore had little influence on anything.

The Legislature, somewhat dismissive of their argument, nevertheless retained the belief that the rebellion had been set in motion by Underhill, and the "Underhill Meetings" supported by the European-led JBU. Though it was clearly proved that these ministers were not involved in the uprising, they were nevertheless believed to have been involved in the dissemination of relevant information concerning the "rebellion" to their congregations and surrounding communities. Five European Baptist ministers were singled out as being culpable: Reid, Maxwell, Dendy, Hewitt, and Henderson, the last two having preached in Killick's chapel in Morant Bay, which no doubt provided the necessary additional proof of "guilt by association." Threatened in this way, the BUGB, BMS, and European-led JBU sought to

---

44. Bleby, *Reign of Terror*, 90–91.
45. Bleby, *Reign of Terror*, 166.
46. Bleby, *Reign of Terror*, 169.

mollify their accusers by joining with the ministers of other denominations, and electing to abandon their EBS colleagues.

Fortuitously for these groups of Baptists this was not too difficult, the BMS being able to confirm that there had in fact been no European Baptist-led witness in the region prior to 1866, when

> Sir Henry Storks, head of the Special Commission . . . urged upon Dr Underhill the importance of opening Mission stations in this neglected region. In March, 1866, Mr Phillippo and Mr Thomas Lea were sent out as a deputation by the Baptist Union. . . . The deputation's report having been sent to England, the Committee voted a sum of money to establish stations in and around Morant Bay itself. . . . Very soon the Rev William Teall . . . left his loved people at the far west of the island, and took in hand this pioneer work in the extreme east . . . gradually winning "dark St Thomas" for the Kingdom of Light.[47]

The entire BMS then went on the "offensive" in order to protect their missionaries and ministers. Tucker later documented some of the disparaging remarks made by BMS missionaries in regards to members of the EBS describing the region and the work of the EBS in Saint Thomas as

> The neglected and backward state in which the bulk of the population lived in comparison with more favoured parts of the island; another is the presence of workers of that sect, whose origin is probably due to negro immigrants from America, and which is known as the Native Baptist Church. Some of these churches are communities of earnest, hard-working people of, that labouring class, supporting their own pastor, who in many cases, is not a college-trained man; but others are discreditable and unworthy, and should more properly be called fanatic than Baptist-Churches where morality is not insisted upon as a sine qua non for membership, and much religious hysteria and crude African superstition mingle with the worship and practices of the members.[48]

They dared to describe the EBS as a church "where morality is not insisted on," when in reality, it was not until the arrival of the EBS that many "Christian" plantation owners were forced to not only accept, but respect, marital relationships on their plantations, before the EBS would agree to work there. Tucker, realizing the moral injustice of what he and his colleagues were saying, tried to redeem the situation. He made clear that it was not a belief

47. Tucker, *Glorious Liberty*, 84.
48. Tucker, *Glorious Liberty*, 85.

that he personally held about the work of Parson Killick and the members of the EBS. However, by calling all those present in Saint Thomas "Native" Baptists, other groups, missionaries, and the Legislature began to associate the one with the other, seeing the two as being synonymous, and therefore co-opted the term and from then on used it as the way to describe them.

Too late, so quickly had the pioneering work and sacrifices undertaken by past and present members of the EBS in Morant Bay been disparaged. Their previous eighty years of struggle for freedom in Jamaica was rapidly dismissed and overshadowed by this redefinition given to them by the BMS and other missionary organizations. For example, Woolridge, the leader of the LMS, on first arriving in Kingston in 1835, acknowledged the movement as being synonymous with that of the BMS, stating that

> In a list of the city's chapels he included Lyle's and Killick's, classified as Baptist with those of Mr Gardner and Mr Tinson of the BMS.[49]

However, in 1865 the very same LMS organization rather unfavorably declared Killick and Lisle to be "black men, ignorant, disreputable and unrecognized."[50] Edmondson, the Methodist District Chairman, went further, declaring that

> In almost every Parish a number of uneducated, and I fear unprincipled men, having risen up as native Preachers, chiefly of the Baptist persuasion. They have formed churches and become their ministers. Most of them are utterly incapable of instructing the people in the great principles of Gospel Truth; and it is highly probable that they have dwelt much on the claims of classes, and have represented the Black as an oppressed race, who ought to defend themselves. I have heard of language like the following as used by a black preacher—"You are black and I am black, and you ought to support your own colour." "The blacks are seven to one of the others, and they ought to have the Island."[51]

BMS missionaries in Jamaica simply concurred with these sentiments, while at the same time expressing their own frustrations, stating that

> It is aggravating at times to hear all these spoken of as Baptists, as if forming one company or denomination with ourselves.[52]

---

49. Gordon, *Our Cause*, 71.
50. Gordon, *Our Cause*, 71.
51. Stewart, *Religion and Society*, 167.
52. Tucker, *Glorious Liberty*, 85.

They then added further insult to injury by joining with the other denominations in choosing to send an

> Address [to] Governor Eyre expressing their gratitude for his prompt suppression of the rebellion. . . . Rev East [President of Calabar College] published his sermon to his Rio Bueno Baptist congregation on "Civil Government: What the Bible says about it: A sord for our Times." The sermon had been delivered in reaction to Morant Bay. The published version was prefaced by J.M. Phillippo. The theme was that the Christian religion should make its adherents lovers of the law, order, and government. East gave thanks to God that the wicked ringleaders of the Morant Bay Rebellion had been put to death.[53]

So, the BMS by their actions had chosen, in response to persecution, to turn their backs on a relationship which had lasted for over fifty years. Forgotten was the fact that not only had they inherited many, if not all of their churches and congregations from this movement, but that EBS members had, when called upon, sacrificed their own lives in order to enable the BMS to continue to preach the gospel in Jamaica. Underhill, he of the famous letters of support, also used the weight of his office to enforce the condemnation, and given his influence, his words are worthy of being fully documented here, for they were perhaps the final nail in the coffin for the public face of the EBS and relationships with African Jamaican Christians who, after Morant Bay, wanted no part in the white man's God and the white man's Christianity.

Preaching at Belvoir Street Chapel in Leicester in January 1866, his sermon, which was widely reported in the press, contained the following statements:

> And now a few brief words with regard to the relations and conditions, as illustrated by this recent struggle. You are quite aware that our missionaries have had to endure a vast amount of reproach, and it is very startling that the Government should charge upon them any participation in the lamentable affair. There are about 21 or 22 white brethren, and as many native brethren, labouring for us. In all the numerous meetings (and they amount to about 25), there were only two instances in which the Baptist Missionaries either took part, or signed a requisition from the people. The real fact is, there is a larger proportion of the clergymen of the Church of England than of our brethren all put together; and I am very surprised that the

---

53. Stewart, *Religion and Society*, 173, 174.

Government should charge us with any portion of the rebellion. Then, again, the very scenes of the outbreak are in a part of the island in which we have no missionary station whatever. I believe it is now upwards of twenty years since a missionary of our society appeared in the district. There were, I believe two missionaries in the district—an independent missionary and a black man. It has been known for years as a Church of England district. It is a district that has been considerably populated by captured Africans in the course of the immigration experiments. They obtained permission to bring to Jamaica persons captured in slave ships. Our name as Baptists has been brought into disrepute because of some other men calling themselves Baptists. It so happened that there was a very good black man who came to Jamaica to preach to the people while they were then slaves, and who gathered a very considerable congregation in Kingston. These persons have gradually spread over the island, and seem to have planted themselves in the district of St Thomas-in-the-East, and these men have maintained a good many foolish practices; and there has always been (so to speak) a kind of gulf between our brethren and these native Baptists. Many of them joined our communities, but we have always held ourselves aloof from any communication with them. This body of ancient Baptists has been sustained by the planters of Jamaica; and if you go through their accounts, you will find no grants for the maintenance of our mission societies, but not a few grants for the societies and chapels of those native Baptists. I do not pretend to say that while the planters have supported these native Baptists only, they have done wrong; but I do say that after they have supported them, I think that it is too hard, in a great crisis like the present, to turn round and charge us with the disloyalty which belongs almost exclusively to themselves. In fact, the blacks in our missionary neighbourhood are almost paralyzed with the sorrowful transactions which have taken place.[54]

So, Underhill gave permission for the EBS to be seen as no more than a sorry bunch of ignorant Africans who practiced a false religion. Imagine then how far the high and mighty fell when, having "disassociated themselves so adamantly"[55] from having had any kind of relationship with the EBS, the truth of the atrocities carried out to those very same people came to light. Phillippo, and then Underhill, tried to backtrack, and apparently the latter, forgetful of his own actions, chose to criticize the actions of local

54. Underhill, "Dr Underhill," 8.
55. Tucker, *Glorious Liberty*, 169.

The Final Roar of the EBS: Saint Thomas in the East (1865)

BMS missionaries in Jamaica, admonishing and then correcting them. Underhill stated that, while they had been:

> True to the history in acknowledging the independent origin of the Native Baptists in the 1780s in the preaching of freed slaves from the United States, but [they] seemed to distort the cooperation between the native group and the original BMS missionaries, especially Burchell, by claiming there had never been any union with them, a claim that was true only in a formal or institutional sense.[56]

The BMS also directly criticized the actions of the JBU, whose words "could be interpreted as justification of the government's unnecessary brutality."[57] While it had not been unexpected that, given Eyre's influence, the actions of the EBS were more than likely to have been condemned by those of other denominations, it must have been something of a disappointment for them to hear it from those with whom they had had such a close working relationship for so many years. Both the BMS and the JBU had let down the EBS, their white missionaries and ministers, being clearly seen as being in step with the desires of Empire.

So, what of the EBS? Well, the lion had roared for the final time in Morant Bay, as the first Baptist mission, a part of the global Baptist family, simply became just another bunch of heathen "native" Baptists lost in the annals of time. Members scattered and were prominent in the social, political and religious history of Jamaica no more. They were quickly expunged not only from the memories of those religious organizations which were familiar with them, but from the British-inspired history books. This was in many ways a very sad end to a people and a movement which for over eight decades had led the way in providing unflinchingly transparent advocacy for a people and a nation, for the glory of God.

---

56. Tucker, *Glorious Liberty*, 167.
57. Tucker, *Glorious Liberty*, 174.

Chapter 12

Legacy

I BEGAN THIS BOOK by telling the story of those commissioned to operate and run the slave colony of Jamaica on behalf of the Crown, as legislated and led by the British Parliament. Every day control was therefore placed in the hands of those to whom they had ceded control: the governor, colonial legislature, Jamaican Assembly, and the plantocracy. Their duty was to operate the slave colony by maximizing profit, no matter the cost in terms of human lives, as there was a neverending supply of African bodies being made available to them. However, at the conclusion of this book, some eighty-three years later, after the intervention of George Lisle and his cadre of leaders of the EBS, despite building an army of believers and establishing congregations in every parish on the island, while a level of freedom had been gained, politically and socially little seemed to have changed.

The Crown was more in charge than ever, with Jamaica becoming a Crown colony, directly ruled from Britain, and maintaining both the class system and colorism within society. The planters, merchants, and traders had either become politicians and businessmen, retaining ownership of much of the land in Jamaica, or they had taken their vast wealth to Britain, where they were able to join the upper echelons of society, living once again as masters of all that they surveyed. Such was the gratitude of a grateful nation for the wealth on which Britain was built that there was hardly a town or city in which they lived that did not have statues erected in their honor, schools named after them, or the finest universities, after having received bountiful endowments, naming "chairs" in their name.

In terms of the church too, little had changed. The CofE was still in charge, but with the support of white British missionary agencies leading Black majority churches as they in turn sought to fulfill the wishes of the Crown in their new Jamaica. The EBS, having had its name expunged from the history books, had meant that not even members of the JBU, who had been richly blessed with lands and buildings, had until recently known little, if anything, of their existence, and the extent to which they had fought to establish not only Christianity on the island, but were instrumental in making it available to all. Happy were they to celebrate BMS missionaries, such as Knibb, Webb, and Phillippo, whose names hung proudly at the entrances of many churches established by Baker, Gibb, and others. The events in Morant Bay, on all levels political, social, and religious, therefore seems like a tragic end to a brave people who had fought the good fight of faith to the end, with little or no legacy to show for it.

However, this is far from the truth in regards to Lisle and the EBS. They were not politicians seeking man's praise or affirmation. Neither were they a civil rights movement whose victories could be chalked up along a timeline of successes. They were an evangelistic movement, dedicated to sharing the gospel, the good news of Jesus Christ, to all who would listen. Their belief had been a simple one: that if they could encourage the people, through the sharing of their own experiences and God's word, that what God had done for them in bringing about their emancipation, God in turn could do for them, if only they stretched out their hands to heaven. So, rather, the question has to be asked: Did they achieve their goal? Is there a spiritual legacy which remains even until today, despite the nation's enforced ignorance in regards to the movement?

Well, our first clue as to whether they achieved their goal, and perhaps the most striking clue, is that despite the colonial leadership being seen as the "victors" for removing the EBS from the public arena, to this day the British government and many descendants of the mulattos and coloreds, who became the new leadership of Jamaica, seem at the very worst to have a fear of all who call themselves Jamaicans, and at best are wary of African Jamaicans as a race. Enlightenment thinking had taught the British and Western Christianity that they were not simply culturally superior to those whom they had colonized, but had a culture which the "heathen" would want to embrace. They had expected a docile, willing people, but instead were repeatedly faced with a people, enslaved Africans who demonstrated a superiority, not only spiritually, but morally and ethically, through adherence to a faith which they refused to deny. Let me explain by reflecting on their ministry of over the eighty years, and how through the ages the legacy of the movement, though invisible to many, has evolved and brought forth new leaders who have never forgotten the hope of Ps 68:31.

The EBS were Pentecostals in terms of their interpreting of the Scriptures, and so they understood that they "wrestled not against flesh and blood, but principalities and powers."[1] They therefore had to make sure to leave the people with the foundations necessary on which they could build their faith, so that it would not be shaken, extinguished, or defeated. To this end Lisle's Covenant was read every week, thereby ensuring that they were all on the same page. Then, the enslaved in turn learned to place their faith not in a man or a woman, but in God, for it was only God, they believed, who was able to deliver them from the shackles of their enslavement.

Through the freedom which had to take the gospel to every parish, the people soon came to understand that through Jesus Christ, two freedoms were being offered to them, firstly, the possibility of their physical freedom on earth. Then secondly, if that could not be achieved, through their faithfulness to the ways of Christ, they would have an eternal freedom to look forward to. Either way, they could once again be free to be with friends and family on earth or, in death, be reunited with ancestors long since gone, hence the elaborate "Nine Night" celebrations. It was a win-win situation as far as they were concerned, especially given that the lives which they were being forced to live was a hell on earth, without remission.

The leaders of the EBS were their model, each one showing them that no matter what the plantocracy or the British government tried to do to them, they would stand tall for Jesus Christ, even if that meant death, as was the case concerning George Lewis. Being faithful to God was all that mattered, and so they would walk miles through the night, just to hear the promises God had prepared for them. No matter then how many were bruised, broken or even killed, it was a martyrdom with heavenly rewards, and so convinced were they as to the truth of this that death was preferable to the losing of their eternal salvation. This was unambiguously seen during the genocide of 1865, when at the end of it all even their oppressors understood that the fear of death no longer had power over them. Many did not seek death, but if it was to be, then they declared like Old Virgil that if they were to die, then they should just hang them high, so that they could go to their father in heaven.

Yet, one may interject and say that, as Lisle's generation of leaders were all gone by 1828, as were the next generation after the troubles of 1831–32, then surely their faith must have been due in no small part to the BMS missionaries who were with them for over thirty years, and most significantly led them to emancipation and beyond. However, the evidence demonstrates

---

1. Eph 3:12 (SFLB).

that while the enslaved attended many BMS-led churches, it was not always for the reasons one might assume. Firstly, many were illiterate, and therefore, if they were to continue to be able to hear the stories of the wonders of Jesus, then they needed to be in those churches in order to be able to hear it. Secondly, as you will recall, in the early years of the CSL, when EBS ministers were prevented from preaching, we know that many attended the CofE, and other permitted churches, in order to not just hear the word but in order to strategize and socialize without fear of the authorities. So, the BMS to many of them would in many instances have been no different. Apart from Thomas Burchell, who many believed treated them as equals, they would attend other churches, gladly accepting anyone who would tell them stories of faith and the hope that could be had in Jesus Christ.

However, having gone to the white man's church, they clearly did not necessarily imbibe the white man's theology, as was seen many times when they came into conflict with them. This was especially true when the BMS stressed the need for them to accept their enslaved position, as God-given according to 1 Cor 7:20, 21. However, many being able to read the Bible for themselves, they knew that, had the missionaries done a proper exegesis of the whole text, and especially vv. 22–23, they too would have known that God was declaring all men, no matter the status in which they came to Christ, to be equal and free. However, should one choose to become a slave to someone, it was better to choose to be slaves of God rather than slaves of men. The BMS therefore could not dissuade them from continuing to express the belief that God meant for them to have both their physical, as well as their spiritual, freedom. Such contentious issues were therefore often not spoken about, until they were forced to do so, as was the case concerning Sam Sharpe in 1831. Yet we see that once their own freedom was jeopardized, the BMS soon found the necessary evidence, be it courtesy of William Carey, by which they believed that they had permission to challenge leaders in Jamaica.

Africans simply wanted to hear the word of God, and relied on the Holy Spirit to bring understanding in the days and weeks following. We see this reliance on, and trust in, the Holy Spirit when Sharpe, and then Gordon, at the time of their individual executions, spoke words of prophecy—insights, given by God, as to the things to come, for those whom they were leaving behind. We also see it in the revival of 1861 to 1862, when so thrilled were the people that God was visibly interceding in their lives, as well as speaking to their hearts, confirming to them that they no longer had need of white missionaries, or any white minister. The Spirit of God was writing his truth directly in their hearts and lives, in ways beyond that which was achieved by most of the BMS missionaries.

I am further convinced that, as evangelicals who believed in a culturally acceptable way to live the Christian life, the BMS, like the missionaries before them, not only did not understand the theological position of these Africans, they had no interest in doing so. Nevertheless, they, and especially William Knibb, seemed to understand the significance of invoking both Africa and Ps 68:31 (as Lisle had done), in order to keep them on his side. This at various crucial times enabled Knibb to claim greater levels of support than he may actually have had, including when he engineered a change of direction in the BMS Committee concerning the establishing of an African mission.

No matter the hardship and distractions, the enslaved and leaders of the EBS kept their eyes solely on God's promises. We learn two further things about the faith which they had in God from their period of freedom and equality. When emancipation finally came, and many African Christians found that their old masters had fallen on hard times, there was a generosity of spirit which saw many of them offering accommodation, and even providing care for their wayward offspring. This indefatigable spirit was much to be admired in contrast to the bitterness of many of the planters who, despite their compensation, seemed only concerned with revenge. These African Christians had found the pearl of great price, and were not willing to trade it by harboring bitterness, anger, or resentment against those who had once tortured and oppressed them.

Then, while the events of 1865 had clearly put an end to the public face of the EBS, it also nevertheless served to demonstrate to all that they were a people of faith who exemplified and brought to life the pages of the Bible, their actions declaring time and again their belief that

> For if we live, we live to the Lord; and if we die, we die to the Lord. Therefore, whether we live or die, we are the Lord's.[2]

Despite everything, they were not beaten, deflated or destroyed, and this engendered a fear which was real for many of the white inhabitants of Jamaica, the colonial government, and leaders who were, in the main, a people who either had no active faith in God, or saw everything simply in terms of power, control, empire, and caste. The might of the British Empire therefore could be seen to have had a hollow victory, having repeatedly failed to defeat these Christians who had imbibed the messages of the EBS and so were not solely invested in a person or a movement, but God. They were a force to be reckoned with, and while the Empire could and did so easily break their bodies, it could not break their will, or their belief in the God of the Bible, the God of the Ethiopian. Their success was such that the

---

2. Rom 14:8 (SFLB).

footprint of the movement continued to be seen through the years in many diverse groups and individuals, even to the present day.

MISSIONARY AND RELIGIOUS ACTIVISTS

John Edward Ricketts (1857–1908)

John Edward Ricketts appears from current research to have been a unique missionary in many respects in that though he attended Gibraltar and Stewart Town Baptist Churches, in Saint Ann (today a part of the JBU), in 1887 he went from there as a missionary to the Congo and then Nigeria, under the auspices firstly of the American Baptist Missionary Union (ABMU) and then the Southern Baptist Convention. Interestingly, the archives of the American Baptist Historical Society describe Ricketts as having been a member of an American Baptist Church in Jamaica, which had been established by Lisle's Ethiopian Baptists movement. This is worthy of further investigation, as present in Jamaica at that time was the Jamaica Missionary Board and the BMS, neither of which became vehicles for his missionary career.

Ricketts was a part of a group of "Africans" who benefitted from philanthropic sponsorship, which enabled him to attend the now-defunct African Institute in Colwyn Bay, Wales. The institute had been set up:

> Specifically for the training of African . . . equipped to work independently of Western denominational missions or else in a nondependent partnership with White missionaries . . . [it] brought together Africans from various African colonies and Liberia, as well as African Americans . . . [teaching by] the first decades of the twentieth century . . . that the road to heaven did not lead through Europe.[3]

Here once again Ethiopianism was raising its head in another form, though unfortunately for Jamaica, Ricketts never returned from Africa to put his beliefs into action in a land which by then was becoming increasingly imitative of British Christianity and British cultural values.

Marcus Garvey (1887–1940)

Marcus Garvey could be said to have been a man who lived well before his time. He, like Gordon, emphasized Black consciousness long before it was articulated in the public arena some fifty or so years later, by such people

---

3. Fischer-Tine and Gehrmann, *Empires and Boundaries*, 202–3.

as Steve Biko (South Africa) and Malcolm X (North America). Garvey, however, was one of the earliest people who took this Jamaican notion of Black consciousness to a global audience. He was a child of emancipation, and so benefited from the brief period of educational growth, attending school from the ages of seven to fourteen years old. Thoughts of God and Christian formation had therefore always been a part of his developing years, but as an adult he developed his own concepts of God, sin, and the humanity of the African Jamaican. One of Garvey's earliest challenges was confronting the Western notion of sin, which for him did not originate in disobedience to authority or sexual promiscuity, but rather, "sin . . . was the loss of identity by black people."[4]

Responding to developing Black cultural alienation Garvey preached a gospel which encouraged his people to

> Affirm blackness as God's gift to black people, since God had created humanity in his own image.[5]

His resistant reading of the Bible did not lead him to articulate a theological position which respected the status quo but rather one which challenged for a new order. For this he was rejected, in his homeland by his own people, his peers, the Jamaican middle classes who took offence when he used the terms "negro" and "Black" to describe all peoples of African descent. They, having been enculturated into British cultural values, saw the use of such a term in their regard as insulting, believing that it should only be used to describe those who were of a "lesser" social status than themselves.

Garvey was a pioneer of the Pan-Caribbean nationalist movement whose ideas took root amongst Jamaica's working and under classes after his death. Then his theories were adapted by a new generation of people who reinterpreted them and used them as the basis for what later became the Rastafarian Movement. Ironically, Garvey found a warm welcome amongst African Americans, who respected his ideas to such an extent that they have since acknowledged him as being one of the "founding fathers" of the American Civil Rights Movement of the 1960s.

Alexander Bedward (1859–1930)

Alexander Bedward began his ministry on December 22, 1891, inheriting a community, in a district known as 67 August Town, in the then-parish of Saint David (now Saint Kingston). They practiced rituals similar to Zion

---

4. Erskine, *Decolonizing Theology*, 110.
5. Erskine, *Decolonizing Theology*, 109.

Revivalism, but with other rituals drawn primarily from the CofE and British cultural practices. Bedward believed that the best way to conquer the colonizer was to develop a command of his culture and embrace it as one's own, thereby nullifying any effect of superiority it could continue to engender.

Harping back to the days of the Morant Bay Riot he named his church the Native Baptist Free Church, emphasizing Black identity, and preaching against the injustices of the government. Bedward, as a result, built up a significant following, which by its very numbers had the potential to challenge the minority colonial government. This made him an enemy of the governor of Jamaica, who had him "sectioned" in 1895, before imprisoning him in an asylum in 1921, where he died of bronchitis in 1930. Like Garvey, his theories were also adapted and adopted by those who went on to establish Pan-Caribbean nationalism and the Rastafarian movement.

Rastafari

When Independence came to former British colonies in the Caribbean, the winds of change brought a renewed determination by Caribbean peoples to define their cultural identity, as Jamaicans, Barbadians, Trinidadians, etc., and in Jamaica, Rastafari, reggae, and particularly the music of Bob Marley emerged as not only a new spiritual voice, but a political one also. Rastafari was a new religious movement which wanted nothing to do with what they saw as the white oppressor's government and their white God. In fact, so opposed to them were they that they created a whole new lexicon of words to dilute the language of their oppressors.

Rastafari's initial support came primarily from amongst the dispossessed and downtrodden, the poor. History teaches us that Leonard Howell, considered to be the founding father of the movement, made himself an enemy of the state when he set up a friendly society named the Ethiopian Salvation Society in 1937, and then located his Rastafari movement in Saint Thomas before relocating it to Kingston. One of his leaders, Joseph Hibbert, proudly declared his links with the EBS in 1917 when he stated that he had learned his early lessons of faith in one of their chapels in Kingston. The colonial government, in response, fearing that Rastafari was the resurrection of the EBS, especially after they refused to pay taxes (reminiscent of the tax riots of 1865), made a calculated decision to persecute members of the movement. Howell received two years of hard labor in 1934, before being imprisoned on charges of sedition. He was also confined to a lunatic asylum variously from the 1930s to the 1950s, the government hoping that in so doing they would destroy the movement.

However, rather than destroy the movement, it galvanized the movement, increasing year on year until it became a global movement. Foundational to the beliefs of Rastafari was (and is) the scriptural text of Ps 68:31, which they used as the means to reclaim their African identities with thoughts of a Black Jesus, and a Black God, Jah, directly challenging the stereotypical, Eurocentric picture of a Middle Eastern Jesus. Overtime it has become the prime motivator in the search for a true Caribbean cultural identity, and such is its power that many of those who have observed the privileging of English cultural values in Jamaica have now acknowledged the fact that Rastafarianism, more than any other movement, has been the preserver and maintainer of Jamaican cultural identity.

Charismatic/Pentecostal Movements

Revivalist "Bands" and Zion Revivalism

Revivalist "bands" and Zion Revivalism, which emerged after the 1861 to 1862 revival, came to the fore and soon developed into the leading Christian grouping on the island, having roots in both African religious practices and the EBS. However, as successful as Zion Revivalism was, the colonial government refused it the right to license its own ministers, thereby negating their ability to establish legitimated churches which could serve the needs of the majority of the people. They therefore sought new ways by which they could gain both their religious freedom and social equality. They soon found it in a larger movement of Pentecostalism from America.

Pentecostalism

There had been an enduring belief in African Jamaican Christian mythology since the Morant Bay Riots in 1865 that one day their deliverance would come from America. Education, missionary activity, and travel to Panama and North America exposed African Jamaicans to the wider world, enabling them to come to the realization that the British Empire was not the only system of power in the world. They learned that the United States of America possessed similar, if not equal, power and influence in the world around them, and so to North America they looked. It was probably no surprise to the faithful, then, when in 1917 Evangelist J. Wilson Bell sent an invitation to the Church of God (CoG), Cleveland, somewhat reminiscent of the one sent by George Lisle and Moses Baker almost one hundred years earlier, asking them to come and assist the people of Jamaica.

There were other Black Pentecostal organizations in Jamaica at that time but it would seem that none of them possessed what the CoG had: the ability to stand up to the colonial system and the power to license their own ordained, globally accepted, and accredited ministers. The CoG responded by sending evangelist J. S. Llewellyn to Jamaica in April 1918. However, the early years saw little growth, for though theologically the CoG emphasized orthodox Pentecostalism, with an emphasis on singing, music, and baptism in the Holy Spirit, similar to that believed by African Jamaicans, they were in fact found to be as conservative and as exclusive in their cultural practices as their European Christian counterparts.

However, following the Second World War, when the CoG offered Jamaicans the opportunity to have their own accredited ministers accredited, they embraced the CoG. The CoG in turn, true to its word, provided the necessary financial backup to build churches, and sent globally recognized healing evangelists such as T. L. Osborne to encourage them. The CoG then gained favor by reintroducing to Jamaica clapping and the use of musical instruments, including drums, into services, together with such practices as jumping, "falling," or being "slain in the spirit," and being lost in moments of ecstasy. There were healing services, all-night prayer meetings, and water baptism which took place in rivers and streams, which many converts saw as being a continuation of the ministry of the EBS.

African Jamaicans grew to fully embrace this movement, which they could identify with, as a legitimate form of worship, able once again to meet their physical, social, emotional, and spiritual needs, one worshiper proudly echoing the words of worshipers long since passed as he stated the reasons why he attended the Pentecostal church:

> Why the people flowing to the New Testament Church of God the more, it was divine healing. Anywhere we went and preached that brought people that was sick and we prayed for them, and they got healing you see. Then the people them, believe the church for the healing more, even more than the preacher. That goes a lot to the physical, you know, because many of the people them, want that power. Yes man, when the Spirit preaches you feel it, you feel it all over your body. The body feel good. I mean, if you go in the church and the Spirit of God is not in the church, you cyan operate. You just sit down listening, but when the Spirit of God come in, you can turn the body in the Spirit.[6]

In embracing CoG practices, Jamaica appears to have finally come full circle, returning to the practices of the EBS, thereby confirming to them

---

6. Austin-Broos, *Jamaica Genesis*, 79.

once again God's acceptance of their experiences, social, religious, and cultural practices.

Independent Baptists

We know that once Parson Killick took over the leadership of the Windward Road Chapel, he changed its name to the Independent Baptist Chapel, and just as the enslaved watched over the remains of Sam Sharpe until he was given a Christian burial, it would seem that the indigenous independent Baptist groups, with no links to the JBU, see themselves as the keepers of the legacy of George Lisle. Some congregations were established before 1865, while others came about shortly after, but we know that under Killick their numbers remained high, but because they remained a movement banned by the colonial government until well into the twentieth century, there are few records. However, we do know that they were "despised and rejected" by white leaders of the JBU, and many of their African Jamaican brothers and sisters who attended those churches. These independent Baptists, nevertheless, having seen white leadership at its worst, were determined to go it alone, despite the mockery which they received for

> Trying to maintain themselves without white leadership . . . regarded even by many of the Negroes themselves as impossible. They throng the popular churches pastored by white men and have heretofore regarded other Baptists as very ignorant and superstitious and derisively dubbed the First Church [Lisle's Church] "John Crow."[7]

THE FEARFUL

Britain

Yet, we are not done yet. Turn the clock forward another decade, and we are in Britain, in the 1960s, when a great influx of British Commonwealth citizens began to arrive in England. Step forward the white peoples' "champion" and conservative member of Parliament, Enoch Powell. Powell clearly knew the history of the EBS and the mental strength of African Jamaicans, sounding the alarm at the arrival of so many citizens. In 1968 he even went as far as to declare that there may well be "rivers of blood" as a consequence. He, as we now know, was harping back to the 1833 and 1835 parliaments,

---

7. Parrish and Jordan, "Report of the Commission," 120.

and 1865 views of Governor Eyre, who feared that to give Africans freedom would almost certainly result in violence against the respective white populations. Powell continued to fear being persecuted in a simlar way that past British governments had persecuted African Jamaicans.

Jamaica

Returning to Jamaica, it was in the 1970s at the height of his fame when global icon Bob Marley purchased a property a few doors away from the residence of the Prime Minister of Jamaica. This caused great concern; history speaks of how Marley was ostracized by his white neighbors, and though he was both Scottish and Africa Jamaican, a colored, he was seen as having deserted his own because of his empathy for the Black majority. In order to cover up for their prejudice, his antagonists blamed his "rural" background for their hostile behavior towards him. When Marley was asked how he felt about it, he simply responded, "Sistah, I bring the ghetto uptown." To this day, he is loved the world over but treated with indifference by the leaders of a Jamaica who, in semi-independence, never hesitated in rewarding the duplicitous actions of William Knibb with a medal of honor for his services to Jamaica, while Marley, since his death in 1981, has thus far received nothing.

Finally, we move forward to June 2015. Jodi Stewart-Henriques, a member of one of the oldest "planter" families, and the wife of Jamaican rapper Sean Paul (a fellow colored), made quite derogatory comments in a national newspaper about her neighbor, the globally admired and then eight-time Olympic and world champion Usain Bolt. Her complaint was that

> Between the bikes, loud horrid music, parties and screams I wish he went back to where he came from. He's a horrible neighbour. . . . He takes his nasty behaviour with him everywhere. He's the ultimate party clown. . . . I honestly cannot believe the set of UPT (uptown) that have him as poppy show in the parties or their boat.[8]

What had Usain Bolt done to receive such vitriol, one may ask? Well, the story behind the story was that she was not simply complaining about Bolt as a person, but more so about the fact that he, a "lower caste" African Jamaican, had been able to afford and move into one of, if not the most, exclusive neighborhoods in Jamaica: Norbrook. She believed that he had forgotten his place, his social status, as one who had no right to consider themselves equal to any other caste or group in society, and was only placed

8. Jerkins, "Usain Bolt," para. 9.

on the earth to be controlled by their superiors and, of course, to serve. Bolt, having receiving permission to fulfill his potential through the church which he grew up in, which was located in an area dominated by the EBS, by just being successful destroyed the enduring myth which Jodi Stewart-Henriques was alluding to.

CONCLUSION

So, did the EBS achieve their goal of inspiring a people to believe in God. The answer has to be yes, and while few in Jamaica of today may fully understand their evolution, it is clearly understood by the British government and the coloreds and mulattoes of Jamaica who continue to fear what might happen if African Jamaicans Christians (who have established more churches per square mile than even the United States of America) are able to look back and see who they were becoming, and still have the potential to be, if they walked in obedience to the God of Ps 68:31.

In conclusion, then, the majority of African Jamaican Christians, having looked at European Christianity, refused to be colonized in the same way, in which Fanon described many other colonized nations had been subject to, in that:

> The Church in the colonies [was] the white people's Church, the foreigner's Church. She does not call the native to God's ways but to the ways of the white man, of the master, of the oppressor. And as we know in this matter many are called and few are chosen.[9]

While many may not know how or why their congregations came into being, their chapels are, however, a constant visible legacy, a reminder to all, that once there was an indefatigable group of African American ex-slaves and African Jamaicans, enslaved and free, who, led by one George Lisle, both inspired and raised an army of believers in the most heinous of all British slave colonies—women and men who were willing to lay down their lives so that Africans in Jamaica could not only hear the good news of the gospel, but be made free from their shackles and chains, both physical and spiritual.

---

9. Fanon, *Wretched of the Earth*, 32.

Chapter 13

Epitaph

How then shall this story end? Who gets the last word? Well, I believe that the last word has to be said of George Lisle, the pioneering leader of a team who could so easily have chosen another path, but chose to serve Jamaica instead. Yet, while this is the concluding chapter of this book, it is not the conclusion to the story, but rather an attempt to tell a part of the story of the legacy of George Lisle. The work of Lisle and his Ethiopian Baptists, his contribution to Christianity, our understanding of mission, and life in Jamaica has until the publication of this book been largely left unacknowledged. They were not represented in many Jamaican or British history, or books on Baptist history, and their names do not adorn the walls of many of the churches of the JBU, who have been "educated" to proudly celebrate their BMS "founders." Yet as this book now demonstrates, theirs was a glorious history, one which not only led to the establishment of Christianity amongst the African Jamaican population, but fought for and laid the foundations for freedom.

George Lisle came from humble beginnings on the slave plantations of Virginia, where he learned about Christianity from his parents Nancy and Lisle. His faith was birthed in the bosom of the American South, where he learned to negotiate his existence as an enslaved African Christian, and it grew to adulthood in the crisis of the American Revolutionary War, where he learned how to be a pragmatist in order to develop the skills which were needed for ministry amongst a powerless Black population, facing an all-powerful white population.

Lisle then took this ministry to Jamaica, where he demonstrated a mature Christian faith, leadership skills, and a determination to succeed when faced with a plantocracy and an Anglican Church which saw the Christian faith as closed to Black people, white being the only acceptable God-given order of things. So loved was he by many of his leaders that many of them, in freedom, adopted his first name: George Gibb, George Lewis, George Vineyard, and in Nova Scotia, David George. He was the pastor's pastor, leading a cadre of leaders in the USA, the Bahamas, Britain, Sierra Leone, and Jamaica, as well as being the father of an innumerable number of saints named and unnamed in this book, who did indeed stretch out their hands to God, wherein they found salvation, healing and deliverance.

As the two worlds collided over eight decades, the casualties were many and almost always were Ethiopian Baptists, and yet they never lost heart. Persecutions came in the form of violence and murder, particularly as Laws were enforced that were designed to lead to the demise of the movement, but they never lost courage or the desire to simply worship their God. These Ethiopian Baptists should therefore be credited with preserving the integrity of the gospel of Christ at a time when it was being discredited by the close association between the plantocracy and the CofE. They taught the wider society that all human beings were made in the image of God, and worthy of the salvation offered by God.

He was a visionary leader who saw his task as enabling his African brothers and sisters to receive the truth of the gospel for themselves, and despite the attempts of the Jamaican Assembly, the plantocracy, and the CofE to prevent him from establishing an inclusive church, available to all, he triumphed. Lisle and his colleagues, Black, colored (mulatto), and white, demonstrated a maturity of faith which saw them, through the use of his Covenant, receiving support not only from the wider Baptist family in England and America, but "sympathetic" members of the plantocracy, the Jamaican Assembly, and the British aristocracy in the most trying of circumstances. He then used the permissions which he received to negotiate agreements that the enslaved could be educated and have their common law relationships legalized as marriage, with the benefit of developing a family unit, even if "ownership" remained in the hands of the planters.

History also shows us that Lisle and his EBS welcomed the missionaries of the BMS to work with them and assist them in their mission in Jamaica. BMS records clearly show the leading role which Lisle and his people took in evangelizing the nation and how many of those early missionaries, Rowe, Compere, Tinson, and Burchell, became Ethiopian Baptists in all but name, as they too sought to encourage and accept the contextualization of those Baptist churches which they inherited, in the likeness of its African adherents.

His passion and energy never seemed to wane. We see him in 1822, at the grand old age of seventy-two years old, visiting Britain, in order to seek assistance for the work in Jamaica. While there, despite receiving a somewhat lukewarm and perhaps dismissive response to his visit to the BMS, he nevertheless showed his generosity of spirit on his return to Jamaica in 1826. Learning that BMS missionary Joshua Tinson substituted for him while he was away, in gratitude, assisted him in establishing a ministry in Kingston.

Lisle died in 1828, but not without leaving a strong vibrant church. While he and his team may have "gifted" the BMS approximately 20,000 members, it is clear that the EBS remained, going from strength to strength as they regrouped and continued his work, once again across all the parishes of Jamaica. Taking into consideration the numbers within each congregation in the 1820s, it is likely that there were far more people who belonged to the EBS, or EBS-inspired churches, than those who were in the BMS. He had clearly raised a missionary movement which, even in death, was far from being an insignificant "Native" religion. We know that what he taught his adherents went on to being established in not just one or two, but three generations of believers, whose faith was repeatedly tried; in 1831–32 during the "Baptist War," during apprenticeship and the failures of the NEG, and finally in Morant Bay. Each generation not only stood their ground, but testified to the goodness of God, and proved faithful, even when faced with martyrdom. They, like Lisle, never gave up, and were never found wanting.

His legacy then continues even to the present day, as Jamaicans, having experienced the truth of God's promise for them, have themselves established ministries, handing the baton to diverse groups of indigenous African Jamaican-led religious expressions. Individuals and churches which have been led by bold men and women in each of their organizations and situations have, in their own ways, put on the mantle of Lisle, whether knowingly, or unknowingly. All that is therefore left to do is to thank God for the life and ministry of George Lisle, the first Baptist missionary to the world. Of the many accolades which he received during and after his lifetime, we are fortunate that a few remain. Thanks to the faithfulness of the Independent Baptists and the NBC, a picture of his tombstone, erected by Parson Kellick, has been preserved, though his remains are believed to have been scattered. It was placed on his tomb in the burial ground where he was laid to rest, close to his beloved Windward Road Chapel.

Drs. Parrish and Jordan at Rev. Lisle's Grave, Kingston, Jamaica, March, 1915.

Drs. Parrish and Jordan at Rev. Lisle's Grave, Kingston, Jamaica, March 1915, *New York Public Library,* **accessed https://digitalcollections.nypl.org/items/ ee4cd680-15a6-0132-0775-58d385a7bbd0**[1]

While the then-British-led Jamaican government had managed to "successfully" extinguish his story from public view, and the trustees of his beloved chapel had demolished it in 1907,[2] those who knew of him first and

---

1. Citation: "In memory of the Revd George Lisle. The founder of the Baptists in Jamaica in the year of our Lord 1783. He was indeed a burning and shining Light who have borne the burden and heat of the day. His race is run. His warfare accomplished, and he has exchanged the sorrows of the wilderness for the joy of heaven in the year 1828. This tomb is erected by the Members of the Independent Baptist Chapel now under the Rev William Killick his successor. Blessed are . . . Source: New York Public Library.

2. Unfortunately, just as the demise of the public face of the EBS was tragic, so too was the demise of the church. The trustees of 1907, were not in fact members of the

were also inheritors of his ministry sought to give him the belated reverence due to him. They have left us epitaphs in the form of a poem, reflections, and a monument, each of which continues to speak of his work, his life, his ministry, and all those throughout the world, who now live in his legacy:

MUSINGS

1
Methinks I hear faint voices,
That come from the cold dead past.
Bringing memoirs of the faithful
From a sea of forgetfulness—vast

2
They chant like ancient minstrelsies
Of a sable race of men.
And tell of worthy tributes
The world has withholden from them.

3
The air is rife with the music,
But the sound that strikes my ear
Is a song of loving service
That all world should hear.

4
A song of human chattel
In which men use to trade,
And it seems as I gaze in the distance
A scroll before me is laid.

5
Adorned with the faded features
Of one whose life was spent,
In sacrificial service,
For human betterment.

6
From the chant of mysterious voices
I catch the trend of his life,
Of struggle and toil and sorrow,
Of hardship and suffering and strife.

---

church, and though there was little damage to the structure of the chapel following the hurricane of that year, they chose to demolish the whole building, embezzling the funds, while retaining ownership of the three acres, it resulted in the building of a much smaller chapel, seating approximately forty to fifty people, which remains to the present day. Parrish and Jordan, "Journal," 121.

> 7
> He preached mid jeers and curses
> That men might see the light.
> And daily as he labored
> Endeavored to do the right.
> 8
> While yet the vision lingers
> I see him suffer shame.
> See him fettered and led away
> Without one bit of blame.
> 9
> But when I fain would close my eyes
> To hide from view, the sight.
> Behold the shackles fall away,
> Loosened by God's own might.
> 10
> Then free indeed from bondage
> Of spirit and of frame.
> Still sorrowing and rejoicing,
> He labors again in His name.
> 11
> I listened enrapt by the voices
> That sang the song to me.
> Wondering as I looked anon
> Whose face is this I see.
> 12
> And then, methought in fancy,
> As I gazed and gazed a while.
> Beneath the painted picture
> I saw the name—*George Lisle*.[3]

This man doubtless has long since finished his labours and has entered the saints' rest . . . but he will be remembered, and his name honored, both here and in Jamaica while memory holds its place. Whatever the Negro Baptists here and in Jamaica are, they owe it to his humble beginning. And whatever may be written of either of us, it cannot be complete if his name is left out. His record is here, there and in heaven.[4]

In conclusion, then, Jamaica was fortunate to have been the home of George Lisle, the first Baptist missionary to the world. He not only believed in the truth of the Bible, but had an unyielding faith in the God of the Bible. He was a true apostle of Jesus Christ who led a people which, when faced

3. Henderson, "Musings," 150–51.
4. Love, *History*, para. 7.

with violence, imprisonment, and martyrdom, were never found wanting. As a nation, Jamaica may never know what it might have become under the spiritual guidance of Lisle's EBS, but one thing is certain: whether they were Black or white, all who were touched by his ministry were all the better for it.

George Lisle Monument.[5]

---

5. FMBNBC, "George Lisle Monument," 149.

Appendix 1

Punishments

"A Negro Hung Alive by the Ribs to a Gallows." Published Dec. 1, 1792 by J. Johnson, St Paul's Church Yard, London, accessed June 17, 2022. https://www.gutenberg.org/files/65715/65715-h/65715-h.htm.

294 Appendix 1

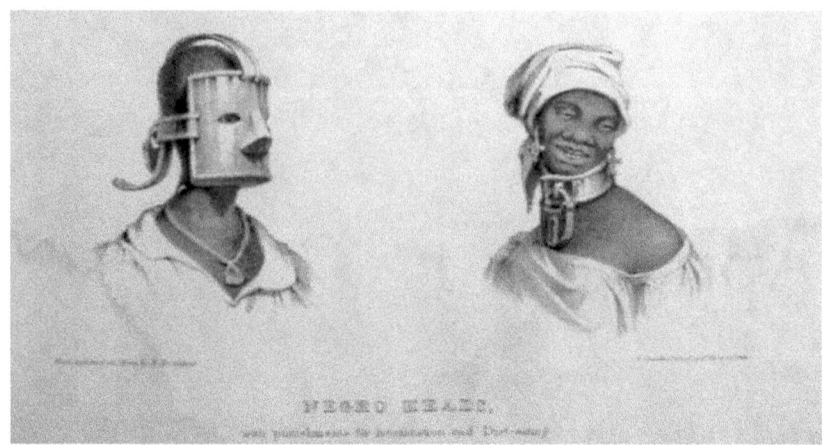

"Negro Heads, with Punishments for Intoxication and Dirt Eating." *Slavery Images: A Visual Record of the African Slave Trade and Slave Life in the Early African Diaspora*, accessed June 16, 2022, http://slaveryimages.org/s/slaveryimages/item/2992.

Flagellation of a female Samboe Slave, London, Published Dec 2, 1793, by J. Johnson, St. Paul's Church Yard, accessed June 17, 2022. https://www.gutenberg.org/files/65715/65715-h/65715-h.htm.

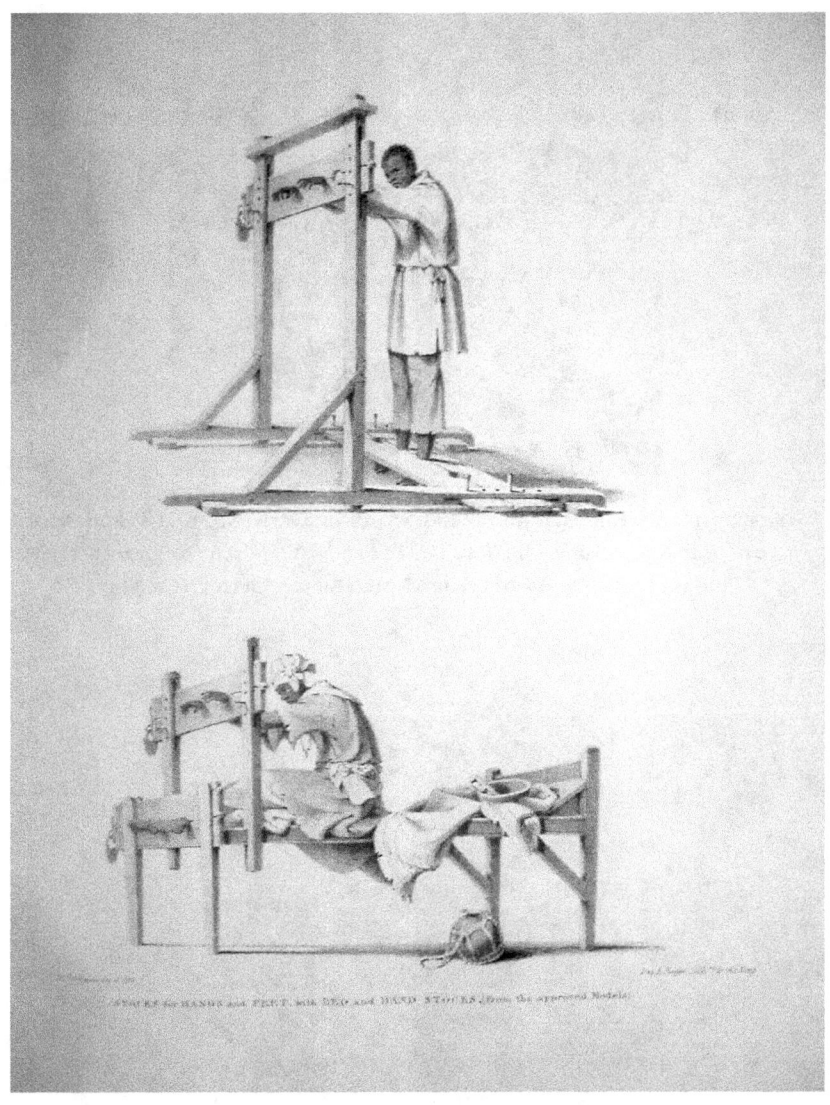

"Punishment of Children in Stocks, Trinidad, 1836," *Slavery Images: A Visual Record of the African Slave Trade and Slave Life in the Early African Diaspora*, accessed March 9, 2022. http://slaveryimages.org/s/slaveryimages/item/1232.

"Whipping of a Slave, French West Indies, 1840's." *Slavery Images: A Visual Record of the African Slave Trade and Slave Life in the Early African Diaspora*, accessed June 16, 2022. http://slaveryimages.org/s/slaveryimages/item/3107.

"A Female Negro Slave, with a Weight Chained to Her Ankle," published Dec. 1, 1792 by J. Johnson, St Paul's Church Yard, London, accessed June 17, 2022. https://www.gutenberg.org/files/65715/65715-h/65715=h.htm.

The Horrid Torture of Impalement[sic] Alive as a Punishment on Runaway Slaves. Published September 1808, Yale University Library, accessed at https://collections.library.yale.edu.

Appendix 2

Rebellions

1678—Caused by prolongation of martial law
1684—First serious one
1686—Sanguinary, at Clarendon
1691—Many white people murdered
1702—Eastern districts
1717—Repeated attempts causing great alarm
1722—Musquito Indians introduced to quell it
1734—The negro town Nanny taken
1736—Under Cudjoe
1739—Under Quaco, in Trelawney
1740—Speedily subdued
1745—Conspiracy to assassinate the whites
1758—In Trelawney
1760—Under Tacky; 60 whites, 400 negroes killed
1765—Coromantees the insurgents
1766—In Westmorland
1769—Conspiracy discovered in Kingston
1771—Conspiracy; assembly of 300 surprised by the militia
1777—Followed by thirty executions
1782—St. Mary's, under Three-Fingered Jack
1795—Trelawney Maroons
1796—Maroon war; 600 transported
1798—Under Cuffee; great destruction of rebels
1803—Conspiracy to murder the whites discovered

1807—Conspiracy of a very serious character
1807—Mutiny of the black troops
1809—Conspiracy against the whites in Kingston[1]

---

1. Madden, *Twelvemonth's Residence*, 2:248–49.

Appendix 3

Story of an African Taken into Slavery

ROBERT MADDEN ON A visit to Jamaica, came to understand how one enslaved man, a doctor, came to be enslaved. He wrote:

> I had a visit one Sunday morning very lately, from three Mandigo negroes, natives of Africa. They could all read and write Arabic; and one of them showed me a Koran written from memory by himself-but written, he assured me, before he became a Christian. . . . One of them, Benjamin Cockrane, a free negro who practised with no little success as a doctor in Kingston, was in the habit of coming to me on Sundays, to give me information about the medical plants and popular medicine of the country; and a more intelligent and respectable person, in every sense of the word, I do not know. As an Arabic scholar, his attainments are very trifling, but his skill as a negro doctor, one of the English physicians of Kingston assured me was considerable. He had lately known him called to a young lady, where with his herbs and simples he had effected a successful cure of a serious malady. When he comes to me, he drives in his own gig attended by his servant. His history is that of hundreds of others in Jamaica, "except these bonds," which he, by extraordinary industry and good conduct, had managed to shuffle off. I took down the heads of his story pretty much in his own words, as he related it to me in the presence of the attorney-general, to whom I made him known, as I had likewise done to Dr. Chamberlain; and I believe both these gentlemen will vouch for the fact that

there is at least one negro in the world who is an intelligent, well-educated, right-thinking man, and not so very nearly connected with the lower class of brutes, as the reverend of the 'Annals of Jamaica' would lead us to infer. Cockrane says his father was a chief in the Mandigo country; he was sent to school, but was too idle a boy to become a scholar. "Plenty of books in the Mandigo country, but not much schools; the great schools are farther up the country. He began to learn to be doctor in Mandigo country: -nobody taught him first: he noticed for a long time what plants did harm to the cattle, and how they did them harm: he noticed what herbs they were fond of when they were sick, and he tried a great many of the good herbs for a long time, till he found which did most good to sick people. His village go to war with another village near sea-coast—plenty of ships there then to carry away poor black man-other village beat his—people ran away, but plenty taken prisoner and carried down to the sea, and he among them. Well, when ship came near Tortola, the English admiral pursued and took her—there were 360 slaves on board—were distributed in the King's service, and all were to be free in seven years. When he got free, came to Jamaica, there make him a slave again—take him up for one runaway. When the Duke of Manchester Governor, applied to him to make him free;—asked him what for these people make him slave—he no slave. The Duke told him the commissioner had a right to make him slave—(I presume the seven years' service might not have been considered expired)—sent back to Antigua; but the commissioners there gave him free. Came back again to Jamaica—but some people told him he had no right to be free—they made him slave again, and he remained slave three years, till governor got him free. Was in Barbados when Lord Cockrane was there, and when he gone away, the people called him Cockrane. Since he got free, he try to serve God every day for so much goodness to him. And why for no? who made the white man's heart?—God.—And who made the black man's heart?—God. Why should not black man serve God as well as white man? And every day him get up and go where him choose, and do what him like; very much goodness to be thankful for to him good Father."[1]

---

1. Madden, *Twelvemonth's Residence*, 1:127–30.

Appendix 4

The Covenant of the Anabaptist Society

Received orders of the Baptist Church in America the 17th of December 1777—began in Kingston Jamaica December 25th, 1783—elders appointed in Kingston for the said Anabaptist Church in Jamaica and was ordained by them on the 25th of December 1795.

1. We are of the Anabaptist persuasion because we believe it agreeable to the Scriptures. Proof:—(Matt.3 v1–3; 2 Cor. 6 v 14–18).

2. We hold to keep the Lord's Day throughout the year, in a place appointed for Public Worship, in singing psalms, hymns, and spiritual songs, and preaching the Gospel of Jesus Christ. (Mark 16 v 2, 5, 6).

3. We hold to be Baptised in a river, or in a place where there is much water, in the name of the Father, and of the Son, and of the Holy Ghost. (Matt. 3 v 13, 16, 17; Mark 1 v 15, 16; Matt. 28 v 19).

4. We hold to receiving the Lord's Supper in obedience according to His commands. (Mark 14 v 22–24; John 6 v 53–57).

5. We hold to the ordinance of washing one another's feet. (John 13 v 2–17).

6. We hold to receive and admit young children into the Church according to the Word of God. (Luke 2 v 27–28; Mark 10 v 13–16).

7. We hold to pray over the sick, anointing them with oil in the name of the Lord. (James 5 v 13, 14, 15).

8. We hold to labouring one with another according to the Word of God. (Matt. 18 v 15–18).

9. We hold to appoint Judges and such other Elders among us, to settle any matter according to the Word of God. (Acts 6 v 1–3).

10. We hold not to shedding of blood. (Gen. 9 v 6; Matt. 26 v 51–52).

11. We are forbidden to go to law with another before the unjust, but to settle any matter we have before the Saints. (1 Cor. 6 v 1–3).

12. We are forbidden to swear not at all [sic]. (Matt. 5 v 33–37; Jas. 5 v 12).

13. We are forbidden to eat blood, for it is the life of a creature, and from things strangled, and from meat offered to idols. (Acts 15 v 29).

14. We are forbidden to wear any costly raiment, such as superfluity. (1 Pet. 3 v 3, 4; 1 Tim. 2 v 9–10).

15. We permit no slaves to join the Church without having a few lines from their owners Consent and of their good behaviour. (1 Pet. 2 v 13–16; 1 Thess. 3 v 13).

16. To avoid Fornication, we permit none to keep each other, except they be married according to the Word of God. (1 Cor. 12 v 2; Heb. 13 v 4).

17. If a slave or servant misbehave to their owners they are to be dealt with according to the Word of God. (1 Tim. 1 v 6; Eph. 6 v 5; 1 Pet. 2 v 18–22; Titus 2 v 9–11).

18. If any one of this Religion should transgress and walk disorderly, and not according to the Commands which we have received in this Covenant, he will be censured according to the Word of God. (Luke 12 v 47–48).

19. We hold, if a brother or sister should transgress any of these articles written in this Covenant so as to become a swearer, a fornicator, or adulterer; a covetous person, an idolater, a railer, a drunkard, an extortioner or whoremonger; or should commit any abominable sin, and do not give satisfaction to the Church, according to the Word of God, he or she, shall be put away from among us, not to keep company, nor to eat with him. (1 Cor. 5 v 11–13).

20. We hold if a Brother or Sister should transgress, and abideth not in the doctrine of Christ, and he, or she, after being justly dealt with agreeable to the 8th article, and be put out of the Church, that they shall have no right or claim whatsoever to be interred into the Burying-ground during the time they are put out, should they depart life; but should they return in peace, and make a concession so as to give satisfaction, according to the word of God, they shall be received into the Church

again and have all privileges as before granted. (2 John 1 v 9–10; Gal. 6 v 12; Luke 17 v 3, 4).

21. We hold to all the other Commandments, Covenants, and Ordinances, recorded in the Holy Scriptures as are set forth by our Lord and Master Jesus Christ and His Apostles, which are not written in this Covenant, and to live to them as nigh as we possibly can, agreeable to the Word of God. (John 15 v 7–14).

In witness whereof we have hereunto set our respective hands and seals this thirteenth day of June in the year of our Lord, one thousand seven hundred and ninety: William Wilson, John Liele, George Liele Jnr., Amos Stiles, Charles Price, John Harris, John McIntire, James Pascall, John Baptist, George Good, William Good, James Cargill, Hannah Liele, Diana Price, Ann Lindsay, Jane Williams, Silvia Stiles, Sarah Savage, Elizabeth Gordon, Elizabeth Good, Mary Brown, Lucy Liele, Elenor Bonner, Sabina Johnson. Witnesses Joseph Spencer and George Liele.

We bind ourselves, under an affirmation, to do duty to our King, Country, and Laws, and to see that the affixed Rules are duly observed.[1]

---

1. Anabaptist Society, "Elders and Rules."

Appendix 5

Roll of Honor African Baptist Assistants

James Alexander Clarke
Thomas
Thomas Laing
James Pascall
Moses Hall
Cupid Wilkin
Harry Brown
John Duff
Thomas McKean
John Allen

J Cunningham
Robert Hamilton
William Duggan
John Davis
Peter Lovermore
John Gilbert
Joseph Sylva
Thomas Peart
Robinson
John Pascal

Appendix 6

Roll Call of the First African Jamaican Ministers Who Attended Calabar College

Richard Merrick
Joseph Merrick
Robert Graham
J Campbell
Francis Johnson
Thomas Henry
Thomas Smith
Robert Ellis Watson
Angus Duckett
Edwin Palmer
WML McLaggan
Ellis Fray
Joseph Gordon
Richard Dalling
Alexander Brown

James Barrett
James B Service
Henry Bartholomew Harris
James Gordon Bennett
John James Steel
Patrick O'Meally
Daniel Gregg Campbell
George Moodie
Francis Pinnock
Samuel Holt
James Maxwell
Robert Adolphus Facey
J J Porter
Windsor Burke
William Mengie Webb

Appendix 7

Working toward Emancipation, 1837

"Water-Jar Sellers," *Slavery Images; A Visual Record of the African Slave Trade and Slave Life in the Early African Diaspora*, accessed March 9, 2022, http://slaveryimages.org/s/slaveryimages/item/2313

308   Appendix 7

"Milkwoman," *Slavery Images: A Visual Record of the African Slave Trade and Slave Life in the Early African Diaspora*, accessed March 9, 2022, http://slaveryimages.org/s/slaveryimages/item/2317.

"Chimneysweeper," *Slavery Images; A Visual Record of the African Slave Trade and Slave Life in the Early African Diaspora*, accessed June 16, 2022, http://slaveryimages.org/s/slaveryimages/item/2315

310   Appendix 7

"Lovey," Seller of Flowers and Puppeteer. *Slavery Images; A Visual Record of the African Slave Trade and Slave Life in the Early African Diaspora*, accessed June 16, 2022, http://slaveryimages.org/s/slaveryimages/item/2316.

Appendix 8

Emancipation Day— August 1, 1838, Song Sheet

HYMNS FOR THE NEGRO JUBILEE, 1838

On this bright glorious morning

1

On this bright, this glorious morning,
As the Sun illumes the skies,
Disencumbered, disenthralled,
See the sons of Africa rise!
Hallelujah, Hallelujah!
Hallelujah, Praise the Lord!

2

Now, indeed, the chain is broken;
God has heard his people's pray'r!
Come, ye freed men, come adore Him,
Let us to his House repair.
Hallelujah, Hallelujah!
Hallelujah, Praise the Lord!

3
There, in strains of true devotion,
Let your grateful spirits rise;
'Tis His goodness has redeemed you:
Seek that you the boon may prize.
Hallelujah, Hallelujah!
Hallelujah, Praise the Lord!

4
What return can you now render
For His love who sets you free?
Hearts and lives to Him devoted,
By your conduct let us see.
Hallelujah, Hallelujah!
Hallelujah, Praise the Lord!

5
Heavenly Father, we now praise thee,
For thy kind restraining care,
Long display'd towards this people,
Keeping them from every snare.
Hallelujah, Hallelujah!
Hallelujah, Praise the Lord

6
To thy care we still commend them;
Still they need thy guiding hand:
Angel of the Cov'nant save them;
Lead them safe to Canaan's land.
Then they'll praise Thee,
Then they'll praise Thee,
When redeemed from ev'ry sin.

HYMN II

O Lord upon Jamaica shine

1
O Lord upon Jamaica shine,
With beams of heavenly grace;
Reveal thy power through all our coasts,
And shew thy smiling face.

2
Amidst this Isle exalted high,
Do thou our glory stand;
And like a wall of guardian fire,
Surround this favour'd land.

3
Soon let thy name from shore to shore
Sound all the earth abroad'
And distant nations know and love,
Their Saviour and their God.

4
Earth shall obey her Maker's will,
And yield a full increase;
Our God will crown this chosen Isle
With fruitfulness and peace

HYMN III

Hark the song of new-born gladness

1
Hark the song of new-born gladness
Rolls along the Western Sea,
Thousands from despair and sadness
Hail the dawn that sets them free;
Great Jehovah,
Thine this day of Jubilee

2
Thou didst hear thy people crying,
For their brethren o'er the wave,
Thou hast heard the bondsman sighing
He is free who slept a slave;
Thine the glory,
Thine alone the power to save.

3
Child of woe thy chain is broken,
Heal thy wounds, and dry thine eyes;
All fulfill'd that God has spoken,
See the Sun of Freedom rise;
Glorious morning,
Justice triumphs—SLAVERY dies.

4
Ev'n the oppressor calls thee brother,
Pleased no longer with thy groan,
And the happy negro mother
Now may call her child her own;
God of wonders,
Thine the triumph—Thine alone.

Appendix 9

Christian Rituals—Prayer Meetings and Facing Death

PRAYER MEETINGS:

During the disturbances in 1832 daily prayer—meetings were held in many of the places of public worship in those districts to which the outbreak had not extended. They were generally crowded to excess. During the space of a fortnight a prayer—meeting was held every day in the chapel at Spanish Town, at twelve o'clock, and this notwithstanding the contumely, the scorn, and punishment to which the people were subjected; and on one occasion while engaged in earnest sup plication that the unhappy man who had been induced to perjure himself against the missionaries, and on whose evidence their lives depended, might be brought to repentance, a messenger arrived, announcing that their prayers were fully answered, thus literally fulfilling the promise, "It shall come to pass that before they call I will answer, and while they are yet speaking I will hear." In towns and in districts where there is a concentrated population, a minister can at almost any time, and at a comparatively short notice, insure an attendance at a special prayer-meeting amounting to Isaiah xv. 24. On the 17th of February, 1833, Samuel Stennett, on whose affidavits Messrs. Burchell and Gardner had been committed, sent for his uncle, Mr. George Scott, a respectable person at Montego Bay, and declared to him that he had sworn falsely against the missionaries, and that he had been bribed to do so.

"The scarlet fever was raging dreadfully in Kingston when I was there," says Dr. Newbegin. "Entire families were times swept away. It was so bad, indeed, that not a day passed without a funeral—often two during twenty four hours in connexion with the church at East Queen-street, under the pastoral care of the Rev. Samuel Oughton. A public notice was given on the Sunday that a prayer-meeting would be held for the especial purpose of supplicating Almighty God on behalf of the suffering people. The time for meeting was half-past four o'clock, A.M., which was long before daylight. As many as 1500 people assembled. There was very great devotion, and many strove earnestly with the Spirit." Independently of the meetings for united family devotion on the estates, in numerous cases each separate house has its family altar. Nor is this practice confined to the country—it is almost universally current in the towns, where social prayer meetings are so numerous and common; thus, in traversing the streets after dark, the voice of prayer and praise is heard in every direction. These habits are pursued abroad as well as at home. Wherever they went, and wherever familiarly known, the purity, the fervour, the resolution, and the constancy of their devotion, were universally apparent. On a certain occasion the author, when at one of his country stations, hearing that some tradesmen who were then slaves were come to work on a plantation in the neighbourhood, employed them on the mission premises during their own time, on which account he provided them with sleeping accommodation. On rising before daylight on the first morning after they had lodged on the premises, he overheard one of them in fervent prayer, and on inquiry found that all of them (half a dozen in number) belonged to the church under the pastoral care of a missionary brother, the Rev. J. Merrick, now of Western Africa, whose station was about ten miles distant. These brethren were entire strangers to the writer until this discovery was made; and this he found was their habitual practice wherever they took their abode for the night. In some cases it was customary for Christian negroes employed in field labour to hold a prayer-meeting during their hour of cessation for refreshment, in the middle of the day, selecting some secluded spot for the exercise. It is customary for the Christian negroes, both in town and country, whenever practicable, emulating the conduct of David, Daniel, and others of the Old Testament saints, to engage in private exercises of devotion three times a day. The moment they awake in the morning, which is often long before the dawn, they are on their knees: this is repeated at noon, and again on retiring to rest. Many are in the habit of praying thus whenever they awake in the night, and the writer has known some who, from constant habit, awoke almost invariably at a certain time, and poured forth their prayers in the stillness and solitude of the midnight hour. To such a degree is this duty in general recognised, that in the towns, on the occurrence of a hurricane, or the shock of an earthquake, the voice of prayer is heard in almost every house, and frequently from the middle of the streets. Under these circumstances it will be readily conceived that social prayer meetings are numerous and frequent. At these meetings among themselves females commonly engage as well as males, and their prayers are oftentimes distinguished by astonishing fervour and natural eloquence. In connexion with the Spanish Town district there are, on a moderate calculation, 280 every week, three or four being held during that period by each class respectively, under the superintendence of subordinate native agency. This estimate will probably apply to the greater part of the larger churches and congregations on the island, as also to the majority of those of smaller dimensions, in a corresponding degree. On the supposition that these meetings averaged 100 per week, at 100 of the principal stations, there would be 10,000 social prayer-meetings during every week of the year.[1]

FACING DEATH

An interesting individual of colour, arrested by the hand of death in the prime of life, shortly after a severe relative bereavement, sent for the writer to visit him. In the early part of his affliction, and for many previous years, he went about to establish his own righteousness, not submitting to the righteousness which is of God by faith. His views became gradually clear and comprehensive, and a short time before he died his mind was filled with joy unspeakable. Looking at his children, who were soon to be left orphans, he said, "For a long time I feared I could not leave them; the thought was like a dagger to my heart; but now I can give them up without a pang; the Lord will provide for them. I can trust his promise, he cannot lie. I am now ready." Then clasping his hands, and looking upward in ecstasy, he exclaimed,

---

1. Phillippo, *Jamaica*, 338–41.

"Come, Lord Jesus, come quickly! Why tarry the wheels of thy chariot? " A fit of coughing seized him as the result of this effort, and he ruptured a blood-vessel. A swoon succeeded, from which recovery seemed impossible. But he rallied; and looking around with astonishment on his weeping relatives and friends he uttered at intervals, as his breathing allowed him, "And am I come back again? -Oh, what happiness have I enjoyed! I have been in Heaven! I have heard the angels sing! I have seen the Lamb in the midst of the throne: o, that you could have seen what I have seen! Alas! that I am here again; but it will be only for a moment. This has been but a foretaste of the glory that yet remains-a sip of the river of life; what will it be to drink of it through eternity?" He now summoned his remaining strength, and addressed all present with an earnestness and sweetness of manner almost seraphic, and soon after expired, with a hope full of immortality?" Similar to the dying experience of this individual were the last moments of an aged female, who for many years had eminently adorned the doctrine of God her Saviour. Her calmness—her heavenly mindedness—her almost complete abstractedness from the world—her love to Christ, and zeal for his glory, in the salvation of her fellow-creatures, had been long remarkable, but towards the closing scene of her life all the graces of the Spirit seemed matured and ripened. Being greatly respected in the town and neighbourhood, numbers of persons of all classes successively crowded around her bed to take a last farewell. Her chamber seemed the verge of Heaven. She was often in raptures indescribable. These feelings were caught in some degree by her pious attendants, and the intervals from pain and repose were passed in reading passages of Scripture, in singing, holy conversation, and prayer. She seemed assimilated to the spirits of the just made perfect—in a mortal body, indeed, yet detached from mortality in the midst of her relatives and friends, yet wholly separated from them. The careless and gay amongst her visitors were struck with astonishment at the happiness she enjoyed, and at the fervour and force of her appeals and exhortations to them, and many, as well as the servants about the premises, seemed involuntarily to say, "how sweet and awful is this place! Let me die the death of the righteous, and let my last end be like his." She died singing those beautiful lines beginning, "See the kind angels at the gates Inviting me to come." in which she was joined, at her request, by the Christian friends whom she had now summoned around her bed.[2]

2. Phillippo, *Jamaica*, 408–10.

Appendix 10

Chapels, Monuments, and Grave Stones

Jericho Baptist Chapel, Clarendon. Photograph by D. Morrison.

320 Appendix 10

Old Baptist Chapel Montego Bay, destroyed 1832, accessed at Brunel University, London Archives, England.

William Knibb Memorial Baptist Chapels, before and after 1832. Photograph by D. Morrison, Falmouth, Jamaica.

Chapels, Monuments, and Grave Stones 321

Bedward Chapel, 1900s. Photograph courtesy of D. Morrison.

Bedward Chapel today. August Town, Jamaica. Photograph by D. Morrison.

Old Salters Hill Baptist Chapel ruins, St James. Photograph by D. Morrison, St James, Jamaica.

Monument to Crooked Springs Baptist Chapel and the 1831 Baptist War. Photograph by D. Morrison, Salter's Hill, St James, Jamaica.[1]

1. To The Glory of God. This monument is sacredly dedicated to commemorate the 200-year anniversary (1791–1991) of the establishment of the Salter's Hill Baptist Church by Moses Baker, an ex-American coloured. The first church known as Crooked Spring Baptist Church, was three miles from this site, was favoured by Samuel Vaughn. A prudent plant came. A new church was built on this site in 1829, opened on December 27, 1831, but burnt down on January 4, 1832 by the St James militia in retaliation for the lighting of the freedom torch which was lit by the Tulloch Castle, Kensington Estates, on December 26, 1831 to signal the start of the slave rebellion known as the Sam Sharpe rebellion, also called the "Baptist War."

Thomas Burchell Headstone, Photograph by D. Morrison, Abney Park Cemetery, Stoke Newington, London, England.

Bibliography

PRIMARY SOURCES

Jamaica

Anabaptist Society, George Liele Pastor, est. 14th October 1796. "Elders and Rules of the Anabaptist Society." *LOS Deeds* 432, folio 288, 1796.

Liele, George. "Indenture Deeds for Windward Road Chapel." *LOS Deeds* 372, folio 207, 1798.

———. "Sale of Windward Road Chapel." *LOS Deeds* 451, folio 164, 1798.

———. "The Purchase of Casar by George Liele." Indenture Papers, 1795.

———. "Trust Deeds Windward Road Land." February, 1791.

———. "Sale of Kitty from George Liele Snr to John Lisle." Indenture Papers, 1795.

Morton, David. "Land Sale to George Liele, Kingston." *LOS Deeds* 372, folio 207, 1789.

Simpson, John. "Indenture Contract Papers for the Sale of Kitty to George Liele." Indenture Papers. Kingston, 1793.

———. "Indenture Papers for the Sale of Kitty to George Liele." Indenture Papers. Kingston, 1794.

Smith, J. H. "Indenture Papers." *LOS Deeds* 384, folio 161, 1794.

Swigle, Thomas Nicholas. "Deeds." Thomas Nicholas Swigle and Francis Swigle land sale to George Liele: 521, folio 212, 1804.

National Library of Jamaica

"History Notes: Information Notes on Jamaica's Culture and Heritage." https://nlj.gov.jm/history-notes/history-notes.htm#emancipation.

Britain

Magazines/Journals/Internet

Baker, Moses. "An Account of Moses Baker, a Mulatto Baptist Preacher near Martha Brae in Jamaica." *The Evangelical Magazine* 11 (1803) 365–72.
———. "Account of Moses Baker, of Jamaica." *The Evangelical Magazine* 12 (1804) 469–72.
"The Case of Mr George William Gordon." *The Law Magazine & Law Review, or, Quarterly Journal of Jurisprudence* 22.43 (1866–67) 28–83.
Headsman. "1865: Paul Bogle." https://www.executedtoday.com/2012/10/24/1865-paul-bogle/.
Johnson, William John, ed. "Evangelical Christendom: Its State and Prospects." *Evangelical Alliance* 15.2 (1861) 632.

The British Newspaper Archives

Gordon, Robert. "Negro Riots." *Daily News*, January 26, 1866.
———. "Robert Gordon, Letter to the Editor." *Daily News*, January 26, 1866.
O'Connor, Major-General. "The Black Rebellion in Jamaica." *London Magnet*, November 20, 1865.
Underhill, Dr. "Dr Underhill, Belvoir Baptist Chapel, Leicester." *The Leicester Chronicle*, January, 6, 1866.

SOAS, University of London

Alloway, Rev. LMS Missionary, Ridgemount, Jamaica, W.I. "Letter to LMS." November 6, 1860.
Fletcher, Duncan. LMS Missionary Chapleton, Jamaica, W.I. "Letter to LMS." February 19, 1861.

Turner Collection, University of Birmingham

Banbury, Rev. T. "Jamaican Superstitions or The Obeah Book (1894)." Portland: Banbury, 1894.
Beckwith, M. "Chapters on Religion." Black Roadways, 1929.
Cundall, F. "On Myalism." *Journal of the Institute of Jamaica* 2.6 (1899) 587–88.
Hutton, Joseph Edmund. *A History of Moravian Missions (1922)*. London: Moravian Publication Office, 1922.

Brunel University

British and Foreign School Society. "Specimen of Writing &c. Lancasterian School." Kingston, 1826.

Angus Library, Regent's College, Oxford University

Bailey, George Gibbs. "Letter to Dr John Rippon, Kingston, May 9, 1793." BAR (1790–93), 542–43
Baptist Missionary Society. "Annual Report of the Committee of the Baptist Missionary Society." London: Haddon, 1823.
———. "Committee Meeting." Oxford, May 21, 1822.
Clarke, Jonathan. "Letter from Jonathan Clarke to John C Rippon." July 19, 1790.
Cook, Rev Mr Joseph, "Letter from Rev Cooke to John C Rippon." *Baptist Annual Register*, September 15, 1790.
Dendy, Rev. Walter. "Letter from Walter Dendy to Revd. J Angus." June 9, 1843.
Dutton, Henry John. "Browns Town, St Ann. Letter to Mr Giles, Gaunt House, Standlake, Oxon." March 28, 1840.
Francis, Inez Sibley. "The Baptist in Jamaica (1865)." London: The Baptist Missionary Society, 1842.
Knibb, William. "Journal Entry 28 January 1825."
———. "Letter to Samuel Nichols, from Kingston, Jamaica. March 1825." Knibb Letters.
———. "Letter to England from Kingston Jamaica, March, 1825." Knibb Letters.
———. "Letter to Mr Charles Young." London, December 19, 1839.
Liele, George. "Letter from George Liele, Kingston, Jamaica, to Dr John Rippon." December 18, 1791. Edited by John Rippon. BAR, 1790–93.
———. "Letter from George Liele, Kingston, Jamaica, to Dr John Rippon." May 18, 1792. Edited by John Rippon. BAR, 1790–93.
———. "Letter from George Liele, Kingston, Jamaica, to Dr John Rippon." January 12, 1793. Edited by John Rippon. BAR, 1790–93.
Swigle, Thomas Nicholas. "Letter from Thomas Nicholas Swigle, Kingston, Jamaica, to Dr Rippon." October 9, 1802. Edited by John Rippon. BAR, 1800–1802.
Teall, Rev. W. "Jubilee of the Jamaica Mission." *The Missionary Herald*, January 2, 1865.

British Parliament

Great Britain, Parliament, House of Commons. *State Papers*. Vol. 25. London: Clarke, 1827.
Hansard, House of Commons Debate. *Abolition of Slavery*. Debate, Hansard, 257–360, 1823.
HC Deb 14 May 1833 vol 17. *Ministerial Proposition for the Emancipation of Slaves*. Hansard 1193–262, 1833.
HC Deb 19 June 1835 vol 28. *Abolition of Slavery*. Hansard 918–60, 1835.
HC Deb 30 May 1833 vol 18. *Ministerial Plan for the Emancipation of Slaves*. Hansard 112–66, 1833.
House of Commons Select Committee. *Report from the Select Committee on the Extinction of Slavery Throughout the British Dominions: with The Minutes of Evidence, and General Index, 11 August 1832*. Government, London: Haddon, 1833.
House of Commons, The Slavery Committee. 1833. *A Second Letter from Legion to His Grace the Duke of Richmond*. London: Bagster, 1833.

The National Archives

"Proclamation to the Rebellious Slaves, 2 January 1832." TNA CO 137/181, 111.
"Reward Poster for Sam Sharpe, Colonel Gardiner, Captain Dove and Captain Johnson, 3 January 1832." TNA CO 137/181, 110.

United States of America

Bryan, Andrew. "Letter from the Negro Baptists in Georgia Addressed to The Rev Dr Rippon, Savannah-Georgia, USA Dec. 23, 1800." *The Journal of Negro History*. 1.1 (1916) 86–87.
Foreign Missions Board National Baptist Convention (FMBNBC). "George Lisle Monument." *Thirty-Sixth Session Journal of the National Baptist Convention* (September 6–11, 1916) 149. http://media2.sbhla.org.s3.amazonaws.com/aaa/nbc/NBC_1916.pdf.
Henderson, Pearl K. "Musings." *Thirty-Sixth Session Journal of the National Baptist Convention* (September 6–11, 1916) 149. http://media2.sbhla.org.s3.amazonaws.com/aaa/nbc/NBC_1916.pdf.
Livingston, Philip. "A Bond for the Manumission of a Slave, 1757." https://www.gilderlehrman.org/history-resources/spotlight-primary-source/bond-manumission-slave-1757.
Marshall, V. D. M. "The Journal of Negro History, Vol. I. Jan. 1916." https://www.gutenberg.org/files/13642/13642-h/13642-h.htm.
Parrish, C. H., ed. "Drs Parrish and Jordan at Rev. Lisle's Grave. Kingston, Jamaica." Louisville, KY: Mayes Print, 1915. From the New York Public Library Digital Collections, New York, USA. https://digitalcollections.nypl.org/items/ee4cd680-15a6-0132-0775-58d385a7bbd0.
Parrish, C. H., and L. G. Jordan. "Report of the Commission of the Foreign Mission Board." *Journal of the Thirty-Fifth Annual Session of the National Baptist Convention, Held with the Baptist Churches of Chicago, Ill., September 8–13, 1915* (1915) 115–23. http://media2.sbhla.org.s3.amazonaws.com/aaa/nbc/NBC_1915.pdf.
Woodson, Carter Godwin. ed. *The History of the Negro Church*. Washington, DC: The Associated Publishers, 1921.
———, ed. "Letter from the Negroe Baptists in Georgia Addressed to The Rev Dr Rippon, Savannah-Georgia, USA Dec. 23, 1800." *The Journal of Negro History* 1 (1916) 366.
———. *The Journal of Negro History* 1.1 (1916) 1–462. https://www.jstor.org/journal/jnegrohistory.

Printed Primary

Assembly of Jamaica. *Slave Law of Jamaica: With Proceedings and Documents Relative Thereto*. London: Ridgeway, 1828.
Baptist Ministers, eds. *The Baptist Magazine for 1817*. Vol. 9. London: Button, 1817.

Baptist Missionaries. *A Narrative of Recent Events Connected with The Baptist Mission in the Island Company also A Sketch of the Mission from Its Commencement in 1814, to the End of 1831*. Kingston: Jordan and Osborn, 1833.

Benedict, David. *A General History of the Baptist Denomination in America, and Other Parts of the World*. Vol 2. Boston: Manning & Loring, 1813.

Bleby, Henry. *Death Struggles of Slavery: Being a Narrative of Facts and Incidents which Occurred in a British Colony*. London: Hamilton, Adams, 1853.

———. *The Reign of Terror: A Narrative of Facts Concerning Ex-Governor Eyre, George William Gordon, and the Jamaica Atrocities*. London: Nichols, 1868.

Brooks, Walter Henderson. *The Silver Bluff Church: A History of Negro Baptist Churches in America*. Washington, DC: Pendleton, 1910.

Buchner, J. H. *The Moravians in Jamaica: History of the Mission of the United Brethren's Church to the Negroes in the Island of Jamaica from the Year 1754 to 1854*. London: Longman, Brown, 1854.

Burchell, William Fitzer. *Memoir of Thomas Burchell: Twenty-Two Years a Missionary in Jamaica*. London: Green, 1849.

Buxton, Charles, ed. 1849. *Memoirs of Sir Thomas Fowell Buxton*. London: Murray, 1849.

Clark, Dendy, et al. *The Voice of Jubilee: A Narrative of the Baptist Mission, Jamaica*. London: Snow, 1865.

Clarke, John. *Memorials of Baptist Missionaries in Jamaica, including A Sketch of the Labour of Early Religious Instructions in Jamaica*. London: Yates & Alexander, 1869.

Cornford, Philip Henry. *Missionary Reminiscences: or, Jamaica Retraced*. Leeds: Heaton, 1856.

Dillon, Rev. J. T. *Centennial Review of the First Baptist Church Montego Bay, Jamaica 1824–1924*. Kingston: The Gleaner, 1923.

Ellis, J. B. *Diocese of Jamaica: A Short Account of Its History, Growth and Organisation*. London: SPCK, 1913. http://anglicanhistory.org/wi/jm/ellis1913/17.html.

Findlay, G. G., and W. W. Holdsworth. *The History of the Wesleyan Methodist Missionary Society*. Vol 2. London: Epworth, 1921.

Hill, Richard. *Lights and Shadows of Jamaican History: Being Three Lectures, Delivered in Aid of the Mission Schools of the Colony*. Kingston: Ford & Gall, 1859.

Hinton, John Howard. *Memoir of William Knibb: Missionary to Jamaica*. London: Houlston & Stoneman, 1847.

Love, Emanuel King. *The History of the First African Baptist Church: from Its Organization, Jan 20th 1788 to July 1st, 1888*. Savannah, GA: The Morning News Print, 1888.

Madden, Richard R. *A Twelvemonth's Residence in the West Indies: During the Transition from Slavery to Apprenticeship*. Vol 1. London: Cochrane, 1835.

———. *A Twelvemonth's Residence in the West Indies: During the Transition from Slavery to Apprenticeship*. Vol 2. London: Cochrane, 1835.

Martin, Robert Montgomery. *Statistics of the Colonies of the British Empire in the West Indies, South America, North America, Asia, Australia, Asia, Africa and Europe: From the Official Records of the Colonial Office*. London: Allen, 1839.

McCornock, Mr. *The British and Foreign Anti-Slavery Reporter*. Vol. 3. London: Lancelot Wild, 1840.

Miles, William Augustus, ed. *A Second Letter from Legion to His Grace the Duke of Richmond, Chairman of the Slavery Committee of the House of Lords, Containing an Analysis of the Anti-Slavery Evidence Produced before the Committee.* London: Bagster, 1833.

Parliament. *Slave Law of Jamaica; With Proceedings and Documents Relative Thereto.* London: Ridgeway, 1828.

Phillippo, James Mursell. *Jamaica: Its Past and Present State.* London: Snow, 1843.

Ross, Henry James. *Thoughts on the Objectional System of Labour for Wages in the West Indian Colonies: And on the Necessity of Substituting a System of Tenancy and Allotment of the Staple Cultivation.* London: Hatchard, 1842.

Senior, Bernard Martin. *Jamaica as It Was, as It Is, and as It May Be; Comprising Interesting Topics for Absent Proprieters, Merchants.* London: Hurst, 1835.

Smith, James. *William Knibb: Missionary in Jamaica: A Memoir.* London: Alexander & Shepherd, 1896.

Thome, Jas A., and J. Horace Kimball. *Emancipation in the West Indies: A Six Months' Tour in Antigua, Barbados and Jamaica in the Year 1837.* New York: The American Anti-Slavery Society, 1839.

Tucker, Leonard. *Glorious Liberty: The Story of a Hundred Years Work of the Jamaica Baptist Mission.* London: The Baptist Missionary Society, 1914.

Underhill, Edward Bean. *Life of James Mursell Phillippo, Missionary to Jamaica.* London: Yates & Alexander, 1881.

———. *The West Indies: Their Social and Religious Condition.* London: Jackson, Walford & Hodder, 1862.

Waddell, Hope Masterton. *Twenty-Nine Years in the West Indies and Central Africa: A Review of Missionary Work and Adventure 1829–58.* London: Nelson, 1863.

Wesley, John. *Thoughts upon Slavery.* Dublin: Whitestone, 1775.

SECONDARY SOURCES

"African American & Black Canadian Family History." https://www.archives.com/genealogy/family-heritage-african-american.html.

Akin, Daniel. "The Cross and Faithful Ministry as Seen in the Pastoral and Missionary Ministry of George Liele." August 24, 2010. https://www.danielakin.com/wp-content/uploads/2010/08/Galatians-6.11-18-The-Cross-And-Faithful-Ministry-As-Seen-In-The-Pastoral-And-Missionary-Ministry-Of-George-Leile-Manuscript-ds1.pdf.

Asante, Molefi Kete, and Ada Fazama, eds. *Encyclopedia of Black Studies.* London: Sage, 2005.

Austin-Broos, Diane J. *Jamaica Genesis: Religion and Politics of Moral Order.* London: The University of Chicago Press, 1997.

Bacchus, M. K. *Utilization, Misuse, and Development of Human Resources in the Early West Indian Colonies.* Ontario: Wilfrid Laurier University Press, 1990.

Barrett, L. E. "African Roots in Jamaican Indigenous Religion." *Journal of Religious Thought* 35 (1978) 7–26.

———. *The Sun and the Drum.* Kingston: Sangsters, 1976.

Beckles, Hilary, and Verene Shepherd, eds. *Caribbean Slave Society and Economy: A Student Reader.* Kingston: Randle, 1991.

Bisnauth, Dale. *History of Religion in the Caribbean*. Kingston: Kingston, 1989.
Bland, Sterling Lecaster, Jr., ed. *African American Slave Narratives: An Anthology*, volume 3. Westport, CT: Greenwood Publishing, 2001.
Brathwaite, Edward. *Folk Culture of the Slaves in Jamaica*. London: Beacon Books, 1979.
Brathwaite, K. *The Development of Creole Society in Jamaica 1770–1820*. Oxford: Clarendon, 1971.
Briggs, John H. Y. "Baptists and the Campaign to Abolish the Slave Trade." *Baptist Quarterly* 42 (2014) 260–83.
Catherall, Gordon A. "Bristol College and the Jamaican Mission: A Caribbean Contribution." *Baptist Quarterly* 35.6 (1994) 294–302. https://biblicalstudies.org.uk/pdf/bq/35-6_294.pdf.
———. "Thomas Burchell, Gentle Rebel." *Baptist Quarterly* 21.8 (1965) 349–63. https://biblicalstudies.org.uk/pdf/bq/21-8_349.pdf.
Charet, Matthew. *Root of David: The Symbolic Origins of Rastafari*. Delhi: ISPCK, 2010.
Chevannes, Barry. *Rastafari: Roots and Ideology*. New York: Syracuse University Press, 1994.
Curtin, Philip D. *Two Jamaicas, 1830–1865*. Cambridge: Harvard University Press, 1955.
Davis, Kortright. *Emancipation Still Comin': Exploration in Caribbean Emancipatory Theology*. Maryknoll, NY: Orbis, 1990.
Early, Joseph, Jr. *Readings in Baptist History: Four Centuries of Selected Documents*. Nashville: B & H, 2008.
Edwards, David L. *Christian England: From the 18th Century to the First World War*. Vol. 3. Grand Rapids, MI: Eerdmans, 1984.
Erskine, Noel Leo. *Decolonizing Theology*. Maryknoll, NY: Orbis, 1981.
Fabre, Genevieve, and Klaus Benesch, eds. *African Diasporas in the New and Old Worlds: Consciousness and Imagination*. Amsterdam: Rodopi, 2004.
Fanon, Franz. *The Wretched of the Earth*. London: Penguin Classics, 2001.
Fein, Charlotte Phillips. "Marchus Garvey: His Opinions About Africa." *The Journal of Negro Education* 33.4 (1964) 446–49.
Ferguson, Sinclair B., and David F. Wright, eds. *New Dictionary of Theology*. Leicester: InterVarsity, 1993.
Fischer-Tine, Harald, and Susanne Gehrmann, eds. *Empires and Boundaries: Race, Class and Gender in Colonial Settings*. New York: Routledge, 2008.
Frye, Alex. "Formerly Enslaved People End Apprenticeship Practices in Trinidad, 1832–1838." https://nvdatabase.swarthmore.edu/content/formerly-enslaved-people-end-apprenticeship-practices-trinidad-1832-1838.
Futrell, Samantha Erin. "They Came Up Out of the Water; Evangelicalism and Ethiopian Baptists in the Southern Lowcountry and Jamaica, 1737–1806." Master's thesis, Liberty University, 2013.
Gerloff, Roswith. "The African Diaspora in the Caribbean and Europe from Pre-Emancipation to the Present Day." In *The History of Christianity: World Christianities c. 1914–2000*, edited by Hugh McLeod, 219–35. Cambridge: Cambridge University Press, 2006. https://www.glopent.net/iak-pfingstbewegung.aspx/Members/RoswithGerloff/african-diaspora.pdf.
Gordon, Shirley C. *God Almighty Make Me Free: Christianity in Preemancipation Jamaica*. Blacks in the Diaspora. Bloomington, IN: Indiana University Press, 1996.

———. *Our Cause for His Glory: Christianisation and Emancipation in Jamaica.* Kingston: University of the West Indies Press, 1998.

Griffith-Hughes, Elisabeth. "The Mighty Experiment: The Transition from Slavery to Freedom in Jamaica 1834–1838." PhD diss., The University of Georgia, 2003.

Hall, D. G. "The Apprenticeship Period in Jamaica, 1834–1838." *Caribbean Quarterly* 3.3 (1953) 142–66.

Harvey, David. *Paris, Capital of Modernity.* New York: Routledge, 2004.

Hayford, Jack W. *Spirit-Filled Life Bible.* Nashville: Nelson, 1991.

Heuman, Gad. "The Legacy of Slavery: The World of Jamaican Apprentices." Ninth Annual Gilder Lehrman Center International Conference, Yale University, New Haven, Connecticut, November 1–3, 2007. https://glc.yale.edu/sites/default/files/files/Heuman.pdf.

Holmes, Edward. "George Liele: Negro Slavery's Prophet of Deliverance." *Baptist Quarterly* 20.8 (1964) 340–51.

Homiak, Jake. "Dread History: The African Diaspora, Ethiopianism and Rastafari." http://www.smithsonianeducation.org/migrations/rasta/rasessay.html.

Horowitz, Michael M. *Peoples and Cultures of the Caribbean.* Garden City, NY: The Natural History Press, 1971.

Jasanoff, Maya. *Liberty's Exiles: American Loyalists in the Revolutionary World.* New York: Vintage, 2012.

Jerkins, Morgan. "Usain Bolt: What the World's Fastest Man Means to Jamaica." *Rolling Stone*, July 28, 2016. https://www.rollingstone.com/culture/culture-sports/usain-bolt-what-the-worlds-fastest-man-means-to-jamaica-99518/.

Jiang, Wenbo. "Impacts of Haitian Revolution on Jamaica." *The History of Jamaica* (blog), November 6, 2011. https://wjiang2.blogspot.com/2011/11/impacts-of-haitian-revolution-on.html.

Jones, Pip. *Satan's Kingdom: Bristol and the Transatlantic Slave Trade.* Bristol: Past & Present, 2007.

King, Ruby. "Education in the British Caribbean: The Legacy of the 19th Century." http://www.educoas.org/portal/bdigital/contenido/laeduca/laeduca_121/articulo5/index.aspx?culture=en.

Levy, David, and Sandra J. Peart. "The Secret History of the Dismal Science. Part I. Economics, Religion and Race in the 19th Century." *The Library of Economics and Liberty*, June 4, 2001. https://www.econlib.org/library/Columns/LevyPeartdismal.html.

Lincoln, C. Eric, and Lawrence H. Mamiya. *The Black Church in the African American Experience.* London: Duke University Press, 1990.

Lowe, Turkiya. "Silver Bluff Baptist Church, Silver Bluff, South Carolina (1773–)." *BlackPast* (blog), January 18, 2007. https://www.blackpast.org/african-american-history/silver-bluff-baptist-church-silver-bluff-south-carolina-1773.

Mathieson, W. L. *British Slavery and Its Abolition 1823–1838.* London: Longmans, Green, 1926.

Morrison, D. "Reaching for the Promised Land: The Role of Culture, Issues of Leadership and Social Stratification within British Caribbean Christianity." PhD diss., University of Birmingham, 2012.

Nielsen, Euell A. "First African Baptist Church, Savannah, Georgia (1773–)." *BlackPast* (blog), January 17, 2007. https://www.blackpast.org/african-american-history/first-african-baptist-church-savannah-georgia-1777/.

Parish, C. H., ed. *Thirty-Sixth Journal of the National Baptist Convention*. Nashville: Sunday School Publishing Board, 1916.
Parry, J. H. A., et al. *A Short History of the West Indies*. 4th ed. Oxford: Macmillan Education, 1987.
Payne, Ernest A. "Baptist Work in Jamaica in Jamaica Before the Arrival of the Missionaries." *Baptist Quarterly* 7.1 (1934) 20–26. https://biblicalstudies.org.uk/pdf/bq/07-1_020.pdf.
Ransford, Oliver. *The Slave Trade*. Newton Abbot: Readers Union, 1972.
Robertson, James. *Gone Is the Ancient Glory: Spanish Town, Jamaica, 1534–2000*. Kingston: Randle, 2005.
Rodriguez, Junius P., ed. *Encyclopedia of Slave Resistance and Rebellion*. 2 vols. Westport: Greenwood, 2007.
Rooke, Patricia T. "Evangelical Missionary Rivalry in the British West Indies: A Study in Religious Altruism and Economic Reality." *Baptist Quarterly* 29.8 (1982) 341–55. https://biblicalstudies.org.uk/pdf/bq/29-8_341.pdf.
Russell, Horace O. *Foundations and Anticipations: The Jamaican Baptist Story 1783–1892*. Columbus, GA: Brentwood Christian, 1993.
———. "The Missionary Outreach of the West Indian Church to West Africa in the Nineteenth Century with particular reference to the Baptists." PhD diss., University of Oxford, 1972.
Schweninger, Loren, ed. *Black Property Owners in the South, 1790–1915*. Urbana: University of Illinois Press, 1997.
Sernett, Milton C. *African American Religious History: A Documentary Witness (The C. Eric Lincoln Series on the Black Experience)*. London: Duke University Press, 2000.
Shannon, David T. *George Liele's Life and Legacy: An Unsung Hero*. Macon, GA: Mercer University Press, 2012.
Sinalo, Caroline Williamson. *Rwanda after Genocide: Gender, Identity and Post-Traumatic Growth*. Cambridge: Cambridge University Press, 2018.
Stewart, Robert J. *Religion and Society in Post-Emancipation Jamaica*. Knoxville: The University of Tennessee Press, 1992.
Tyson, Thomas N., et al. "Accounting, Coercion and Social Control During Apprenticeship: Converting Slave Workers to Wage Workers in the British West Indies c. 1834–1838." *Accounting Historians Journal* 32.2 (2005) 201–30. https://www.accountingin.com/accounting-historians-journal/volume-32-number-2/accounting-coercion-and-social-control-during-apprenticeship-converting-slave-workers-to-wage-workers-in-the-british-west-indies-c-1834-1838/.
Walvin, James. *Black Ivory: A History of British Slavery*. London: Fontana, 1992.
Ward, J. R. *British West Indian Slavery, 1750–1834: The Process of Amelioration*. Oxford: Clarendon, 2001.
Whelan, Timothy D. *Baptist Autographs in the John Rylands University Library of Manchester, 1741–1845*. Macon, GA: Mercer University Press, 2009.
Whitt, Michael. *Free Indeed! Trials and Triumphs of Enslaved and Freedmen in Antebellum Virginia*. Vol. 50. Virginia: Virginia Baptist Historical Society, 2011.

Index

Abolition of the Transatlantic Slave Trade, 20, 68, 101
Adelphi Plantation. *See* Stretch and Sett Plantation.
African Methodist Episcopal Church, 37
American Baptist Missionary Union, 25, 27, 277
American Revolutionary War, 39–45, 285
Anabaptist, 58, 59, 65, 75, 302–304
Apprenticeship System, 80, 178, 183–195, 211, 220, 287
Ashton, Susanna, 55

Bailey, Robert, 261
Bailey, William, 261
Baker, Moses, 47, 48, 55–57, 82–87, 90, 93, 98, 101, 103, 105, 115–116, 323
Baker, Mrs Moses. *See* Susanna Ashton.
Baptist Missionary Union, xiii, 277
Baptist Union of Great Britain, 44, 266
Baptist War, 85, 116, 126–146
Beckford, Thomas, 262
Bedward, Alexander, xiii, 278–279, 321
Black River, 137
Bleby, Henry, 144, 252–253, 259
Bogle, Paul, 251–52, 254, 255, 258, 266
Bolt, Usain, 283–84
Bridges, Rev George Wilson, 186
Briscoe, Captain, 262
Bryan, Andrew, 38, 44, 79, 80
Buchner, Rev, 93–94, 95
Buckhead Creek Baptist Church, 35

Burchell, Thomas, 80, 114–16, 129, 141–43, 153–54, 157, 158, 159, 160, 163, 164, 169, 194, 201, 212, 213, 214, 215, 216, 217, 223–24
Burke, William, 262
Burke County, 35, 48
Buxton, Fowell, 76, 127, 189, 195, 201, 210

Calabar College, 212, 269, 306
Calabar High School for Boys, 212
Canning, George, 172
Carey, William, xiii, 44, 161–62, 167, 275
Carleton, Guy, 41
Casar. *See* James Pascall.
Case, Mrs, 156
Catholics, 20, 67, 90, 122
Chinese, 247
Church Covenant, 58, 72, 75, 85, 102, 103, 228, 274, 286, 302–304
Church of England, 10–12, 14, 18, 20, 27, 39, 127, 148, 150, 151, 161, 170, 186, 234, 241, 244, 252, 273, 275, 279, 286
Church of God, 280
Clarendon, 14, 198, 199, 204, 221, 298, 319
Clarke, John, 81, 84, 90, 97, 98, 114, 140, 162, 229, 256
Clarke, Henry, 246, 248
Class and Leader System, 84
Class System, 7–14

Cockrane, Benjamin, 300–301
Colonial Church Union, 150–61, 201, 204
Committee, Baptist Missionary Society, 76, 102, 105, 106, 107, 112, 117,163 124, 161, 164, 210, 212, 214, 228, 267, 276
Committee, Jamaican House of Assembly, 122, 123, 176, 177
Committee, Parliament, 166, 170, 171, 173, 174, 176, 189, 194, 195
Compere, Lee, 90, 103, 105–108, 162, 286
Consolidated Slave Bill, 66
Consolidated Slave Act, 62
Consolidated Slave Laws, 68, 69, 71, 78, 82, 90, 94, 98, 100, 121, 128, 275
Cooke, Stephen, 52, 53, 57, 72, 83
Coolies, 247
Cooper, Miss, 113, 138–140
Cornford, Philip Henry, 128, 135, 140, 144, 145, 146, 219
Coultart, James, 86, 87, 108
Coultart, Mrs, 108–109
Crole, Rev James, 249, 266
Crooked Spring Chapel, 56, 82–84, 165, 323
Cudjoe, 21
Cunningham, Nathan, 221

Dancing, 19, 29, 68, 109–110, 237
David, 136–38
Death Rituals, *See* Nine Nights
Dendy, Walter, 158, 215, 229, 266
Dowson, Thomas, 228
Dr Do Me Good, 206

East Queen Street Baptist Chapel, 88, 90, 91, 105, 117, 164
Elija, 12
Emancipation, Black, 198–199, 211, 217, 219–222, 232, 247, 273, 276, 307–10
Emancipation, Black Hymn Sheet, 222, 311–14
Emancipation, Mulatto and Colored, 181–183

Ethiopianism, 36, 39, 50, 277
Eyre, George, 230, 232–33, 239, 241–45, 248–259, 263–65, 269

Fairfield, 235
Falmouth, 55, 82, 104, 154, 157, 165, 213, 220
First African Baptist Church, Savannah, 41–42
Flamstead, 56, 83, 125
Fonthill, 259
Free Towns and Villages, 195–99

Gardner, Francis, 141, 142, 157, 268, 315
Garvey, Marcus, 277–78
Gaulphin Plantation, 36
George, David, 43, 286
Georgia, 34–35, 40–44, 48, 107
Ghana. *See* Gold Coast.
Gibb, George, 48, 54, 80, 84, 91–93, 113, 273, 286
Gibraltar, 204, 277
Gilbert, John, 48,54
Gold Coast, 23, 217
Gordon, George William, 233, 240–43, 248, 251, 254, 275
Gordon, Robert, 234, 258
Graham, Richard, 260
Graham, Robert, 81
Gray, Lady, 82, 83
Great Jamaican Revival, 235–39
Gully Chapel. *See* East Queen Street Baptist Chapel.
Gurney's Mount, 221

Haitian Revolution, 61–62
Hall, Moses, 136–38, 305
Hall, Prince, 37
Hanover Street Baptist Chapel, 112, 266
Hibbert, Joseph, 279
Hinchelwood, Mr, 261
Hobbs, Colonel, 259–60
Holy Spirit, The, 20, 53, 84, 97, 145, 236, 237, 275, 281
Hospital, 90
House of Assembly, 52, 54, 122, 135, 148, 158, 176–78, 184, 233, 257

Index   337

Hub and Spoke Evangelism, 48, 56
Hudson, Mrs, 141–42
Huxley, Thomas, 254

Illustrations, 2, 4, 5, 6, 9, 13, 18, 22, 25, 29, 32, 35, 36, 42, 46, 54, 109, 110, 111, 115, 126, 134, 140, 160, 163, 179, 187, 199, 215, 221, 222, 225, 227, 238, 241, 253, 257, 263, 265, 288, 291, 293–97, 307–10, 319–24
Indians. *See* Coolies.
Ireland, Rev James, 33

Jackson Town, 168
Jamaica Baptist Union, 247, 249, 266–67, 271–73, 277, 282, 285
Jamaica Missionary Board, 277
Jamaican Legislature, 66, 104, 166, 176, 187
Jericho Baptist Chapel, 140, 319
Jewish Faith, 67, 122
Judson, Adoniram, 44
Junor, Fanny, 262

Kellick, Parson William, 48, 163, 164, 193–94, 233, 244–45, 266, 268
Kingston, 17, 46, 47–55, 57, 62, 66, 71, 75, 76, 85, 86, 88, 90–91, 94, 105, 111–12
Kingston Council, 66, 90
Kingston Race Course, 50
Kingston Tabernacle, 241, 249, 251, 266
Kirk, Presbyterian, 67, 122
Kirkland, Colonel Moses, 42, 45
Kirkland, Mr, 262, 263
Kitty. *See* Catherine Lisle.
Knibb, William, 15, 117, 163–170, 181, 226, 228, 231
Knibb, Thomas, 76

Lancasterian School, 206
Lang, Brother, 94, 96
Latrobe, Charles, 202
Lewin, Mr, 144, 145
Lewis, George, 46, 93–97, 235, 274, 286
Liberty Grave, 221
Liberty Tree, 221

Lisle, Catherine, 75, 80
Lisle, George, 31, 32, 34, 47, 71–77, 282, 285, 288, 291
Lisle, Lucy, *See* Lucy Price.
Liguanea, 55
London Missionary Society, 236, 268
Loyalists, White, xiv, 43, 45, 47, 60, 61, 142, 143, 155, 157
Lucea, 142–43, 155, 157

Madden, Richard Robert, 25, 192, 193, 300
Magee, Martha, 78
Manchester, 93, 95, 198, 199
Manchester Mountains, 97
Manumission, 21, 41, 186
Maps, 1, 23, 34, 45, 49, 70, 131, 209
Marchioneal, 76, 112
Marley, Bob, 279, 283
Maroons, 21–22, 84, 113, 134, 135, 184, 255, 258, 261–62, 263, 264
Methodists, 18, 19–20, 66, 68, 72, 20, 54, 55, 66, 68, 72, 102, 201, 203, 207, 239–240, 266, 268
Monklands, 260
Montego Bay Baptist Chapel, 84, 86,104, 116, 126, 128, 133–35, 154, 157, 164, 220
Moore, Rev Matthew, 19, 20, 39
Moravians, 19, 39, 93–94
Mount Carey, 223–224
Myalism, 28

Nanny, of the Maroons, 21
Negro Education Grant, 200–218
Negro Villages, 246
New Providence, Bahamas, 44
Nine Nights, 30, 65
Nova Scotia, 22, 43

Obeah, 28
Old Carmel, 94, 95

Palmer, Rev Edwin, 266
Parliament, British, 5, 6, 67, 76, 101–102, 127, 161, 170–79, 182, 185, 189, 190, 191, 192, 194, 195, 201, 272, 282

Pascall, James, 48, 81, 304, 305
Peart, Robert, 95–96
Pembroke Hall, 93
Pentecostal, 53, 148, 280–82
Peters, Jesse, 44
Phillippo, James, 93, 112, 124, 138, 203, 207, 208, 212, 228–29, 264, 266, 267, 269, 270, 273
Port Maria, 93, 243
Powell, Enoch, 282
Presbyterian, 67, 122, 134, 143, 219, 241
Price, Charles, 233, 255–58
Price, Lucy, 45, 80, 257, 304
Providence Rhode Island, 33
Punishments, 14–17, 33, 68, 184, 187, 195, 205, 242, 293–97

Quaker, 55, 201

Rankin, George, 260
Rastafari, 279–80
Rebellions, 17, 127, 128, 133, 134, 250, 298–99
Resistance Hymn, 84
Retrieve Plantation, 131
Revivalists, 280
Ricketts, John Edward, 277
Rippon, John, 39, 44, 55, 57–59, 68
Rivers of Blood, 190, 282
Roach, Rev, 266
Rodney Hall Court House, 92
Rowe, John, 59, 103, 107, 286
Royal Adventurers of England Trading to Africa, 4
Runaways, 22, 62
Russell Hall Plantation, 91
Ryland, John, 59, 101, 161

Salt Spring Estate, 133
Salter's Hill Baptist Chapel, 116, 134–35, 142, 154, 165, 166, 215, 229, 323
Sam Sharpe Rebellion, See Baptist War.
Savannah, 39, 41–44
Savannah Baptist Association, 44
Schools, 50, 52, 182, 200–206, 212, 278
Seasoning, 15, 234
Service, Rev James, 266

Sharpe, Henry, 33, 35, 39, 42
Sharpe, Sam, 85, 116, 126–133, 140, 142, 144–46, 153, 154, 164, 166, 167, 182, 247, 275, 282, 323
Silver Bluff Baptist Chapel, 36, 43
Slave Code, 11

South Carolina, 34, 36, 40–44, 48, 57
Sparkes, James, 261
Speed, Johnson, 261
Spence, George, 143
Spencer, Herbert, 254
Spring Valley, 92
St John's Chapel. See East Queen Street Baptist Chapel.
Stennet, Samuel, 244
Stewart Town Baptist Chapel, 155
Stony Gut, 242, 251, 259, 260
Stretch and Sett Plantation, 55
Swigle, Thomas Nicholas, 39, 48, 57, 86, 87–91, 98
Swiney, Sam, 167
Tables, 191, 206, 216
Taylor, Alick, 262
Taylor, Daniel, 262
Telfer, John, 261
Telfer, Rebecca, 260
Ticket, Baptist, 84, 113, 118, 214, 215
Ticket-of-leave, 64, 94
Tinson, Joshua, 76, 103, 108, 111, 112–13, 124, 141, 212, 286
Treadwheel, 187–89
Tyrer, George, 262

Underhill, Dr E B, 124, 228–29, 232–33, 247–49, 266–70

Vaughan, Samuel, 82, 83, 90, 104, 323
Victoria, Queen, 248, 250, 266
Vineyard, George, 48, 57, 90, 98, 286
Virgil, Old, 135
Virginia, 33, 34, 40, 57, 285
Vyvyan, Richard, 174, 176

Waddell, Hope Masterton, 132, 147, 148
Wages, 139, 215, 218
Walker, Robert, 261
Wesley, John, 12

Wilberforce, William, 101, 103, 200
Williams, Hannah, 43
Williams, Mr, 67
Windsor Lodge, 135, 142
Windward Road Chapel, 53, 54, 73–76, 282, 287

Winn, Isaac Lascelles, 55, 56
Wolverine, 254

York, Duke of, 4

Zion Revivalism, 280

www.ingramcontent.com/pod-product-compliance
Lightning Source LLC
Chambersburg PA
CBHW070228230426
43664CB00014B/2243